The Origins of War
in Early Modern Europe

'I told him the happiness of the world was in few hands, and very late experience had proved how much the fate and dispatch of the great affairs of it depended upon the character and mutual confidence of those who transacted it.'

Philip Yorke reporting conversation with the French foreign minister, 1748.

The Origins of War
in Early Modern Europe

Edited by
JEREMY BLACK
Lecturer in History
University of Durham

JOHN DONALD PUBLISHERS LTD
EDINBURGH

To
Jonathan Dent and William Salomon

ISBN 0 85976 168 1

Exclusive distribution in the United States
of America and Canada by Humanities Press
Inc., Atlantic Highlands, NJ 07716, USA.

Phototypeset by Quorn Selective Repro, Loughborough.
Printed in Great Britain by Bell & Bain Ltd., Glasgow.

PREFACE

' . . . a Prince who has a hundred thousand men in his hands and many pretensions, may from day to day expect events, which may be improved by a good Politician.'
Earl of Stair on Frederick the Great.[1]

'Ask each party in the state of war, why the sword is drawn? It will be answered, to obtain a safe, honourable and lasting peace. Yet, though peace is the pretended object of all hostilities; we shall find the means, to attain this object, are as different and contrary, as the policy, interest, ambition and passions of each belligerent power.'
Monitor, 6 November 1762

I first conceived the idea of this volume when sitting on a park bench in Munich on a heavy evening in August 1983 after the Hauptstaatsarchiv had shut. I must have been very tired because I little anticipated the complexity of the task. It rapidly became apparent that in one volume it would not be possible to study all the types of wars that affected European powers between 1500 and 1800, even assuming that a generally acceptable typology could be constructed. It also became obvious that different views existed as to how best to tackle the question. That was simply from the perspective of a group of historians, leaving aside the varied methods of others disciplines, trenchantly reviewed recently by Tim Blanning.[2] Rather than only presenting one view, this volume deliberately offers several, on the principle that that is the only healthy way to approach the problem. In particular, the powerful and thoughtful essays of William Roosen and Karl Schweizer present a perspective that is more informed by current theoretical work among political scientists and more ready to use their analytical devices than that of several contributors including the editor. The essays in this book, all written by scholars carrying out research on the topic at present, offer, individually, reassessments of particular conflicts or groups of conflicts that represent a significant contribution to the history of international relations in the early modern period. This is not a subject that is very fashionable at present nor regarded by many historians as of great importance, but as the essays make clear, war was a central activity of the countries of the period, and the conduct of foreign policy integral to the political history of the age. Collectively the essays offer an attempt to redress the overwhelming emphasis on conflicts in the last two centuries in studies on the causes of war. This effort has been made because it is felt that it is misguided for theoretical and general work to be based on such a circumscribed chronological period, and because it is possibly time to look afresh at many of the conflicts of the early-modern period and at the international relations of that era. The essays in this book are by no means the last word on the subject, but hopefully they will inspire fresh work in an unduly neglected field. Many students appear to find the available literature rather limited and unreflective, a situation reminiscent possibly of a letter Philip Yorke sent to his uncle from The Hague in 1777:

'Professor Pestel to whom I have mentioned what your Lordship said in a former letter, that I might read in a number of books the History of Europe from the Peace of Westphalia, agrees entirely with you with respect to the circumstances of facts that have happened, but says that what he had in head was of a different nature, and not to be found in any book that he knows of, which was to give a sort of system of policy, and of the present Ballance of Europe, drawn from the facts that have happened since the period mentioned, a study which he says is entirely new, and not followed in our universities'.[3]

Jeremy Black

NOTES

1. Stair, commander of the British forces in the Austrian Netherlands (*Pay Bas*, modern Belgium) and Ambassador to The Hague, to Robert Trevor, Envoy Extraordinary at The Hague, 13 Jan. 1743, Aylesbury, Buckinghamshire County Record Office, Trevor papers, vol. 33.

2. T. C. W. Blanning, *The Origins of the French Revolutionary Wars* (1986), pp. 1–35, 205–6.

3. BL. Add. 35378 f. 20.

ACKNOWLEDGEMENTS

The wide scope of this work and the escalating cost of domestic and foreign research entails a lengthy list of acknowledgements. I would first like to thank the contributors who have faced a difficult task and much lightened my load by their good humour, promptness, and intelligent treatment of their brief. I regret greatly that not all those who agreed to offer an essay were able to do so, and I am particularly sorry that Roy Clayton was forced to withdraw from the project. I am grateful for the encouragement offered by several scholars who were unable to participate, especially Simon Adams, Jonathan Israel and Bob Stradling. Drafts of part of the book were read by Leopold Auer, Lawrence Brockliss, Peter Dickson, Robert Evans, Jeremy Gregory, Michael Howard, Colin Lucas and John Stoye. Their helpful remarks were of great value and their encouragement most important. I owe much to Her Majesty the Queen, Prince Kinsky, Earl Waldegrave, Lady Lucas, the trustees of the Wentworth Woodhouse papers, John Weston-Underwood and Richard Head for permission to consult their manuscripts. Wendy Duery, Janet Forster and Joan Grant typed drafts and a final version with a helpful forbearance only those who know my handwriting can appreciate. I am grateful for assistance from the British Academy, the British Council, the German Academic Exchange Scheme, the Staff Travel and Research Fund of Durham University, the Twenty-Seven Foundation and the Zaharoff Foundation. The Warden and Fellows of Merton College, Oxford provided crucial hospitality, as did my parents, Peter Bassett, Richard Berman, John Blair, Tony Brown, Hilmar Brückner, Jonathan Dent, Robert Gildea, Anthony Gross, Dan and Stella Hollis, Peter Hore, Harold James, James Kellock, Max King, James Lawrie, Jeremy Mayhew, Jon Parry, William Salomon, Paul Smith, Peter Spear, Mark Stocker, Peter Tibber, Alan Welsford and Paul Zealander. John Tuckwell has proved more than just a publisher. Without Sarah's support and encouragement this book would not have been written.

Jeremy Black

CONTENTS

NOTES ON THE CONTRIBUTORS

Jeremy Black,   Lecturer in History, University of Durham. Publications include *British Foreign Policy in the Age of Walpole* (Edinburgh 1985); *The British and the Grand Tour* (1985); *The English Press in the Eighteenth Century* (1987); *Natural and Necessary Enemies: Anglo-French Relations in the Eighteenth Century* (1986); ed., *Britain in the Age of Walpole* (1984); co-ed., *Essays in European History in honour of Ragnhild Hatton* (1985).

Steven Gunn,   Junior Research Fellow, Merton College Oxford; graduate of Oxford (Merton); author of several articles on early-sixteenth century England, and a thesis on Charles Brandon, Duke of Suffolk.

Stewart Oakley,   Senior Lecturer in European History, University of East Anglia, Norwich. Has also taught at the universities of Exeter, Edinburgh and Minnesota. Publications include *The Story of Sweden* (1966); *The Story of Denmark* (1972); *Scandinavian History 1520–1970: a List of Books and Articles in English* (1984); and articles on Gustavus III of Sweden and the peasantry of Scandinavia.

David Parrott,   Lecturer in History, University of York; graduate of Oxford (Christ Church and Wolfson); author of a thesis on 'The Administration of the French Army during the Ministry of Cardinal Richelieu' (Oxford, 1985), and an article on strategy and tactics in the Thirty Years' War.

Karl Roider,   Professor of History, Louisiana State University, Baton Rouge. Author of *The Reluctant Ally: Austria's Policy in the Austro-Turkish War, 1737–1739* (1972); *Austria's Eastern Question, 1700–1790* (1982); *Thugut, Austria, and the French Revolution* (forthcoming); ed., *Maria Theresa* (1973).

William Roosen,   Professor of History, Northern Arizona University. Author of *The Age of Louis XIV: The Rise of Modern Diplomacy* (1976); Editor of the *Proceedings of the Western Society for French History*.

Karl Schweizer,   Associate Professor of History, Bishop's University, Quebec. Co-ed., *The Devonshire Political Diary 1757–1762* (1982);

Francois de Callières: The Art of Diplomacy (1983), Co-ed., *Essays in European History in honour of Ragnhild Hatton* (1985).

Paul Sonnino, Associate Professor, University of California, Santa Barbara. Publications include *Louis XIV's view of the Papacy 1661-1667* (1966); ed., *Frederick the Great's Anti-Machiavel* (1981).

Claude Sturgill, Professor of History, University of Florida, Gainesville. Publications include *Marshal Villars and the War of the Spanish Succession* (1965); *Claude le Blanc: Civil Servant of the King* (1976); *La Formation de la Milice Permanente en France, 1726-1730* (1977); *L'Organisation et l'Administration de la Maréchaussée et de la Justice Prévôtale, 1720-1730* (1980).

Philip Woodfine, Lecturer in History, Huddersfield Polytechnic. Currently engaged in work on the War of the Jenkins' Ear.

ABBREVIATIONS

Add.   Additional Manuscripts in the British Library.
AE.   Paris, Quai d' Orsay, Archives du Ministère des Affaires Etrangères, recently renamed Relations Extérieures.
Ang.   Angleterre.
BL.   London, British Library, Department of Manuscripts.
CP.   Correspondance Politique.
(os)   Old Style.

All books are published in London except where otherwise stated. The New Year is always taken as starting on 1 January.

INTRODUCTION

Jeremy Black

'... there is not a Foreign Minister, who resided at his Majesty's Court during the course of the last winter, that was not convinced of the King's resolution to prevent the French succours from landing in North America ... it is not to be believed, the court of France could have suffered itself to be so grossly imposed upon, as to be made to believe, that a superior fleet would quietly stand by, and be tame spectators of the debarkation of so considerable a force, known to be sent, in order to support the most violent measures, and unjust pretensions, that ever were set on foot; or that His Majesty would suffer the French to take by force, that which the King refused to yield them by treaty, while he had it in his power to prevent them.'

British Secretary of State, Earl of Holderness, explaining peacetime attack on French fleet.[1]

'Among savages the means of intercourse are restricted to tribes who are neighbours, and hostilities confined in the same manner. As knowledge increases the means of intercourse extend, and nations not in immediate vicinity, learn to mingle in each others affairs. The history of European nations proves this, among whom treaties offensive and defensive have been constantly extending and multiplying for the two last centuries, as their intercourse has increased, and, wars, without becoming less frequent, have become far more general, bloody, and expensive. The balance of power, a notion springing up among statesmen towards the end of the fifteenth century, has been a principal cause both of the frequency and the extensiveness of modern wars; the religious distinctions which divided Europe after the period of the reformation have also been the cause or the pretext of frequent hostilities; and the supposed dignity of crowns, an expression the more dangerous from the obscurity of its meaning, has been constantly enumerated among the reasons for nations unsheathing the avenging sword.'

James Currie, 1793.[2]

Violence was endemic in early-modern Europe. It was a common means of settling disputes between individuals, groups and countries. This reflected the values of a society, or rather group of societies, that was more prepared to accept violence than European society in the twentieth century. It is difficult to gauge the significance of these values for the international relations of the early-modern period, but the purpose of this introduction is to suggest that they were of great importance and that they played a major role in causing the frequent wars of the era. Attention will be devoted to the role of religious and dynastic considerations, and it will be argued that international relations in the period after the Peace of Westphalia of 1648 were not substantially different to those prior to 1648. Furthermore it will be suggested that the standard conceptualisation of international relations, one developed in the nineteenth century, cannot be applied to the early-modern period without difficulty, and that this affects the study of the

1

causes of war. For the purposes of this book the early-modern period is understood as that from the beginning of the sixteenth century to the outbreak of the French Revolutionary Wars in 1792, though there was of course continuity in behaviour and interests across both divides. The Eurocentric perspective of the book reflects the particular abilities and interests of the contributors. It does not imply that struggles between European and non-European powers or those among the latter were of no significance. However, if the values of European society are regarded as of some importance, then clearly there is a case for treating wars between European powers separately, particularly as different values pertained in their treatment of non-European states. The Ottoman Empire was a special case both because of its European land-frontier and because of the developing habit of treating it as part of the European system.

In considering the values of early-modern European society the first two spheres for assessment are religion and dynasticism, the Church and the Crown. Rather than pressing wholeheartedly for peace the principal moulder of public opinion, the clergy, had a distinctly ambivalent attitude towards the idea of war.[3] This was possibly appropriate in a Christendom that was under threat from an expansive aggressive non-Christian power, the Ottoman Empire (Turkey). Though the Austrian Habsburg conquest of Hungary in the 1680s marked the end of any serious threat of a Turkish advance into central Europe, conflict continued between the Turks and the Christian powers for much of the following century. It was not simply the territories directly bordering the Ottoman Empire that were affected by this conflict. As Holy Roman Emperor successive Austrian Habsburgs were able to enlist the support of many German princes, and the conquest of Hungary was in many respects one of the greatest German political achievements of the seventeenth century. A large number of German princes, including the rulers of Baden and Bavaria and the future George I of Britain, took part in the conflict.

Italian and Iberian powers were principally concerned by maritime struggles, usually with the states of North Africa, uneasy tributaries of the Ottoman Empire. These were still serious in the eighteenth century. Coastal regions of Italy witnessed extensive preparations and regular alarms, privateering was incessant, and Spain launched a series of attacks on North Africa. Her conquest of Oran in 1732 and failures at Algiers in 1775 and 1784 were among the greatest amphibious operations of the age.

If a crusade-type struggle with the infidel was a laudable form of war in the eyes of clerics, so also were wars against heretic Christians. In one respect the early-modern period in Europe can be defined as the age of religious wars. Doctrinal and ecclesiastical disputes giving rise to conflict between Christian powers were not of course a novel product of the Reformation. If relations with Byzantium are included, they had been a significant factor in international disputes over the previous half-millennium. Had the Protestant German powers been defeated by the Emperor Charles V, a not impossible eventuality, then the Reformation would have been even more clearly seen in a pattern of medieval politico-religious disorder. However it was not, not least because of divisions among the Catholic powers, particularly Britain, France and Charles V. French willingness to support the cause of the German Protestants in the War of the Schmalkaldic League and to ally with the Turks set a pattern for the early-modern period, one in which warring blocs did not equate with religious divisions. Thus the French supported the Dutch and the Swedes against the Habsburgs, just as they were later to ally with George I against Spain in the War of the Quadruple Alliance and with Frederick II (the Great) of Prussia against Maria Theresa of Austria in the War of the Austrian Succession.

These links did not however prevent the habit of presenting international relations in a religious light. As generations of school-children who have answered the question 'What part did religion play in the Thirty Years' War?' will know, this is an issue that has greatly agitated historians of the early seventeenth century. However, it then seems to be discarded as a topic of serious enquiry. It is generally accepted that religious perspectives ceased to have any major significance with the Peace of Westphalia, the agreement that, in ending the Thirty Years' War, provided considerable safeguards for the Protestant German princes. It is possibly this belief that has led to a tendency to treat 1648 as a crucial date in studies on the history of international relations. The Longmans series on the history of the European states system begins with 1648. However, Westphalia is an inappropriate date for several reasons. It did not mark, as has often been suggested, the end of significant Habsburg power. The extraordinary resilience of Spain and the domestic disorders in France known as the *Frondes* enabled the Spanish Habsburgs to reverse their recent territorial losses dramatically in the years immediately after 1648. The Austrian Habsburgs, as a result of domestic and international developments, were to be stronger in the period 1683–1733 than they had ever been before.

If Westphalia neither represented a fundamental change in the fortune of individual states nor, as has been claimed recently,[4] witnessed the beginning of a novel form of European international relations, a states system, it could also be suggested that it is inappropriate to treat it as the beginning of a new age in attitudes to international relations. By stressing the supposed end of religious factors in international relations in this period, historians have helped to divide these relations in early modern Europe into two eras, one from approximately 1517 until 1648, the other from then until the French Revolution. The former is identified with conflicts that arose from developments at the beginning of the era, the consolidation of Habsburg power and the Reformation. Religious differences are regarded as of considerable importance in this age. The latter era is seen as a secular age and the methodology that has been used to describe it is one that is essentially derived from the late nineteenth century, when states appeared to operate their foreign policies in a cool and dispassionate fashion, unaffected by ideology. This view was an inaccurate assessment of the international relations of the period, an assessment that throws interesting light on how the intellectuals of the age wished to believe that diplomacy operated. Because all the European great powers of the nineteenth century — Britain, France, Austria, Russia and Prussia — were already distinct and important actors on the international stage in the period 1648–1792 it was understandable that the diplomatic relations of the earlier age should be treated in terms of the analyses and attitudes that appeared to be most appropriate for the later period.

The resulting treatments varied with the skill and interests of particular historians, but the general stress was on policy and long-term planning carried out rationally and in accordance with an unemotional *raison d'état* by monarchs without illusions, pre-eminently Frederick the Great, and by European chancelleries that were bureaucratically distinct and independent and capable of generating informed policies. Thus, as Paul Sonnino shows, historians of the foreign policy of Louis XIV, the principal late-seventeenth-century topic that engaged the interest of historians two centuries later (to the serious detriment of work on eastern Europe), searched for some policy that would reduce the varied moves of Louis to a consistent, rational plan by which these moves could be explained, judged and linked to subsequent episodes of French foreign policy.

In such a form of analysis war tended to be regarded as a device of deliberate policy, the decision to resort to it based either on a rational consideration of national advantage, or, in the case of rulers or ministers who were to be condemned for folly, on a failure to make such an assessment. There was little sense of ideology and domestic pressures for conflict were generally ignored, with the exception of states, such as Britain, whose system of government led them to be regarded as conspicuously different from those described as absolutisms. The *mentalités* that affected the conduct of foreign policy were rarely discussed, but when they were, they were judged to be, what was implicit in the vast bulk of the scholarship, a matter of *raison d'état*, a machiavellian assessment of opportunities and interests that was illustrated by the publication of Frederick the Great's *Politische Correspondenz*.[5]

Different scholars will discern different attitudes towards international relations in past ages. In general, however, diplomatic historians tend to pay too little attention to these attitudes. Many take them for granted and are understandably disinclined to study them. In contrast to the ordered series of diplomatic papers, material on attitudes to foreign policy tends to be more diffuse and is often ambivalent in meaning or difficult to assess the importance of. More crucial is the difficulty of establishing a methodology by which past attitudes can be defined and their significance assessed. Possibly as a result most diplomatic historians, particularly those of the eighteenth century, continue to hold the assumptions outlined above.

There is clearly much of value in the attitudes underlying late nineteenth-century studies of diplomatic history, but it can be suggested that they have led to a failure to consider adequately the relevant *mentalités* of the period. In an important recent lecture Michael Howard has drawn attention to what he calls 'a cultural predisposition to war' and referred to 'bellicist' societies.[6] It could be suggested that such a predisposition existed throughout the early-modern period. War appeared natural and inevitable, and a right way to adjudicate disputes. This essay does not have space to discuss adequately the way in which this cultural preference for violence reflected the mores of society. It is difficult to determine how far state success in seeking to acquire a monopoly of violence influenced attitudes. It is also difficult to assess the impact of the critics of war, who became more vocal in the eighteenth century. Howard has argued that there was a distinct change in mood, 'For Louis XIV and his court war was, in his early years at least, little more than a seasonal variation on hunting. But by the eighteenth century the mood had changed. For Frederick the Great War was to be preeminently a function of *Staatspolitik*, and it has remained ever since'.[7]

Howard's writings on the causes of war are very persuasive, but it could be argued that here he has made an error, possibly misjudging a shift in sensibility. Just as it is too easy to interpret changes in artistic fashion, religious practices and the style of kingship in the eighteenth century as fundamental alterations, so it is necessary to be cautious in assessing signs of 'modern' behaviour in the international relations of the period. Frederick the Great's conduct was not obviously a new departure. What was possibly novel was the fashion in which he chose to conduct the European public relations exercise then expected from all major powers,[8] and in particular his cultivation of some of the leading foreign intellects of the age, the French *philosophes*. Arguably more significant in leading to the assumption that Frederick represented a new departure was the bulk and availability of his surviving correspondence and the use made of it by historians. But possibly this was no more than the effect of a change in style in the eighteenth century that led some monarchs to write more, producing for example a massive growth in the amount of surviving royal correspondence between the reigns of Georges I and II of Britain and that of George III.

Two major elements of international relations in the age of Frederick the Great that were far from novel and that suggest that possibly the eighteenth century should be seen as part of the early-modern period rather than a precursor of nineteenth-century diplomacy were the role of dynastic concerns and the continued habit of discussing relations in religious terms. The latter has received relatively little attention, although place was found for religion as a significant ideological factor in Anglo-Prussian relations in the mid-eighteenth century in Manfred Schlenke's subtle attempt to place these relations in more than just a diplomatic context.[9] Although it would be difficult to present the century from the French Revocation of the Edict of Nantes in 1685 to the formation of the Fürstenbund (League of Princes) in 1785 by Frederick the Great as a way to organise north-German Protestant opposition to the Emperor Joseph II, as a period of religious conflict, it would be foolish to ignore the significance of religious considerations in engendering hostility and, if only often for contemporaries, explaining action. Much of this hostility stemmed from anger at the treatment of coreligionists in other countries, and this could often lead to diplomatic intervention, and resultant tension as in the Palatinate in the late 1710s, when a German religious war appeared imminent.[10] Recalcitrant religious minorities, such as the Huguenots in the Cevennes mountains of France or the Hungarian Protestants, obtained some foreign assistance for their armed resistance. The Hanoverian decision in 1730 to support the Protestant townspeople of Hildesheim against their Catholic Wittelsbach Prince Bishop led to tension and military action.[11] The religious situation in Europe was generally unstable, particularly in the Empire, Poland and the Habsburg lands, where Catholicism in the early eighteenth century continued its advances of the previous century.[12] The Imperial Vice-Chancellor from 1705 to 1734, Count Frederick Schönborn, sought to use Imperial authority for the cause of Catholicism. In some respects Frederick the Great's invasion of the Austrian province of Silesia in 1740 represented the first significant successful Protestant counter-offensive in the Empire since the Thirty Years' War, and Frederick certainly presented it as a move designed to help the Silesian Protestants.[13] The confrontations and wars of the period were indeed seen in religious terms by many commentators. The Austro-Spanish treaty of Vienna in 1725 was presented in Protestant Europe as a Catholic plot, visible evidence of a powerful sinister conspiracy that supported the Jacobite pretender to the British throne and the Polish Catholics responsible for such atrocities as the so-called Thorn massacre of 1724. The Austro-French *entente* in the late 1730s led to discussion of the need for a Protestant alliance, reminiscent of similar suggestions in the early 1720s.[14] Lord Harrington, a British Secretary of State, pressed a Prussian envoy in 1740 on the need to form a plan 'as a bulwark to the Protestant religion in particular', and the issue of religious leagues frequently emerged in the diplomatic correspondence of the period.[15] The Seven Years' War was widely portrayed in propaganda as a religious conflict, a development that was in keeping with the stress on religious animosity in the domestic publications of several states.[16]

It was of course true that the alliances of the period rarely conformed to confessional lines exactly. The Alliance of Hanover, negotiated in 1725 to confront the new Austro-Spanish pact, linked Britain and Prussia to France, and in the following year Prussia switched alliance. Sweden fought Prussia in the Seven Years' War and Denmark and the United Provinces remained neutral. Count Osterman, the Russian foreign minister, observed in 1740 with reference to the Jülich-Berg succession dispute, 'religion is more talked of, than really minded in transactions of this kind'.[17] It would be foolish to exaggerate the significance of religious animosity in causing wars in this period; it was more likely to be resorted to in order to encourage support for and to explain a conflict that had already begun, a situation not too dissimilar from that pertaining prior to 1648. However, the largely unstudied topics of religious animosity in eighteenth-century diplomacy and discussions of foreign policy suggest that it would be mistaken to differentiate the period too sharply from the pre-Westphalian age. They also help to account for the generally uncritical response of the clergy of the period to warfare. Sensing a new critical attitude, historians have devoted attention to the published works of the *philosophes*. These were clearly of some significance, playing a role in the development in the independent United States of America of a belief in the concept of just wars in which it was essential to seek alternative means of resolving conflicts before embarking on war. However, this belief, which was of scant assistance to the native Indians, also had Christian roots, which were arguably of greater significance. It is possible that, rather than the writings of the *philosophes*, a better guide to the dominant ideology of the age could be found in fast-day sermons held to secure divine intercession, or the pageantry of victory: *Te Deums*, processions, fireworks, addresses. Defeats in the early stages of the Seven Years' War, with the French 'encamping almost at our gates', did not lead Edward Weston, a career bureaucrat, experienced in diplomatic negotiations, to criticise the war. Instead in 1756 he wrote an anonymous pamphlet entitled *The Fast* in which he called for a national fast day to win divine support for a country enervated by immorality and irreligion.[18] National fast days were held in Britain in all but one of the years of the War of American Independence. George III declared 13 December 1776 a day of 'General Fast and Humiliation' because of 'the just and necessary Measure of Force which we are obliged to use against our rebellious subjects'. The 1776 fast day led to over forty printed sermons. Newspapers such as the *Monitor* frequently saw Providence at work in the Seven Years' War. Some of the religious ceremonies and language were doubtless a matter of convention, but in searching for any supposed changes in eighteenth-century attitudes to war it is necessary to remember that Europe was still a fundamentally religious society and that most ethical problems were expressed in religious terms.

Unlike Edward Weston, George Frederick Handel was no gloom and doom merchant. The more favourable international situation of late 1743 allowed him to exercise his talents by writing the *Dettingen Te Deum*, first performed at the Chapel Royal in London on 27 November (old style) 1743. His celebration of the Royal hero as victor was part of a long European tradition of exalting majesty in its most impressive function, the display of power. This display ranged in style and form, from medals to the foundation of chivalric orders for the nobility under royal patronage, but it was a constant feature of the period. War was not the sole sphere in which such display could occur, but it was one that best served the aggressive dynastic purpose that illuminated so many of the states of the period. Handel's triumphal piece looked back to such works as Philippe Quinault's libretto for Lully's 1677 opera *Issus* which presented Louis XIV as Neptune and referred both to the seizure of Messina and to a French engagement off the coast of Sicily in the spring of 1676. The dynastic theme in the diplomacy of the period and in the attitudes that conditioned its formulation and execution serves like its religious counterpart to link the post and pre-Westphalian periods. It has been argued that the early-modern period witnessed the origins and growth of the modern impersonal state. There is not space to discuss this interpretation fully, but it could be suggested that it can be queried on the grounds that insufficient evidence has been advanced to support the theory, that much of it relates to the writings of a small group of arguably unrepresentative thinkers, and that the political *practice* of the age was still essentially monarchical in a traditional fashion across most of Europe. A revisionist stress on limited change carries with it the danger that the essentially static nature of such an interpretation makes it difficult to explain change. Nevertheless, such a stress appears to be justified in the case of international relations and is arguably also appropriate for domestic affairs. There were significant alterations in particular aspects of international relations, such as the firmer grasp of the nature of a linear frontier associated with improved mapping and, possibly, a more definite perception of the nature of political sovereignty. However, the crucial role of the monarch in most European societies, including Britain, throughout the eighteenth century, and the dynastic perspective of monarchical ambitions ensured a basic continuity in the conduct of international relations. Clearly this perspective varied by individual. Childless Frederick the Great was less obviously interested in dynastic affairs than say Louis XV with his determination to support his son-in-law Don Philip in Parma. Dynastic concerns did not exclude other interests. They did however remain a central feature of international relations. If proprietary dynasticism describes the attitude of most monarchs to their countries it is not surprising that they were willing to use their resources for territorial accumulation. They did so in the context of court cultures that were predisposed to war, seeing it as a heroic endeavour. Not all monarchs sought war, but most engaged in it at some time, a tendency possibly increased by a demographic structure which often led to young men succeeding to thrones. Louis XIV, Peter the Great, Charles Emmanuel III of Sardinia, Charles III of Spain, as King of Naples, and Frederick the Great were all examples of young monarchs who took aggressive steps that were not 'necessary' in terms of the diplomatic situation at the time. This argument cannot be pushed too far: Philip V of Spain was not the sole instance of a ruler aggressive until his death, and one London newspaper pointed out in 1758 that the monarchs of the neutral powers in the Seven Years' War were generally younger than those of the combatant states.[19]

Imbued with bellicist values, monarchs faced a European situation made unpredictable and turbulent by the whims of dynastic luck. Frederick the Great feared wrongly in 1749 that a general war would follow the death of Frederick I of Sweden.[20] It was no accident that most of the major wars of the eighteenth century prior to the French Revolution and a good many of the quarrels that did not lead to war take their name from succession disputes, ranging from the relatively minor to that over the Spanish Succession which involved the largest empire in the world. Many other conflicts arose as a result of these succession disputes. The European element of the Seven Years' War was essentially an attempt to reverse the verdict of the War of the Austrian Succession; Philip V's invasion of Sardinia in 1717, Sicily the following year and Naples in 1734 attempts to reverse the exclusion of Spain from her Italian empire at the end of the War of the Spanish Succession.

These dynastic claims could be regarded as an opportune sham. Robert Vyner referred in the House of Commons in 1741 to 'one of those imaginary titles, which ambition may always find to the dominions of another'.[21] The fraudulent manufacture of some pretensions and the willingness of states to barter claims for 'equivalents', other benefits to which they did not have a legal right, lends some substance to this charge. It is possible to present monarchs and ministers as adopting pretensions to serve their long-term plans, in short of using dynasticism for the sake of *Staatspolitik*, and much of the debate surrounding Louis XIV's foreign policy revolves around this analytical device. However, it is more reasonable to assume that when monarchs said they were pursuing dynastic claims they were not all being disingenuous, accepting of course that prudential considerations could affect the extent to which these claims were pushed.

The pursuit of land and heiresses linked the monarch to his peasants. As wealth was primarily held in land and transmitted through blood inheritance it was natural at all levels of society for conflict to centre on succession disputes. Peasants resorted to litigation, a method that was lengthy and expensive, but to which the alternative was largely closed by state disapproval of private violence. Monarchs resorted to negotiation, but the absence of an adjudicating body and the need for a speedy solution once a succession fell vacant encouraged a decision to fight. Most of the dynasties ruling in 1650 or 1750 owed their position to the willingness of past members of the family to fight to secure their succession claims. George I was willing to fight in 1714 should a pro-Stuart coup seek to prevent him inheriting the British throne. He had to fight the Jacobites the following year, just as the Bourbons had to fight to gain France, Spain and Naples, and the Romanovs to hold Russia, the Braganzas Portugal and the Vasas Sweden. Although peaceful successions of new dynasties did take place, war and inheritance were often two sides of the same coin; a problem exacerbated by varying and disputed succession laws and by the need in marital diplomacy to avoid morganatic marriages.

Conflict over territory was not solely linked to issues of dynastic inheritance. Disputes over ownership of territory were matched by quarrels over boundaries. Drawing up a memoir for domestic consumption on the causes of the Anglo-French conflict of 1755, the experienced French foreign office bureaucrat Le Dran attributed it first to the ambiguity of the clauses in the Peace of Utrecht (1713) concerning the cession of Nova Scotia to Britain.[22] The absence in most countries of a non-military police force at the disposal of central government ensured that minor territorial disputes could lead to the use of troops. French operations against smugglers on the Savoyard frontier, including the pursuit of fugitives over the border, inflamed relations on more than one occasion. In 1756 the British Minister Onslow Burrish reported, 'A Quarrel has happened between the Elector of Bavaria and the Count of Oetingue Wallerstein, concerning an Estate in the Circle of Swabia, belonging to Count Contardini, which He had offered to sell to His Electoral Highness. The Bailiff, who is said to have a large Sum in His Hands, refused to liquidate his Accompts with His Lord, and was protected by Count Oetingue. Contardini complained to the Elector of Bavaria, and desired His Protection; upon which a Corporal with five soldiers were sent to take Possession of the Castle; and in Consequence of this Count Oetingue ordered one hundred and fifty Men to dispossess Them; but the Bavarian Soldiers barricaded the Castle, and killed five of the Count's Men . . . and a Bavarian Officer has since been sent with a Party of Soldiers to secure the Possession of the Place'.[23]

Six years earlier a dispute between the Elector Palatine and the Archbishop-Elector of Cologne over inundations from the Rhine led to the use of troops to demolish some controversial sluices. In both cases the matter was settled without further conflict. It was difficult for small states to sustain the burden of military operations and this encouraged them not to push minor disputes to extremes, unless they received external support. Furthermore, the existence in the Empire of federal institutions with jurisdiction over disputes between princes made it easier to settle disputes by compromise or to avoid them becoming a significant conflict.[24] The 1756 dispute was referred to the Swabian Circle, the regional assembly for the local rulers.

No such agency existed for the major powers, and in issues of dynastic inheritance it was harder to compromise as considerations of honour were involved. It is difficult to assess the significance of such considerations, which were mentioned frequently in the diplomatic correspondence of the period. In the same letter in which he remarked that 'il est encore moins permis aux Souverains qu'au reste des hommes de présenter l'illusion sous les apparences de la vérité', Rouillé, the French foreign minister in 1755, informed the French envoy in Spain that Louis XV wished to keep the peace he had given to Europe, 'mais il ne craindra jamais de faire la guerre, quand sa gloire ou ses engagemens avec ses alliés l'y forceront'. Two months later he wrote to the envoy at The Hague, 'Nous désirons la paix, maix nous ne lui sacrifierons pas l'honneur et les intérêts de la nation francaise'.[25]

The impact of such considerations in the courts of Europe, where policy was made, is difficult to assess, but the issue cannot be ignored by arguing that it is impossible to arrive at the psychological profile of particular groups.[26] An interesting attempt to use the psychological approach is E. H. Dickerman's article on Henry IV of France's personal, particularly sexual, problems and perceived inadequacies in the late 1600s and how these led him to take an aggressive stance in the Jülich-Berg dispute.[27] Evidence for such an approach is usually unreliable and the conclusions necessarily tentative. However, that does not make the method pointless, and before the subject is dismissed out of hand it is worth pointing out that most historians working on international relations use psychological terms, such as aggressive, without explicitly considering the bases for their judgments.

A habit of viewing international relations in terms of concepts such as glory and honour was a natural consequence of the dynastic commitments and personal direction that a monarchical society produced. It reflected traditional notions of kingship and was the most plausible and acceptable way to discuss foreign policy in a courtly context. Such notions also matched the heroic conceptions of royal conduct in wartime. In his essay Steven Gunn shows how the example of Henry V was a powerful one at the court of Henry VIII. John Hale has recently rather surprisingly stated that by 1611 personal royal service in wartime 'was coming to be considered something of an eccentricity'.[28] This would have amazed subsequent Swedish monarchs and German rulers, as well as William III and George II of Britain, Louis XV on the way to Metz, Peter the Great, and Victor Amadeus II at the siege of Turin. Thus the *mentalité* of the bellicist early-modern-European monarchical society can be discerned. This matches the observation reached from a different perspective of Joseph Schümpeter that it was in the nature of absolute monarchies to be war machines. Writing of Transylvania, Peter Sugar has recently suggested that the rulers of that turbulent principality indulged in 'constant aggressive wars' in order to establish themselves domestically, that they strove to achieve a 'goal in foreign affairs that went beyond those required by religious or even Transylvanian ends' and that there was an 'overwhelming interest of absolute princes in foreign affairs'.[29]

The bellicist nature of the society of the period helps to explain why great-power wars were more frequent in the early-modern era than subsequently.[30] It does not necessarily explain why particular wars began. At this point it is possibly appropriate to face two insoluble problems of definition, first that of war, and second that of the beginning of a war. As a specialised form of organised mass violence war is and was commonly defined as a conflict between two sovereign states. Aside from the range of conflict that that definition comprehends in terms of the number and intention of the combatants and the type and duration of the conflict, it is also possible that sovereignty may entail too exclusive a definition. The position of major rebellions, such as the Dutch revolt or the Hungarian risings against the Habsburgs, is particularly difficult. The sovereignty of the ruler in individual states did not preclude traditions that bad kingship could be redressed by rebellion. Some risings, such as the Hungarian revolt under Rakoczi (1704–11), involved organised struggle between armies and were a significant feature in the international relations of the period. There is also the problem of assessing when it is reasonable to cease talking of a rebellion, as in the Dutch revolt against Philip II, and begin considering it as a war. Many domestic campaigns, as with the French action against the Huguenots in the 1620s, entailed a military commitment that was equal to that of a foreign conflict. Rebellion leading to an independent state with a sovereign right to wage war was rarely successful, though Portugal and the United Provinces gained such a status. European early-modern history is littered with instances of polities that failed to become independent states: Bohemia in the 1620s, Catalonia in the 1640s, Transylvania, Hungary and the Ukraine in the 1700s. It is difficult to determine which of these struggles can be regarded as wars. It is similarly difficult to assess conflicts that were clearly civil wars, in which domestic violence reflected not a demand for fiscal amelioration, as in so many peasant uprisings, but rather a struggle with distinct political objectives. In several, such as the French civil war in the 1590s and the struggle when Augustus II gained the Polish throne in 1697, the source of the conflict was the identity of the sovereign. Many of these civil wars based on disputed successions were subsumed within larger conflicts. The British civil war which followed the invasion of William III in 1688 was a vicious conflict, particularly in Scotland and Ireland, involving major hostilities lasting over a period of several years. It is usually however treated as part of the Nine Years' War, otherwise known as the War of the League of Augsburg. Similarly the Spanish civil war of the 1700s was a major conflict whose roots were not simply found in the disputes of European diplomacy.

The significance of domestic struggles, their close relationship with international conflicts and the ambivalence of the concept of sovereignty, particularly in the case of disputed successions, makes it difficult to accept the definition of war adopted by writers whose empirical consideration has been devoted to modern conflicts defined as a struggle between two sovereign powers. This is especially the case with central Europe. In the Empire, the Habsburg lands and Italy there was not a clear fusion of political power and sovereign authority, and the ambiguities in the constitutional position of the Emperor in particular help to explain the difficulties of determining when the Thirty Years' War became a war. That contemporaries, both in this and in other struggles, disagreed, the same conflict being termed war and rebellion, was not due to insincerity. There were fundamental differences, often directly related to the cause of the conflict, and these pose problems for historians today, just as they caused jurists at the time to quarrel.

It could be argued that this confusion became less of a problem after Westphalia, and that anyway these conflicts were all functionally wars and should be treated as such. The first is certainly untrue for the period 1650–1715, though possibly less so thereafter. The consolidation of territorial sovereignty in mid-seventeenth-century France and Spain and the definition of Imperial and princely authority in the Empire at Westphalia have led many to assume that 1648–59 witnessed the establishment of a stable state system, albeit one that was to be strained by Louis XIV's actions, and that the domestic authority of these states was clear, at least in foreign policy. In short the states had succeeded in monopolising organised violence. This analysis looks less certain from an eastern-European perspective, and this suggests the problem of adopting a chronology of early-modern European developments based on French developments, a problem that also affects subjects other than international relations. In eastern Europe the century after Westphalia was a period both of major territorial changes between the states and of the unsuccessful struggle of a number of groups — Hungarians, Transylvanians, Ukraineans and Cossacks in particular — for independence. The fluidity of territorial boundaries in eastern Europe gave greater opportunities for these groups, as did the existence of buffer zones between the major empires. In such a situation the identification of a sovereign authority capable of declaring war is largely an irrelevant question.

The situation in eastern Europe changed in 1709–11. The defeat of Charles XII of Sweden by Peter the Great at the battle of Poltava in 1709 spelled the end of his hopes to reorder the fluid territorial system of eastern Europe at Russia's expense, and, in particular, to create an independent Ukraine under Mazepa. The end of Rakoczi's rebellion signalled a new age in Hungary. Austria and Russia, both now expanding powers, had no real interest in semi-independent buffer zones. Ukrainean and Hungarian separatism became a matter of pathetic exiles dreaming of a different Europe. The simultaneous crushing of Catalan autonomy helped the new Bourbon monarchy in Spain to show that it also was unwilling to tolerate semi-independent regions, while the defeat of the Jacobite rebellion of 1715, though not strictly comparable, was followed by a period of increased direction from London of Scottish affairs.

Thereafter it could be argued that the distinction between foreign war and domestic rebellion was clearer in most of Europe, though in some areas, particularly Poland, the position was still ambiguous. The attempt to partition the Austrian empire in 1740–2 was an attempt to transfer territories between sovereign states, rather than to create new ones by encouraging rebellion. However, the major changes that were envisaged at this point are a salutary rejoinder to those who would argue that in the eighteenth century warfare was about very little. The rulers of the period could conceive of major alterations in the territorial structure of Europe. However, they lacked the military muscle to carry them out, a close parallel to their domestic situation.

The argument that all major conflicts were functionally wars and should be treated as such represents for the early-modern period a major qualification of the definition of war as a military struggle between sovereign states. It also leads to a massive expansion in the number and type of conflicts that have to be considered. All significant policing operations involved troops and the numbers used were often large: 20,000 men were sent to put down the Breton rising of 1675, a force larger than the armies of many independent states. In the Rakoczi rising 85,000 Hungarians were killed in battle, and in 1711 the number of Austrian troops deployed in Hungary may have reached as high as 52,000, nearly half of the entire army.[31] The Pugachev rising in Russia of 1773–4 led to pitched battles. The battle of Tatischchevo of March 1774 was an engagement between 9,000 men and 36 guns under Pugachev and 6,500 men and 22–25 guns under General P.M. Golitsyn.[32] To restrict the definition of war to a conflict between sovereign states therefore fails to take note of major military commitments. The alternative however causes significant problems for the study of the causes of war.

Clearly military operations took place along a continuum stretching from formal war to actions against smugglers. Formal war did not necessarily entail greater commitments or problems than domestic action, though particularly after the early 1710s it generally did so. There is much in common between domestic and international conflicts. In both cases it was not necessary for 'war' to begin with a specific move, a point well made in the case of international conflict by David Parrott, and in both sustained hostilities were often not sought. Negotiations could precede conflict, and the latter was often ended by a settlement that was essentially a compromise, reflecting the manner in which the struggle had revealed the strength and determination of the combatants. The increased unwillingness and inability of powerful domestic groups to take differences with the central government to the point of violence, particularly in western Europe, arguably makes this parallel less appropriate for the eighteenth century. Nevertheless, it is one that poses a serious question to the existing definition of war.

The functional definition of war in terms of the use of military force is itself not without its problems. In particular, contemporaries were generally able to differentiate between the policing and war functions of the armed forces. Furthermore, in terms of the *mentalité* of courtly society earlier referred to there was a relatively clear distinction. Glory and honour could be gained through suppressing domestic discord, but it was primarily a function of defeated foreign rivals. Domestic conflict could be a serious problem, but it was in the attitude of the rulers concerned (and in that of most other monarchs) a matter of rebellion not war. This tended to remain the case for other rulers even when ideological factors, principally religious considerations, led to attempts to interpret rebellions in a more favourable light.

That wars were therefore generally regarded as armed conflicts between states did and does not necessarily make it easy to determine when they began.

Declarations of war often followed hostile acts. The British attacked a Spanish fleet off Sicily in 1718 and a French squadron in the Atlantic in 1755, and did not declare war subsequently in either case for several months. In May 1756 the Earl of Holderness, one of the British Secretaries of State, wrote to Robert Keith, the Minister Plenipotentiary in Vienna: 'Notwithstanding the repeated hostilities of the French in North America, in time of profound peace; their infractions of the most solemn treaties, by the reparation of Dunkirk; and their open menaces, and immense preparations against these kingdoms; His Majesty has, hitherto, confined himself to the Defence of His Dominions, and the meer detention of the French ships, and cargoes, without confiscation, from the hope, that an accommodation might still be brought about, and that France would have shewn an inclination to agree upon reasonable terms; in which case, their ships and cargoes might still have been entire, and open to restitution. But all hopes of that kind being now vanished, from the answers returned by the court of Versailles to those of Madrid and Berlin; and France having on the contrary, by an attack on the island of Minorca, (the possession of which is of so great consequence to the commerce of these kingdoms,) rendered it impossible for His Majesty, consistent with what he owes to his subjects, and to his own honour, to remain any longer within the bounds, which, from a desire of Peace, he had thus prescribed to himseif; It is with the greatest reluctance and concern, that the King finds it now indispensably necessary to shew his resentment, by a Declaration of War; and, at the same time, to call upon His Allies who have guaranteed His Majesty's Dominions, by the Treaties of Utrecht and Aix La Chapelle, to perform their engagements'.[33]

Seventeen years earlier Francis Whitworth, one of the MPs for Minehead, wrote to the other, Thomas Carew: ''tis certain if taking of ships and killing of men be a state of war, we are now without a formal declaration in a war — and I dare say as we have been forc'd by the Spaniards to these vast expences we shall not pick up the sword till ample satisfaction is made us for all the injuries and insults they have shewn our merchants'.[34]

Conflict without a formal declaration of war could occur more easily at sea than on the continent, and it was particularly common in the colonies. In 1718 a dispute arose over the island of Canso off Nova Scotia. French fishermen were driven from the island by the British and several of their boats were seized. Three years later the island was retaken after a French attack. The British Royal Africa Company complained frequently of attacks by other European interests. In October 1723 the Portuguese destroyed their trading station at Cabinda, two years later the Company complained about French action on the Guinea coast, and in 1728 Dutch attacks upon their ships led to demands for naval protection and the despatch of a British warship.[35] Britain was then an ally of all three powers, and colonial hostility proved compatible with European alliance, particularly as the issue did not arouse much domestic interest. The same was the case with an Anglo-French quarrel over St. Lucia in the 1720s and with Anglo-Dutch differences in the East Indies in 1750.[36] If hostilities were restricted to the colonies,[37] it was less easy for battles to be fought in Europe without a declaration of war.

However, it was by no means rare. States did attack others without any such declaration, and it was possible to engage in wars as auxiliary powers. It was under the latter guise that George II fought Marshal Noailles at Dettingen in 1743; war was not declared between Britain and France until the following year.

Declarations were often delayed for diplomatic reasons or never made because the use of military force was seen as a reasonable intervention in the domestic affairs of another power. As most alliances contained provisions for defensive mutual assistance only, it was felt necessary on many occasions to avoid the first declaration of war. There might also be domestic reasons for such a course of action. This did not necessarily preclude actions that might be judged as aggressive, as in the case of Britain in 1755, and it did not prevent states from being deserted by some of their allies, as Austria was in 1733. Certain states claimed a right to intervene in the affairs of weaker neighbours, as eighteenth-century Russia did in those of Poland, and their military actions were deliberately not accompanied by any declaration of war.

Accepting the distinction between hostilities and war, a British pamphlet of 1755 nevertheless thought it possible to ascertain the exact cause and commencement of conflict, '... a Distinction which is understood in modern Policy, but is not authorised by the Law of Nations, between Reprisals and Hostilities, and between Hostilities and War. For, whether that Distinction is understood or not, our present Conduct certainly may be justified, and reconciled to the Principles of the purest Equity. If we are making Reprisals, who made them necessary? If we are committing Hostilities, who gave the Provocation? And if we are even carrying on a War, who is to blame? Certainly, the Party who committed the first Injustice, by his Conduct, authorized Reprisals to be made upon him. If he continues to support the Injustice by Force, it is immaterial by what word you term the Operations against him, whether by that of *Hostilities* or *War*'.

Participating in the lively debate on the causes of the Anglo-French war of 1793, John Bowles argued that 'The party who declares war or begins the attack, is undoubtedly, *prima facie*, the aggressor, and the presumption in favour of the other party. This evidence, however, is not conclusive. A state may be obliged to declare war, in order to redress an injury, for which no reparation could be obtained by treaty. Thus in 1790, if Spain had refused satisfaction for the attack made by her on our settlement at Nootka Sound, we should have been justified in declaring war, and in so doing, we should not, strictly speaking, have been the aggressors. But there can be no doubt that the *onus* lies upon the party who first resorts to violence to justify the attack, by proving that he has sustained an injury, for which he had in vain demanded satisfaction'.[38]

The pro-British conclusion of the 1755 argument was dubious with regard to Anglo-French hostilities in North America.[39] The method was also a questionable one in arriving at the causes of wars. There was no shortage of 'injustices' for powers that wished to feel aggrieved; many survived from previous peaces, as Stewart Oakley demonstrates in his chapter.[40] Instead it is often unclear why individual issues emerged as causes of significant controversy at particular points, for most did not. It is furthermore often unclear at what point action taken over such issues can be classified as war, especially if there was no declaration of hostilities or one only after conflict had continued for a period. This point can be illustrated from David Parrott's account of Franco-Spanish relations in the early 1630s. It is equally pertinent in such cases as relations between Britain and Spain in the 1580s, Britain and France in the mid-1750s[41] and Russia and Turkey in the mid-1780s. The Russian annexation of the Crimea in 1783 hardly improved tense relations with Turkey. Russian military expansion in Pontic Europe was well advertised: in 1787 Catherine the Great and the Emperor Joseph II visited the new naval base at Kherson. Trouble had developed two years earlier in the Caucasus, an unstable buffer zone, when Russia and Turkey were drawn in to support competing Georgian factions. By 1786 relations were deteriorating rapidly, and in May the Russian envoy at Constantinople delivered a memorial demanding compliance with Russian demands over Georgia. France, which enjoyed good relations with both powers, sought to solve the disputes without success, and in January 1787 Choiseul-Gouffier, the French envoy, reported a new aggressive Russian stance over Georgia. The following month he noted warlike steps by both powers.[42] The French envoy in Vienna and his Austrian counterpart in St. Petersburg had warned that the Turks could be provoked to the point of risking war,[43] and in August 1787 the Turks declared war. The immediate precipitants were the news of revolts within the Austrian dominions and drought in Russia, the departure for Egypt of Gazi Hassan, the principal opponent of war and possibly encouragement from the British envoy.[44]

In the case of the Russo-Turkish conflict there was a definite declaration of war, but it is arguable that hostilities in the Caucasus predating this declaration mark the true beginning of the conflict. It could also be suggested that the state that formally began the war was not the one with the most aggressive intentions. It is frequently difficult to determine when in a series of hostile acts, often carried out with violence by armed forces, war can be said to begin. Anglo-French relations in 1742-4 are an obvious example. This was also a problem that puzzled contemporaries. Not all wars of course began in this fashion. Abrupt changes of policy and plans signalled by major military moves, as in the Prussian invasion of Silesia in 1740 and the French attack on Austria the following year, were clearly different in type. They best correspond to the model of a conflict begun by a specific act of policy. A.J.P. Taylor wrote of 'the more prosaic origin of war: the precise moment when a statesman sets his name to the declaration of it'.[45] However, it could be suggested that this model, which corresponds more closely to the reality of nineteenth-century wars, is inappropriate for many wars over the preceding three centuries.

The model of war begun deliberately by a specific act of policy is that which has been discussed most fully by theorists of the causes of war. There is little sympathy for the idea of a war begun by accident,[46] nor sufficient discussion of the problem, for contemporaries and historians, of determining when a war began. If the latter problem is probed it could be suggested that a central question for study is not which among a number of disputes and attitudes, each of which were regarded by different contemporaries as the cause of war, was in fact the crucial issue,[47] but rather why at a given moment the range of hostilities and issues that made war a constant possibility, and conflict often a constant reality, led to serious hostilities. In some cases this was clearly due to an act of state policy whose intended result was a major war. However, it could be argued in the majority of early-modern cases that war happened as a result of a series of acts whose intention was not to cause a major conflict, and indeed the point at which these acts became a war was and is often unclear. A case could be made for discussing the Thirty Years' War, the War of the League of Augsburg, and the War of the Spanish Succession in these terms. This argument does not imply that the study of specific triggers of conflict should be discarded, but rather that it is necessary to match it by a full consideration of whatever is held to constitute the international 'system'. The latter comprised not only the range of interests and issues that divided and united states, but also the attitudes that affected the conduct of policy, or, rather, the attitudes whose furtherance policies were designed to obtain.

This approach is advocated by William Roosen and Karl Schweizer in their important essays when they call attention to the structural characteristics of the state system of the period. Their suggestion is a valuable one, provided that it is not adopted as a mechanistic or reductionist analysis. Schweizer's list of structural characteristics is essentially one of economic and political strengths, interests and trends. Roosen's scope is more extensive and he attaches weight to the attitudes, fears and misunderstandings of the decision makers. It can be suggested that such a structural approach is of great value provided it does not lead to the argument of inevitable conflict. It is at this point that the crucial distinction between hostility and war is so useful. Hostile interests, whether economic, political, religious or ideological, do not have to lead to war. The conflicting political interests of France and Austria between 1648 and 1756, and their colonial and commercial counterparts between Britain and the United Provinces between 1609 and 1688, were both important in the several wars between the respective powers, but they did not prevent peace. Furthermore, periods of peace were not simply opportunities to prepare for a fresh war. They could witness significant cooperation, as between Britain and France in 1716–31 or France and Austria in 1727–8. Such developments cannot be fully explained by reference to a structural model that concentrates on interests. If political differences drove Louis XIV to attack the United Provinces in 1672, they did not prevent close cooperation with William III in replanning the map of Europe in the late 1690s. If commercial and colonial disputes between Britain and Spain, exacerbated by a domestic British agitation, helped as Philip Woodfine shows to drive the two powers to war in 1739, they had failed to do so a decade earlier and did not prevent close relations between the two powers in the early 1750s. If structural political interests led France to seek Prussia's alliance against Austria in 1733–5 and gain it in 1725 and 1741, they did not prevent her from joining Austria to attack Frederick the Great in 1756. In 1727 the Wolfenbüttel diplomat Schleinitz had referred, in a letter to the French foreign minister, to 'les difficultés presque insurmontables qui naturellement se trouveroient à fixer et à concilier les vues et intérêts de la maison d'Autriche et celle de Bourbon'.[48]

One of the dangers with a determinist structural approach is that it can display a questionable interpretation of evidence. If a system and its development are defined, then it is all too easy to assume that events that correspond to the system are explained by it and prove it, and that those that do not are due to deviations from the model.[49] In the case of early-modern international relations such deviations can be explained in terms of the personal idiosyncrasies of particular monarchs, an interpretation also employed by contemporaries when accounting for the analytical faults of their comparable model, one based on the concepts of natural interests and the balance of power.[50] To regard a war as a structural crisis in the international system, because it occurred in a period of transition within that system, is to beg several questions. What if the war had not occurred? Are not all systems continually in a period of transition? Aside from being conceptually questionable such theories are possibly too general to be of any particular use, and when they do descend to issues that can be discussed factually the results are often unfortunate. Employing George Modelski's long cycle of world leadership theory, William Thompson has recently produced a table of 'global succession struggles', in which the 'global war period' 1689–1713 witnessed an attempt by France to replace the United Provinces as the world power.[51] The Habsburgs, France's principal rival in the wars of the period, are not mentioned. Modelski's portrayal of eighteenth-century Britain as the 'world power' would have been scant comfort to the British ministers fearing French invasion in 1744–6 and during the early disastrous stages of the Seven Years' War, but as Modelski presents France as embroiled in continental affairs it is not surprising that he does not discuss these fears.[52] In contrast to theories such as Modelski's, Charles Doran urges caution in the selection of individual variables, such as particular types of military spending, as crucial determinants of national strength.[53] Discussing negotiations for the end of the War of American Independence with Joseph II in 1782, the British Envoy Extraordinary in Vienna, Sir Robert Murray Keith, noted, 'He [Joseph] said, *at once*, and with an animated tone — you seem to calculate probabilities, (as I have often done) by weighing the great considerations of state policy, national honour, and national advantages. This thing cannot be true, because it would be impolitick, — that event must happen because all our *data* are in favour of it. But you forget that in the present crisis, it is not the interests of France, of England, or of Holland which hold the balance, but the personal wishes, and hopes of John, Andrew, or Peter, the ministers of those different countries. Mr. Fox had his views in accelerating peace — Mr de Vergennes believes he can attain the pinnacle of favour by concluding that work — we must now see what Lord Shelburne thinks, and if the establishment of his administration requires peace or war'.[54]

Reporting on Spanish policy in 1733, the British Minister Plenipotentiary, Benjamin Keene, observed: 'where passion and chance have so great a hand in matters, as they have in this country, it is as difficult to reduce their actions to system, as it is hazardous to say the same situation will last for 24 hours'. The following year Keene reported on the explanation advanced by the leading Spanish minister José Patiño, in conversation with many diplomats, for the Spanish attack on Austria in 1733: 'that their declaring war was not the effect of any scheme laid with France *de longue main*, but the work of a pique improved by the French'.[55]

It is facile perhaps to raise empirical queries concerning theories advanced for a broad timespan. The willingness of scholars to advance such theories for such a difficult subject is praiseworthy and they can produce illuminating perspectives. It is clearly important to discuss the topic of the causes of early-modern European wars at a level more general than that of individual conflicts. Scholars who do not do so nevertheless implicitly use concepts derived from their interpretation of the period. If relations between states are conceived of within a structural model stressing competing interests, this model is not invalidated by periods of peace or cooperation between the states. Such periods can be regarded as ones when it was possible to reconcile competing interests without formal conflict; they do not prove the weakness of the competitive element. Such an interpretation accords with studies such as those of Clausewitz and Blainey which treat war as a specialised form of power struggle.[56]

In casting doubt on the reductionist and determinist characteristics of certain theoretical suggestions it is not necessary to discard all attempts to consider the structural characteristics of the international relations of the era.[57] In particular it is surely important to devote more attention to the attitudes of the age, while accepting that these were neither uniform nor unchanging and while avoiding any attempt to create a new reductionist and determinist model. One of the more worrying aspects of the use of models in work on the early-modern period is that they are sometimes employed by scholars who have clearly little interest in the surviving evidence concerning the conduct of affairs. This may owe something to the impact of economic reductionism and to the work of scholars, such as Braudel and Wallerstein, who have generally treated politics as epiphenomena, matters of limited and essentially transient significance. Such an approach is of debatable value. In the case of international relations a failure to consult archival material can easily lead to a schematic interpretation of developments.[58] However, the principal impression created by early-modern archives of many types is that of the ignorance, uncertainty and unease of contemporaries, whether concerning the actual or anticipated fiscal resources of the state, the confessional loyalty of subjects or the aspirations of other powers and their likely response to moves. In place of glib assumptions about policy, archives enable one to glimpse the hesitations of the past, the choice between possible steps whose impact could not be assessed. While eschewing determinist viewpoints, such an approach does not necessarily lead to a perspective in which it is assumed that policy depends exclusively on the views of monarchs and ministers. Nevertheless, it is naturally these views that emerge as most significant in a study of the available documentation. The Saxon envoy in Spain was instructed in 1725 to investigate ministerial views on foreign policy, court cabals, and the financial and military affairs of Spain, and told that without understanding the internal state of a court it was impossible to form a sound judgment of its foreign policy.[59] In assessing the significance of *mentalité*, the effect of concepts such as glory and honour or of ideas such as the balance of power, it is necessary to ascertain what they meant to specific individuals at specific junctures. Such concepts were neither uniform nor unchanging in their impact, and it is changes in attitudes to the use of the power that are still a relatively uncharted field. While the views of Erasmus and Rousseau, More and Kant, Hobbes and Voltaire, Montesquieu and Clausewitz have all been discussed, little attempt has been made to assess their impact. Arguably the subject suffers, as so many others do, from the great man obsession, the concentration on the ideas of a small number of usually atypical thinkers, a study facilitated by, and possibly in some measure due to, their availability in print. Diplomatic archives are not usually regarded as a promising field for scholars of political thought. They are exceedingly bulky; poorly, if at all, indexed; and the theoretical reflections they contain are fragmented and peripheral to the often ephemeral nature of the reports. However, far from being unreflective, many diplomats were able and perceptive.[60] That many, such as the Marquis de Mirepoix, French envoy in Vienna in the late 1730s, prided themselves on their skill in such court arts as dancing and display, did not prevent them from using their social entrées at the highest level of court society to acquire important information. Lord Waldegrave, the British envoy at Vienna from 1728 to 1730, possessed a skill with cards that was believed to help him in this respect. In an age when courts were the centres of government, social skills were essential. Precisely because the writers and recipients of diplomatic correspondence were men of power and because their letters were not intended for publication, they are an excellent source for the attitudes of early-modern politicians. Many were greatly concerned about the source and use of political power in other countries. It is therefore through studying the correspondence of such men that the international relations of the age can be better understood.

One of the most striking aspects of early-modern discussion of international relations is the capriciousness which was seen to dominate them. Possibly this owed something to the Christian legacy, the habit of seeing providence at work. Commenting on the dramatic turns of fate that affected Peter the Great and Charles XII of Sweden, George Tilson, a British bureaucrat, wrote in 1722, 'a Pruth as well as a Frederickshall are the short ways Providence has to set bounds to ambitious and turbulent Princes'.[61] It is more likely that the notion of capriciousness was sustained by the chance factors integral to dynastic politics, and, in a lesser degree, to the wealth of the community in the shape of the harvest, and to military operations. The unpredictability of the policy of individual states was a frequent theme in the correspondence of the period,[62] as was the rapidly altering nature of the 'system'.[63] Doubtless there were reasons why diplomats unable to account for the activities of particular states, and ministers of monarchs keen to avoid pressure to declare themselves should refer to unpredictable change, but nevertheless the predominant impression is one of a perception of kaleidoscopic change. Partly the changes were seen as structural, responses to significant alterations in what was seen as a European system. Thomas Robinson, British Minister Plenipotentiary in Vienna, explained diminished Austrian interest in British views in 1732: 'such is the present system of Europe, and so changed it is from what were the interests of Princes thirty years ago, since the acquisitions of the Muscovites and the share they have now in the affairs of Europe joined to the pretention of the House of Saxony to the succession of the Emperor that whatever use his Imperial Majesty has for the Maritime Powers, with respect to Italy, and Flanders in particular, and even to his other hereditary countries in general, yet with respect to the latter, and still more with respect to Silesia, Bohemia and even Hungary, this court thinks it has less need of the Maritime Powers, than of Muscovy, and Prussia, to keep the King of Poland in awe'.[64]

More common was a sense not of structural change, but of wilful unpredictability, William Fraser, a former British Under Secretary, writing in 1785 of 'these strange disjointed times. Where there is no System, but that of striving to ... overreach.' This helped to produce an impression of an unstable international situation, with violence as an ever-present threat. Regretting the French revolutionary wars, the veteran British diplomat William Eden, Lord Auckland, wrote of his wish to see the world restored 'to peace, or at least to that old state of Disorder which was a Paradise in comparison of the present "Infernalité".[65] The effect of this situation on the policy of individual powers and its role in producing conflict is difficult to assess. A tense and uncertain international situation did not necessarily lead to war.[66] On the other hand it did encourage a constant anticipation of conflict. This helped to lead to the vigorous pursuit of alliance partners and active negotiations of treaties that is a constant feature of the period.[67] It also had an effect in encouraging the growth of armed forces in those states that could afford them. A 'military revolution' has been discerned in the period 1560–1660,[68] and, though detailed accounts of military campaigns in the period 1650–1700 induce considerable caution in accepting such an interpretation, it is nevertheless the case that military costs were a major item in state expenditure in early-modern Europe.

The unpredictable nature of international relations encouraged war. Tim Blanning has argued that the reciprocal nature of war is crucial, that the victim of a predator has a choice of submitting and avoiding war. In common with Geoffrey Blainey, he had also claimed that the decision to prefer war to peace is taken by the two parties concerned because they have different assessments of their respective power.[69] However, as Quincy Wright has pointed out, it is unlikely that war can be 'decided by highly intelligent generals without any bloodshed'. In the early-modern period the difficulty of translating diplomatic strength into military achievement and the rapidly altering nature of international alliances ensured that it was usually worthwhile for states that felt themselves to be weaker to fight or fight on. When Lord Stair, the British Ambassador at The Hague, urged war with France in April 1742, writing 'I flatter myself that before the end of summer, His Majesty may be in a condition with his other friends, to make the peace of Europe upon such terms, as he himself shall think proper, such a peace as France will not be able to break thro' for a great many years',[70] he was being optimistic in his usual fashion, but it would have been quite possible in the diplomatic situation of the time to make two valid assessments, one concluding that France should yield, the other that Britain should not attack. Given the fast-changing international situation of the period, war was not a particularly effective way of testing the 'power relationship' between states. Swedish successes in the first eight years of the Great Northern War, and the collapse of the anti-Swedish coalition in 1716–17 vindicated to a certain extent Swedish obduracy in the face of substantial odds. Aside from those prudential considerations it was difficult in the court culture of the age to surrender claims that were felt to be good.

Although it was possible to assess power in terms of the size of armed forces and the number of allies, such an assessment was both a poor guide to the results of a war and no reason why conflict should be avoided. Rather than constructing a general theory around this issue of different assessments,[71] it would be more appropriate in the case of early-modern Europe to draw attention to features in the international relations of the period and the perception of these relations, the existence of a bellicist society, and the fact that some monarchs wanted war and profited from it at least in terms of territorial gains. Attention is thus still devoted to the courts of the period, but it is important to try to get a more sympathetic perspective than Blanning's somewhat mechanistic view that 'it is the repeated inability of decision-makers to get their sums right which lead to repeated wars'.[72] Wright pointed out the need for an historical assessment of such misjudgments, though he possibly underestimated the difficulty contemporaries faced in gaining accurate information about the actions and views of other states. Wright argued that 'false images depend not on misinformation about the immediate situation, but on prejudiced conceptions and attitudes rooted in distant history, in the national culture, or in the minds of important persons in the decision-making process'.[73]

Naturally no general theory can account for all the wars of the period, while no typology of early-modern warfare commands general assent. The range of issues in dispute was vast, many of them apparently trivial, but often pregnant with possibilities. Reporting tension between the Austrian government of Milan and the Duke of Parma in 1733, Robinson wrote of 'new troubles upon the Po. One of them is as much as if the inhabitants of Milbank would have the ferry boat constantly on their side of the water, and should send in the night time a couple of sturdy watermen to undo it from the posts at Lambeth and bring it over to Westminster upon which the Archbishop should order the first Westminster sculler that should be found plying at Lambeth to be seized by way of reprisals'.[74]

This collection of essays is intended to open a debate on a subject that has received very little attention for the early-modern period. There is a need for an intermediate level of research between studies of all wars at all times, which are usually very implausible to the historian, and examinations of particular conflicts that often draw implicitly on assumptions about the causes of wars in a given period. Rather than borrowing concepts wholesale from existing theoretical studies, the majority of which simply address themselves in practice, if not in pretension, to the late-modern period,[75] it is necessary to consider the particular nature of early-modern international relations, without assuming that these are unchanging and without creating a deterministic model. In considering the implications of the bellicist nature of society it is important to probe the importance of the triumphal use of force in conferring greater acceptability on monarchs and bringing political success to ministers. If major wars were indeed more common in the early-modern period than subsequently, as the mathematical work of J.S. Levy would suggest[76] (and there is no doubt that the picture is the same for minor wars however defined), then it is necessary to study the social and cultural aspects of European society that made this possible. The suggestion of this introduction is that the bellicist nature of society and the characteristic features of international relations, including in particular the way in which they were perceived, made it easier to bridge the hostility/war dichotomy employed by certain modern theorists, and that this dichotomy itself is not a helpful way of viewing relations between many states. Other scholars will possibly not agree with this tentative conclusion, but if this book encourages debate and furthers research its purpose will have been achieved.

NOTES

Unless otherwise stated all dates are in new style.

1. Holderness to Robert Keith, Minister Plenipotentiary at Vienna, 28 Aug. 1755, BL. Add. 35480.

2. [Currie]. *A Letter, Commercial and Political Addressed to the Right Hon. William Pitt* (Dublin, 1793), pp. 5–6.

3. J. R. Hale, *War and Society in Renaissance Europe 1450–1620* (1985) pp. 35–7; D. Napthine and W. A. Speck, 'Clergymen and Conflict 1660–1763', *Studies in Church History* 20 (1983).

4. D. McKay and H. M. Scott, *The Rise of the Great Powers 1648–1815* (1983), p. 1.

5. 46 volumes (Berlin, 1879–1939). The publication of the papers of Peter I (the Great) of Russia began in 1887, that of the *Recueil des Instructions données aux Ambassadeurs et Ministres de France depuis les Traités de Westphalie jusqu'à la Revolution Française* in 1884.

6. M. Howard, *Weapons and Peace* (1983), p. 6.

7. M. Howard, *The Causes of Wars and other essays* (1983), p. 13.

8. For an important study of an earlier public relations campaign, J. Klaits, *Printed Propaganda under Louis XIV: Absolute Monarchy and Public Opinion* (Princeton, 1976).

9. Manfred Schlenke, *England und das friderizianische Preussen 1740–1763* (Freiburg, 1963).

10. K. Borgmann, *Der Deutsche Religionstreit der jahren 1719–20* (Berlin, 1937).

11. Count Törring, Bavarian foreign minister, to Count Ferdinand Plettenberg, first minister of the Elector of Cologne, 24 Dec. 1729, Münster, Staatsarchiv, Dep. Nordkirchen, NA. 148; Chauvelin, French foreign minister, to Chavigny, French envoy at the Imperial Diet, 23 Jan., 22 Feb., 7 Mar. 1730, AE.CP. Allemagne 376; Gansinot, Wittelsbach envoy at The Hague, to Törring, 14 Nov., Plettenberg to Törring, 28 Dec. 1730, Munich, Bayerisches Hauptstaatsarchiv, Kasten Schwarz 17313, 17223.

12. W. R. Ward, 'Power and Piety: the origins of Religious Revival in the early eighteenth century', *Bulletin of the John Rylands Library* 63 (1980).

13. *Politische Correspondenz* I, 298–301; Frederick to George II, 30 Jan. 1741, F. V. Raumer, *König Freidrich II und seine Zeit 1740–1769* (Leipzig, 1836), p. 109.

14. J. Black, *British Foreign Policy in the Age of Walpole* (Edinburgh, 1985), p. 120.

15. Harrington to his fellow Secretary of State, the Duke of Newcastle, 6 July 1740, PRO. 43/90; Bussy, French envoy in London, to Amelot, French foreign minister, 17 May 1741, AE.CP Ang. 412; Titley, British envoy in Copenhagen, to Harrington, 5 Sept. 1741, PRO. 75/81; *Politische Correspondenz* II, 272, 355; L'Hôpital, French envoy in Naples, to Montaigu, French envoy in Venice, 28 Jan. 1744, Paris, Bibliothèque Nationale, Nouvelles Acquisitions Françaises, 14916.

16. J. Black, 'The Challenge of Autocracy: The British Press in the 1730s', *Studi Settecenteschi* 3–4 (1982–3); J. Black, 'The Catholic Threat and the British Press in the 1720s and 1730s', *Journal of Religious History* 12 (1983); J. Black, 'Richard Rolt, 'Patriot' Historian', *Factotum* 16 (1983); W. Fryhoff, 'De Paniek van Juni 1734', *Archeif voor de Geschiedenis van de Katholieke Kerk in Nederland* 19 (1977).

17. Edward Finch, British envoy in Russia, to Harrington, 1 Nov. (os) 1740, PRO. 91/26.

18. R. C. Stuart, *War and American Thought: From the Revolution to the Monroe Doctrine* (Kent, Ohio, 1982); J. Black, 'Religious Subjects don't sell: Edward Weston and the Economics of publishing in 1756–7', *Factotum* 21 (1985).

19. J. H. Lind, 'Ivan IV's Great State Seal and His Use of Some Heraldic Symbols During the Livonian War', *Jahrbücher für Geschichte Osteuropas* 33 (1985); numerous examples of the exaltation of victorious power among exhibits recorded in catalogue *Prinz Eugen und das Barocke Österreich* (Vienna, 1986); on the impersonal state, J. H. Shennan, *The Origins of the Modern European State, 1450–1725* (1974), *Liberty and Order in Early Modern Europe. The Subject and the State 1650–1800* (1986); H. H. Rowen, *The King's State: Proprietary Dynasticism in Early Modern France* (New Brunswick, 1980). On maps I have benefited from numerous conversations with Peter Barber and from the help of David Buisseret. P. Solon, 'Frontiers and Boundaries: French Cartography and the limitation of Bourbon ambition in seventeenth-century France', D. Buisseret, 'Cartography and Power in the Seventeenth Century', *Proceedings of the Western Society for French Historical Studies* 10 (1982); N. G. d'Albissin, *Genèse de la frontière franco-belge. Les variations des limites septentrionales de la France de 1659 à 1789* (Paris, 1979). On the crucial role of British monarchs, Black, 'British Foreign Policy in the Eighteenth Century: A Survey', *Journal of British Studies* (1987) discusses recent work; *Owen's Weekly Chronicle*, 22 Ap. 1758.

20. *Politische Correspondenz* VII, 12.

21. W. Cobbett, *Parliamentary History of England from . . . 1066 to . . . 1803* (36 vols., 1806–20), XII, 167.

22. AE., Mémoires et Documents, Ang 41 f.54.

23. Burrish to Secretary of State Earl of Holderness, 29 June 1756, PRO. 81/105.

24. M. Hughes, The Imperial Supreme Judicial Authority under the Emperor Charles VI and the crises in Mecklenburg and East Frisia (Ph.D., London, 1969).

25. Rouillé to Duras, 11 Jan., Rouillé to Bonnac, 6 Mar. 1755, AE.CP. Espagne 517, Hollande 488.

26. The problem of the psychological approach for the historian is discussed in T. C. W. Blanning, *The Origins of the French Revolutionary Wars* (1986), pp. 1–8.

27. E. H. Dickerman, 'Henri IV and the Juliers-Cleves Crisis: the Psychological Aspects', *French Historical Studies* 8 (1974).

28. Hales, *War and Society*, p. 31.

29. J. Schümpeter, 'Zur Soziologie der Imperialismus, *Archiv für Sozialwissenschaft und Sozialpolitik* 56 (1918–19); O. Subtelny, *Domination of Eastern Europe. Native Nobilities and Foreign Absolutism 1500–1715* (Kingston, 1986), p. 56; P. F. Sugar, *Southeastern Europe under Ottoman Rule, 1354–1804* (Seattle, 1977), pp. 165–6.

30. J. S. Levy, 'Historical Trends in Great Power War, 1495–1975', *International Studies Quarterly* 26 (1982), p. 289.

31. C. W. Ingrao, *In Quest and Crisis: Emperor Joseph I and the Habsburg Monarchy* (West Lafayette, Indiana, 1979), pp. 158–9. Recent work on this conflict includes L. and M. Frey, 'The Rakoczi Insurrection and the Disruption of the Grand Alliance', *Canadian-American Review of Hungarian Studies* 5 (1978) and articles in the *Acta Historica Academiae Scientiarum Hungaricae* 22 (1976), particularly G. Razso, 'La situation militaire générale et la guerre d'indépendance de Rakoczi'.

32. I. de Madariaga, *Russia in the Age of Catherine the Great* (1982), p. 248.

33. Holderness to Keith, 11 May 1756, BL.Add. 35480.

34. Whitworth to Carew, 2 Oct. (os) 1739, Taunton, Somerset Record Office, Trollop-Bellow papers, Box 16 0B8.

35. H. C. Hart, 'History of Canso', *Collections of the Nova Scotia Historical Society* 21 (1927), pp. 3–6. Africa Company memoranda, 13, 28 Feb. (os), 4, 18 Dec. (os) 1724, 18 Mar. (os) 1725, 18 Mar. (os) 1726, PRO. 35/48, 54, 55, 61; Secretary of State Viscount Townshend to William Finch, envoy at The Hague, 10 June (os) 1726, PRO. 84/290; Africa Company to Burchett, Secretary of the Admiralty, 28 May (os), 6 June (os), 3 Aug. (os) 1728, PRO. ADM 1/3810.

36. Newcastle to Holderness, envoy at The Hague, 2 Jan. (os), Holderness to Newcastle, 6, 23 Jan. 1750, PRO. 84/454.

37. William Lorimer to Sir Ludovick Grant, 17 May 1754, Scottish Record Office, GD. 248/182/1/43.

38. Anon., *Reflections upon the Present State of Affairs* (1755), pp. 53–4; Bowles, *French Aggression, Proved from Mr. Erskine's "View of the Causes of the War"* (2nd ed., 1797), p. 11.

39. There is an extensive literature on the topic. Significant works include T. C. Pease (ed.), *Anglo-French Boundary Disputes in the West, 1749–1763* (Springfield, Illinois, 1936), M. Savelle, *The Diplomatic History of the Canadian Boundary, 1749–63* (New Haven, 1940); D. S. Graham, 'The Planning of the Beausejour operation and the approaches to war in 1755', *New England Quarterly* 41 (1968); D. S. Graham, British Intervention in Defence of the American Colonies, 1748–56 (PhD., London, 1969); J. E. Stagg, Protection and Survival: Anglo-Indian Relations 1748–63. Britain and the Northern Colonies (PhD., Cambridge, 1984); T. R. Clayton, 'The Duke of Newcastle, the Earl of Halifax, and the American Origins of the Seven Years War', *Historical Journal* 24 (1981).

40. *Old England* 13 May (os) 1749; *Owen's Weekly Journal* 15 Ap. 1758; *Monitor* 28 June 1760.

41. Governor William Shirley of Massachusetts to the Earl of Halifax, President of the Board of Trade, 20 Aug., Lieutenant-Colonel Charles Lawrence, Lieutenant-Governor of Nova Scotia, to Halifax, 23 Aug. 1754, S. Pargellis (ed.), *Military Affairs in North America 1748–1765* (New York, 1936), pp. 25–9.

42. M. S. Anderson, 'The Great powers and the Russian annexation of the Crimea, 1783–4', *Slavonic and East European Review* 37 (1958–9); A. W. Fisher, *The Russian Annexation of the Crimea 1772–1783* (Cambridge, 1970); Sir Robert Ainslie, British envoy in Constantinople, to the Foreign Secretary, the Marquis of Carmarthen, 25 Jan., 11 Mar., 10 June, 24 July, 9 Aug., 10 Nov., 9 Dec. 1786, 11, 15 Jan., 10, 23 Feb. 1787, PRO. FO. 78/7, 8; Segur, French envoy in St. Petersburg, to Vergennes, French foreign minister, 1, 9, Sept. 1786, Noailles, French envoy in Vienna, to Vergennes, 13, 18 Nov. 1786, Choiseul-Gouffier to Vergennes, 25 Jan., 10, 23 Feb., Memorandum read at Conseil d'Etat, 28 Feb. 1787, AE.CP. Russie 119, Autriche 351, Turquie 175; D. M. Lang, *The Last Years of the Georgian Monarchy 1658–1832* (New York, 1957), pp. 205–11; A. Bennigsen, 'Un mouvement populaire au Caucase au XVIIIe siècle: la "Guerre Sainte" au Sheikh Mansur', *Cahiers du Monde Russe et Soviétique* 5 (1964).

43. Noailles to Vergennes, 15 June 1785, Segur to Vergennes, 22 Sept. 1786, AE.CP. Autriche 349, Russie 119.

44. S. J. Shaw, *Between Old and New: The Ottoman Empire under Sultan Selim III 1789–1807* (Cambridge, Mass., 1971), pp. 25–8; J. M. Black, 'Sir Robert Ainslie: His Majesty's Agent — provocateur? British Foreign Policy and the International Crisis of 1787', *European History Quarterly* 14 (1984).

45. A. J. P. Taylor, *How Wars Begin* (1980), p. 14.

46. Blanning, *French Revolutionary Wars*, p. 25.

47. Much of the work devoted to specific conflicts, such as the War of the Spanish Succession, revolves around this question.

48. Schleinitz to Chauvelin, 16 Sept. 1727, AE.CP. Brunswick-Hanovre 46.

49. For a comparable attack on Wallerstein's model of early-modern world economic relations, T. Skocpol, 'Wallerstein's world capitalist system: a theoretical and historical critique', *American Journal of Sociology* 82 (1983), p. 1088.

50. J. Black, 'The theory of the balance of power in the first half of the eighteenth century: a note on sources', *Review of International Studies* 9 (1983).

51. W. R. Thompson, 'Uneven Economic Growth, Systemic Challenges, and Global Wars', *International Studies Quarterly* 27 (1983), p. 347.

52. G. Modelski, 'The Long Cycle of Global Politics and the Nation State', *Comparative Studies in Society and History* 20 (1978), p. 222.

53. C. F. Doran, 'Power Cycle Theory and the Contemporary State System', in W. R. Thompson (ed.), *Contending Approaches to World System Analysis* (Beverly Hills, 1983), p. 178; Thompson, 'Cycles, Capabilities, and War. An Ecumenical View', in same book, p. 146.

54. 'Heads of a Conversation with the Emperor at the Augarten on the morning of 19 August 1782', BL.Add. 35526.

55. Keene to Charles Delafaye, Under Secretary in the Southern Department, 16 Feb. 1733, Keene to Newcastle, 10 May 1734, PRO. 94/116, 119.

56. Carl von Clausewitz, *On War*, edited by M. Howard and P. Paret (Princeton, 1976); G. Blainey, *The Causes of War* (1973).

57. There is an interesting theoretical discussion in G. A. Craig, 'The Historian and the Study of International Relations', *American Historical Review* 88 (1983), p. 7.

58. I. Wallerstein, *The Modern World-System* (2 vols., New York, 1974, 1980); I. Wallerstein, 'The States in the institutional vortex of the capitalist world-economy'; A. R. Zolberg, 'Strategic interactions and the formation of modern states: France and England', *International Social Science Journal* 32 (1980), p. 689. Braudel of course had considerable experience of diplomatic archives.

59. Instructions to Feraty de Valette, 17 Ap. 1725, Dresden, Hauptstaatsarchiv, Geheimes Kabinett, Gesandschaften, 2797.

60. An interesting study of one such diplomat, successively Sardinian envoy at The Hague and Vienna, is A. Ruata, *Luigi Malabaila di Canale. Riflessi della Cultura Illuministica in un Diplomatico Piemontese* (Turin, 1968).

61. Tilson to Charles Whitworth, Minister Plenipotentiary at Berlin, 4 Mar. (os) 1722, BL. Add. 37389.

62. Villeneuve, French envoy at Constantinople, to Marquis de Caumont, 28 July 1735, Paris, BN. NAF. 6834.

63. Edward Finch, British Envoy Extraordinary in Stockholm, to Lord Harrington, Secretary of State for the Northern Department, 27 Feb. 1739, reporting the opinion of Frederick I of Sweden, PRO. 95/87.

64. Robinson to Harrington, 16 Ap. 1732, PRO. 80/87.

65. Fraser to Keith, 7 June 1785, BL. Add. 35534; Auckland to Sir James Bland Burges, Under Secretary at the Foreign Office, 9 Feb. [1793?], Bodleian Library, Bland Burges papers, 31; James III, pretender to the British throne, to the Duke of Wharton, on a Jacobite mission to Vienna, 14 Ap. 1725, Windsor Castle, Royal Archives, Stuart Papers 81/94; Ossorio, Sardinian envoy in London, to Gansinot, Wittelsbach envoy in The Hague, 3 Oct. 1730, Robinson to Harrington, 19 Nov. 1738, PRO. 107/2, 80/132; Chavigny, French envoy in London, to Bussy, French envoy in Vienna, 30 Jan., Chavigny to Chauvelin, 16 Feb. 1733, AE. CP Autriche, supplement 11, Ang. 379; Wachtendonck, Palatine envoy in London, to the Sulzbach minister von Schall, 21 July 1733, Munich, Bayerisches Hauptstaatsarchiv, Kasten Blau 88/1; Tilson to Robinson, 16 Aug. 1736, BL. Add. 23798.

66. St. Saphorin, British representative in Vienna, to Whitworth, 16 May 1722, BL. Add. 37389.

67. Gansinot to the Bavarian minister Baron Malknecht, 9 Dec. 1732, Munich, Kasten Schwarz 17321; R. C. Snyder, 'Some Recent Trends in International Relations Theory and Research', in A. Ranny (ed.), *Essays in the Behavioral Study of Politics* (Urbana, Illinois, 1962), p. 104.

68. M. Roberts, *The Military revolution, 1560–1660* (Belfast, 1956).

69. Blanning, *French Revolutionary Wars*, pp. 26–7; Blainey, *Causes of War*, pp. 245–6.

70. Q. Wright, 'The Nature of Conflict', *Western Political Quarterly* 4 (1951), p. 205; Stair to the Secretary of State for the Northern Department, Lord Carteret, 27 Ap. 1742, PRO. 87/8.

71. L. L. Farrar (ed.), *War* (Santa Barbara, California, 1978), p. xiv; D. R. Rapkin, 'The Inadequacy of a Single Logic Integrating Political and Material Approaches to the World System', in Thompson (ed.), *Contending Approaches*, p. 257.

72. Blanning, *French Revolutionary Wars*, p. 28.

73. Q. Wright 'Design for a Research Project on International Conflicts', *Western Political Quarterly* 10 (1957), p. 267.

74. Robinson to Edward Weston, Under Secretary in the Northern Department, 27 May 1733, PRO. 80/96.

75. Some degree of industrialisation is a structural prerequisite for Organski's interesting transition model, A. F. K. Organski, *World Politics* New York, 1968), Organski and J. Kugler, *The War Ledger* (Chicago, 1980).

76. Levy, 'Historical Trends', *International Studies Quarterly*.

1

THE FRENCH WARS OF HENRY VIII

Steven Gunn

Richard Corbett of Assington in Suffolk went to war in 1523, and wisely made his will beforehand. In its preface he explained why he thought he was going: 'to wait upon the right noble prince, Charles duke of Suffolk, into the parts of France, there to war upon the French men, being the king's my said sovereign lord's ancient enemies, according to his high commandment'.[1] Corbett's phrasing poses neatly the question of why Henry VIII made war on France. Was Henry's 'high commandment' a rational decision formed by a coherent foreign policy? Was it an emotional decision, born of an atavistic antipathy to the neighbours across the Channel shared by king and people alike? Or was it dictated by internal pressures, pressures articulated through the great men about the king like the duke of Suffolk? Was it indeed the king's own decision at all, or merely the performance of England's inescapable role in the emerging international system of early modern Europe?

For whatever reason, Henry VIII was a warrior king. He spent roughly a quarter of his reign in open war with the French. He came to the throne in April 1509; by the end of the year he had reinforced Calais, ordered general musters, commissioned new artillery, expanded and upgraded his father's small bodyguard of courtiers, the king's spears, and initiated an expansion of the navy which would quintuple its forces by 1515. He had also begun discussions with France's most powerful neighbours for an alliance against her.[2] Henry emerged from the diplomatic maze two years later, in November 1511, as part of an impressive, though by no means universal, 'Holy League' against the French. The ensuing encounters with the French fleet were inglorious, and a campaign to reconquer Guienne from Spanish bases in 1512 was a fiasco. But in 1513 Henry himself led an army from Calais to the conquest of Thérouanne and Tournai. Another large invasion was planned for 1514, but the inconstancy of his allies and the generous offers of the French prompted Henry to make peace in August 1514. In 1522 England entered the first of many conflicts between Francis I, king of France since 1515, and Charles V, ruler of the Netherlands, king of Spain and, since 1519, Holy Roman Emperor. That year produced only a vicious raid through Picardy, but 1523 saw an English army, within reach of Paris, forced to turn back by the failures of Charles V's forces elsewhere. In 1524 another major expedition was held ready to exploit any success by Charles's lieutenants, but was never launched. The defeat and capture of Francis at Pavia early in the following year raised hopes of English annexations in France, but tax revolts and imperial reticence led Henry to exploit the French predicament by offering peace rather than war. For the next fifteen years England had generally to court the French: Charles V's loyalty to his aunt, Catherine of Aragon, and to the Papacy which Henry had first to coerce, then to abandon in his search for a divorce, necessitated it. But Charles could not ignore Henry's potential as an ally, and 1543 brought England back to the offensive against France. In 1544 Henry invaded in person, took Boulogne, and was promptly abandoned by the Emperor, who wanted to turn his back on France and crush the German Protestants. Until June 1546 Henry fought on alone, determined to keep Boulogne; six months from the end of his life he made a peace under which his conquest would remain English until 1554, when the French might buy it back.

Henry lived in an unstable Europe. The agglomeration of feudal lordships into nation-states had produced great powers capable of rapid and devastating military action, but still left independent enclaves capable of tempting the powers into expansionism or provoking an unexpected war. These flashpoints — Gelderland, Sedan, Savoy and Navarre amongst others — came under the subjection or close tutelage of the great powers by 1559, initiating a rather different system of international relations.[3] But in Henry's reign they were still free enough to cause trouble. At the time of Henry's accession the international system was still further weighted towards conflict by the fact that Venetian expansion across the Italian mainland had reached the limit at which no power with Italian interests felt safe; in 1509 her rivals combined to humble Venice but soon fell out, strewing the diplomacy of the ensuing years with their mutual recriminations, and continuing grudges against the Most Serene Republic. Roman policy was aggressive under the warmongering Julius II, while France's Louis XII sought to dominate northern Italy. Finally, arrangements for the Spanish succession poisoned the relationship between Ferdinand of Aragon (sole ruler of the united Spanish kingdoms since 1506) and the Holy Roman Emperor Maximilian (paternal grandfather of Ferdinand's heir Charles) to prevent their cooperation against France. The deaths of Louis, Ferdinand and Maximilian brought no respite. For Charles V united Spain and the Empire to encircle France and aspire to European hegemony, and war was inevitable. Louis's successor Francis I reacted to this challenge to the position France had retained for nearly half a century as Europe's strongest nation-state, and Charles had to test whether the great potential of his patchwork empire could be realised in effective military strength.

The European system bred wars; but England's place in that system by no means forced her to participate. The French valued English quiescence, and from 1475 to 1550 were happy to buy it, with pensions of £5,000 or £10,000 a year. If left alone, the French were highly unlikely to attack England — their only serious expedition against the mainland in Henry's reign took place in 1545 to hamstring the English defence of Boulogne — and even Calais was rarely considered as a possible prey. The French kings coveted firstly Milan, secondly Naples, and thirdly an expanded northern and eastern frontier. Even in wartime, direct action against England was limited to skirmishes around Calais and the briefest of naval raids. So the draftsman of the 1545 subsidy bill rather exaggerated Henry's achievement in enabling his subjects to live 'out of all fear and danger as if there were no war at all, even as the small fishes of the sea in the most tempestuous and stormy weather do lie quietly under the rock or bank side, and are not moved with the surges of the water'.[4]

Of course it was traditional French strategy to attack England indirectly, by activating the old alliance with Scotland. Continental chroniclers pictured a king of Scots who said 'Whatever it pleases the king of France to command me, I shall do it'.[5] Yet the French often tried to calm the Scots when ancient hatred, border incidents and Scottish piracy combined with Henry's patronising and hamfisted attempts to manipulate Scottish affairs to inflame Anglo-Scottish enmity. When England set herself against France, the Scots could seek a French alliance with confidence, as they did in March 1512. When Henry tried to restrain France by the threat of war, Francis stimulated Scottish anglophobia, as in the years after 1515. When Henry tried to crush Scotland into subservience, as he did after the death of James V in 1542, the French could not stand idly by. But in 1532-34 Francis I did his best first to prevent, and then to settle, a war between Henry and James, exercising more pressure on the Scots than on the English. Henry could not expect the French to abandon the Scots entirely; but he did not have to reckon that his problems with his northern neighbour would force him into war against France.

Nor did he face consistent French support for pretenders to his throne. In wartime the French used any weapon that came to hand, and in 1522-23 these included the Yorkist claimant Richard de la Pole. But in peacetime De la Pole was shuffled off French territory and often ignored, and after his death in 1525 Henry was even less likely to be stirred up to war by French intervention in English dynastic struggles, as Edward IV, for example, may have been in 1475.[6] The break with Rome did create the threat that Francis and Charles would cooperate to depose Henry for religious reasons, and the rapprochement of 1538-40 between those monarchs caused Henry immense concern: the construction of a chain of coastal fortifications, and anxious attempts to court the German Protestants, testified to the danger of such isolation. But there was no obviously suitable replacement for Henry, and little enough trust between Francis and Charles. Francis had no great interest in crusading against England, and Charles could crusade against the Turks or the Empire's Protestants instead. Though the threat of 1538-40 was serious, it was not likely to recur too often. The rivalry of Valois and Habsburg dominated European politics, and it was a rivalry which apparently left England free to stand aside or choose when and where to become involved.

The primacy of the Habsburg-Valois struggle gave Henry still greater freedom, in that he could wait for wars to break out before committing himself. In 1521 Henry's minister Cardinal Wolsey knew that Charles V would offer better terms for an English alliance once he was already under the strain of war. He also knew that Charles's assaults would have weakened France before England mounted an attack.[7] Before 1519 Henry was dogged by the difficulty of assembling reliable offensive alliances against France — in 1510 his councillors explained to Spanish ambassadors that the young king had renewed his father's treaty with France because he had as yet no alliances enabling him to do otherwise — but Charles V's position made it easy for Henry to enter or leave European conflict as it suited him.

Henry liked the idea that he could 'have the said Emperor bound' to make war on France, 'and he to be at his liberty', and in 1521–25 Wolsey and the king were perhaps over-careful to preserve their freedom of action.[8] The fact that Henry's heir or heiress throughout his reign was a minor, and that Francis and Charles were always either marriageable themselves or had young offspring available, reinforced this freedom by enabling the construction of marriage-alliances which need never prove binding. Invasions could be mounted or aborted at relatively short notice, and this too brought flexibility. Planning against France was complicated by the desire to neutralise the Scottish threat before crossing the Channel, but compared with his contemporaries Henry enjoyed a free hand. Unlike Charles V, he had no need to write himself memoranda complaining that 'Peace is beautiful to talk of but difficult to have, for as everyone knows it cannot be had without the enemy's consent'.[9]

However much Henry prized his freedom, it was not respectable for him to make war of his own mere 'will and appetite'. Wolsey, asking Parliament for taxation in 1523, for example, had to parade a long list of *casus belli*.[10] These were provided in abundance by the French need to strike first against Charles V, exploiting their standing army and interior communications to attempt a crippling early blow. In 1521–22 and 1542–43 Henry's hesitation enabled French offences against neutral England to pile up, and these were then used to justify a declaration of war. Naval conflict between France and the Netherlands inevitably led to the capture of English merchants and the confiscation of their goods, while French naval movements threatened the Channel Islands. Border incidents around Calais were bound to occur, as the Franco-Flemish frontier met the coast there. French suspicion of English intentions could lead to more clearly hostile actions, the withholding of the pension and even, in 1522, the arrest of the entire English wine fleet at Bordeaux. This might look like a gradual escalation of hostilities drawing England into war: the French attacked the Netherlands in July 1542, by the end of the month English merchants had been arrested, by August the French soldiers of Boulogne were taunting the English garrison of Guines with comments like 'You Englishmen be all naught', by September there were problems over the hot pursuit of Frenchmen by Netherlanders into the Calais Pale and vice versa, and in February 1543 an alliance was duly formed between England and the Habsburgs.[11] But the apparently smooth succession of events is deceptive. In 1536, when Henry was happy to stay on the sidelines of the European conflict, there were problems with plundering Netherlanders returning through the Pale, and the French confiscated an English ship. But Henry's minister Cromwell made equal fuss about infringements of English neutrality by each side, and no-one mentioned the fact that the French pension had been unpaid for several years since it was better spent subsidising the German Protestants.[12]

Henry could certainly avoid war if he wished. On the other hand, if he chose to make war it would almost inevitably have to be against France. Henry did not seek consistently to maintain the balance of power, doing his best to kick Francis I while he was down in 1525. Yet he probably did see unrestrained French expansionism as a political and a moral evil. In 1512–13 the 'inordinate appetite' of the French king, his 'damnable ambition' to control the church and his fellow princes, was condemned in Henry's propaganda as a threat which must 'needly be extermined'.[13] In 1516 Henry tried secretly to fund Swiss opposition to French control in Italy. In particular he wanted to preserve the Low Countries from further French encroachment. In August 1542 the English Council hurriedly prepared to help the Netherlands when it looked as though the French would tear them apart in a triple invasion. This was sound strategy — Henry VII had resisted the growing French control of the Channel seaboard, and Elizabeth would do the same — but it also reinforced Henry's honour. For he enjoyed exercising an avuncular protection over the Low Countries, having himself named a guardian of the future Charles V in 1513 and protector of the Netherlands in 1522. It is probably unfair to separate the seaboard question — a matter of 'real English interests' — from that of Henry's international standing, though there are signs that some of his subjects were developing a view of war which conceived of the national interest in narrower strategic and economic terms.[14]

In fact England was more closely tied to the Low Countries than Henry liked to admit: here the international system did constrain him. As England's export trade came to depend increasingly on the sale of cloth at Antwerp, so the maintenance of a close relationship with the Netherlands grew in importance. In the fifteenth century the English alliance was regarded as natural in the Netherlands, and the war between Philip the Good of Burgundy and Henry VI after 1435 was difficult, indecisive and brief. Yet Henry VII had been able to cut off the cloth trade from 1493 to 1496 to force Maximilian not to support the Yorkists. In 1528 Henry VIII tried to do the same, buying French support for his pressure on the Pope. But the policy was no longer practicable. Not only did customs revenues collapse, despite attempts to transfer the cloth trade to France, but unemployment in the cloth industry presented serious threats to public order. In Mons it was said that Henry had beheaded numerous merchants for opposing his policy. The truth was more prosaic: he was forced to conclude a truce. Henry was reluctant to enter into war against the Low Countries, and did so only because it seemed the best way to pursue his divorce; but the collapse of his policy showed that he had less room for manoeuvre than he imagined.[15]

Henry was bound to the Dutch in other ways. Until 1514 he was obliged to help them by the planned marriage between Charles and his sister, Mary, a match so valuable that Henry was loath to jeopardise it. This drew Henry into assisting the regent Margaret of Austria against the French-backed duke of Gelderland in 1511, before he committed himself against France. England's obvious economic interests in the protection of the Low Countries, and the venerable tradition of intervention to protect Flanders from French aggression, also made the defence of the Netherlands a convincing justification of war to place before Parliament, since their destruction would be 'to the inestimable loss and damages of this realm'.[16] So badly did Henry need the assistance of the Dutch in transport and victualling that no campaign in northern France was practical without at least the benevolent neutrality of their government. Thus direct Anglo-French conflict in 1516–18 was out of the question because Charles's councillors, led by Chièvres, were resolutely francophile. For most of Henry's reign the anglophiles were in the ascendant in the Netherlands. Margaret of Austria herself confessed to a confidant that 'I have always been and still am a good Englishwoman', and leading nobles like Buren, Fauquembergues and Du Roeulx were proud to be counted 'a right Burgundian, a true man to his master and a friend to England'.[17] They encouraged English aggression against France and did their best to support English campaigns. All too often, though, they found it impossible to fulfil the unreasonable promises made on their behalf by the distant Charles V; and they understandably distorted Henry's campaigns by distracting his armies to the defence of their own vulnerable frontiers.

Nonetheless, they were the best allies Henry had, and the problems of transport, shipwreck and victualling which attended even campaigns based on Calais and blessed with their help show that Henry's best hope of making war without disaster (and with more prestige than invasions of Scotland brought) was to fight in northern France. An obvious target beckoned for any invasion begun at Calais. The shape of the French border with the Low Countries, redesigned by the French gains of 1477, channelled English ambitions south towards Boulogne as the obvious way to expand the Calais Pale. Just before the French took Boulogne in 1477, John Paston had commented, 'God forfend that it were French, it were worth £40,000 that it were English'.[18] Henry shared Paston's sentiments, though Boulogne cost him nearer a million. In 1513, 1514, 1522 and 1523 the king contemplated or even pressed for a siege of Boulogne, while the raids of his Calais garrison reached the walls of the town. If the capture of Boulogne in 1544 was 'the most extraordinary' of Henry's 'nonsensical actions', it was one he had had a long time to think over.[19] In fact the expansion of the Pale, whether by the capture of Boulogne or of Ardres (planned in October 1543), or the cession of Boulogne and other towns in a peace settlement (demanded in 1525 and 1543) was the most sensible aim of English aggression against France.[20] After 1453 Calais had held firm at a time of dire English weakness and great French strength: an enlarged Calais was more likely to endure under English control than another foothold elsewhere. Boulogne in particular presented a realistic target should Henry choose war.

There were other reasons why Henry's aggression was best vented on the French. His subjects disliked foreigners in general, rioting against alien merchants and falling out readily with foreign mercenary soldiers in Henry's pay. But they reserved a peculiar hatred and contempt for the French. A Spanish merchant noted cheerfully that 'the best word an Englishman can find to say of a Frenchman is "French dog" '. True to form, Sir William Paget, putting the finishing touches to the 1546 peace treaty, fulminated against 'these false dogs'.[21] Antipathy was reflected at deeper levels of the language. The duke of Norfolk, expressing the absurdity of his rumoured arrest for treason in 1536, said that the day he deserved to be in the Tower 'Tottenham shall turn French'. Hostile caricatures of the English were rife in medieval French literature, and reappeared in the 1520s. Similarly English writers mocked the French as a nation of downtrodden and perfidious peasants, and the English court spurned as 'French vices and brags' the affectations brought back from Francis's court by young Englishmen in 1519. In 1523 English soldiers greeted the news that the rebel duke of Bourbon would assist them by warning that 'never was Frenchman true to England'. In 1514 Sir John Wiltshire was not surprised that a French priest in Calais refused to celebrate Henry's victories. 'I cannot blame him,' declared Wiltshire, 'he did like a true Frenchman.'[22]

Such sentiments were carried through into action. We might doubt the resolve of the English noble who allegedly commented, after meeting the French at the Field of Cloth of Gold, that if he had a drop of French blood in his body, he would cut himself open to get rid of it. But at the Battle of the Spurs in 1513 many French nobles surrendered to the Netherlanders because the English were killing Frenchmen rather than taking prisoners. In the same year Londoners attacked the servants of the Venetian ambassador in the streets because Venice had made peace with France. Such hostility enabled Henry to use public opinion as an excuse for a tough stance in negotiations with the French, as he did in 1514.[23] It also helped offset the reluctance of many of his subjects to go to war. High desertion rates, and mutinous demands to return home once campaigning conditions deteriorated, gave substance in Henry's reign to the spectre of national military decline which haunted English thinkers. The tenantry went to war out of a sense of duty and (largely unfulfilled) hope of plunder, the very poor because the king's meagre wages were better than nothing.[24] But at least there was less reluctance to fight the French than there would have been to fight less natural enemies.

It was also easier to motivate the nobility and gentry to fight in France than elsewhere. Chivalry looked backwards for examples: the duke of Suffolk dismissed a claim for a share in the ransoms from the battle of Solway Moss because 'never the like demand hath been read of in any chronicle, nor heard tell of in any country'. Lord Berners translated Froissart's chronicles because of 'the great pleasure that my noble countrymen of England take in reading the worthy and knightly deeds of their valiant ancestors'.[25] By and large those deeds had been done against the French. Where the Burgundian dukes had had to cobble together a national chivalric tradition from tales of Lotharingian princelings and Flemish crusaders, English printers could sell poems about Agincourt in the 1530s, and English heralds collect chronicles of the Hundred Years' War.[26] Even at moments when English and French nobles jousted together to celebrate peace between their nations, there was an edge of patriotic competition: at Paris in 1514 the tourneying English lords 'had ever on their apparel red crosses to be known for love of their country'. The alliance with the Turks, developed by France from the 1530s, provided a boost not only to the anti-French rhetoric of proclamations and treaties with the Habsburgs, but also to the anti-French aggression of English nobles who took the defence of Christendom seriously. As the reign went on, the nostalgia of military men lower down the social scale, like Elis Gruffydd of the Calais garrison, concentrated on Henry's early campaigns against the French. Even Tudor bureaucracy found precedents helpful, and among Thomas Cromwell's papers in 1533 was 'A view of King Edward III for his retinue in France and Normandy, and of his charges there'.[27]

England's history, and the passions it engendered, made it easy for Henry to make war on France. But what motivated him to do so? War stimulated Henry's intellect, for he was fascinated by gadgetry of all kinds and especially by new weapons and developments in fortification. It stimulated still more his sense of honour. The court of his father Henry VII shared with that of the Low Countries a Burgundian culture which interpreted honour in highly martial terms — leading to the depiction at Richmond Palace of a succession of English kings 'appearing like bold and valiant knights' rather than in the panoply of kingship — and the early Tudor conception of honour in general laid a great stress on war. Honour dominated the rhetoric of Henry's foreign policy.[28] In part this made his wars an 'extension of tournament by other means', an opportunity to set up all his tents on the expectation of battle, or appoint his jousting companions to major commands. Henry was undoubtedly fond of the trappings of chivalry, a fondness in no way discouraged by his father, who created him earl marshal at the age of three and allowed him to joust publicly in 1508.[29] But the chivalric overtones of the quest for honour did not imply that Henry approached war as a dilettante.

To fight honourably could constrict Henry's options. Commitments were better carried out once made, for as Henry's ambassador Sir Robert Wingfield told Maximilian, Henry was not 'so light or of so little resolution as to arm' himself 'at all pieces, and then call for a pillow'. Treaties should not lightly be abandoned, for 'of all worldly losses, and specially in a prince, honour and credence is the most'. If a peace were to be broken, Henry should be seen to be in the right, to 'save his worldly honour, and also discharge his conscience to God'.[30] If a victory were to be won, Henry might best go in person, 'to have the honour of so high an enterprise', as Lord Admiral Sir Edward Howard invited him to do when the French navy was trapped before his fleet in April 1513. But on that occasion the Council dissuaded Henry from joining Howard, not wanting to put the king 'in jeopardy upon the chance of the sea', and honour rarely dictated action totally at odds with common-sense. In his correspondence, as in his autobiographical fiction, the Emperor Maximilian reconciled a chivalrous quest for honour with a relentless and politically shrewd aggrandisement of himself and his house, apparently without hypocrisy or conscious incongruity.[31] Henry VIII could seek to do the same.

To ascribe honour to oneself was merely pride: honour had to be validated by the approval of society. For Henry this confirmation came from several sources. After the 1513 campaign flattering letters flowed in from Italian princes and cities. Henry's ambassadors reported the responses of other courts, Cardinal Bainbridge writing that in Rome 'his glory is ... esteemed to be immortal'. During the campaign the nobles of the Low Countries, the doyens of that same Burgundian chivalry imbibed by Henry at his father's court, were 'all full of courage to serve the noble king of England'.[32] Indeed, it was the mark of a chivalrous king — Arthur and Edward III were examples — to be able to attract other knights to one's service. Henry made much of men like Guyot de Heulle, 'an esquire of Burgundy', who participated in feats of arms at the English court, was knighted by the king in 1512, fought in at least five English continental expeditions between 1511 and 1523, and was rewarded with a pension of £100.[33]

Battle was the greatest test of honour. The dominance of pitched battles in European warfare between 1450 and 1530 sprang largely from the dominance of chivalric aspirations in the military mind.[34] This could give English strategy an appearance of aimlessness, as armies roamed across France offering battle. In 1513 Henry was keen for battle, but managed only a successful skirmish. In 1522 the earl of Surrey devastated the French countryside in the attempt to provoke a battle, but achieved only the satisfaction of marching through France 'unfoughten withal'. To defy an enemy and prove him too craven to fight was a recognised act of prowess — one Flemish noble boasted of three months inside France without any opposition — but French generals realised that the English were strongest in defence and refused to attack. Instead they taunted the English with treating war (dishonourably) as a holiday occupation: in 1544 the captain of Montreuil told his besieger, the duke of Norfolk, to enjoy his hunting and hawking while the mild weather lasted, 'and by winter, according to the old English custom, you will go home to your kinsmen'.[35] Of course it lay within the bounds of honour to do as Henry did in 1544, and pursue conquest by siege when the chances of forcing the enemy to battle were minimal.

Henry's foreign policy was generally consistent with his code of honour, and when it was not, he was troubled, for instance over breaking his oath to keep the peace in 1521.[36] He claimed to hold the crusade as the highest form of warfare, as chivalry dictated he ought to do, and in 1511 he assisted Lord Darcy and other enthusiasts — of whom there were many — to campaign against the Moors. Though it was impractical for him to crusade in person, he came as close as he could to a crusade in his first war against France, fighting to defend the Roman church against the schismatic Louis XII. Much of his domestic and international propaganda then concentrated on the need to free the Pope from oppression, and Henry's recourse to negotiation in 1514 was in part a response to the peace initiatives of the new Pope, Leo X.[37]

Henry's chivalry defined his relationship with other monarchs, and above all with Francis I. Like the knights of romance, they veered from undying brotherhood to mortal combat and back again, along a path of eager competition in the quest for honour. Their ambassadors and councillors spoke of the natural friendship between two princes 'whom God and nature have made to be and remain good brothers and friends together', since 'more conformity is betwixt them than in or amongst all other christian princes'.[38] But even before his accession Francis was eager to hear about (and outdo) Henry's achievements in the lists, and Henry was devastated by the upstaging brilliance of Francis's first invasion of Italy and victory at Marignano.[39] Most international relations were a matter of personal relationships between monarchs, with wars declared over betrayals of promise and personal slights, but the rivalry between Henry and Francis was an especially intense case.

Henry's relationship with his forbears also mattered greatly to him. It was not enough to be 'the most valiant prince under heaven' in his own age; he aspired also to be 'the most goodliest prince that ever reigned over the realm of England'.[40] Henry felt his closest competitor to be Henry V, and consciously took him for a model. Each was the son of a troubled usurper, seeking to identify the new dynasty with the nation by an aggressive foreign policy. Each was a devout defender of the church (if necessary against papal power), each an enthusiastic advocate of naval power, each a stern military disciplinarian. Henry V showed more personal courage, at least on the battlefield, and certainly worked far harder at the less exciting administrative details of kingship. But Henry VIII did not let these differences deter him from an almost ritualistic imitation of his namesake.[41]

It was sound policy perhaps to do as Henry V had done, and start the reign with a generous attitude to dynastic rivals, restoring or promoting to titles the Courtenays, Staffords and Poles. There might have been some political purpose in executing the long-imprisoned Edmund de la Pole before crossing to France in 1513, though the parallel with Henry V's execution of the Southampton plotters on the eve of the Agincourt campaign must have been in the king's mind. It was as good for the morale of the troops in 1513 as it had been in 1418 to see the king walking round on a wet night encouraging the watches. It was natural to do as Henry V did and hand out conquered French lands to one's closest followers, though in 1513 this could amount only to one castle for Charles Brandon. It was as relevant a statement of England's prominence in the 1520s as it had been in the 1410s to have an Emperor visit the country to consult with the king. But Henry's mimicry went further still. In 1513 a Latin biography of Henry V was translated into English to encourage the king to 'attain to like honour, fame and victory'. One incident on which it dwelt (and of which Henry could have been aware from other sources) was Henry V's encounter with St Vincent Ferrer. The famous preacher had denounced Henry as a cruel warmonger in a sermon at the siege of Caen. Henry calmly called him to a private interview, from which Ferrer emerged to announce that the king was a most christian prince conducting a just war. In 1513 John Colet preached against war before Henry VIII; Henry calmly called him to a private interview, from which Colet apparently emerged to announce that the king was a most christian prince conducting a just war.[42] The badge of that war was borrowed from Henry V: Henry VIII's war propaganda used the Lancastrian red rose. Even the ideal end to the war looked back to 1430. Only one uninformed Fleming and the blustering duke of Bourbon ever spoke of crowning Henry VIII at Rheims. The promise with power to win Henry's heart was a coronation at Paris.[43]

There is a danger of anachronism in asking how seriously Henry took his claim to the French throne, as J. S. Brewer unwittingly pointed out by explaining in 1867 that Tudor Englishmen 'believed as fully in the right and title of their kings to France as we believe in our title to India or Ireland'.[44] To modern eyes Henry's attitude to his title looks suspiciously flexible. At the Field of Cloth of Gold he joked about it. When declaring war in May 1522, he made no special mention of it. Then in 1523 and 1524 he was insistent that Bourbon recognise it. In March 1528 he even told imperial ambassadors that he did not want Charles V to devastate France, since it was his inheritance, for which Francis paid him a pension. This identification of the pension as a rent for English possessions in France, or even for the French crown, was a frequent one.[45] It might be dismissed as a diplomatic ploy, or even a harmless piece of self-deception, but Henry's actions suggest otherwise. In 1512 he was eager to obtain a papal brief transferring Louis XII's kingdom to himself, and his propaganda stressed that the war to defend the Pope was also 'the direct moyen' to 'recover France'. When he concluded peace in 1514 it was only for the lifetimes of Louis and himself, in order not to prejudice his own or his successors' later claims.[46]

Again and again Henry considered plans to attack Normandy and Guienne, England's oldest French possessions, rather than more accessible portions of France. In 1523 Wolsey had to win him over to an assault across the Somme by arguing that the conquest of 'all that is on this side the water of Somme . . . should be as honourable and beneficial unto his grace, and also more tenable, than all Normandy, Gascony and Guienne'. In August 1536 English councillors told Charles V's ambassadors that the Emperor would have to commit himself to placing Guienne and Normandy in English hands if he wanted an offensive alliance. Only during the negotiations for the 1543 alliance did the English Council suggest that Henry would exchange his claim to Guienne (conveniently near Spain) for Charles's claim to the Somme towns, a logical extension of Henry's increasing concentration on the enlargement of the Calais Pale.[47] Earlier in the reign Henry and his commanders treated the claims to France and to the former English territories as more than diplomatic counters. In 1513 he handed Thérouanne over to Maximilian and kept Tournai probably because, as heir to the dukes of Burgundy, Maximilian's grandson Charles rightfully held the first but not the second as a fief from the French crown — Henry's French crown. In the same way Surrey was prepared to abandon the siege of Hesdin in 1522 because the town was part of Charles V's inheritance rather than Henry's French royal possessions. In 1523 Suffolk swore the inhabitants of captured towns to Henry as king of France, and made serious plans to garrison his conquests, realising that his expedition was no mere *chevauchée*.[48]

Henry's treatment of his French claim made sense in the light of the demands of honour and of history. His honour would be compromised if he did not try to claim his right, or abandoned his claim lightly. Henry V had been moved by 'the desire of justice and of his right, which every man is bounden to his power to demand and seek'. Edward III knew that if he demanded his right and was refused, 'if he should then sit still, and do not his devoir to recover his right, he should be more blamed than before'.[49] Henry's right existed, on the other hand, whether he claimed it or not, and like his landowning subjects in their lawsuits over estates, he saw no incongruity in waiting for the best moment to assert his right. Like his subjects, he might accept a pension in return for not pressing his claims for the moment, or might even enter into a close relationship with his rival without finally waiving his claims (as Henry did in 1518).

Indeed, the king's flexibility over his claim to the overlordship of Scotland was even greater than that over France. That did not imply a cynical attitude to either right, merely that the assertion of one offered more exciting possibilities than the other. To realise the right to French land by conquest — even of Boulogne alone — brought undying 'name, fame, honour and renown'. But it was better to recover land to which one had a less debatable right, hence Henry's early concentration on the English duchies. For, again like his subjects, he wanted to have back his ancestors' lands first and foremost. Lord Berners in 1522 begged to have his family's lands (exchanged in the past with the duke of Buckingham) returned to him, rather than a grant of any of Buckingham's other manors. The duke of Suffolk in 1538, in a vast exchange of lands with the crown, asked to keep one half-manor in Norfolk because he held it 'by descent of inheritance from his ancestors'.[50] It was hardly surprising that it took a lifetime of unsuccessful invasions of France for Henry VIII to begin to concentrate wholeheartedly on enlarging the Calais Pale, rather than regaining Lancastrian France.

Henry fought for his right also in the light of his sense of history. At his accession Englishmen and Europeans alike urged him to regain his French inheritance. John Skelton greeted him

> As king most sovereign
> That ever England had;
> Demure, sober and sad,
> And Mars's lusty knight;
> God save him in his right!

Those around him argued frequently from history. In 1510 the Spanish urged that 'as the realm of France was lost by the aid of Spain from your noble predecessors, that now the aid of Spain shall help your highness for to recover your most noble right inheritance in the realm of France'. In 1515 Sir Robert Wingfield lectured Maximilian on John, Edward III, Henry V and the English claim to France. The Battle of the Spurs was noted as especially significant because it 'had not been seen before time, that the English horsemen got the victory of the men of arms of France'. In 1536 ambassador Chapuys urged Henry to join with Charles V to repress the French and then throw back the Turks, tracing the ills of Christendom back to Philip Augustus's declaration of war on Richard I and the consequent loss of the Holy Land. Even Cromwell's propagandist Richard Morison, stirring up the English to throw back the papalist hordes in 1539, referred his readers to Froissart to see how Poitiers and Sluys showed the national ability to beat the French on land or sea.[51] Henry's ability to recover his inheritance was a test of his place in national history.

The places where Henry launched his campaigns reminded him of the fact. Edward III had besieged Tournai and failed; Henry did better. 1342 saw a battle of Morlaix, 1346 a crossing of the ford at Blanche Tâche, just before Crécy; in 1522 Henry's fleet raided Morlaix, in 1525 his army was to have crossed at Blanche Tâche to enter Normandy. The prisoners he took in 1513 paralleled those taken by his forbears: the duke of Longueville was the great-nephew of Charles of Orléans, the most renowned captive of Agincourt. The names of Henry's sons — Henry, then Edward — echoed those of his conquering predecessors. Henry was not alone in his awareness of the past — Edward III had sought to imitate Edward I in strategy as in chivalry — but he was sited at an ideal distance from 1453 for a renewal of the war.[52] His oldest councillors in 1509, Surrey and Foxe among them, were just old enough to remember the national agony at the loss of France, and perhaps wish for revenge. But the harsh realities of a losing war were far enough in the past to make the adventurous campaigns recounted by Froissart an attractive prospect. The prevailing view of the operation of fortune's wheel in history made it conceivable that France had had her day, especially since a fall ought to come after the sort of proud and greedy expansionism pursued by the French crown since 1453. To equal or outdo his ancestors Henry had to fight France. Having fought France and won, even though the only addition to his inheritance was Boulogne, Henry had to keep his gains. As he told those who pressed him to make peace in 1545–46, he had won Boulogne honourably and meant to keep it.[53] Unfortunately Francis I was equally concerned about dying in credit, and would not make peace without Boulogne's return until the nations fought each other to a standstill and their diplomats produced a compromise settlement. Queen Mary's famous despair at the loss of Calais would show the gravity of the sort of irrevocable loss both monarchs feared.

No-one questioned the idea that glory should be Henry's aim. At his accession everyone (except the fallen ministers of his father) rejoiced with Lord Mountjoy that 'Our king does not desire gold or gems or precious metals, but virtue, glory, immortality'. Over the means to achieve glory there was some debate. England's position in Europe made her ruler a prime candidate for the role of humanist peacemaker. Henry enjoyed playing that role when the time was right, as it was in 1518, but he never entered wholeheartedly into the Erasmian critique of war. Though Wolsey may have tried to steer Henry along this path, the difficulty of reconciling Habsburg and Valois, and Henry's own military ambitions, prevented much success. That did not mean that Henry was living in the past. Humanist learning spoke with more than one voice, and a good scholar like John Parkhurst, the future bishop of Norwich, could extol his master the duke of Suffolk with Latin verse epigrams comparing him to Mars.[54] When Henry and his courtiers read the classics, they found war eulogised as heartily as in the medieval romances of 'bold bawdry and open manslaughter' beloved of earlier generations. Though they lived in an age of change, they did not suffer from split personalities. Henry's courtier and general Sir John Wallop had fought the Moors at his own expense in 1516, thrived at the 'Renaissance' courts of Henry VIII and Francis I (as ambassador), and when leading his troops past Thérouanne in 1543 challenged the French garrison to a six-a-side jousting match. To Wallop chivalry was not an anachronistic affectation, but a way of life.[55]

It was a way of life widely shared in the political nation surrounding the king. By 1545 Elis Gruffydd was scathing about the younger gentlemen-captains sent out from England, 'a lot of feckless boys who were sent to school to learn to count money and become auditors rather than soldiers'. But only twenty-two years earlier Lord Berners had been confident that reading his translation of Froissart 'exciteth, moveth and stirreth the strong hardy warriors, for the great laud that they have after they ben dead, promptly to go in hand with great and hardy perils, in defence of their country'.[56] The last phrase was telling. For late medieval chivalry was a nationalised cult, and Henry VIII maintained this. He was visibly a devotee of St George, wearing in his hat a brooch depicting the saint when he landed at Calais in 1513. In July 1531 he gave a poor woman 4s 8d because she asked him for alms for the love of St George. His subjects invoked St George too, from Sir Edward Howard, through Thomas Cromwell's nephew Richard, to a lowly Welsh servant of the earl of Devon. For the select few there was St George's order, the Garter. At least early in the reign, most of those elected had considerable military experience; at every stage those chosen counted election a great honour, and sought it for their friends. Even when away from court, knights kept the Garter feast on St George's day. There is every sign that the Garter was more than a political favour dressed up in tinselled armour.[57]

In 1550 John Coke argued that the lack of a living tradition of chivalric biography in England, in contrast with France, did not prove that England had no heroes: if Sir Edward Poynings, for example, had been French, 'they would have made of his acts a great book'. The same argument applies more generally. The lull in chivalric writing — bar Berners — between Malory, Tiptoft, Caxton and Hawes, and the Elizabethans, has been taken to represent a lull in the 'chivalric tradition' between two 'revivals'.[58] But the English aristocracy between Hawes and Spenser maintained an interest in war and chivalry despite the quiescence of chivalric authors. We do not know what literature the marquis of Exeter owned at his arrest in 1538, but we know he had two St Georges to wear, one on his Garter chain, the other on a black lace, as well as plate decorated with 'a scutcheon of St George', a roll of the statutes of the Garter, two books of the statutes of the Garter, and a roll of the arms of the knights of the Garter. His interest extended to European warfare too, with 'a painted tablet of the siege of Pavia'. Exeter was a jousting courtier, but even Thomas Cromwell owned a 'cloth stained with a table of the taking of the French king'. Such interests were the norm, and it is unwise to dismiss the actions they generated, like Wallop's jousting match, as 'isolated examples . . . of no great importance'.[59] Henry's peers and knights were a late medieval nobility, equipped for war conceptually even if their armour was sometimes rusty.

One section of that aristocracy was especially militaristic. The Calais garrison kept alive the memory of past English triumphs, commemorating Agincourt with an annual procession. They celebrated the arrival of Anne of Cleves in the town by mounting a tournament. They viewed their neighbours at Gravelines with some disdain, but their hostility naturally focused on the French, to the extent that soldiers from the Pale fortresses could be talked into burning French villages by compatriots in the service of Charles V, even during periods of English neutrality. Even the captains were sometimes reluctant to stop raiding when ordered by the royal Council. The garrison's aggression was concentrated on the Boulonnais, and a lifetime of reports from Calais on how easy and advantageous it would be to overrun must have encouraged Henry's designs on Boulogne.[60] There was intense competition for places in the Calais retinue, as the correspondence of Lord Lisle, the deputy from 1533 to 1540, demonstrates. The senior offices were much in demand among peers and courtiers, selling for considerable sums. In part this was because they paid well, but the military duties involved (though not full-time) cannot have been uncongenial, and good service in them offered a route to advancement. Of Henry's four captains of the vital outpost at Guines, three attained peerages and the fourth, Wallop, became a gentleman of the Privy Chamber, a knight of the Garter, and the commander of a substantial army in 1543. In particular Calais provided a prime career for bastards. Forced to make their own way in the world, but endowed with the military enthusiasms and even equipment of their parental households, they thronged the garrisons. Amongst others, illegitimate sons of Lord Berners, Lord Cobham and Sir Edward Poynings followed such careers. Poynings' son Thomas showed what could be achieved, by rising through the hierarchies at Calais and Boulogne to be created a baron in 1545.[61]

Others of Henry's subjects, born with even fewer advantages, had to make a career of military service wherever they could find it. These ranged from the runaway apprentices who fought as freebooters from the Calais Pale between 1522 and 1524, or signed up for the French and imperial armies in 1536 and 1542, through the thirty English cavalry who fought as mercenaries for the Netherlands against Gelderland in 1511, to the forerunners of the Elizabethan professional captains who served in the continental wars of the 1540s.[62] But for the landed classes war offered attractive opportunities even if they had no need to earn their livelihood by it. Piracy paid well for those able to fit out a ship, as William Compton did in 1513. Retaining men for military service shaded over easily into the illegal construction of a feed and badged local affinity. Friends and relatives could be appointed to lucrative captaincies, and assured of a more prominent place in local society by securing knighthoods: the duke of Suffolk saw thirteen of his dependants of various sorts knighted after campaigning under him in 1513, 1523 and 1544.[63] For those in bad odour with the king, military service was a way to regain favour. Henry V's nobles found this after the law and order drive of 1414, as did former Protestant plotters under Mary. Lord Darcy obviously thought his royally-sponsored crusade of 1511 a good chance to win back some of the prominence he had lost since the death of Henry VII, a chance he shared with the Yorkshire friends he took as captains.[64] War was expensive — Darcy spent £4,000 on his crusade and the 1513 campaign, though £1,000 may have been reimbursed by the king — but its dividends could be great. In 1545, after successful campaigns in France and the North, Suffolk was allowed to buy monastic lands at about one-third the price charged him in 1542. Military distinction was one of the most frequent qualifications for entry into the Henrician peerage.[65]

So the political nation was both well attuned to war, and well able to benefit from it. But how far did it push Henry into making war? The French government apparently thought it might do so, and spent freely on pensions to leading councillors and courtiers in the hope of keeping Henry docile. They graded these payments carefully according to the apparent influence of the individual concerned, and continued to pay pensions to councillors after Henry's pension lapsed in the 1530s. Charles V's ambassadors blamed French gold whenever they could not get what they wanted from Henry's Council, and in the war of 1522–25 they undertook to pay the French pensioners annuities of equal value. But such pensions were not secret, unlike the infamous French pensions of Charles II's reign: in 1514 the earl of Worcester asked Henry and Wolsey whether he should accept the French offer of a pension.[66] Wolsey at least was in the pay of both Francis and Charles, and when English councillors divided over foreign policy, there is little sign that their pensions determined the stances they took. Even those with far stronger attachments to one of the powers usually threw themselves into support for a policy they disliked, once it was in operation. Norfolk in 1528 did show signs of sulking, disgusted at a war against Charles V which threatened social stability in East Anglia, cut off his own profits from trade with the Netherlands, and bruised his pride as the self-appointed champion of the traditional Burgundian alliance. But Suffolk fought the French happily in the early 1520s, after an awkward political education from 1515 to 1518 taught him to keep his francophilia under control. His love for France was largely induced by his wife's income as Louis XII's widow, an income some three times the size of his own and liable to interruption by Anglo-French conflict. Such loyalties could not be erased — in 1526 the peace with France enabled Suffolk to congratulate Francis on his release after Pavia and 'offer you what a gentleman can offer, to die at your feet in your service' — but they were usually suppressed once the king's mind was made up.[67]

Of course it was at the point when the king was making up his mind that political influences were at their most important. The question of Henry's relationships with his ministers and courtiers has been a vexed one ever since frustrated ambassadors and rebellious subjects blamed Wolsey, Cromwell or Henry's scheming intimates for policies promulgated in the king's name. Portraits of Henry have ranged from manipulative monster to manipulated mannikin, but at least in foreign affairs the king played a forceful and intelligent — though sometimes capricious — part in the formation of policy. The locus classicus for those who would stress the primacy of politics in the causation of Henry's wars has always been the supposed struggle between war and peace parties in the early Henrician Council, a struggle won by militant nobles and an ambitious Wolsey against peaceable bishops and the advisers of Henry VII. But, as G. R. Elton bluntly put it, there is 'no good evidence' for such an analysis: hence the wild variations in the suggested memberships of the two parties in different writers' versions of the early years of the reign. It was often Henry VII's most trusted servants — Darcy, Poynings and others — who were at the forefront in Henry VIII's first campaigns, and in any case the pacific nature of Henry VII's policy has been greatly overrated.[68]

Later wars were blamed on Wolsey by contemporaries, and have been so by some historians, notably because of the very slim possibility that a grateful Charles V might secure Wolsey's election as Pope. But the king and the cardinal obviously worked closely together, debating possible measures in a way that showed that Henry was well aware of strategic problems and diplomatic subtleties. The king discussed with ambassadors at tedious length when he felt in the right mood, and worked in his own hand on papers concerning war and diplomacy more often than on any other subject except theology. In matters less central to Henry's conception of the role of the monarch it is easier to dismiss Wolsey's policies as mere 'stage-props in the game of manipulation', but in foreign affairs it runs contrary to most of the evidence.[69] Indeed, on occasion the attribution of policies to ministers could be a ploy in Henry's own political game. In 1536 he told the imperial ambassador that the 1528 declaration against Charles V was not Wolsey's responsibility (as Henry had conveniently asserted in the past) but his own, and that it showed how real were his grievances against Charles. Henry knew well enough that it was best for a king not to be unequivocally personally identified with an unpopular or unsuccessful foreign policy: people mentioned the fate of Richard II to him from time to time. He probably realised too that the dominance of his ministers over the minutiae of diplomacy and military administration gave them a significant influence over the way policy was executed. After all, their job was to carry out the king's will intelligently. Similarly, Henry's councillors would not have been worth listening to if their advice did not help him reach decisions. But Cromwell's memoranda on foreign affairs were dotted as much as Wolsey's must have been with notes like 'To know when of the king' and 'In the king's arbitrament'.[70]

Henry was usually more bellicose than his councillors. Early in his reign that was the impression he gave, an impression reinforced by the chivalrous militancy of his young courtiers. Late in his reign the entire council tried to bring Henry round to peace with France, Suffolk and Wriothesley asking Charles V's ambassador to seek a settlement between England and France, and Norfolk and Paget urging the hotheaded earl of Surrey not to 'animate the king to keep Boulogne'. Even after the 1546 peace, Henry ordered William, Lord Grey of Wilton, to destroy a new French fort near Hammes, contrary to the advice of the Privy Council, and was overjoyed at Grey's success. Throughout the reign his advisers voiced preferences in foreign policy for personal reasons, like Suffolk's francophilia, ideological reasons, like Bishop Stephen Gardiner's zeal for the imperial alliance, or even political reasons, like Norfolk's enthusiasm for war in 1542 because it would increase his responsibility and favour through military command.[71] But it cannot be shown that the pursuit of such interests by councillors, courtiers or even ministers was a major cause of Henry's wars. They provided the means, in diplomacy, administration and generalship, to wage war when the king willed it. Sometimes they did so with enthusiasm, but often they counselled against war *en masse* and were rebuffed. Henry's wars were more the result of victories of the king's will over their advice than of one faction of counsellors over another.

The effects of war on politics were greater than those of politics on war. The political infighting between conservative and reformist councillors which troubled 1543 died down when war absorbed all their energies in 1544. Henry used the war more explicitly to appease internal dissension in 1513, when justifying his dictation of a settlement to the bishops in their dispute over probate. Unlike Edward IV, though, he never justified his wars by suggesting that they would turn the harmful energies of his subjects to more constructive ends than their private quarrels, and he thought about the good effects of war on England as little as the bad. Though he knew there were financial restrictions on the war effort, just as he knew there were practical limitations on his strategy, he was prepared to push his servants and his subjects to the limit of what was possible in the search for military success. Even when Henry did acknowledge the existence of problems, he concentrated his interest on overcoming those on the other side of the Channel rather than those of finance, recruitment and supply which affected his country more directly.[72]

To that extent he was irresponsible. In his wartime strategy he was perhaps irrational in modern terms, though not in the eyes of many contemporaries. Henry shared the attitude of his friend Sir Edward Howard, who replied to Breton gentlemen who offered to surrender Brest Castle to him in 1513 if he would stop burning the coastline, 'Nay . . . we are sent hither to make war and not peace'. Yet Henry's overall policy was not senseless. He faced the problem of how to build on the 'unspectacular but substantial strength' achieved by his father's foreign dealings. That strength had no independent existence; it had to be demonstrated among the powers of Europe, and that was what Henry aimed to do, whether by war or peace. To 'have in your hands the conducing of the universal peace in Christendom, to your great merit, high laud, and perpetual renown', as Wolsey described it to the king in 1526, and practised it for him in 1518, was one means to maintain England's leading role on the European stage. To make effective war was the other, and Henry, like Maximilian and other contemporaries, saw war as a first rather than a last resort.[73] Offensive war, or the threat of it, was a defensive measure in general terms — a demonstration that Henry was a force to be reckoned with — even when France and her enemies were absorbed enough in their own quarrels to pose no immediate threat to England.

All too often Henry made ineffective war. In part it was because he followed others in over-assessing England's strength. The Battle of the Spurs reawakened European admiration for the English and their longbow, and as late as 1557 good Frenchmen could claim that one English soldier could beat three French. In March 1543 Marshal Du Biez, the future defender of Montreuil, declared that with five thousand English archers to strengthen his forces he would not fear all the power of the Low Countries.[74] In practice Henry's armies were fragile and unreliable weapons for an aspiring conqueror. Henry also overestimated his enemy's vulnerability. Intelligence reports told him again and again that the over-taxed people of Normandy and Guienne would welcome an English return; that 'the natural inhabitants of Guienne beth affectionate unto your crown of England'; even that the gentlemen of Guienne had flocked to his army to swear fealty to him in 1512. He must have called to mind that Henry VI's last chance in France had been offered by a Gascon revolt. In spring 1514 there was reportedly discontent in Brittany; in early 1523 the French commons supposedly cried 'Vive le roi d'Angleterre', and the Normans apparently told Francis I that they had been better ruled by the English. In autumn 1523 Henry's entire plan of campaign (with some misgivings) was based on the ineffectual revolt of Charles duke of Bourbon, his tenants and friends. Only by 1544 did Henry become disillusioned with the prospect of French rebellions, and this was another cause of his concentration on Boulogne.[75]

That concentration also marked Henry's conviction that he had often fought as others' stooge, and was now determined to win territory and honour for himself alone. He had fortunately avoided some schemes which were totally to the advantage of his allies: the projected Anglo-French attack on Spain in 1514, which might well have won Navarre for Louis XII but never half of Castile for Henry and Catherine, and the Anglo-French descent on the Low Countries of 1528, which could have won little from the Pope for Henry, but might well have moved the French border north.[76] Henry did better out of war against France than he would have done from these enterprises, but not much better. In 1512 he helped Ferdinand of Aragon conquer Navarre. In 1513 he punished the citizens of Tournai for their repeated insolence to Maximilian: as a Valenciennes chronicler put it, the Emperor saw 'that in the English he had a big stick with which to correct them'. Well into 1514 Henry paid a large force of mercenaries to stay in the Low Countries, waiting for his next campaign, but also defending Margaret of Austria. She begged him not to disband them, for she was well aware that England's other allies could hide from French attack behind the Pyrenees or the Alps, but she could only shelter behind an English army. In 1523 she took the chance to conquer Friesland while the English again covered her frontier. In 1524 both Margaret and Charles V were keen for the English to invade to take the pressure off their own campaigns, but Henry and Wolsey were increasingly wary.[77] The king took the lessons in international politics learnt in these first fifteen years on beyond the fall of Wolsey. In 1536 he avoided commitment to either France or the Empire, but kept his options open by apparently serious negotiations with each side. In 1543–44 he waged war with a clearer impression than Charles V of what he wanted and how to get it, and on his own terms he was successful.

Henry's subtlety increased with age, until he resembled the father-in-law who had led him into his first war: Ferdinand of Aragon, who, as an English envoy put it, 'by his policy and long drifts ... attaineth many things to other men's pains'. But the strength of Charles V meant that Henry could never be as successful as Ferdinand. Charles's enmity for France made it easy for Henry to do what his father-in-law found hard, to coordinate an alliance to attack the French from all sides. But even when Henry thought, as in 1522, that he could fight a winning war in alliance with Charles until Francis would buy England out of the coalition against him, he miscalculated. The English tail could not wag the Habsburg dog enough to enforce a joint strategy to England's benefit; but neither could Henry extract any other than financial concessions by peace negotiations with the French, which hardly made any war worth fighting in the first place. After a lifetime of fruitless cooperation, Henry's selfish concentration on Boulogne in 1544 was entirely understandable.[78]

Henry's England had been outgrown by the Habsburg hybrid, and by a France made strong by a solid tax-base, a standing army and an increasingly firm alliance with the Swiss; meanwhile the Burgundian unification of the Low Countries, completed by Margaret of Austria and Charles V, gave even England's traditional ally against France a powerful mind of her own. Henry VIII could not be Henry V, and by the end of his reign he surely knew it; yet he fought on. Two possible explanations for this present themselves. The first is that Henry was incompetent, the plaything both of wilier continental statesmen and of his own short-sighted and factious advisers. Certainly he often fought others' wars for them, though that was sometimes unavoidable if he wanted to fight a war at all. Certainly his government seemed uncoordinated in its foreign relations, jerking about from promises to one power to commitments to another. But often that can be shown to be Henry's rough-and-ready form of diplomatic subtlety, rather than the result of wild swings in a factional conflict. In 1540–41 Gardiner was negotiating an imperial alliance, the Howards a French one; in 1545–46 Gardiner was negotiating an imperially-sponsored peace, Paget a Protestant-sponsored one. Yet Henry was fully in control of each set of talks. In 1536, with only one dominant minister talking to both sets of ambassadors, the impression of deception rather than incoherence is stronger still. Even in the early years of the reign, Bainbridge at Rome found himself ordered to negotiate an anti-French accord as though English policy were unquestioningly hostile to France, while at the same time other English envoys were confirming Henry VII's treaty with Louis XII, and the young king was apparently far from committed to a French war.[79]

It seems clear that Henry was not forced into war by the machinations of foreign rulers or of his own councillors and courtiers. Nor was he drawn irresistibly into war by the machinery of the international system. Henry chose war. He chose war although he apparently had little to gain. His conquests were financial disasters — Tournai cost twice as much to garrison and fortify as it paid in tribute and French compensation for its return — and while Boulogne was a town worth taking, lesser acquisitions like Thérouanne could readily be dismissed as 'ungracious dogholes' by subjects who chose to criticise royal policy. Henry did apparently miscalculate the advantages to be gained by war, a mistake readily made in a Europe changing its diplomatic face beyond all recognition. Yet few of his subjects complained.[80] Some may have thought the king stupid but refrained from saying so, but most shared with Henry a view of war and of kingship which did not measure achievement in such a simplistic way. For Henry the often useful generalisation that wars are fought for power would have been a blasphemy against the code of knightly honour. Francis I understood that, pronouncing after his crushing defeat at Pavia that all was lost except honour. Court chroniclers understood that, knowing that the total number of spears broken was a good measure of a joust's greatness: honour, unlike power, was not a divisible substance but one that could reproduce itself. Henry fought in the hope of real conquests and of a real extension of the power of his nation, his dynasty and himself: he fought among the ambitious monarchs of a state-building Europe. But he also fought in the shadow of his ancestors, those warrior-kings who looked down at him from the portraits at Richmond Palace, for an honourable place in the history of his country and the annals of prowess.

NOTES

1. Norfolk Record Office, Norwich, NCC Wills 161 Multon. Spelling and punctuation have been modernised in all quotations, and other languages translated into English. All

dates are old style, with the year beginning on 1 January. I should like to thank Dr G. W. Bernard, Mr C. S. L. Davies, Mr P.J. Gwyn and the editor for helpful comments on this piece.

2. *Letters and Papers, Foreign and Domestic, of the Reign of Henry VIII* (hereafter *LP*), ed. J. S. Brewer *et al* (1864–1932), I, i. 168, 244, 260, 264, 287, 325 (*LP* references are to document numbers unless otherwise stated); C. S. L. Davies, 'The English People and War in the Early Sixteenth Century', *Britain and the Netherlands*, vi, ed. A. C. Duke, C. A. Tamse (The Hague, 1977), p. 1.

3. J. R. Hale, *War and Society in Renaissance Europe, 1450–1620* (1985), p. 24.

4. D. L. Potter, 'The Duc de Guise and the Fall of Calais, 1557–1558', *English Historical Review*, xcviii (1983), 483; *Statutes of the Realm*, ed. A. Luders *et al* (1810–28), 37 Henry VIII c. 25.

5. R. Macquereau, *Traicté et Recueil de la Maison de Bourgoigne*, ed. J. A. C. Buchon (*Chroniques et Mémoires sur l'Histoire de France* xvi, 1838), p. 23.

6. J. R. Lander, 'The Hundred Years' War and Edward IV's 1475 Campaign in France', in his *Crown and Nobility 1450–1509* (1976), pp. 220–41.

7. P. J. Gwyn, 'Wolsey's Foreign Policy: the Conferences at Calais and Bruges Reconsidered', *Historical Journal*, xxiii (1980), 760–1, 768.

8. *Calendar of Letters, Despatches, and State Papers, relating to the Negotiations between England and Spain*, ii, ed. G. A. Bergenroth (1866), p. 42; *State Papers, Henry VIII* (1830–52), i 41; G. W. Bernard, *War, Taxation and Rebellion in Early Tudor England* (Brighton, 1986), pp. 9–11.

9. D. M. Head, 'Henry VIII's Scottish Policy; a Reassessment', *Scottish Historical Review*, lxi (1982), 1–24; K. Brandi, *The Emperor Charles V* (1939), pp. 219–20.

10. *LP* III, ii. 2957.

11. *LP* XVII. 560, 571, 649, 915, 952, 1005, 1114, 1220, XVIII, i. 50, 114, 142.

12. *LP* X. 1157–9, XI. 161, 286, 306; D. L. Potter, 'Foreign Policy in the Age of the Reformation: French involvement in the Schmalkaldic War, 1544–1547', *Historical Journal*, xx (1977), 527.

13. *Tudor Royal Proclamations*, ed. P. L. Hughes, J. F. Larkin (New Haven and London, 1964–69), i, no. 73; *The Gardyners Passetaunce*, ed. F. B. Williams, jr. (The Roxburghe Club, 1985), p. 3.

14. *LP* III, ii. 2636, 2958, XVII. 593–4; R. B. Wernham, *Before the Armada* (1966), pp. 58, 82, 315–6; *Le Journal d'un Bourgeois de Mons*, ed. A. Louant (Brussels, Commission Royale d'Histoire, 1969), p. 20; C. S. L. Davies, 'English People and War', p. 14.

15. M.-R. Thielemans, *Bourgogne et Angleterre . . . 1435–1467* (Brussels, 1966), pp. 427–8; R. L. Storey, *The Reign of Henry VII* (1968), pp. 82–4; W. G. Hoskins, *The Age of Plunder* (1976), pp. 184–90; *Bourgeois de Mons*, pp. 288–9; *State Papers*, i. 281, 286.

16. E. Hall, *Hall's Chronicle* (1809 edn.), pp. 522–3; Macquereau, *Traicté et Recueil*, p. 21; J. Le Patourel, 'The Origins of the War', *The Hundred Years War*, ed. K. Fowler (1971), p. 32; *Statutes of the Realm*, 3 Henry VIII c. 22.

17. *LP* I, i. 1793, ii. 2009, 2404, XVII. 496; S. J. Gunn, 'The Duke of Suffolk's March on Paris in 1523', *English Historical Review*, ci (1986), 596–634; Brandi, *Charles V*, pp. 75, 164.

18. *Paston Letters and Papers of the Fifteenth Century*, ed. N. Davis (Oxford, 1971–76), i. 502.

19. Quotation from L. B. Smith, *Henry VIII: the Mask of Royalty* (1971), p. 158; *LP* I, ii. 1925, 3018, III, ii. 2360, 3320; Hall, *Chronicle*, pp. 568, 641, 679; C. G. Cruickshank, *Army Royal* (Oxford, 1969), p. 28.

20. Bernard, *War, Taxation and Rebellion*, p. 30; *LP* XVIII, i. 754, ii. 249.

21. *Chronicle of King Henry VIII of England*, ed. M. A. S. Hume (1889), p. 120; S. R. Gammon, *Statesman and Schemer* (Newton Abbot, 1973), p. 106.

22. *LP* I, ii. 2854, XI. 233; cf. M. P. Tilley, *A Dictionary of the Proverbs in England in the Sixteenth and Seventeenth Centuries* (Ann Arbor, 1950), no. T 444; P. Rickard, *Britain in Medieval French Literature* (Cambridge, 1956), pp. 163–89; J. G. Russell, *The Field of Cloth*

of Gold (1969), p. 189; J. Coke, 'The Debate Between the Heralds of England and France', *Le Débat des Hérauts d'Armes*, ed. L. Pannier, P. Meyer (Société des Anciens Textes Français, 1877), pp. 77–9; Hall, *Chronicle*, pp. 597–8, 663.

23. Russell, *Field of Cloth of Gold*, p. 188; Macquereau, *Traicté et Recueil*, p. 35; *LP* I, ii. 1970; T. Rymer, *Foedera, Conventiones, Literae et cujuscunque generis Acta Publica* (3rd edn., The Hague, 1745), vi. 61.

24. J. J. Goring, 'Social Change and Military Decline in Mid-Tudor England', *History*, lx (1975), 185–97; C. S. L. Davies, 'English People and War', pp. 6–8.

25. *State Papers*, v. 317; *Sir John Froissart's Chronicles . . . translated . . . by John Bourchier, Lord Berners* (1812 edn.), ii. iii.

26. Y. Lacaze, 'Le rôle des Traditions dans la Genèse d'un Sentiment National au xve Siècle: La Bourgogne de Philippe le Bon', *Bibliothèque de l'Ecole des Chartes*, cxxxix (1971), 303–85; N. H. Nicolas, *History of the Battle of Agincourt* (3rd edn., 1833), Appendix, pp. 69–77; College of Arms, London, MS M6 bis ff. 55–60; MS M9 *passim*; MS R36 ff. 42–55. I am grateful for permission to cite material in the College of Arms.

27. Hall, *Chronicle*, p. 572; *LP* VI. 229 (ix, G), XVII. 361; *Tudor Royal Proclamations*, i, no. 220; S. J. Gunn, 'The Life and Career of Charles Brandon, duke of Suffolk, c.1484–1545', Oxford University D. Phil. thesis, 1986, p. 217; M. B. Davies, 'Boulogne and Calais from 1545 to 1550', *Fouad I University, Bulletin of the Faculty of Arts*, xii (1950), p. 75.

28. G. Kipling, *The Triumph of Honour* (Leiden, 1977), p. 59; M. E. James, 'English Politics and the Concept of Honour, 1485–1642', in his *Society, Politics and Culture* (Cambridge, 1986), pp. 311–2; Smith, *Henry VIII*, p. 161.

29. C. S. L. Davies, 'English People and War', p. 14; M. L. Bruce, *The Making of Henry VIII* (1977), p. 195, and sources cited there.

30. *LP* I, ii. 1884; E. Dudley, *The Tree of Commonwealth*, ed. D. M. Brodie (Cambridge, 1948), pp. 26–7; *State Papers*, i. 35.

31. Hall, *Chronicle*, p. 536; P. S. Fichtner, 'The Politics of Honor: Renaissance Chivalry and Hapsburg Dynasticism', *Bibliothèque d'Humanisme et Renaissance*, xxix (1967), 567–80.

32. James, 'Concept of Honour', p. 312; D. S. Chambers, *Cardinal Bainbridge in the Court of Rome, 1509 to 1514* (Oxford, 1965), p. 50; Macquereau, *Traicté et Recueil*, p. 27.

33. Hall, *Chronicle*, pp. 515, 523, 527, 659; *LP* I, ii, Appendix 26, II, ii, pp. 1444, 1479, III, ii. 2636, 3288.

34. M. G. A. Vale, *War and Chivalry* (1981), p. 171.

35. *LP* I, ii. 2125, III, ii. 2500, 2526, 2636, 2958, XVII. 614; *Mémoires du Maréchal de Florange*, ed. R. Goubaux, P.-A. Lemoisne (Société de l'Histoire de France, 1913–24), i. 137; M. B. Davies, 'The "Enterprises" of Paris and Boulogne', *Fouad I University, Bulletin of the Faculty of Arts*, xi (1949), 55.

36. *State Papers*, i. 85–6.

37. Hall, *Chronicle*, p. 520; Chambers, *Bainbridge*, p. 37; *Gardyners Passetaunce,· passim; The Anglica Historia of Polydore Vergil*, ed. D. Hay (Camden Society lxxiv, 1950), p. 223.

38. College of Arms MS R36 f. 34r; *LP* III, i. 629.

39. *LP* I, ii. 3387, II, i. 1113.

40. 'Account of Henry VIII's Expedition into France, A.D. 1513', ed. W. C. Trevelyan, *Archaeologia*, xxvi (1836), 476; Hall, *Chronicle*, p. 609.

41. *Henry V: the Practice of Kingship*, ed. G. L. Harriss (Oxford, 1985), *passim*; D. R. Starkey, *The Reign of Henry VIII: Personalities and Politics* (1985), p. 43.

42. *LP* I, ii. 2391; Gunn, 'Charles Brandon', p. 38; Coke, 'Debate Between the Heralds', p. 98; *The First English Life of King Henry the Fifth*, ed. C. L. Kingsford (Oxford, 1911), pp. 4, 67, 126, 130–2; R. P. Adams, *The Better Part of Valor* (Seattle, 1962), pp. 69–71.

43. *Gardyners Passetaunce*, p. 3; *LP* III, ii. 2715; Bernard, *War, Taxation and Rebellion*, pp. 22, 32; Chambers, *Bainbridge*, p. 39; Gunn, 'March on Paris', p. 63.

44. *LP* III, i, p. cxl.

45. *LP* III, ii. 2292; Bernard, *War, Taxation and Rebellion*, pp. 12, 21, 33; Hall, *Chronicle*, p. 746; *Tudor Royal Proclamations*, i, no. 220.

46. Chambers, *Bainbridge*, pp. 38–40; *Gardyners Passetaunce*, p. 10; Rymer, *Foedera*, vi. 61.

47. *LP* I, i. 945, III, ii. 1762, 2201; Bernard, *War, Taxation and Rebellion*, pp. 34–5; *State Papers*, i. 135; *LP* XI. 285, XVII. 468.

48. *LP* III, ii. 648; Gunn, 'March on Paris', pp. 616, 619.

49. *First English Life*, p. 93; *Froissart's Chronicles*, p. 41.

50. Head, 'Scottish Policy', pp. 5–9; Smith, *Henry VIII*, p. 160; *LP* III, ii. 2027; Gunn, 'Charles Brandon', p. 261.

51. *LP* I, i. 278, 329, 570, 572, II, i. 1165, X. 1069; J. Skelton, *The Complete Poems*, ed. P. Henderson (2nd edn., 1948), p. 132; Hall, *Chronicle*, p. 550; R. Morison, *An Exhortation to Styrre all Englyshemen to the Defence of theyr Countrye* (1539), sig. B iv v.

52. J. J. Scarisbrick, *Henry VIII* (Harmondsworth, 1971 edn.), p. 59; Bernard, *War, Taxation and Rebellion*, p. 35; J. Vale, *Edward III and Chivalry* (Woodbridge, 1982), p. 93.

53. *LP* XX, ii. 431.

54. Adams, *Better Part of Valor*, p. 39; Gwyn, 'Wolsey's Foreign Policy', pp. 756, 758, 760; Scarisbrick, *Henry VIII*, chapter 4; J. Parkhurst, *Ludicra, sive Epigrammata Iuvenilia* (1573), p. 19.

55. *The Dictionary of National Biography*, ed. L. Stephen, S. Lee (2nd edn., 1908–09), xx. 609–12; *LP* XVIII, i. 979.

56. M. B. Davies, 'Boulogne and Calais', p. 27; *Froissart's Chronicles*, i, preface (unpaginated).

57. James, 'Concept of Honour', p. 333; Cruickshank, *Army Royal*, p. 14; *LP* I, ii. 1748, V, p. 755, VI. 352, XI. 1016; 'Expedition into France, A.D. 1513', p. 476; Gunn, 'Charles Brandon', pp. 7, 107, 151–2, 200, 337.

58. Coke, 'Debate Between the Heralds', pp. 95–6; A. B. Ferguson, *The Chivalric Tradition in Renaissance England* (Washington, 1986).

59. PRO. SP 1/138 ff. 105–6; *LP* XV. 1028 (6); Cruickshank, *Army Royal*, p. 200.

60. Adams, *Better Part of Valor*, pp. 249–50; *LP* I, ii. 2974, III, ii. 2301, 2326, XI. 452, XVI. 34, XVII. 849, XVIII, i. 97.

61. *The Lisle Letters*, ed. M. St C. Byrne (Chicago and London, 1981); H. Miller, *Henry VIII and the English Nobility* (Oxford, 1986), pp. 179, 184; M. B. Davies, 'Boulogne and Calais', p. 21. The other captains of Guines were Nicholas, Lord Vaux, William, Lord Sandys, and William, earl of Southampton.

62. Hall, *Chronicle*, pp. 646, 669, 686; *LP* X. 934, 969, 1172, XI. 436, XVII. 533, 691, 1091, 1106; Archives Départementales du Nord, Lille, B 2316/125847; C. S. L. Davies, 'English People and War', pp. 9–10.

63. *LP* I, i. 1316 (8), ii. 1957–8; S. J. Gunn, 'The Regime of Charles, Duke of Suffolk, in North Wales and the Reform of Welsh Government, 1509–25', *Welsh History Review*, xii (1985), 475; *Idem*, 'Charles Brandon', pp. 40, 294; *Idem*, 'March on Paris', p. 629.

64. E. Powell, 'The Restoration of Law and Order', *Henry V*, ed. Harriss, pp. 71–2; C. S. L. Davies, 'England and the French War, 1557–9', *The Mid-Tudor Polity*, ed. J. Loach, R. Tittler (1980), p. 163; *LP* I, i. 725, 728, 837, 1363.

65. *LP* I, i. 880, ii. 2576; Gunn, 'Charles Brandon', p. 298; Miller, *English Nobility*, pp. 14–37.

66. *LP* I, i. 734, ii. 3427, III, i. 1321 (iii), XI. 800.

67. Gunn, 'Charles Brandon', pp. 83–90, 93–4, 123–4, 212. For information on Norfolk's trading interests I am grateful to Mrs S. Vokes.

68. G. R. Elton, *Reform and Reformation* (1977), p. 35; Starkey, *Reign of Henry VIII*, pp. 48–9, 57–9; Adams, *Better Part of Valor*, p. 41; Wernham, *Before the Armada*, p. 83; M. J. Tucker, *The Life of Thomas Howard, Earl of Surrey and Second Duke of Norfolk, 1443–1524* (The Hague, 1964), pp. 93–101. For an important reinterpretation of Henry VII's attitude to war, see I. Arthurson, 'The King's Voyage into Scotland — the War that Never Was', *England in the Fifteenth Century*, ed. D. T. Williams (forthcoming, 1987).

69. Quotation from Starkey, *Reign of Henry VIII*, p. 63; Bernard, *War, Taxation and Rebellion*, pp. 40–5; Gunn, 'March on Paris', pp. 47–9.

70. *LP* XI. 285, 479; K. J. V. Jespersen, 'Henry VIII of England, Lübeck and the Count's War, 1533–1535', *Scandinavian Journal of History*, vi (1981), 260.

71. *LP* I, i. 880, 1475, XVII. 770, XX, i. 689, ii. 455; *Polydore Vergil*, pp. 163, 197; *A Commentary of the Services and Charges of William, Lord Grey of Wilton*, ed. P. de M. G. Egerton (Camden Society xl, 1847), pp. 3–9; G. Redworth, 'The Political and Diplomatic Career of Stephen Gardiner, 1538–1551', Oxford University D.Phil. thesis, 1985, *passim*.

72. Redworth, 'Stephen Gardiner', p. 158; *LP* I, i. 1642; Lander, 'Edward IV's 1475 Campaign', pp. 229–30; Bernard, *War, Taxation and Rebellion*, pp. 53–5.

73. Hall, *Chronicle*, p. 533; S. B. Chrimes, *Henry VII* (1972), p. 273; *State Papers*, i. 168; Gwyn, 'Wolsey's Foreign Policy', pp. 755–60, 772; H. Wiesflecker, *Kaiser Maximilian I* (Munich, 1971–81), iv. 151.

74. C. Gaier, 'L'invincibilité anglaise et le grand arc après la guerre de cent ans: un mythe tenace', *Tijdschrift voor Geschiedenis*, xci (1978), 379–85; *LP* XVII. 295.

75. *LP* I, i. 1081, 1359, 1665, ii. 1971, 2782, III, ii. 2770, 2799; Gunn, 'March on Paris', pp. 609, 629.

76. *LP* I, ii. 3476–7; Gunn, 'Charles Brandon', pp. 157–8.

77. Macquereau, *Traicté et Recueil*, pp. 22, 30, 38–9; *LP* I, ii. 2609, 2633, 2646; Bernard, *War, Taxation and Rebellion*, pp. 18, 48.

78. *LP* I, i. 1326, 1447, III, ii. 2450.

79. Redworth, 'Stephen Gardiner', pp. 78, 165–75; Chambers, *Bainbridge*, pp. 22–9.

80. C. G. Cruickshank, *The English Occupation of Tournai, 1513–1519* (Oxford, 1971), p. 279; *LP* III, ii. 2958; Bernard, *War, Taxation and Rebellion*, pp. 3–7.

2

WAR IN THE BALTIC, 1550–1790

Stewart Oakley

Since the middle of the nineteenth century, when a British squadron operated against Finnish coastal defences during the Crimean War,[1] the waters of the Baltic have been free of armed conflict, and since that time the only international clashes near its shores have been during the Second Schleswig-Holstein War between Denmark, Prussia and Austria in 1864 and the Winter War between Finland and the Soviet Union in 1939–40. Sweden, the country with the longest Baltic coastline, has been at peace since 1815.

In the later sixteenth century and throughout most of the seventeenth, however, the Baltic area was the scene of intense rivalries between its bordering states which left it undisturbed for only brief periods. The eighteenth century after 1721 was more peaceful, but even then only the 1730s and the 1770s were entirely pacific. Ironically, of the eighteenth century wars fought there, only one (that between Sweden and Russia in 1788–90) had little connection with larger European conflicts, while of those in the seventeenth only two (Denmark's and Sweden's intervention in the Thirty Years' War after 1624 and Sweden's war with Brandenburg-Prussia in 1674–9) were linked at all closely with events outside the Baltic. Before the emergence of Russia as the leading Baltic power at the beginning of the eighteenth century, the area was to a large extent politically self-contained; its wars were fought mainly between the powers surrounding it: Sweden, Denmark, Russia and Poland. Its commercial links with the world outside became increasingly important from the late fifteenth century, and, as will be seen, trade through it with Western Europe formed an important element in its conflicts. Baltic states also had important political interests outside the Baltic: Denmark in northern Germany, Poland in central and southern Europe, Russia in south-east Europe and the Black Sea. But conflicts between these states rarely impinged on the rest of the continent, while the conflicts of the rest of Europe rarely spread to the Baltic. It is significant that only after the conclusion of the War of the Spanish Succession, in which, of the Baltic powers, only Brandenburg-Prussia played any active part, did non-Baltic states take much interest in the progress of the Great Northern War, which continued for another six years.

The clashes which began in the Baltic in the middle of the sixteenth century can be traced to the final break-up of the Kalmar Union, which had, at least nominally, united the kingdoms of Denmark, Norway and Sweden-Finland under a ruler in Copenhagen before the revolt of Gustav Vasa against the latter in 1520, to the expansion of Muscovy under Ivan III and Ivan IV towards the Baltic, to the collapse of political authority in the south-eastern Baltic (Livonia) after the

Reformation and to the growing importance of the Baltic for the economy of Western Europe, which made control of its trade a desirable objective for rulers in constant need of means to fill their depleted treasuries. For the first hundred years Sweden, almost continuously at war, formed the central pivot of conflict. Denmark disappeared from the scene during the last two decades of the sixteenth century and in the first decade of the seventeenth, but was otherwise involved in all wars up to 1660. Russia played only a subsidiary role after 1617, and Poland, a formidable contestant until the third decade of the seventeenth century, then became a victim. In the later seventeenth century before 1700, the emergence of Brandenburg-Prussia added a new element to the pattern, and Sweden found itself on the defensive in the midst of an increasingly unfavourable international situation. But of this none of its neighbours were able to take advantage until the end of the 1690s, and even then only Russia was able fully to exploit the situation. Denmark abandoned all hope of regaining the position in the Baltic it had been able to boast a century before, and from the end of the Great Northern War enjoyed almost a century of peace, interrupted only briefly and largely bloodlessly in 1788–9. Poland, even under the Saxon kings, found itself outmanoeuvred by its eastern neighbour, and Sweden's rather pathetic attempts in the course of the eighteenth century to exploit Russia's preoccupations outside the Baltic to win back some at least of what had been lost only confirmed its position in the second rank of powers and caused further loss of territory.

The final break-up of the Kalmar Union left the Scandinavian world divided into a western part, comprising Denmark, Norway and Iceland ruled from Copenhagen and an eastern comprising Sweden and Finland ruled from Stockholm. Of these the former was undoubtedly the dominant. In possession of most of what is now southernmost Sweden (the provinces of Skåne, Halland and Blekinge), Denmark could control all shipping passing in and out of the Baltic through The Sound and The Belts. Since 1429 such shipping had had to pay tolls at Elsinore. With the island of Gotland also under its control, its king could also threaten sea communications between Stockholm and the southern Baltic. With the eastern frontier of Norway thrust almost to the Baltic north of the Swedish capital, the whole of northern Sweden, whose frontier with northern Norway was ill-defined before the middle of the eighteenth century, could be isolated. Sweden's only access to the sea outside the Baltic was a small strip of territory at the mouth of the Göta river, on which stood the fortress of Älvsborg. In the east the frontier between Finland and Novgorod had been delineated by treaty in the fourteenth century, but the scattered population on either side of it paid it scant attention, and conflict along it was frequent. It was thus in Sweden's strategic interests to deprive Denmark of as much as possible of its land base to the east of The Sound, to drive back the Norwegian salient in the north and to acquire Gotland. All this had been achieved by 1660. In the east it was to Sweden's advantage to secure a stable frontier in Finland, especially at a time when Russia was emerging as an aggressive European power, and to prevent the establishment of a potential or real enemy on the southern shore of the Gulf of Finland. These aims it achieved temporarily by the 1620s, but its position in Livonia had to be abandoned again one hundred years later. While neither Denmark nor Sweden offered a serious threat to Muscovy, it was long an ambition of Muscovy's rulers to secure access to the Baltic on as broad a front as possible both to enjoy the benefits of direct trade with the West and to strengthen Muscovy's position in the face of the sprawling republic of Poland-Lithuania, its most formidable adversary.[2] Because of internal weaknesses, Russia had to wait until the early eighteenth century for this. Poland in its turn had longstanding claims of overlordship in Livonia which it was tempted in the late sixteenth and early seventeenth centuries to assert, but then had to abandon.[3]

By the middle of the sixteenth century, the once-powerful Hanseatic League was swiftly declining in power and influence. Lübeck's fleet could still make the city a useful ally in the middle of the sixteenth century, but it ceased to be of consequence after the 1560s. Brandenburg-Prussia did not become a Baltic power until the middle of the seventeenth century, when it acquired the poorer eastern part of Pomerania. After this one of its ruler's principal aims in foreign policy was to acquire, for both strategic and economic reasons, the wealthier western part and particularly the mouth of the Oder with the port of Stettin from Sweden, a task not fully accomplished until after the end of the period.[4] Of the other German states bordering the Baltic, neither Pomerania, which disappeared as an independent entity in 1648, nor Mecklenburg was of any consequence in international affairs. The duke of Holstein-Gottorp, who shared the territories of the duchies of Schleswig and Holstein with the king of Denmark, was, however, of some importance at various times because of Sweden's interest in supporting him against the Danish king's claims of sovereignty and in using his lands as a link between its territories gained on the Baltic and North Sea at the end of the Thirty Years' War and as a threat to Denmark from the south. The only gain made by Denmark as a result of its participation in the Great Northern War was the acquisition of the Gottorp lands in Schleswig, a gain guaranteed by the Western great powers. But when the duke was adopted as heir to the Russian throne in the 1740s, Russia took over his claims, which nearly led to war between Denmark and Russia twenty years later. Not until the 1770s was a settlement of the question finally reached.

Of extra-Baltic powers concerned with and influencing Baltic affairs in the period, the Dutch and British were most affected by their commercial interests in the region, in particular with supplies of 'naval stores' on which their fleets depended for their existence, and on the trade in Baltic grain which was the mainstay of Dutch economic hegemony. Both sought because of this to maintain peace at sea, and both were strongly opposed to the dominance of one power which might be in a position to dictate disadvantageous terms in exchange for allowing freedom of navigation; hence in the seventeenth century they generally supported Swedish expansion at the expense of Denmark up to the point when it seemed that Sweden was establishing a *dominium maris Baltici*. They were also, however, anxious for similar reasons to prevent any leading Baltic power from joining their enemies and would ideally have liked to enjoy the friendship of each, an end difficult to achieve because of the intense rivalries in the region; close association with one state was only too likely to drive another into the opposite camp. A Dutch fleet relieved a Copenhagen besieged by the Swedes in 1658, and a British squadron was sent to the Baltic at the end of the Great Northern War both to protect merchant shipping and limit Russian gains.[5] The Dutch in the early seventeenth century also had to prevent the establishment on the southern shore of the Baltic of bases from which Spanish ships might operate against their commerce.[6]

France's only serious commercial concern in the Baltic was to prevent its enemies from obtaining thence supplies of commodities which might strengthen their war potential; the interference with Scandinavian shipping to which this led might strain relations between it and Denmark and Sweden.[7] As with the Maritime Powers, it sought to keep the friendship of the Baltic powers and to prevent their aiding or at worst joining any alliance directed against it. But Sweden was in French diplomacy from the 1630s cast in a more specific and positive role. Its general opposition to the Habsburgs and its acquisition of bases on the south coast of the Baltic made it a valuable ally in the struggle against Austria, the northern link in the eastern *cordon sanitaire* of which Poland should form the central and the Ottoman Empire the southern sections.[8] In the eighteenth century, when the Austro-Russian alliance became the most stable element in European diplomacy, Sweden, with its common frontier with Russia in Finland and the ambitions of many Swedes to wreak revenge for losses sustained at the end of the Great Northern War, could before the Diplomatic Revolution be looked to to draw Russian forces away from central Europe by a diversionary attack. Unfortunately Sweden was by this time militarily too weak to fulfil this role very effectively; it failed lamentably in the war in Finland in 1741–43, as after the Diplomatic Revolution it did little to harm France's enemy Brandenburg-Prussia in the Pomeranian War of 1757–62. Of the other European powers, only the Emperor entertained some interest in Baltic affairs in the seventeenth century, particularly in assisting the Poles against the armies of Gustavus Adolphus and Charles X.

From the late fifteenth century the Baltic became increasingly important as a centre of international trade. The growth of population in Western Europe led to a burgeoning demand for the grain of Poland and the German Baltic lands, and the expansion of merchant and naval fleets increased enormously the value of Polish timber, Livonian hemp and flax, and Finnish tar. High-quality Swedish iron and the copper of which Sweden had almost a European monopoly also attracted more and more merchants' attention.[9] The growing value of the trade in the area made control of the rivers along which it flowed — from the Neva in the east to the Oder in the west — and of the ports through which it passed — from Narva to Wismar — increasingly desirable for powers for which the financing of administration and war was becoming a more and more pressing problem. The extent to which economic motives rather than motives of strategy or prestige played a part in the aims of Danish, Swedish, Russian or Polish statesmen of the sixteenth and seventeenth centuries has long been disputed.[10] Economic considerations were less likely to appeal to wide sectors of a population when it was thought necessary to justify a war and may thus have been misleadingly played down in contemporary propaganda, while in some areas, like the south-eastern Baltic, strategic and economic advantages so often coincided that it is difficult to disentangle the two. In Swedish and Russian expansion, however, there can be no doubt that the control of trade routes was an important driving force.[11]

The ability of the state to pursue its ideal interests is confined within certain parameters governed by its political and social structures and economic resources. In the sixteenth century the kingdom of Denmark-Norway had a population of about three-quarters of a million. The economy of Denmark itself was almost wholly agricultural. Its grain was not of the highest quality, and much of it was needed to feed its sister kingdom, which suffered from a deficit. But in the sixteenth and early seventeenth centuries it conducted a lucrative trade in cattle with north Germany and the Netherlands,[12] and had extensive timber and more limited mineral resources to call on in Norway. Its greatest asset, however, was its geographical position at the entrance to the Baltic, and in the eighteenth century a large merchant marine could exploit the long period of neutrality enjoyed by Denmark in the midst of European conflict. But until the eighteenth century Danish society was dominated by a small nobility, which shared the landed estates with the crown, so that the majority of the rural population were tenants of one or the other. The development of overseas trade in the eighteenth century did, however, create a society of rich merchants in the capital, and a growing number of estates passed into the hands of the bourgeoisie. The nobility also dominated administration. The power of the king in Denmark was before 1660 limited by the fact that the crown was elective; each successive monarch had, as the price of his election, to agree to a charter which confirmed the privileges of the nobility and bound him to consult his Council on all important matters of state. With the introduction of hereditary and absolute monarchy in 1660/1, these restrictions were removed. From the middle of the eighteenth century, however, the character of the rulers meant that power passed in practice to powerful ministers. While the crown was elective, the king's most effective weapon against a Council which opposed his foreign policy was his position as duke of Schleswig-Holstein, for as such he was not bound by his election charter; he could as duke conduct a policy which, however, could hardly leave his kingdom unaffected. He also had at his disposal the income from the Sound tolls and access to financial resources outside the Treasury, which again gave him a freer hand in the conduct of foreign policy than might at first appear.[13] Militarily Denmark was the most formidable power in the Baltic in the sixteenth century. Its fleet remained a significant element even in European politics up to the Napoleonic period,[14] but on land it continued to rely on expensive mercenary forces long after the Swedes had evolved an effective national force. The weaknesses of Danish state finances always restricted the scope of the country's foreign policy.

Not until the eighteenth century did the latter factor so obviously apply to Sweden. In many respects its resources were little better than those of Denmark-Norway, its population at the beginning of the period certainly smaller. But it managed to develop and husband them to better advantage. Poorer agriculturally than Denmark, it was generally able to feed itself until the later seventeenth century, when it came to rely on imports of grain from Livonia. And it did have at its disposal the rich mineral deposits — especially of iron and copper — in the Bergslagen region north-west of Stockholm. The iron was not only a valuable export but could be used as the basis of an indigenous armaments industry, and in the early seventeenth century copper exports played a large part in financing the Swedish war machine. As in Denmark, Swedish society was dominated by a landowning nobility enjoying a monopoly of high office in central and local administration. The Estate of Nobles also dominated the Diet (*Riksdag*), which, unlike the equivalent body in Denmark, where it met infrequently before 1660 and then not at all, had become an accepted organ of government in the seventeenth century and an organ to which the crown had to turn for approval of significant new legislation and above all for extraordinary taxation. This was true even during the period of absolutism in the last two decades of the seventeenth and first two decades of the eighteenth century. Before this, although the crown was hereditary, the constitution made for an uneasy balance between King and Council with, as during the regencies for Queen Christina (1632–44) and for Charles XI (1660–72), the Council sometimes in the ascendant and at other times, as under assertive monarchs like Charles X (1654–60), the king in charge of policy. The death of Charles XII in 1718 ushered in the so-called 'Era of Liberty', when the monarch was reduced to little more than a figurehead and the Council became the servant of the Diet. Foreign policy was largely dictated by the Diet's Secret Committee, of which the Chancellor was not a member. In 1772 king Gustavus III restored the crown's authority; foreign policy, especially after 1780, was his particular sphere. These frequent constitutional changes had profound effects on the conduct of the country's relations with foreign powers, especially in the Era of Liberty, when the two main opposing political groupings — the Hats and the Caps — chose different views on the most desirable alignment for Sweden to adopt in foreign relations and when there was considerable foreign interference in Swedish politics.[15] Unlike Denmark, Sweden relied basically on an army recruited locally, although in the sixteenth century and during the large-scale operations in Germany in the 1630s and 1640s this was strongly reinforced with hired mercenaries. Sweden's navy was generally inferior to that of Denmark-Norway and was sadly neglected for much of the eighteenth century due to financial weakness. For long periods even in the seventeenth century the military machine was heavily dependent on French subsidies, which might involve entry into a war which was not in Sweden's true interests, and the doctrine that war should feed itself encouraged the occupation of enemy territory for other than purely tactical reasons. Sweden was, however, able successfully to prevent deep enemy incursions into Sweden proper, though not into Finland, occupied twice by Russian troops in the eighteenth century.

Muscovy's strength lay in its reserves of manpower (although the size of its population before the eighteenth century must not be exaggerated)[16] and in its great expanse of territory which could easily swallow up an invading army. In quality its army and administrative machine were distinctly inferior to those of either of the Scandinavian monarchies before the eighteenth century, and while the power of the tsar did give its policy some consistency and continuity, it was not immune to the effects of palace intrigue, which might lead to new advisers gaining the ear of the sovereign or to a change of tsar; the murder of tsar Peter III in 1762 saved the Baltic from a potentially disastrous conflict.

Poland also had the advantage of its large area, which might prove impossible for any contemporary army to hold down effectively, as the Swedes found under both Charles X and Charles XII. In the sixteenth and early seventeenth centuries it was also a military power of some significance; its noble cavalry in particular, while it might lack sophistication, was certainly a match for Sweden's in the early 1620s.[17] Even the constitutional weaknesses of an elective monarchy, in which, unlike in that of Denmark, foreign powers felt free to intervene on the death of any monarch, were not apparent until the middle of the seventeenth century.

When Brandenburg-Prussia became a Baltic power in the middle of the seventeenth century, its noble-dominated estates could, through their power of the purse, limit considerably the ruler's freedom of manoeuvre in foreign policy, but by 1700 they had ceased to play any significant role in the latter, which was dictated by the elector. A poor nobility, while it dominated administration, was closely bound to the monarchy, on which it depended for its daily bread. A succession of military-minded monarchs built up an army larger per head of population than any other in the Baltic region.

The conflict in the Baltic which was to last almost a century began with the capture of the port of Narva by tsar Ivan IV in 1558. This was followed by an advance into Estonia, which led the nobles of the area and the burghers of the city of Reval (Tallinn) to appeal for help to neighbouring states concerned to prevent Russian control of the southern shore of the Gulf of Finland.[18] Foremost among these was Sweden. Its king, Gustav Vasa, had just concluded peace with Muscovy and was not anxious to resume the war. His son Erik, who succeeded him in 1560, intelligent but temperamentally unstable, had ambitious plans for his new realm including the diversion of Baltic trade through it to avoid The Sound, a marriage alliance with England and a general strengthening of Sweden's position against Denmark. He eagerly took up the offer of sovereignty in exchange for military aid.[19] In Denmark there was also a change of ruler at this time. Frederik II, as ambitious as Erik XIV, dreamed of restoring the Kalmar Union and was concerned to counter the establishment of Swedish power in Livonia. His father Christian III had been as reluctant to aid the Livonians as had Gustav Vasa, although his chancellor Johan Friis had been keen to intervene; the Danish terms were at this stage too high for the delegates to swallow. Frederik, however, purchased the island of Øsel from its bishop for his brother Magnus. This might have provided a useful base for further operations on the mainland, but in practice the move turned out to have little diplomatic or military significance; Magnus accepted offers of overlordship over western Estonia, but, with little support from home, was unable to defend his acquisition against the Russian advance.[20] The establishment of Sweden in the north in 1561 and Erik's proclamation of a blockade of Narva brought Denmark and Russia together the following year and Denmark and Poland in 1563.[21] After the Russian capture of Narva, the Order of

Teutonic Knights in Livonia turned for help to Poland, which claimed a general overlordship over the area and had a particular interest in the fate of the great port of Riga. It could be expected to oppose not only the Russian advance but also any Scandinavian interference there; a six-year truce between Muscovy and Poland expired in 1562.[22] The scene was thus set for a four-cornered struggle in which the constant factors were the opposition of Denmark and Sweden and of Russia and Poland.

The ostensible reasons for the outbreak of war between Denmark and its Lübeck ally on the one side and Sweden on the other in 1563 — the dispute over the use of three crowns on the national coat of arms, the right of passage through The Sound, the arrest of ambassadors — obscured the true nature of the rivalry: Denmark's desire to contain Sweden within its historic boundaries and ultimately to impose control over the whole of Scandinavia, and Sweden's urge to break out of the ring of Dano-Norwegian territory to west and south.[23] With the accession of Erik's half-brother John to the Swedish throne during the war, the nature of the struggle changed. While under Erik Sweden had clashed head-on with Poland while avoiding outright conflict with Russia, to which commercial concessions were even made,[24] under the new king, married to a Polish princess and united to her family also financially, the two powers joined in a common assault on the Muscovites which resulted in the capture of Narva by Pontus de la Gardie in 1581.[25] To exploit the new situation peace was made with Denmark in 1570. The latter now withdrew from the struggle for the rest of the century partly because of financial exhaustion and partly because of the character of the state's leadership, first under a disillusioned monarch, Frederik II, and then under a regency for his son, Christian IV (born 1577, 1588–1648), dominated by a nobility without foreign ambitions.

Even under John III Swedo-Polish relations were not particularly close; the two powers' interests in Livonia were impossible to reconcile. Rivalry again became enmity as a result of the revolt against John's son Sigismund after he succeeded his father in 1592.[26] Already elected king of Poland in 1587 after promising to return Estonia to Polish sovereignty, Sigismund's accession to the Swedish throne promised the creation of a truly dominant Baltic power which would not only threaten Denmark but might impose its will on Muscovy. But Sigismund's Catholicism aroused fears in the Swedish Protestant nobility led by the king's uncle Charles, and their successful rebellion added a dynastic element to the two countries' rivalry in Livonia; the brief union again split asunder, and Sweden was left alone to face three contenders for Baltic dominion.[27] Its task was made easier by the internal confusion in Russia in the years following the death of Ivan IV. Not only did Charles secure peace with Russia in 1595, by which the latter gave up its claims to Livonia, but he was able in 1609–11 to extend his quarrel with Sigismund to the gates of Moscow itself.[28] He failed to impose his own candidate permanently on the Russian throne, but the Poles had as little success. After the accession of Michael Romanov in 1613 Swedish forces had to retire, and in Livonia Charles (Charles IX from 1603) managed only with difficulty to maintain the Swedish position, which was little more advanced than in 1561.[29]

Denmark returned to the scene after the coming of age of king Christian IV in 1596. In him were reborn the old Danish ambitions to revive the Kalmar Union. For some years he struggled in vain to persuade his council to support his plans to take advantage of his rival's preoccupations in the East, but meanwhile sources of friction between the two powers accumulated, in particular the right to collect taxes from the inhabitants of the far north of the Scandinavian peninsula, where there was no clear frontier, and Swedish interference with trade to Narva and Riga. In 1611 Christian finally, having secured his financial position so as to be able to support at least the opening campaign from his own resources, outmanouevred his critics, and war broke out between the two countries with a Danish attack on the Swedish port of Kalmar. Before his death in the same year Charles was desperately fighting a war on three fronts.[30]

The young Gustavus Adolphus of Sweden (1611–32) was able to conclude peace with Denmark in 1613 on rather humiliating terms (the Treaty of Knäred) and with Muscovy in 1617 on terms which at least deprived the latter of access to the Baltic for the rest of the century (the Treaty of Stolbovo). For a decade he would be able to concentrate his energies on Poland.

The spread of the Thirty Years' War, beginning with the Bohemian revolt in 1618, towards the Baltic in the early 1620s created new problems for the Scandinavian powers. Christian had long been seeking to strengthen his position in north-west Germany to balance Swedish advances in Livonia; he asserted Danish claims to sovereignty over Hamburg and sought to instal his sons in the secularized bishoprics of Bremen, Verden, Halberstadt, Osnabrück and Paderborn. The advance of Catholic forces northward toward the Lower Saxon Circle threatened his position there. As a German prince (in Holstein) he could not but be concerned by the Emperor Ferdinand II's high-handed treatment of the Elector Palatine. How far purely religious issues played a part in his calculations is more difficult to determine. The leading Lutheran prince in Germany had, after all, joined the Emperor in crushing the Bohemian rebellion, and there was no immediate threat to the religious settlement in Denmark; there was no Catholic claimant to the Danish throne. But just because Christian was not noted for his piety, sympathy for the fate of fellow Protestants must not be discounted as a motive for intervention.[31]

With Sweden the case was rather different. Gustavus had less of a direct interest in northern Germany. On the other hand a Catholic and Imperial victory there would greatly strengthen Sigismund in Poland and not only place the whole Swedish position in Livonia in jeopardy, but would encourage the Polish king to make a bid for the Swedish throne itself. Gustavus did not, however, have sufficient forces at his disposal to intervene in Germany while the campaign against Poland still raged, and did not trust Christian, should he act alone or without firm guarantees from his allies, not to seize the opportunity of Sweden's engagement to open a new campaign to secure his throne.[32]

These considerations explain the attitudes of the two monarchs to the invitation made to them by the anti-Habsburg coalition. Christian's decision to intervene was very much a personal one; his election as captain of the Lower Saxon Circle was secured against the opposition of a large number of its members, and he went to war against the wishes of his council. But the decision was not as foolhardy as has often been claimed. The forces at his disposal were a match for those of the Catholic League, and he had made careful financial provision for at least one year's campaigning from sources outside the control of the council.[33]

Christian's defeat in 1626 made Gustavus's position much more perilous. By 1628 the whole German Baltic littoral, with the exception of Stralsund, was under Imperial control, and the Austrian general Wallenstein had at his disposal ports from which a Spanish or Imperial fleet could not only harass Dutch shipping but also convey Polish troops in an attack on Sweden. The Swedish king's first step was to throw troops into Stralsund, although it was rather the activities of the Danish fleet which compelled Wallenstein to raise the siege, and to seek to extricate himself from the Polish scene.[34]

For a short time there was some hope that a settlement might be reached in Germany (at the congress of Danzig) without Swedish intervention, which was not anticipated with any eagerness by most German princes. When negotiations failed to materialise, however, Sweden's course was inevitable. As Jerker Rosén has pointed out, 'since Sweden found itself already *de facto* at war with the Emperor both in Poland and in Germany, it was not a question of war or peace' but of whether to fight the war on German soil.[35] Gustavus's aims in 1630 were, however, limited, and he began the new campaign with no great expectations; the forces at his disposal were, after all, small, and none of the leading German princes, not even his own brother-in-law in Brandenburg, seemed willing to conclude any binding agreement with him. In many respects his prospects seemed even less bright than had Christian's in 1624. He had, on the other hand and unlike Christian, solid backing from his council and the Swedish nobility for the enterprise, an efficient administrative machine evolved by his chancellor Axel Oxenstierna and a well-trained and experienced national army. He sought at this stage little more than a restoration of the status quo after the end of the Bohemian revolt, compensation in money or territory for his efforts and a base or bases on German soil which would insure against an attack on his dominions.[36] The possession of Pomerania, to which Sweden had claims on the death of the present ruler in any case, would fulfil these aims; revenue from trade down the Oder would provide *satisfactio*. Only as military success followed military success did more ambitious plans for a coalition of German Protestant princes (a *corpus evangelicorum*) under Swedish leadership and even of the Imperial throne emerge.[37] Much was made in Swedish propaganda at the time of the defence of Protestantism. As with Christian IV, it is difficult to assess how important an element this was in Sweden's entry into the war. Gustavus's attachment to his faith appears to have been sincere, but the religious issue was so closely allied with the dynastic that the two elements cannot be convincingly separated.[38]

After his withdrawal from the war in 1629 (the Treaty of Lübeck), Christian sought to preserve what was left of the Danish position in northern Germany and to counter the extension of Swedish power in the region. His interference with the passage of Swedish ships through The Sound, his sheltering of Gustavus

Adolphus's widow after she had fled from Sweden, his despatch of an embassy to Madrid, all had aroused Swedish suspicions by 1643 to such an extent that the regency for the young queen Christina (1632–54) decided to order Torstensson in Bohemia to march from the gates of Prague to invade Jutland.[39] The peace of Brömsebro in 1645, by which Denmark surrendered the islands of Gotland and Ösel as well as the province of Halland (if nominally for only thirty years), can be said to mark the replacement of Denmark by Sweden as the leading Baltic power. It was now rather Denmark which was threatened by Swedish encirclement.

After the Westphalian settlement (1648), the gains from which were to involve Sweden in the following years in German affairs and German rivalries to an extent hardly consonant with its own interests, peace reigned in the Baltic for six years. Sweden was ruled by a queen who had sought to extricate her realm from the German conflict at a rate which seemed indecent to many of her advisers and had no desire to embark on a new war, especially as the ancient dispute with Poland was not yet settled in a final peace treaty. Internally Sweden also faced the task of absorbing the territory gained at Brömsebro and Westphalia and the disbandment of the great army of which Sweden was the paymaster.[40] Denmark was still recovering financially and economically from the second occupation of her mainland in twenty years, and the new king Frederik III had his hands bound by a strict election charter imposed by a council which had no desire for foreign adventures.

Russia had played little part in Baltic or central European affairs since the peace of Stolbova, but its support of the Ukrainian cossacks against the king of Poland now brought it back on the scene with an advance into Poland (1654) which threatened the break-up of the republic and the establishment of Russian troops on the Baltic. By 1655 developments in Poland were becoming threatening to Sweden, and the new monarch Charles X (1655–60), a soldier who had commanded Swedish troops in Germany at the end of the Thirty Years' War, was not the man to sit idly by and see the situation deteriorate further. A large-scale mobilisation was in any case necessary and a large military force was most easily maintained on occupied territory. He had before him the choice of offering Poland assistance against the Russian advance in exchange for territorial concessions on the Baltic littoral, in particular the ports which Sweden had controlled during the truce of 1629–35, the income from which had helped so much to sustain the war in Germany, or to go to war against Poland with the same objective. An offer to Poland was made but rejected, and Charles consequently plunged into a campaign which proved both the military weakness of Poland and the difficulty of inflicting a decisive defeat on it.[41] Charles's difficulties encouraged Frederik of Denmark, now in a much stronger position vis-a-vis his council than at the beginning of his reign, to strike at Sweden directly with the object of regaining control of both sides of The Sound (1657). After compelling the Danes to make peace at Roskilde in 1658, Charles undoubtedly toyed with the idea of destroying Danish independence and ridding his realm once and for all of the threat of Danish revanchisme. It was with this end in view that he renewed the war almost at once, at a time when he still had to face Russia, Poland, Brandenburg and the Emperor.[42]

The 'Northern Hundred Years War' ended with the series of peace treaties concluded in 1660/1 by which Denmark acknowledged Sweden's possession of the provinces of Halland, Blekinge and Skåne but regained control of central Norway and Bornholm, surrendered at Roskilde, and Poland, threatened by Russia, surrendered its claims to the Swedish throne and Livonia. Russia made peace with Sweden on the basis of the status quo at Kardis in 1661, but continued its war against Poland for a further six years. The focus of European diplomacy now moved decisively westward to centre on the ambitions of the France of Louis XIV; the Baltic area, though still of great commercial importance, was for the succeeding four decades diplomatically something of a backwater. The rulers of Denmark abandoned dreams of the revival of the Kalmar Union, even temporarily of regaining the lost provinces in southern Sweden to concentrate on the reconstruction of the kingdom after the introduction of absolute monarchy. Sweden, weakened by a regency government which had to answer for its policy to a mature king Charles XI in 1672 and divided within itself, sought to protect its leading position in the Baltic without antagonising its neighbours. For Sweden, above all Denmark must be isolated. Poland and Russia again turned from the Baltic to deal with the threat of a revived Turkey. The Great Elector of Brandenburg was concerned with the assertion of authority over his estates and with his obligation to the Emperor to defend the Empire against French threats. The Maritime Powers, having helped to prevent complete Swedish domination of the Baltic, were mainly concerned with preserving the peace of the area.

The only breach in the peace in the later seventeenth century had little to do with Baltic questions. During the years of continuing Habsburg-Bourbon rivalry, a rivalry in which religious differences played little part, two alternative policies were argued over in the Swedish council. One party saw Swedish interests as best served by a continuing close association with France, a power which was sufficiently remote not to pose any sort of threat to Swedish territory and yet wealthy enough to pay subsidies to support the country's military establishment in its far-flung European territories. Another party favoured alliance with the Dutch and the Emperor to limit the French threat to international peace. The temporary dominance of the latter view led Sweden to join the Triple Alliance in 1667 and to sign the Hague Guarantee Treaty in 1669.[43] The chancellor Magnus Gabriel de la Gardie, however, favoured the French connection, and on the eve of the opening of the Dutch War secured a French alliance (1672) which carried with it the promise of much-needed subsidies in exchange for a commitment to maintain a military presence in Pomerania sufficient to discourage Brandenburg from assisting France's enemies. But when Brandenburg entered the war against France, the latter refused to pay subsidies until Sweden acted, and in 1674 it was consequently possible to maintain such a force only by crossing the border into Brandenburg and commencing hostilities.[44] In this way Sweden found itself engaged in a war from which it could hope to gain little benefit. News of the Swedish defeat at Fehrbellin (1675) led Frederik III to arrest the duke of Gottorp, in alliance with Sweden since 1661, and prepare to cross The Sound. Only with difficulty were Danish troops again dislodged from the old Danish provinces, where the unpopularity of the Swedification policy practised by the new rulers in Stockholm provided them with much support among the inhabitants. That Sweden lost at the peace of St. Germain in 1679 only a strip of territory in Pomerania was due to French pressure on behalf of its client at the negotiations, a lesson which was lost neither on the Swedes nor on the country's jealous neighbours.[45]

A potentially dangerous situation arose as early as 1683, when an offensive alliance was signed between Denmark, Brandenburg and France against Sweden. After 1679, under the leadership of chancellor Bengt Oxenstierna, Sweden had moved towards the Emperor and the United Provinces, whose fleet had so menaced communications between Sweden and Pomerania in the previous conflict, while Brandenburg and Denmark had moved in the opposite direction. Denmark again occupied the Schleswig territories of the duke of Gottorp in 1682. Fortunately for peace in the Baltic only Denmark was eager for conflict; France failed to ratify the agreement.[46] Brandenburg subsequently reverted to its Imperial allegiance, and Denmark, unable to act alone against Sweden, found itself isolated. The position in Gottorp, however, continued to poison relations between Denmark and Sweden, and again nearly caused war at the end of the decade. An alliance between Sweden and Brunswick-Lüneberg and intervention by the Maritime Powers, now united under William of Orange, forced Denmark to give way at the treaty of Altona in 1689 and to evacuate the duke's territories.[47] Attention was again diverted to central Europe, where not only Brandenburg but Danish and Swedish troops were engaged against France in the Nine Years' War.[48]

The return of peace in 1697, however, opened a new phase in the Baltic struggle and placed Sweden in a parlous situation. The securing of full powers by the ambitious Peter I revived Russian ambitions to secure a Baltic coastline while the election of Augustus of Saxony to the throne of Poland at the same time provided that country with a ruler who sought a success in foreign policy to strengthen his position at home. Denmark had at last the allies it needed for a war of revenge. In 1698 was concluded the first of a series of treaties between the three powers aimed at depriving Sweden of the lands it had gained in the course of the century and of its position in the Baltic. The time seemed especially propitious for the allies. The death of Charles XI in 1697 raised the prospect of a lengthy regency for his son Charles XII, and of the lack of decisive leadership associated with this form of government. Harvest failures (which decimated the population of central Finland) seemed likely to undermine the country's economy and with it its military strength as well as to cause discontent in the lower orders, and the protests of Livonian nobles against the resumption of royal lands suggested widespread discontent among the upper.[49] In 1700 Denmark reoccupied the Gottorp lands, Saxon troops marched into Livonia, and Russian troops laid siege to Narva. The Great Northern War (1700–21) had begun.

That it continued for over twenty years was due partly to the preoccupation of the Western powers in the War of the Spanish Succession, which, for example prevented Charles from striking at Saxony itself until after Blenheim had removed the French threat to southern Germany, partly to Charles's refusal to conclude a compromise peace which would have left his enemies in a position to strike again when the situation seemed favourable, partly to a series of accidents and miscalculations during the Russian campaign which deprived the Swedes of a decisive victory over Peter; the defeats at Poltava and Perevolotjna were the direct cause of the reformation of the anti-Swedish coalition.[50] On the other hand the war might well have lasted even longer had Charles not been killed in 1718 and had the preoccupations of the Western powers in the last year not prevented them from giving Sweden the support it asked for.

The settlements at the end of the war left Sweden with only the gains made from Denmark before 1661 and a small foothold on the southern shore of the Baltic in the shape of a Pomeranian bridgehead and the port of Wismar. While of no real economic or strategic advantage, the latter German possessions, together with Sweden's role as a guarantor of the Peace of Westphalia, always threatened to drag it into central European affairs in which it now had no real interest. The loss of Livonia in particular rankled with Swedish statesmen, but there was little hope of gaining any territory at Russia's expense without the support of a strong ally and a wider conflagration which would divert Russia's now formidable military force from the northern quarter. Denmark, having gained nothing from the war except a guarantee of the Gottorp territories in Schleswig, entered on nearly a century of neutrality. Schleswig was, however, to create a threat of war in the Baltic within a few years of the peace of Nystad. The marriage alliance between the young duke of Gottorp and Peter the Great's daughter provided him during the brief reign of Peter's wife with Russian support for his claims not only to his lands in Schleswig but also the Swedish throne as the son of Charles XII's elder sister. Sweden acceded to the Hanoverian alliance in 1727, and a British naval squadron sailed the Baltic in 1726 and 1727, but in the latter year the death of Catherine I deprived the duke of Russian assistance. The crisis passed.[51]

Conflict again threatened in 1733 with the outbreak of the War of the Polish Succession; the siege of Danzig in 1734 by the Russians brought a French squadron into the Baltic.[52] Neither Scandinavian power was directly involved, but activists in Sweden saw Russia's preoccupations in Poland as an opportunity to attack, and they were restrained with more and more difficulty as the years passed. In 1738, now organised as the Hat party, they seized control of the Diet and Council and began to prepare for a revanchist coup with French support. With the end of the Polish crisis France ceased to be interested in a Baltic war, but the situation changed with the outbreak of the War of the Austrian Succession in 1740.[53]

France now became interested in the possibility of a diversionary attack on Russia from Finland, while the hope of support from Elizabeth should she gain the Russian throne in her planned coup d'état, of which the Swedish ambassador in St. Petersburg was fully informed, held out to the Swedes the prospect of territorial gains at little cost. When Elizabeth, having seized the throne, turned on her erstwhile allies and ordered vigorous resistance to be offered to the advancing Swedish troops, it was too late.[54] The inadequacy of Swedish preparations for the war became all too apparent. The Hats saved themselves from disaster and the possible loss of Finland only by accepting the Russian candidate, the tsarina's nephew Adolf Fredrik of Gottorp, as heir to the Swedish throne in the peace settlement.[55] And the Baltic crisis continued when Russian troops were sent to help defend Sweden against any possible attack from Denmark, disappointed by the failure of king Frederik to secure the election of his son as heir. When Adolf Fredrik proved less malleable than had been envisaged, and Sweden did not become the Russian satellite expected, a new Russo-Swedish war threatened. Vigorous action by Prussia and France and pressure on Russia by Britain and Austria helped Sweden to weather the storm. The end of the crisis was marked in 1751 by an agreement between Denmark and Sweden over the Gottorp claims and the peaceful accession of Adolf Fredrik.[56]

In 1757, however, the Swedish Council was persuaded reluctantly to conclude an alliance with France and Austria which dragged Sweden into war in Germany in the hope of regaining from Prussia the territory lost in Pomerania. The situation had certain parallels with that in 1675.[57] And the outcome was somewhat similar. Fortunately on this occasion Denmark had no wish to exploit Sweden's preoccupations. The death of tsarina Elizabeth in 1762 indeed created a perilous situation for Denmark. Tsar Peter III, duke of Holstein-Gottorp, now in command of a large army with which to pursue his claims to his house's lands in Schleswig, hastily concluded peace with Prussia and turned against Denmark. Only his death prevented the outbreak of conflict, and the cost of the armament necessary to face the Russians put a heavy strain on Denmark's financial resources.[58]

The coup d'état carried through by Gustavus III of Sweden (1771–92) in 1772 created considerable tensions in the Baltic. Russia, Denmark and Prussia had guaranteed the old constitution which Gustavus had now overthrown and threatened to intervene to restore it. Gustavus certainly feared an attack. Russia, however, preoccupied as it was with the first partition of Poland and with war against the Turks and apprehensive of British and French naval preparations, drew back, while France fully supported the new regime.[59] The rest of the decade was a peaceful one. Gustavus was preoccupied with establishing his control and carrying through his reform programme, while none of the other powers had any interest in upsetting the equilibrium. But in the background lay an agreement reached between Denmark and Russia in 1773 by which they would intervene in Sweden to restore the status quo when the time seemed ripe. And in the early 1780s Sweden itself became a destabilising element. Gustavus, disappointed by the opposition which his policies had aroused, particularly within the nobility, sought to restore his popularity by means of an aggressive foreign policy.[60] He planned in 1783 to launch a surprise attack on Denmark with the aim of winning Norway, where he tried to foster separatist tendencies. When, however, he was warned by Catherine II that she would not countenance such a move and when the expected war between Russia and Turkey after the former's occupation of the Crimea failed to materialise, he turned to the idea of an assault on Russia itself.[61] To hopes of a prestigious victory to silence the opposition at home was added a wish to put an end to Russian support for that opposition and in particular for the small independence movement in Finland led by the Sprengtporten brothers. His war aims were never clearly specified. The moment seemed propitious for the planned sea and land assault on St. Petersburg after war broke out between Russia and Turkey in 1787. But the preparations for the attack again proved inadequate, and when the Finnish officer corps mutinied, Denmark reluctantly fulfilled its treaty obligations to Russia by declaring war on Sweden.[62] There was, however, little fighting between the Scandinavian monarchies, and Denmark only too readily accepted British mediation backed by threats from Brandenburg-Prussia.[63] The situation in France, with which the rulers of both Sweden and Russia were much concerned, made possible the conclusion of peace at Värälä on the basis of the status quo in 1790.

War and the threat of war in the Baltic in the early modern period had a multiplicity of causes. All the wars between Denmark and Sweden in the seventeenth century were primarily attempts by the former to restore a position lost as a result of war or rebellion. At least as late as the Kalmar War of 1611–13 Danish rulers entertained dreams of restoring the unity of Scandinavia which the Swedish revolt of 1520 had destroyed. In 1613 Denmark emerged as still the dominant power in the Baltic. In the years following, however, the balance shifted decisively in favour of Sweden, a situation which Christian IV attempted to counteract by strengthening his position in northern Germany — a policy which helped to bring him into the Thirty Years' War — and by working to limit Swedish gains after his defeat. This brought about the humiliating war of 1643–5, after which Danish rulers sought every opportunity to exploit Swedish embarrassment to regain the territory lost until re-entry into the Great Northern War after Poltava. Sweden's wars in the eighteenth century, especially that against Russia in 1741–3, but also the Pomeranian War of 1757–62 and the Finnish War of 1788–90, contained the same element. Poland's long conflict with Sweden in the seventeenth century stemmed immediately from the break-up of the union formed by Sigismund's accession to the Swedish throne, but behind it lay also the dispute between the two countries over claims to Livonia.

Swedish expansion during the century after 1560 was to a large degree an attempt to improve a strategic position and ensure against attack by an immediate neighbour, in particular Denmark, which even after Sweden had replaced it as the leading Baltic power, was always suspected of plotting to regain the status it had lost and tied down Swedish forces in the south of the country even in time of peace. Poland, although not in itself a formidable threat, might exploit an Imperial victory in Germany to launch an invasion of Sweden itself. And once territory had been won there was always the temptation to seek further territory to protect what had already been gained and to be drawn on further than the danger or the resources at one's disposal really warranted. There is certainly an element of this in Charles X's Polish campaign.

But certainly Sweden's ambitions were not wholly confined to strategic considerations. While economic aims played little part in the propaganda of the time and were not so dominant as some modern historians, not all of them professed Marxists, would claim, an opportunity to control the increasingly active trade routes flowing into and through the Baltic was something which the surrounding states, faced as they were by rising costs of administration and the maintenance of a military establishment, could not ignore. Russia's attempts to break through to the Baltic in the sixteenth and seventeenth centuries may have been partly for reasons of prestige, but the urge to exclude middlemen in its overseas trade was also strong.[64] Sweden's reaction was also partly dictated by fear of Russian competition in the Gulf of Finland. Efforts by its rulers to establish complete control of Russian and Polish trade were, however, frustrated by the movement of trade routes out of Swedish control northward to Archangel and westward to Poland, whose coastline Sweden could exploit only for the six years following the Truce of Altmark of 1629.[65]

It is also difficult in the seventeenth century to separate religious issues from other considerations. Poland, the only Catholic country on the Baltic was certainly a threat to the religious as well as the dynastic settlement in Sweden as long as its kings maintained their claims to the Swedish throne, and during the Thirty Years' War a Catholic-Imperial victory might give it the strength to realise this threat which it otherwise lacked the resources to do.

The Baltic does not offer an example of a pre-emptive strike in its pure form. Sweden's attack on Denmark in 1643 was partly to discourage a Dano-Imperial alliance to impose a peace settlement which was against Swedish interests. Charles X's invasion of Poland in 1655 was partly to prevent Russian penetration to the Baltic, and his renewal of the war in 1658 seems to have been aimed at ridding Sweden once and for all of the Danish threat to the heartland.[66]

Conflict might be caused by the need to maintain a larger military establishment than could be supported in peacetime. The doctrine that *bellum se ipse alet* was certainly one likely to appeal to Charles X in 1655, and the difficulties of supply faced by the Swedish commander in Pomerania in 1674 led him to cross the border into Brandenburg and thus precipitate hostilities, although in this case pressure from Sweden's French ally to fulfil treaty obligations was as important.

The personal ambitions of rulers like Ivan IV and Peter I, Christian IV and Gustavus III, and Augustus of Saxony might also lead to war against the wishes of the majority of their subjects; no Danish war in the seventeenth century was precipitated by the pressure of councillors on monarchs. In conflicts between Sweden and Denmark and between Sweden and Russia, however, popular enthusiasm against a traditional enemy was not difficult to arouse; the attack by Denmark on Sweden in 1788 did much to rally his subjects behind Gustavus III. Foreign adventure might also serve to distract attention from domestic difficulties and strengthen a monarch's position at home. Augustus of Saxony counted on the conquest of Livonia in 1700 to improve his hand in dealing with his new subjects with the aim of introducing firmer government, while Gustavus III's attack on Russia in 1788 was aimed partly to restore his waning popularity.

On a number of occasions, finally, Baltic countries were drawn into war simply by the need to fulfil their treaty obligations to other Baltic or to non-Baltic powers. The alliances between Sweden and France in 1672 and 1757 seemed to promise valuable subsidies in exchange for a largely passive role in Pomerania but in each case dragged Sweden into a conflict with Brandenburg. And Denmark's pact with Russia in 1773 obliged it, because of Gustavus III's aggression in Finland, to break its neutrality on the only occasion between the end of the Great Northern War and entry into the Napoleonic conflict on the French side after the British attack on Copenhagen in 1807.

NOTES

1. Erik Hornborg, *Kampen om Östersjön* (Stockholm, 1945), pp. 415–9.

2. Artur Attman, *The Struggle for Baltic Markets: Powers in Conflict 1558–1618* (Gothenburg, 1979), pp. 10–11 (note 2), 12; Walther Kirchner, *The Rise of the Baltic Question* (Westport, Conn., 1954), p. 101.

3. Attman, p. 10; Kirchner, pp. 198–206.

4. What remained of Swedish Pomerania was in 1814 exchanged with a defeated Denmark, which immediately sold it to Brandenburg-Prussia (Johan Feuk, *Sverige på kongressen i Wien 1814–1815* (Lund, 1915), pp. 58ff.).

5. R. C. Anderson, *Naval Wars in the Baltic 1522–1850* (1910), pp. 195–206.

6. Waldemar Carlsson, *Gustaf II Adolf och Stralsund 1628–juli 1630* (Uppsala, 1912), p. 11.

7. G. N. Clark, *The Dutch Alliance and the War against French Trade 1688–1697* (Manchester, 1923), pp. 122–3.

8. Hilding Danielson, *Sverige och Frankrike 1727–1735* (Lund, 1920), p. 88; Andrew Lossky, *Louis XIV, William III and the Baltic Crisis of 1683* (Berkeley, Los Angeles, 1954), p. vii.

9. Attman, pp. 7–8.

10. Michael Roberts, *The Swedish Imperial Experience 1560–1718* (Cambridge, 1979), pp. 26–42; Attman, pp. 208–14.

11. Göran Behre, Lars-Olof Larsson and Eva Österberg, *Sveriges historia 1521–1809* (Stockholm, 1985), p. 67.

12. E. Ladewig Petersen, 'The Danish cattle trade during the sixteenth and seventeenth century', *Scandinavian Economic History Review* XVIII (1970), pp. 69–70, 84–5.

13. E. L. Petersen, 'Defence, war and finance: Christian IV and the Council of the Realm 1596–1629', *Scandinavian Journal of History* 7 (1982), pp. 280, 287–9.

14. The Danish fleet seized by Britain in 1807 was made up of some 20 battleships and 15 frigates (Anderson, p. 319).

15. M. Roberts, *The Age of Liberty: Sweden 1719–1772* (Cambridge, 1986), pp. 35–58.

16. The Russian population in 1725 has been estimated at 13,000,000, less than that of France, and 'until the later seventeenth century she was almost certainly weaker in manpower than Poland-Lithuania' (B. H. Sumner, *Survey of Russian History* (1947), p. 345).

17. Michael Roberts, *Gustavus Adolphus: A History of Sweden 1611–1632*, vol. II (1958), p. 196.

18. Kirchner, pp. 101–7.

19. Attman, pp. 13–14, 45; Kirchner, pp. 165–75; Roberts (1979), p. 9.

20. Attman, pp. 13, 76–7, 98; Kirchner, pp. 126–44.

21. Attman, p. 147; Kirchner, p. 144; Walther Kirchner, 'A milestone in European history: the Danish-Russian treaty of 1562', *Slavonic and East European Review* XXXII:2 (1944), pp. 39–48.

22. Attman, p. 77; Kirchner, p. 99.

23. Michael Roberts, *The Early Vasas* (Cambridge, 1968, i), pp. 210–2, 216; Charles E.

Hill, *The Danish Sound Dues and the Command of the Baltic* (Durham, N.C., 1926), p. 63.

24. Treaties were signed between Sweden and Russia in 1562, 1564 and 1567 (Attman, pp. 64–6, 68, 71).

25. Attman, pp. 75, 99, 147; Roberts (1968, i), pp. 250ff.

26. Attman, pp. 148–51; Roberts (1968, i), p. 260.

27. Attman, pp. 170–1, 174–5.

28. Roberts (1968, i), pp. 453–7; Attman, pp. 183–8.

29. Roberts (1968, i), pp. 394ff; Attman, p. 192.

30. Attman, pp. 175–7, 179–81, 194–5; Hill, pp. 83–4; Petersen (1982), p. 289.

31. Helge Gamrath and E. Ladewig Petersen, *Danmarks Historie* 2 (Copenhagen, 1980), pp. 492–3; Hill, pp. 91–5.

32. M. Roberts, *Gustavus Adolphus and the Rise of Sweden* (London, 1973), pp. 54–60; Axel Norberg, *Polen i svensk politik 1617–26* (Stockholm, 1974), pp. 213–20.

33. Petersen (1982), pp. 300–6; Hill, p. 96.

34. Roberts (1958), pp. 346–56; Carlsson, *passim*.

35. Jerker Rosén, *Svensk historia* I (Stockholm 1962), p. 411.

36. Roberts (1958), pp. 412–4, 417–25; M. Roberts, *Essays in Swedish History* (1967), pp. 82–6.

37. Roberts (1958), pp. 510, 666–73; Roberts (1967), pp. 101–2.

38. Roberts (1958), pp. 418–9; Nils Ahnlund, *Gustav Adolf the Great* (Princeton, New York, 1940), pp. 267–75.

39. Hill, pp. 110–3, 123–4, 131–5; M. Roberts, *Sweden as a Great Power* (1968, ii), pp. 154–60.

40. Roberts (1968, ii), pp. 160–3.

41. Hans Landberg, 'Krig på kredit', in Hans Landberg, *Det kontinentala krigets ekonomi* (Stockholm, 1971), p. 14; Hans Landberg, 'Statsfinans och kungamakt', in *Carl Gustaf inför polska kriget* (Uppsala, 1969), pp. 143–64.

42. Hill, pp. 161–4, 167–9; Roberts (1968, ii), pp. 169–72.

43. Georg Landberg, *Det svenska utrikespolitikens historia* I:3 (Stockholm, 1952), pp. 153–64; Göran Rystad, 'Magnus Gabriel de la Gardie', in Michael Roberts (ed.), *Sweden's Age of Greatness 1632–1718* (1973), pp. 213–4.

44. Harald Bohrn, *Sverige, Danmark och Frankrike 1672–1674* (Stockholm, 1933), pp. 244ff; Landberg (1952), pp. 175–90.

45. Hill, pp. 192–3; Landberg, (1952), pp. 190–203.

46. Hill, pp. 197–8; Lossky, esp. p. 43.

47. Hill, p. 198; Landberg (1952), pp. 230–9.

48. Landberg (1952), pp. 243–5.

49. Jerker Rosén, *Den svenska utrikespolitikens historia* II:1 (Stockholm, 1952), pp. 38–53; Hill, pp. 199–201.

50. R. M. Hatton, *Charles XII of Sweden* (1968), pp. 212–3, 247–8.

51. Olof Jägerskiöld, *Den svenska utrikespolitikens historia* II:2 (Stockholm, 1957), pp. 68, 79–82; Danielson (1920), pp. 10–13, 25–6.

52. Jägerskiöld, pp. 103–5; Danielson (1920), pp. 190–7.

53. Jägerskiöld, pp. 103–40; Richard Lodge, 'The Treaty of Åbo and the Swedish Succession', *E.H.R.* XLIII (1928), pp. 540–1.

54. Jägerskiöld, pp. 139–50.

55. Jägerskiöld, pp. 155–60; Lodge, pp. 554–69.

56. Jägerskiöld, pp. 161–81; J. R. Danielson, *Die Nordische Frage in den Jahren 1746–1751* (Helsinki, 1888), *passim*.

57. Jägerskiöld, pp. 199–202; Erik Armburger, *Russland und Schweden 1762–1772: Katharina II, die schwedische Verfassung und die Ruhe des Nordens* (Berlin, 1934), p. 38.

58. Ole Feldbaek, *Danmarks Historie* 4 (Copenhagen, 1982), p. 267; P. Vedel (ed.). *Correspondance ministérielle du comte J. H. E. Bernstorff 1751–70* (Copenhagen, 1882), pp. IV–V; Armburger, pp. 43ff.

59. Jägerskiöld, pp. 260–7; Roberts (1967), pp. 296–322.

60. Jägerskiöld, pp. 278–80.

61. Jägerskiöld, pp. 289–95; Stewart Oakley, 'Gustavus III's plans for war with Denmark in 1783–4', in R. M. Hatton and M. S. Anderson (eds.), *Studies in Diplomatic History in Memory of David Bayne Horn* (1970), pp. 271–86.

62. Jägerskiöld, pp. 303–22; C. T. Odhner, *Sveriges politiska historia under Gustaf III:s regering* III:1 (Stockholm, 1905), pp. 1–170.

63. Jägerskiöld, pp. 322–4; Odhner, pp. 184–206.

64. Kirchner, pp. 62 (and n.6), 197–8.

65. Attman, pp. 159–173; Roberts (1979), p. 40.

66. Halvdan Koht, 'Scandinavian preventive wars in the 1650s' in A. O. Sarkissian (ed.), *Studies in Diplomatic History in Honour of G. P. Gooch* (1961), pp. 283–6.

3

THE CAUSES OF THE FRANCO-SPANISH WAR OF 1635–59

David Parrott

The frequency and severity of armed conflict throughout history has attracted attention from scholars of many disciplines. Theories concerning the general causes of wars have achieved wide currency, although they frequently prove irrelevant when applied to specific conflicts, or require a substantial distortion of the available evidence to render them applicable. This irrelevance is not surprising; many theories reflect either abstract preconceptions about the nature of human behaviour and political structures, or are based upon a limited number of (usually near-contemporary) historical examples of conflict. Yet this should not serve as an excuse to dismiss general theories of the causes of wars outright. While the theorists may fail in their reductionist intention of providing a single, universal explanation for why wars begin, their proposals remain valuable. For historians concentrating upon a particular conflict are prone to regard its causes from a narrow perspective, implicitly presupposing that the war was inevitable, and that their only task is to explain why it occurred then. Wide-ranging theory, even if largely inapplicable, can challenge the assumption of inevitability, and emphasise that there may be other factors relevant to the causes of conflict which are less immediately apparent to the specialist historian. Moreover there is a branch of theorising about the causes of all wars which cannot safely be ignored without reducing the value of historical research and its conclusions. Drawing upon a much more substantial sample of conflicts, these theorists renounce any attempt to provide a reductionist 'answer' to why wars begin. They concentrate instead upon the attempt to define war itself, to establish its relationship with other forms of political activity, and to determine the decision-making process by which states move from diplomatic hostility to reciprocated military action.

My aim in this chapter is both to examine the causes — in so far as they may be established — of the Franco-Spanish war that broke out in 1635, and to place these causes in the context of theories of conflict. As many issues in the outbreak of this war have been accepted without serious questioning, it may be hoped that theory will provide some insights into its causes. Equally, though the more sophisticated theorists have drawn upon a wide range of historical examples, these rarely extend back before 1700.[1] The omission of examples from the seventeenth century is disappointing, for in some respects the conflicts of this century have much in common with more recent experience. Both periods are characterised by protracted struggles of attrition requiring the highest levels of national commitment.[2] In both periods fundamental political and ideological issues were the subject of conflict. An examination of the Franco-Spanish war may have the additional advantage of bringing such parallels under scrutiny, testing theories of causation against a major conflict which most of these theories did not originally take into account.

The concern to provide a single, all-embracing theory of why wars begin frequently reflects some particular political, sociological or scientific pre-conception.[3] Wars, it is suggested, are caused by the greed, calculation or stupidity of individuals or social groups. These concerns will inevitably prevail over any 'objective' national or strategic interest. This theory could be attached to many of the wars of the sixteenth century. Did Henry VIII's three campaigns in France, above all, his last and most expensive in 1544, reflect any motive other than his personal rivalry with Francis I and his overwhelming vanity?[4] Can the French role in the Italian wars down to 1559 be seen as anything more than an alliance between dynastic aspirations and the greed of a potentially unruly nobility?[5] In both cases it could be argued that there was more to the conflicts than this; but although it would be simplistic to take account exclusively of such interpretations, they should not be ruled out in an attempt to appreciate the causes of sixteenth-century war. A similar view of causation is provided by the assumption that wars reflect the vested interest of institutional forces, whether bureaucracies, officer-corps, or, more recently, that most elusive group of conspirators, the 'military/industrial complex'. The officer-corps had been identified as early as the mid-seventeenth century by that distinguished theorist of the causes of war, Thomas Hobbes, who suggests characteristically that:

> All men that are ambitious of Military command, are enclined to continue the causes of warre; and to stirre up trouble and sedition: for there is no honour Military but by warre . . .[6]

Another view enjoying widespread currency is that the causes of wars are in all significant cases economic, that material interests lie beneath the surface of all decision-making. Seen in retrospect, Elizabeth's war with Spain from 1585 was merely an expansion of the piracy and interloping in the Spanish New World that had been pursued by her subjects during the previous decade. Certainly England appeared less than committed to military support for the Dutch.[7] In turn, Spain's decision not to renew the truce with the United Provinces in 1621 was motivated by concern at increasing Dutch penetration of the Spanish and Portuguese colonial empires.[8]

The opinion that wars reflect purely economic motives may have contributed to the theory that warfare is inherent to certain types of state organisation, whether capitalism, communism, or, in the early modern period, to states whose monarchs were conditioned to regard their territory and subjects as so much inherited property, and who sought to extend their claims whenever this seemed legitimate or practical. Steeped in the tradition of the *Reconquista*, Ferdinand and Isabella found little difficulty in translating the same concept of dynastic expansion to Italy and in justifying the subsequent wars with France which eventually consolidated these gains.[9] This type of theory proposes that the origins of war should not be sought in predictable reactions to external events, but within the state itself. Governments, or certain types of government, choose war as a means to evade the tensions or developing contradictions within their own states. The classic early modern example is perhaps the expansion of the Russian Empire into the West. Its objectives were pursued intermittently, and with variable success; the rhythms of expansion and warfare are best sought in tensions within Russia. Foreign assertion became the main outlet for the pressures created by powerful rulers challenging resistance within the state.[10]

The highest level of generalisation about the causes of war is attained with the quasi-psychological thesis that men, being inherently aggressive, but forced to subsume this impulse in the interests of maintaining an internally ordered society, are 'naturally' disposed to make war on societies outside of their own. Beneath the facade of rational decision-making is an overwhelming temptation to resolve disputes by force, rather than to seek compromise. Long before theories of aggression had been proposed, observers of contemporary events had noted a similar tendency: for Hobbes, this could be attributed to a '... perpetuall and restlesse desire of Power after power, that ceaseth only in Death'.[11] Grotius' programme for restraint in warfare reflected a pessimistic acceptance that conflict would inevitably occur; the best that could be achieved was the drafting of realistic conventions to mitigate its worst consequences.[12] The practical lesson drawn from this assumption of man's propensity to aggression and aggrandisement through force is that certain international state systems prove more likely to encourage warfare than others. The most secure arrangement is taken to be some type of 'balance' between a number of states not locked together in hostile alliances and prepared to act together to curb the aggressive tendencies of any individual power. In practice these groupings of states are rarely so reliable or disinterested that they can provide any permanent stability. The 'Holy League' established in 1495 to resist French expansion in Italy was typical, quickly collapsing into self-interested factions which the French were able to exploit.[13] The worst form of international system is that in which one state is as powerful as any likely combination of its rivals; this state will inevitably exploit the opportunity for the aggressive pursuit of a package of interests and advantage. On the assumption of this theory of innate aggression, it will positively welcome any resultant conflict. The obvious seventeenth-century example is the foreign policy of Louis XIV from 1678. Particularly in the period leading up to the war of the Spanish Succession, it is hard to avoid the impression that Louis, having decided that conflict was inevitable, went out of his way to trample on the sensibilities and challenge the interests of his future opponents.[14] Equally, Sweden after 1631 reveals an aggressive self-confidence and willingness to provoke hostility which went far beyond the rational assertion of her foreign policy interests.[15]

The concern essentially to simplify the origins of warfare, to suggest that a particular general cause can consistently be identified from a synthesis of individual conflicts, represents one approach to the problem. The second variety of theorising about the causes of war is not at all concerned to provide reductionist answers. The aim of these theories is not to simplify historical experience into a few consistent themes, but to ask questions and propose explanations for conflict based upon a more general study of warfare.

As with any consideration of the nature of warfare, the starting point is the work of Clausewitz. In the much-quoted and misunderstood remark that 'War is the continuation of political intercourse with the addition of other means,'[16] and the less familiar statement that 'War is a clash between major interests that is resolved by bloodshed — that is the only way in which it differs from other conflicts.'[17] Clausewitz made a central contribution to the debate about the causes of wars. Both statements emphasise that there is no obvious threshold dividing the peaceful pursuit of objectives from a 'state of warfare'. There is no such thing as a 'military solution', a consigning of responsibility to the High Command when diplomacy fails to achieve its objectives. The awareness that war is a means to a political end should never be relinquished.[18] A decision to go to war is not a straightforward movement from one condition to another, from civil to military objectives. If a government is concerned to pursue a particular aim, and has failed to make any headway against an opposing power through negotiations, it may decide to introduce a measure of force into its hitherto peaceful efforts. The extent to which force will be applied should depend upon the government's perception of the importance of the aim. Equally the government under challenge has the choice of whether or not to respond, and to establish the level of response — again, on an assessment of the importance of the issue involved.

Clausewitz suggests that the consequence of this is that most wars begin as limited engagements in which neither side commits anything approaching its full resources, for the interests at stake are insufficiently great. The implicit consequence of this is that very real doubt can exist about when 'war' may be considered to begin. Does a limited employment of force in pursuit or defence of a particular objective constitute a war? It is, after all, armed conflict between sovereign states, and it would be inappropriate to expect any formal declaration of war in the great majority of cases.[19] Yet how different is this state from that of 'Warlike Peace' described by Raymond Aron,[20] where, for example, the power seeking to put pressure upon another refrains from the use of its own forces, but seeks to incite violence within the other state through sponsoring unrest or revolt? In some cases the distinction appears relatively clear: by encouraging the revolt of the French king's brother, Gaston d'Orléans, in 1632, and by offering him limited financial support, Olivares, the Spanish first minister, did not consider that he was taking the first step on the path to open war.[21] This view appears to have been shared by his French counterpart. Richelieu, who responded, not by direct military action, but by similar support for one of the aristocratic conspiracies in the Spanish Netherlands.[22] Yet in the case of Elizabeth's conflict with the North German towns of the Hanse in 1589, the distinction is far less apparent. What appeared to the Queen to be a legitimate assertion of a Channel blockade in support of the war with Spain appeared to the merchants of the Hanse towns as an act of state piracy — the confiscation of the property of a neutral force on the flimsiest of pretexts.[23]

Moreover in some cases the levels of force will remain small; each side will shy away from an expansion of commitment which would probably be reciprocated. Negotiations resume, or the status quo is respected for the time being. The Cleves-Jülich crisis of 1609–14 is a clear example of this: neither France nor Spain actually wished to push her claims to the point of major conflict after Henri IV had died; such fighting as took place could not be described as war, but merely represented the attempts of both sides to improve their bargaining position before reaching the settlement that both regarded as essential.[24] But in other, more typical, cases both powers progressively increase their commitment to the conflict, which ultimately reaches a level of significance which would qualify it historically as warfare, and may go beyond this towards the final, though in practice unattainable, goal of Clausewitz's 'absolute war'. Yet this move is not automatic: at any point the belligerents could decide that the interests at stake no longer justified the commitment of resources, and could concede the issue to the enemy. While France was prepared to intervene in Scotland on behalf of the Regent, Mary of Guise, in the later 1550s, she was not prepared to push this support to the point of open conflict with England. When Elizabeth challenged the French involvement in Scotland with both naval and land forces in 1560, the French chose not to respond with equivalent force. Given the internal problems faced by the French crown, the possible gains from this foreign involvement did not appear to justify the cost.[25]

The typical historical assumption is that nations go to war over their perceived 'vital interests', these being defined tautologically as interests which the state is prepared to assert or defend by fighting.[26] In fact, the interests over which a government decides to employ an initial measure of force may be very much less than objectively vital, even if they may be depicted as such to the rival state which stands to suffer through their assertion. In many cases the interest which motivated the initial application of limited force will not, logically, justify a movement into significant conflict. The political interests at issue between England and Spain in 1625, or in 1656, could hardly be considered in themselves justification for the wars that broke out between these states.[27] Equally the issues at stake may not even justify the military effort of the state seeking to defend the existing situation. Nonetheless, a progressive movement into war takes place.

Two separate considerations are important in this respect. The first concerns the whole question of interests. It is not enough simply to track down the obvious concerns that will be determined by geography and concern for security. 'Vital' interests would appear to imply those necessary for immediate political and economic survival and stability. In fact, perceived interests may be a great deal more sweeping and less subject to rational analysis. The search for security *in the future* can justify present policies of annexation, of conflict aimed at preserving reputation, and of an uncompromising rejection of other states' legitimate interests. Under the general banner of security, policies aimed simply at aggrandisement and power — for whatever particular reason — will be adopted as if they had a rational justification: safety in an unforeseeable future may only be assured by power gained today.[28] The conquest of states and territory on France's border after 1674 could be justified by the desire to develop a protective glacis, an additional line of defence in front of the *pré carré*, the heavily fortified territory just within France.[29] That it was the attempt to maintain this enhanced frontier at the cost of provoking war with the League of Augsburg, which made France's actual defences necessary after 1689, was given little attention by contemporaries. There is rarely an objective correlation between the importance of the interests that provoked the first use of force, and subsequent full-scale warfare. The gulf between the two is bridged by an often irrational and always subjective assessment of the state's long-term security needs in an international environment of assumed instability.

That these 'security needs' can generate so ready a response reflects the other major consideration emerging from theoretical work on the causes of wars. Governments do not take forceful initiatives in politics on the basis of a clear awareness of their own military strength weighed against that of other states. The distribution of power is perceived hazily and subjectively, with a tendency towards over-optimism about the strength of one's own side. In the occasional cases where one side is objectively recognised to be a great deal stronger than its competitor there will be no war; conflicts of interest will be settled by unilateral concessions, for the only effect of resistance would be to compound the loss of a particular interest with more far-reaching military defeat. The reluctant surrender of many of the petty German princes to Gustavus Adolphus' demands after the Swedish army's great victory at Breitenfeld is a case in point. Now that the King of Sweden dominated Germany with an army of over 100,000 men, it would have been criminally irresponsible for these rulers of minor territories to resist demands for political and military cooperation.[30] The only major exception to this is the case where the more powerful state's 'interest' consists in the conquest or substantial annexation of the lesser. In this circumstance many, though not all, states will attempt resistance. Sometimes this will be successful, as the Dutch proved in their resistance to the armies of Louis XIV after 1672. Had the French demands been set lower than the effective destruction of the United Provinces, then it is probable that they would have been conceded by the States General without conflict.[31]

However, it is rarely the case that the protagonists in a political quarrel are capable of assessing their respective strengths. Historians may with hindsight perceive a marked military disparity between two powers or groups of powers, but this was almost certainly not apparent to those involved.[32] Governments who chose to maintain their interests with a measure of military force did so in the confidence that the enemy would prove unwilling to match successive levels of commitment, and that they would be able to win the advantage in any resultant low-level conflict. This was presumably Elizabeth's calculation when she provided support for the Dutch rebels against Spain in 1585. It was certainly Henri IV's grossly over-optimistic assumption when he stepped up hostilities against Spain into open war in January 1595.[33] Rarely is it the case that the government taking this step felt certain of being able to win a decisive victory in a major war with the enemy power. This contingency — a protracted struggle requiring the mobilisation of resources completely disproportionate to any declared objective — is almost never envisaged. It would establish an unacceptably high threshold for the assertion of a state's interests, by making the disparity between limited aims and the likely cost of their achievement evident at the outset. The protagonist who first resorts to force does so in the hope that it will reactivate the processes of diplomacy and call the bluff of the other side. The opponent will now abandon his claim to the interest at stake on the grounds that it seems unattainable, or military action to attain it will prove too costly. In practice, however, the other power will rarely view the situation from the same perspective. The Duke of Savoy's decision in 1588 to overrun the marquisate of Saluzzo, a French dependency, was obviously likely to provoke a strong French response once Henri IV had restored a semblance of internal order to France. Henri had evidently considered that the simple threat of force would be sufficient to persuade Savoy to return the marquisate, or to offer the territory of Bresse as compensation. It seemed unthinkable that Savoy would risk a military confrontation with France over the issue. Yet negotiations dragged on through 1599, and in 1600 Henri launched a full-scale military invasion of Savoyard territory.[34] The Duke of Savoy had been prepared to play for time, and did not consider that Henri's initial threats would be followed by a declaration of war. For although France's absolute material superiority was indisputable, the king could prove reluctant to involve himself in a costly foreign venture which might well encourage renewed unrest amongst a barely-pacified provincial aristocracy. Savoy had reasonable assurances of Spanish support, and was well aware that Henri was reluctant to jeopardise his claim to be the 'protector' of the independent Italian states by making war upon one of them. This example is characteristic; the forceful conduct of negotiations by France, far from resolving a diplomatic conflict, tended to compound it and to lead to a war which both sides would have preferred to avoid.

In these circumstances the outbreak of war itself provides a definitive — the *only* definitive — resolution of ambiguity. The recalcitrance of both sides and the uncertainty about the power which they are prepared and able to deploy in support of their claims requires the test of war, which has been characterised as '(the most useful) formula for measuring international power'.[35] Only immediately after a period of warfare in which one state has emerged as the clear victor can any type of objective hierarchy in international relations be established. Indecisive wars, or simply the passage of time, obscures this hierarchy, and in turn facilitates the tendency towards further wars emerging out of lesser conflicts of interest. Although the Peace of Cateau-Cambrésis between France and Spain in 1559 appeared as a decisive verdict in favour of Spanish power in European affairs, by the 1590s France was no longer prepared to accept this ranking. Only after the 1595–8 war could the Peace of Vervins (1598) restate essentially the same pro-Spanish balance of power.[36]

Certain significant generalisations can be drawn from these considerations. Both states, or groups of states, who subsequently become involved in warfare, have consciously decided that they have more to gain by being prepared to resort to force than by accepting the demands of the opposing power. But while they have chosen to employ force to support diplomacy, they did not make a conscious decision to 'go to war', and indeed the material interests at stake may well seem insignificant set against the costs of large-scale conflict. However, the aim that is immediately at issue will be surrounded by a mass of emotive, ultimately irrational objectives subsumed within the general concept of long-term security. Together with the absence of any clear conception of respective military strengths, this will persuade the government to increase its military stake progressively, until the powers reach the point of open warfare. Once having reached that point, the more emotive, extreme aims take over as the objective for which the war is being fought; peace will only be attained through a decisive victory, or through the mutual and persistent failure of military effort. The original, lesser aim which might have been negotiable at an earlier stage has been replaced by far-reaching demands which require a clear statement of respective national power if they are to be enforced.

How relevant or useful are either of these groups of theories about the causes of war to an understanding of the Franco-Spanish conflict of 1635–59? Does this conflict have anything to contribute to an assessment of the relative value of the generalisations summarised above?

Some of the reductionist theories may contribute to an understanding of this particular conflict. An examination might begin with the theory that the causes of wars should be sought in the self-interest and ambitions of particular groups within society. Were there forces in the state working towards warfare in 1635?

In Germany during this period, fully entrepreneurial armies threw up military elites which had a strong interest in the perpetuation of conflict as a means to realise their initial investment in the levy and supply of their units through direct state payment, war taxes (contributions) and booty.[37] Gustavus Adolphus' disparate mercenary forces were paid and supplied on the principle that *bellum se ipsum alit*.[38] Governments came to regard the perpetuation of war and its expansion into new territory as a financial, rather than a purely military, expedient; the army itself became a cause of war. The commanders of mercenary forces wished to see the war sustained for as long as possible, and in the unfortunate event of its termination, the starting of another as soon as possible. For Wallenstein the disbandment of the Imperial army in 1630 was a major challenge to his personal fortune.[39] The most tenaciously asserted Swedish demand at Westphalia was for a huge indemnity from the German states as the means to pay off the armies, a very high proportion of whose troops were foreign mercenaries, with nothing but a financial commitment to the Swedish cause.[40] While Swedish belligerence in the later seventeenth century can be explained partly in terms of geography and economic 'vital interests', it is reasonable to point out that the Swedish military machine was substantially larger than could be supported by national resources, and thus encouraged expansionist policies which would ensure that the burden fell elsewhere.[41]

This situation of mercenary armies looking to war as a return on capital invested is less clearly apparent in either the Spanish or the French armies. By the seventeenth century, Spanish military administration had been largely decentralized,[42] but the result was not a system of explicit entrepreneurship, at least for the Spanish and Italian forces. Troops might be raised through the efforts and influence of individuals, but the army was subsequently paid through state taxation, allotted by the military treasuries. There was not the sense that war — with attendant contribution-system and plunder — was deliberately envisaged (in the contract) as the means by which the commanding officers would reimburse themselves. The same situation prevailed in France. At least in theory, the officers were the salaried employees of the crown, granted commissions and the necessary funds to raise their unit under the direction of the administration. Most units were raised for the shortest possible period — often only one campaign — and though the officers frequently became indebted in the course of their service, there was, again, no sense in which the administration of the French war-effort would allow them a legitimate opportunity for reimbursement.

In a slightly different sense, however, a case might be made that the overall commanders of both French and Spanish armies tended consistently to favour conflict and precipitous action leading to war, even when this was not the wish of the chief minister. The issue here is more one of timing than overall policy. In 1627 the death of the Duke of Mantua placed the council at Madrid in a dilemma. The legitimate heir to the dukedom was the French Duke of Nevers, but his succession implied the real risk of French intrusion into North Italy. It was the precipitate action of the Spanish Viceroy of Milan who, acting to occupy the Mantuan territories, crystallised the conciliar debate in favour of opposing the succession with force. The Viceroy's action was officially approved by Madrid, and the war of the Mantuan succession opened.[43] Richelieu too was not immune from the over-precipitous actions of his generals. In late 1634 he was persuaded to accept the French occupation of Heidelberg by the army under the command of de La Force, although this brought France into direct confrontation with Spanish and Imperial forces.[44]

However, further examples can illustrate quite the contrary case: the main problem faced by Richelieu in the years after 1635 was not over-impulsive generals, but a High Command that was consistently unwilling to commit itself to any military initiative. Even the 'loyal' generals found themselves hampered by the command structures, by problems of organisation and communication, and by Richelieu's interference. The others, great aristocrats who had no sympathy with Richelieu or his policies and were relatively invulnerable to his threats, were only too prepared to remain on the defensive and to avoid any action likely to enhance the Cardinal's reputation. The theory that the government was being pressed along the path to conflict by belligerent generals appears distinctly unconvincing in the case of France.[45] In Spain too it should be remembered that at the time of the Mantuan crisis it was her most prestigious general, Spinola, who led the opposition to Olivares' war policy,[46] just as it had been Parma who had been most emphatic in opposing the move to open war against England in the years after 1585. Far from being inclined by self-interest to sponsor all military actions by the state, it would appear that in practice experienced commanders with political influence could act as a brake upon the belligerent tendencies of ministers. Against the claim of national interests and security they set the practical considerations of military resources and capabilities.

Are there other groups in the state who might be considered to benefit from war, and would use their influence to encourage the development of hostilities? One possible group are the financiers, especially the small number of great consortia operating at both courts, and upon whom the governments were totally reliant for advances and long-term loans. For a fortunate few who could remain in business, war brought immensely enhanced profits; it also brought a much higher risk of ruin during the conflict, and of some type of forcible restitution after the conclusion of peace.[47] It is certainly the case that after a war had broken out the financiers had as much interest as the ministers in seeing it continued until a favourable peace could be obtained. Financiers were totally identified with the ministry and its policies; the collapse and fall of the one inevitably meant the ruin of the other. It is far less clear that they would positively welcome, or seek to provoke, war. In the first instance, governments, even in times of peace, were still dependent upon the services of financiers. Investment opportunities and profiteering were still substantial, and the environment far more propitious to the long-term survival of the financiers.[48]

More significant, however, is the evidence that the Spanish and French kings and their ministers evolved policy without the slightest realistic consideration of its costs. During the period leading up to the resumption of war with the Dutch in 1621, it was proposed in the Spanish council that the unsatisfactory truce was actually costing *more* than a resumption of hostilities, in consequence of the Dutch penetration of Spanish colonial markets and the 'idle' military presence necessary in the Spanish Netherlands.[49] In 1634, Louis XIII proposed that open war with the Habsburgs would only cost one million *livres* (c. £100,000) per year more than the existing levels of subsidy to Sweden, Holland and the German Princes![50] It is consistently the case that outside the United Provinces and perhaps England, financial 'ways and means' were not influential in determining policy. The role of the financiers in the subsequent conduct of the war might prove crucial; but this gave them no determining voice in policy-making, either for or against war.

If financial considerations played so small a role in determining government policy, it is reasonable to assume that economic objectives would prove equally unimportant as an underlying explanation for warfare. Indeed, the theory that the causes of wars are in essence always economic stands up badly to the specific examples of this period. Wars fought for economic objectives are the exception not the rule, and even the exceptions look unconvincing. Elizabeth I's war against Spain reflected not a desire to facilitate commercial interloping, but a concern at the religious and strategic consequences of Dutch defeat. It was the failure of the English to provide adequate military support on land for the Dutch, and their very limited military and financial resources, which gave the war its specific character of state-sponsored (and largely ineffectual) piracy.[51] Only in the case of the decision to renew the conflict between Spain and the United Provinces in 1621 do we have a war undertaken for economic aims. But even in this case, the issue of whether it was practical to force the Dutch to end their infringements upon the

Spanish monopoly of trade with the New World was heavily overlaid with the legacy of political and religious conflict remaining from the sixteenth century. The Spanish may have abandoned any real hope of regaining control of the Northern Provinces, but the prestige and *reputación* invested in the attempt to obtain a more favourable settlement than that of 1609 cannot be dismissed.

The Franco-Spanish conflict is more characteristic of the period: the war was conspicuous for the lack of any obvious economic concern, and its final settlement in 1659 made no stipulations capable of benefiting French industry or commerce. Richelieu's navy, which might have served to assert a French commercial presence in the New World, was concentrated in the Mediterranean and the Bay of Biscay as amphibious support for the armies. Under Mazarin, the navy was allowed to fall into decay, and France abandoned any possibility of interfering in Spanish commerce.[52] On the Spanish side the complete lack of concern for economic aims is equally evident: the maintenance of the European empire served no economic purpose whatsoever; there was no sense in which the Spanish dominions could be regarded as an economic unit. Had Spain defeated France in the 1630s and maintained her European hegemony, it is impossible to see how this could have provided her with any new opportunities capable of lifting her economy out of its state of chronic underdevelopment. Spanish decline is perhaps most evident in this pursuit of political/military objectives which were so entirely unrelated to the state's real needs.

If the causes of the war owed nothing to underlying economic motives, it is equally apparent that religion played no real role. Though Richelieu's foreign policy involved him in invidious alliances with Protestants and, from the outset, in open war against both Spain and the Papacy, the ideological weapon was one which the Spanish were little inclined to exploit. Olivares could speak of the French as 'heretics',[53] but the sense that the Spanish were involved in a crusade comparable with the struggle against the Dutch in the sixteenth century seems to have been lacking. In France there were certainly considerable scruples about the acceptability of a war waged against the Catholic Habsburgs. Richelieu and his propagandists consumed a great deal of effort trying to persuade the political classes that the Habsburgs simply used Catholicism as a cloak for their political ambitions, and that the true interests of the church would be served by a French victory. The policy in Germany from the late 1620s was intended to facilitate this. It was unfortunate for Richelieu that the magnitude of Swedish success in Germany during 1631/2 left his attempts to create a 'Third Force' of non-aligned, mainly Catholic, German princes in ruins.[54] However, his intention was, and continued to be, the establishment of a Catholic presence in Germany that was independent of the Habsburgs *and* capable of resisting the pressure of any alliance of Protestant states. To the extreme *dévot* opposition in France this was unsatisfactory, and they continued to attack Richelieu for supporting heretics and rejecting the interests of international Catholicism. Richelieu, however, continued to regard religious concerns as peripheral to his foreign policy, as did Olivares. Beneath the rhetoric both had a purely secular concept of the issues involved in the conflict.

What of the theory that states go to war as a means to resolve or evade internal problems, rather than for specific foreign objectives? Intriguingly, some contemporaries give support to such a view, speaking of war as the 'true means of setting the nation at rest ... [by directing towards it], like water in a gutter, all the turbulent humours of the kingdom'.[55] But practical evidence points in the other direction: rulers recognised that warfare would serve only to aggravate disorders and tensions already present in the state and make their control almost impossible. War was too hazardous and expensive by this stage to be seen as the 'soft option', an alternative preferable to over-mighty subjects, banditry and provincial resistance. Although the assassination of Henri IV and the regency of Marie de Medicis made an aristocratic reaction against Henri's forceful and personal style of government inevitable, there appears to have been no serious suggestion in the regency government that Henri's assertiveness over the Jülich-Cleves issue should be pushed forward into warfare.[56] It was recognised then, and on many other occasions, that there was nothing inherently incompatible about foreign war and internal disorder: the one was as likely to aggravate the other as to restrain it. Richelieu, who was unambiguous in his opinion that warfare meant the abandonment of any hope of domestic reform, was more realistic than subsequent historians. The latter have tended to see in the Franco-Spanish war the making of absolutist France, the creation of a centralised and powerful monarchy. The reality was far closer to a pessimistic prediction made by Richelieu in 1630: the state would have to choose between internal reform and foreign war, and the pursuit of the latter implied the abandonment of any attempt to remedy abuses and disorder in the state.[57] The situation from 1635 is that of an alienated regime struggling to enforce its will upon an increasingly recalcitrant nation, which finally reacted in 1648 by challenging the whole edifice of ministerial government. Regardless of what happened after 1660, there can be no real doubt that France was more disordered, unruly and politically fragmented during the years after 1635 than at any time since 1598. Both Richelieu and Olivares chose war, but neither had any illusion that this would be an escape from the internal problems which beset their states, let alone a solution to them.

An apparently more promising monocausal explanation is perhaps that broad assumption of 'natural bellicosity' put forward by some theorists. Admittedly this is usually given an anthropological slant, but could it be applied here in the sense that France and Spain were 'natural' enemies, whose inherent disposition to fight one another was stronger than any rational calculation of the reasons for conflict? Convincing evidence can certainly be produced. France and Spain went to war some sixteen times between 1500 and 1700; on only one occasion (1627–8) did they fight — nominally — on the same side. This view has been strengthened by historians' propensity to interpret the seventeenth century in the light of Franco-Spanish conflict: the first half of the century is marked by the 'Decline of Spain', the second half (down to 1688) by the 'Ascendancy of France'. On closer inspection, however, it proves less evident that France and Spain were set on an inevitable path to conflict before 1635, or that the mid-seventeenth century *had* to be marked by the victorious emergence of one or the other power.

In the period between 1610 and 1635 there are occasions when both powers acted deliberately to prevent the drift towards a general war: 1614, when settlement was reached at Xanten over the Cleves-Jülich dispute: 1624–5, when Richelieu's first trial of strength against Spain was contained in the Valtelline, the Swiss pass connecting Lombardy with the Tyrol, and was abandoned by France: 1629–31, when a two-year conflict was consciously restricted by both sides to North Italy, and a settlement accepted at Cherasco.

Moreover there are significant instances throughout the period where the two governments made efforts to disperse the atmosphere of 'cold war' and tried to build better relations. Up to the Spanish renewal of war with the Dutch in 1621, France's foreign policy had been marked by considerable sympathy for the cause of international Catholicism and the Austrian Habsburgs' struggle against the Bohemian rebels. In 1613 a dispute arose between Spain, on this first occasion championing rather than opposing the Mantuan succession, and Savoy, whose Duke was hoping to profit from a disputed inheritance to seize Montferrat, an outlying dependency of the Mantuan crown. France, instead of following her typical anti-Spanish tradition and supporting Savoy, placed her diplomatic support on the side of Spain. The French ambassador, Rambouillet, negotiated the peace of Asti (June 1615), which provided for the withdrawal of the troops of Savoy, and guaranteed the independence of Mantua — albeit as a Spanish ally. Subsequent attempts by the Spanish to obtain further advantage from this treaty led not to conflict but to renewed French and Papal regotiations.[58]

This French policy of accommodation continued. From the outset of the Bohemian revolt in 1618, Louis XIII had made his support for the Emperor clear; he had emphasised that France would remain neutral in any wider dispute arising from the intervention of Frederick V, the Calvinist ruler of the Palatinate, on the side of the Protestant Bohemian rebels.[59] By early 1620, France had given explicit assurances of military aid to the Emperor, although the state of the French finances and internal concerns — the campaigns against the Huguenots — delayed their assembly and despatch.[60] This military aid never materialised: it was rendered unnecessary when the support of Spain and the Catholic League of German princes, headed by Bavaria, dramatically improved the Emperor's military position. However, French diplomatic pressure contributed significantly to the conclusion of the Treaty of Ulm (3 July 1620), which ensured that the Protestant Union of German states failed to act as a united force in defence of the Bohemian rebels or of the territory of Bohemia's new ruler, Frederick of the Palatinate.[61] At this point the Palatinate was threatened, not by Catholic German princes, but by Spanish forces from the Army of Flanders — a challenge to France's security that would appear to be far more direct than the Jülich-Cleves *casus belli* of 1609–10. It could be argued that the Treaty of Ulm was a French diplomatic miscalculation, reflecting an ill-informed reading of likely events in both Bohemia and the Palatinate. Certainly subsequent events — the battle of the White Mountain in 1621, when the Bohemian rebels were crushed, and the invasion of the Palatinate by the Spanish Army of Flanders — together with Spain's renewed interest in the Valtelline, now that cooperation between the two branches of the Habsburg family had been so triumphantly vindicated, brought about a change in French attitudes. Yet for a crucial period France did not fall into her traditional reflex of opposing the Habsburgs; indeed she pursued policies which would inevitably have the consequence of strengthening the latter's position in Europe. Moreover this willingness to conciliate was not an entirely one-way process. Instead of exploiting the successful rebuff delivered to France over her intervention in the Valtelline in 1624/5, Olivares behaved with considerable restraint. Spain signally refrained from giving support to the Huguenots, whose revolt served as the ostensible reason for Richelieu's abandonment of intervention in the Valtelline. Indeed in 1627, since Spain was now allied with France against England, Olivares undertook quite sincere preparations to send a naval squadron to Richelieu for defence against Buckingham's attempt to raise the siege of La Rochelle.[62] That it proved too late to be of practical assistance should not detract from its significance as an indication of the flexibility of Spanish policy on the eve of the Mantuan crisis.

Such evidence suggests that there was no insuperable force of 'natural' hostility between France and Spain, that especially when acting against a common threat or enemy — rebellion against the Emperor in 1618–20, England in 1627 — they were capable of cooperation and compromise. The growing fervour of Catholicism in seventeenth-century France might have provided support for a more lasting *rapprochement*. France's 'vital interests', which under Richelieu were focused upon lines of communication and European hegemony, might have been redefined by many of his opponents as the re-establishment of Catholicism and the extirpation of heresy throughout Europe — objectives for which the cooperation of Spain was essential. It was still more the case that Spain, heavily encumbered by commitments in the Netherlands and Germany, could ill afford a policy of confrontation with France. While a long-term view of Spanish security *might* justify present action against France, this was by no means certain. Since the mid-sixteenth century, France's power had fluctuated wildly in response to successive domestic upheavals. It was far from clear that these crises had been brought under control during the 1620s or the 1630s. For Spain to put off war today did not bring the inevitable threat of a more powerful and belligerent France tomorrow. There was a good case to be made for a Spanish policy of restraint and limited concession. The death of Louis XIII, the assassination of Richelieu, a major uprising by the great aristocrats or the Huguenots, provincial revolt against royal fiscality and government heavy-handedness: all of these could ensure that France tomorrow was a much less dangerous prospect than she seemed today.

In trying to explain the origins of the war we are left with only one monocausal theory which appears to have any general validity in these particular circumstances. The role of particular groups or interests can be dismissed, as can the structures of the states and a 'propensity to belligerence'. What remains is the attitudes and interests of the two leading statesmen, Richelieu and Olivares, and the nature of their power within the state.

The Franco-Spanish war did not break out solely because it was desired by Richelieu or Olivares for the consolidation of their own power in government. But the attitudes and the political position of the ministers are certainly a factor to be taken into account.

In early 1624, Richelieu, despite having achieved his Cardinalcy (September 1622), appeared as distant as ever from any prospect of gaining political power under Louis XIII. The King remembered Richelieu's association with the Concini, the upstart Italian favourites of the Queen Mother, Marie de Medicis. The Concini had attempted to govern France without regard to the young Louis; Richelieu was their principal ministerial supporter when the King's *coup d'état* of 1617 brought their regime to an abrupt and violent conclusion. Disgraced by Louis in the subsequent purge, Richelieu had played a leading role in the two revolts of the Queen Mother in 1619 and 1620. While the King had been reconciled with his mother, he had expressed his determination never to allow Richelieu into his council.[63] Consequently, Richelieu, while looking for any chance to obtain favour with the King, had not in the meantime abandoned his commitment to Marie de Medicis. Yet within the Council of State tensions were growing between the Brûlarts — Sillery and Puysieulx — and the recently-appointed *Surintendant des Finances*, La Vieuville. Drawing upon the support of the Queen Mother, La Vieuville was able to obtain the dismissal of the Brûlarts. However, in return for this support Marie enlisted La Vieuville's efforts and sponsorship to get Richelieu nominated to the Council. In late April 1624, the combined pressure of the Queen Mother and the most influential member of the Council finally persuaded Louis to accept Richelieu.[64]

Why did Louis consent to the appointment of a figure he so disliked? The most probable explanation is that in the midst of foreign policy failure, greatly aggravated by the pro-Spanish appeasement of the Brûlarts and the incompetence and inexperience of La Vieuville, Richelieu appeared to have the clearest sense of the need for positive action, and possessed the diplomatic skill and forcefulness to carry it through.[65] At a crucial moment of policy failure and the rejection of the existing ministry, Richelieu won over the King 'en lui suggérant des idées de gloire et de grandeur pour la couronne'[66]. The issue over which France had been humiliated was the control of the Valtelline, the pass connecting Spanish Milan with the Austrian Tyrol. Spanish forces, and the skilful manipulation of Papal support by Madrid, had all but given Spain control of the pass, vital to any close cooperation between the two branches of the House of Habsburg. The first four months of Richelieu's presence in the Council were marked by the decision to challenge the Spanish/Papal *fait accompli*, and by the disgrace and imprisonment of La Vieuville, his original sponsor.[67]

Thus in record time Richelieu placed himself at the head of the Council and of a policy which involved France in conflict with Spain. From the very outset of his ministry, the Cardinal's authority rested upon an aggressive pursuit of French interests abroad, and the assertion of the dynastic claims of the crown. Resistance to Spanish power and 'expansionism' was not a new French policy; but it did represent a decisive break with a long period of appeasement and inertia which had begun in 1614/5 and had reached a highpoint in the early 1620s.[68] In the summer of 1624 this aggressive challenge became the determinant of Richelieu's political authority in France. As the consolidation of his personal power first alienated, then created an opposition from many of his old allies and patrons — the Marillacs, the Cardinal de Bérulle, the Queen Mother — so Richelieu became totally identified with his leadership of an uncompromisingly 'hawkish' government faction. His enemies asserted the impiety of his opposition to the Habsburgs and hence to international Catholicism. They stressed the burdens placed upon the state by any involvement in European warfare, and the need for domestic retrenchment. Louis XIII was sensitive to both these charges, yet in the last resort Richelieu knew that the King's highest ambition was dynastic aggrandisement, above all, the possibility of making the gains in Italy that had eluded his Valois predecessors in the sixteenth century. In April 1630, after the capture of Pinerolo, a strategically vital fortress in the Duke of Savoy's territory of Piedmont, Richelieu presented his most celebrated 'choice' to the King: to maintain the fortress and continue the war, or to use Pinerolo as a bargaining counter for a good peace with the Habsburgs and Savoy:

> Si le Roi se résoud à la guerre, il faut quitter toute pensée de répos, d'épargne et de règlement du dedans du royaume. Si d'autre part, on veut la paix il faut quitter les pensées d'Italie pour l'avenir . . .[69]

This declaration is often taken at face value: a statement of two policies that the King might choose between, and which Richelieu would execute. In fact it represents an implicit decision about the personalities in government; the choice for peace and retrenchment would mean the destruction of Richelieu's own authority, just as the pursuit of the war in Italy since 1629 had whittled away the power of his opponents. Ever since 1624 Richelieu had bid for the King's support as the proponent of an expansionist foreign policy; his involvement in plans for domestic reform, when not simply the empty rhetoric required as a gesture of public good faith, subordinated him to the authority and aspirations of elements in government whom he did not control. In the period after the failure of Richelieu's first foreign policy venture, the Valtelline intervention of 1624/5, and in the midst of the protracted and apparently unsuccessful attempt to handle the 'enemy within', the Huguenots, Richelieu took refuge in the espousal of the reformist policies of his enemies. It is in the period between 1626 and 1629 that we see Richelieu's entirely cynical concern with the reformation of the state, culminating in his participation with Michel de Marillac in drafting the great reforming ordinance, the *Code Michau* (1629). Richelieu's low opinion of the value of government-directed reform is clear enough from his *Testament Politique*.[70] The alacrity with which he jettisoned such surplus baggage after the intervention in Italy had secured his position is equally evident. The King's support for war abroad allowed Richelieu to assert an independent position once again, to replace his rivals in government, and to bring forward new *fidèles*, explicitly loyal to the Cardinal and his aims: d'Effiat as *Surintendant des Finances*, the Bouthilliers and the 'reliable' generals, Schomberg and de La Force. In this sense the Mantuan crisis could not have come at a more opportune moment — saving Richelieu's political influence at Court and preventing his power from draining irrevocably into the hands of his enemies.[71]

It was equally the case that having consolidated his power through foreign war, any proposal to wind down conflict would carry a risk of weakening the Cardinal's hold upon the mechanisms of government. At best, it would lead to demands for a more significant role by those 'outsiders' whom Richelieu had been able to exclude on grounds of their limited commitment to the war effort. For even after the 'Day of Dupes' — the celebrated failure of the Queen Mother to obtain Richelieu's disgrace in November 1630 — his enemies, particularly amonst the great aristrocracy, remained firmly committed to extricating France from conflict with the Habsburgs, and used this as the basis of their appeal to the nation. To counter this, Richelieu came to rely upon an increasingly narrow group of *fidèles*, and used the King's support for his policies to treat his opponents with increasing harshness. The Cardinal's critics, particularly after 1635, emphasised that the war was a means to sustain him and his *créatures* in power, and to exclude all others from the King.[72] To a considerable extent they were correct. Richelieu's authority, and that of his successor as *premier ministre*, Mazarin, could only be justified by the necessity of war, and could only be vindicated by a peace settlement sufficiently favourable to compensate for the burdens that they had placed upon the King's subjects and the extent to which they had alienated French society from government policy. As long as such a settlement was not in sight, they were disposed to continue the war. Perhaps this reflected the belief that it was essential for France to fight on to a decisive victory — if this was attainable. Certainly, though, both Richelieu and Mazarin recognised that their authority and fortunes would not long survive the demands of the excluded political elites in a period of peace following upon an unfavourable conclusion to the war.

It is naive to assume that Richelieu, a supremely competent political survivor, approached the question of conflict with the Habsburgs, and its possible development into full-scale war, with a completely objective regard for French interests. The circumstances of his achievement of power, of his relationship with Louis XIII, and of the ground that was increasingly occupied by his opponents, ensured that he was disposed to policies of confrontation and conflict. These certainly reflected the King's preferences for policies of dynastic assertion abroad, but without the polarisation wrought by Richelieu and his political 'system' — the absence of any middle ground — Louis would not have been drawn so inexorably into the struggle with the Habsburgs.[73]

What of Olivares? It could be suggested that the most crucial decision concerning the character of Spanish policy in seventeenth-century Europe, that of resuming the war with the Dutch after 1621, had already determined the policy to be pursued by Olivares. Yet the option of a progressive extrication from European commitments was not completely inconceivable. Moreover, conflict with France, whether in 1625, 1628/9 or 1635, might have been avoided, and protracted war after 1635 might have been cut short, by a willingness to negotiate a favourable settlement. The case is not as straightforward as that of France, however, in that Spain held her extensive empire in Europe, and this could quite conceivably suffer through a reduction of military commitments and a policy of appeasement. Whether the loss of parts of the empire was acceptable opened up another dimension to the debate, and those who stood in favour of *conservación* at all costs were in the overwhelming majority. Nonetheless at times of major setbacks there was no absence of influential support for an abandonment of aggressive military commitments,[74] although their opponents argued that offensive policies were the only effective means to an adequate defence. Olivares himself was increasingly aware of this: as his policies encountered the severe setbacks of the period leading up to his disgrace in 1643, his denials that he had ever supported belligerent policies became increasingly obsessive.[75]

In reality, Olivares' pursuit of aggressive policies of confrontation with his European rivals was as predetermined as that of Richelieu. It was by working with Don Balthazar de Zúñiga, his uncle, and benefiting from his influence over the King, that Olivares consolidated his political predominance; it was also by taking up his policies: military support to the Austrian Habsburgs to suppress the Bohemian revolt and to fight against its sponsor, Frederick of the Palatinate, together with the renewal of the war with the Dutch. It was the ability of Zúñiga to tilt a far from certain balance of opinion at Madrid in favour of these two decisions[76] that had given him sufficient conciliar pre-eminence to capture the support of the new king, Philip IV, and to ensure that his nephew received similar favour.[77] The opposition that Zúñiga had managed to overcome, with such decisive consequences for Spanish policy, remained significant in Olivares' calculations. Though substantially won over by the spectacular run of Spanish successes in the 1620s, opponents of Olivares' direction of affairs grew more vociferous with each setback. He, like Richelieu, was forced to rely upon a narrowing circle of the governing elite, above all those of his own and related families. He too recognised that there could be no renunciation of his war policies without the loss of his own authority. It has been remarked that Olivares' programme for the reformation of the state has a practicality lacking in Richelieu's empty gestures.[78] There is no doubt that until the early 1640s Olivares was faced with a less coherent political opposition than Richelieu. In consequence he was far more prepared to discuss, and even attempt to implement, domestic change than was his French counterpart, for whom reform was explicitly the opposition's policy. Yet in practice, Olivares' assertion that war abroad and reform at home were compatible was unrealistic; by adopting war, Olivares abandoned any real prospect of achieving domestic reform; opposition gradually focused upon the need for peace if Spain were to avoid catastrophe.[79]

Both statesmen came to power as the proponents of an assertive foreign policy; both found that their predominance was tied either to its triumphant vindication or to its continuation to the last extremity. The stakes were the resources of France and Spain, but the game was played both for national interests and power, and, as contemporaries recognised, for the authority, prestige and profit of the chief ministers and their supporters.

Yet although the destiny of both France and Spain lay in the hands of statesmen who were strongly disposed towards aggressive, assertive foreign policies, this can only explain why conflict was probable. It cannot give any complete explanation of why war ultimately broke out. This movement into war can, however, be interpreted through the group of theories examined in the second half of the introductory section: those concerned with establishing the relationship between diplomacy, limited force and open war; with the uncertainties involved in the progressive increase of military commitments; with the shift from specific to general 'interests'; with the uncertainties involved in assessing the military strength of other powers. Applied to the crucial period between the end of the Mantuan conflict in 1631 and the opening of full hostilities in 1635, these concerns can enable us to understand how two powers, apparently with every interest in avoiding full-scale conflict with one another, should have become enmeshed in a twenty-four year war of attrition.

That both states *did* wish to avoid outright war has not been fully accepted. The traditional interpretation, strongly linked to the conviction of 'inevitable' Spanish decline and French ascendancy, assumes that Richelieu sought not to avoid but to postpone war. The Mantuan crisis provided the evidence of France's ability to challenge Spanish claims to European predominance and to defeat them. The treaty of Cherasco was the turning point: after 1631 Richelieu was simply awaiting a favourable moment to strike, holding France on the sidelines while her allies wore down the Habsburg's power in Germany and Holland. When, against all expectations, an Imperialist and Spanish army wiped out the 'New Model' Swedish/Protestant forces at Nördlingen (6th September 1634), Richelieu recognised that the time for active French intervention had arrived.[80]

This orthodox view leaves a lot of loose ends. If Richelieu was now confident that France was a match for the Habsburgs, then why did he not strike immediately after their humiliation at Cherasco, above all, when they were being hard-pressed by the victorious armies of Gustavus Adolphus? It would seem the height of folly not to intervene at a time when an ally appeared to be carrying all before him. If Louis and Richelieu were genuinely concerned about the fate of Catholicism in Germany, then strong military intervention across the Rhine, 'assisting' the Swedes against the Habsburgs, would have been the best means to secure it. It is suggested that French involvement in Germany at this stage would have led to war with Sweden.[81] But political realism would undoubtedly have asserted itself over any sabre-rattling facade adopted by the Swedish King in the presence of ambassadors. By late 1631 he might be indifferent to French subsidies, but he would have no wish to draw another major power into the war against him. Gustavus' political and military judgement had never previously been influenced by Protestant crusading zeal; it seems unlikely that the prospect of French intervention in Germany would have changed this.[82] Much more likely would have been some variation upon the offer made after Gustavus' death, by the Swedish Chancellor, Oxenstierna, in 1634: in return for a joint offensive alliance against the Habsburgs, the Swedes would pull back their troops beyond the Elbe. Henceforth they would concentrate their military efforts in Bohemia and Silesia, and would leave all of the Rhineland and western Germany to France.[83] It seems probable that fear of war with Sweden was less signifiant than some historians have assumed in discouraging Richelieu from open intervention before 1635.

The usual assumption is that the Cardinal, recognising the immense burdens that the war would place upon France, kept out as long as possible. This would be more convincing if there was the slightest evidence that France was better prepared to sustain a major conflict in 1635 than she had been four years previously. With the notoriously corrupt and incompetent Bullion as *Surintendant des Finances* after 1632, the financial plight of the monarchy became progressively worse.[84] The declaration of war followed upon perhaps the gravest financial miscalculation of the reign, involving a massive attempted sale of interest-bearing bonds (*rentes*). These flooded the money market and remained partially unsold, undermining bonds as an orderly and public system of fund-raising, and giving rise to corrupt speculation and 'trade-offs' by the financiers down to 1659.[85]

If Richelieu was not seeking financial stability as a precondition for entering the war, then a political explanation seems equally unlikely. Richelieu never achieved political security. All that could be said is that the very serious challenges to his power came in cycles. One of these cyclical challenges emerged in 1630, with the 'Day of Dupes', the attempt of the Queen Mother and Marillac to remove Richelieu. The reverberations of this 1630 attempt lasted into 1632, when France was invaded by the king's brother, Gaston d'Orléans, while the Duc de Montmorency raised his futile and fatal rebellion in Languedoc.[86] Had Richelieu wished to take advantage of a period of relative domestic calm, then the aftermath of the successful defeat of these revolts in 1632 would have been a good opportunity. Orléans was discredited and in exile, while the executions of Montmorency and — after a lengthy rigged trial — of the Maréchal de Marillac, had given even the most recalcitrant great nobles cause for thought. By 1635 Orléans had returned and had drawn the various noble dissidents into another round of plotting, to culminate in the attempt to assassinate Richelieu during the disastrous campaign of 1636.[87] Naturally, domestic stability is not independent of external circumstances, yet it would seem clear that the situation in 1635 was no more propitious than that of 1633 for a movement into open war. In the light of this deterioration down to 1635, even *had* Richelieu succeeded in deferring intervention into the later 1630s — assuming that the defeat of his allies at Nördlingen had not forced his hand — there is little reason to consider that either the political or financial position of the French government would have improved significantly.

More specific criticisms can also be levelled at this thesis. If France was not prepared to go to war with the Habsburgs while the Swedes and German Protestants were militarily significant, it seems strange that she should take this risk when the Habsburgs had just succeeded in re-establishing their authority across Germany, and when the Swedes, France's major ally, had been 'perhaps definitively disabled'.[88] If, nonetheless, long-term security considerations required that France should respond to the battle of Nördlingen by accepting hostilities, then why did she not declare war until May 1635? The risks of a subsequent winter attack by Habsburg forces were surely far less grave than the further demoralisation of France's allies, who might reasonably come to the conclusion that the French were unwilling to commit themselves to a hopeless cause. Finally, why was the declaration of war, when finally delivered, rendered only against the King of Spain and not the Emperor? The latter's troops had been just as implicated in the successful campaign of 1634, and it was the Emperor who had gained the most from the battle of Nördlingen, regaining the support of the major Protestant princes by the Peace of Prague.

In a recent article Dr. Robert Stradling expresses his reservations about the traditional account of the origins of this war, and offers a far more convincing alternative. Historians have been over-willing to accept the propaganda of both French and Spanish, who concur, for different reasons, in the view that the war was launched by Richelieu as a 'premeditated onslaught upon Spanish European hegemony'.[89] Instead, Stradling proposes that the origins should be sought not with France but with Spain, that the real author was Olivares. Frustrated by France over the Mantuan crisis, Olivares became increasingly convinced that France under Richelieu was the fundamental obstacle to the achievement of any pro-Habsburg settlement in Europe. In this respect the thesis remains uncontentious: Spain since the sixteenth century had always regarded France as the single most serious threat to her empire. However, Stradling also suggests, with no shortage of supporting evidence, that Olivares had come to accept the need for a pre-emptive attack upon France. The European war would not be ended without the acquiescence of France. This could only be achieved by the use of force, either to destroy French military capacity, or better, to bring about the collapse of government and the disgrace of Richelieu. Ever since the French had taken up the Mantuan succession issue, Olivares had been weighing up the possibility of an assault upon France itself,[90] but it was not until 1634 that the form of this invasion took shape. Setbacks in organisation and coordination persuaded Olivares to accept its cancellation until 1635, though not before the concentration of Spanish naval vessels off the Italian coast had led to French fears of an attack upon Provence.[91] By this stage Richelieu was fully aware of Spanish intentions; his claim to have gone to war to frustrate a Spanish assault on France, subsequently dismissed as self-seeking hypocrisy, can be rehabilitated in the light of Olivares' preparations.

This interpretation goes a long way to tackling the inconsistencies in the existing accounts. Above all, it emphasizes the crucial point that Richelieu did not want to go to war with Spain. He did not do so after the battle of Nördlingen, or after the reports of Spanish naval movements in September and October 1634; it was only with the receipt of irrefutable evidence that Spain intended to launch a pre-emptive strike into France in the spring of 1635 that Richelieu and the King were finally persuaded to declare war, and even then they waited for the opening of the campaign season. But while the view that the origins of the Franco-Spanish conflict should be sought with Spain encourages a more convincing treatment of the evidence, it is perhaps the case that no view which seeks to attribute direct responsibility to one side or the other can be wholly satisfactory. We should perhaps return to the concept that there is no easily perceived, clear-cut distinction between peace and war, but a progressive increase in the levels of violence with which political negotiations are supported by opposing powers. Dr. Stradling reverses the typical explanation: it was Olivares who caused the war, with his 'deferred retaliation' for the Mantuan humiliation. Yet perhaps this view, just as much as the traditional interpretation, attributes too significant a role to the conscious decisions of statesmen. It suggests that these two statesmen in particular regarded war as the inescapable consequence of developments well before 1635. But while Richelieu might have assumed that war with Spain was in some sense *ultimately* unavoidable, he did not consider that his policies in the years before 1635 were likely to precipitate this general conflict.

Stradling's argument that Olivares was plotting a pre-emptive strike against France from 1634, and that it was intelligence of this which led Richelieu into a declaration of war on 19th May 1635, is entirely convincing. What I would wish to question is the assumption that this Spanish attack had its roots in the Mantuan crisis of 1629–31. An alternative explanation would give most emphasis to the steady increase in the levels of violence with which conflicting interests were asserted by France and Spain over the intervening period. When relative military fortunes underwent a dramatic shift during 1634, it was all too easy to pass from violent confrontation across the final steps leading into open warfare. The choice was never perceived as a straightforward issue of peace or war. Olivares did not intend to make a formal declaration of war, not because he hoped for the benefits of a surprise attack,[92] but because with France and Spain already enmeshed in a web of confrontation and barely contained conflict, it would not appear to him that he was doing anything beyond asserting Spanish interests more forcefully. It was for France to decide whether to match this new level of commitment and precipitate war, or whether instead to sacrifice her interests and back down from this next stage.

Historians have held divergent opinions about the significance of the Mantuan crisis. Was it an 'unrelieved disaster' for Spain,[93] or an incident with no lasting strategic or political consequences for her policies?[94] This confusion reflects the peculiarity of the outcome in relation to the war itself: while the Treaty of Cherasco gave the French an outright triumph, it concluded a conflict in which France's political and military incapacity could not have been more apparent. Throughout 1629 and 1630, France's efforts had been entirely committed to the Mantuan dependency of Montferrat, a small territory placed between the Spanish Milanese and Piedmont-Savoy. Its main fortress, Casale, had received a French garrison in 1629, and was subsequently besieged by Spanish troops, requiring a massive French commitment in both the 1629 and 1630 campaigns to try to lift the siege. If France were to lose Casale, she lost all ability to influence the Mantuan dispute. If she consolidated her hold upon it, she was no nearer to relieving Mantua itself, isolated on the other side of the Milanese. In fact, if the Habsburgs held firm, France had no real capacity to force a military solution in North Italy. From the outset, Richelieu had miscalculated the insuperable logistical and communications problems involved in maintaining forces in Italy, via conquered, but far from cooperative, Piedmont. He had failed as well in the diplomatic sphere, considering that French threats would keep the Emperor from supporting the Spanish in this theatre. Yet by May 1629, 15,000 Imperial troops were mustered and *en route* for Italy.[95]

Nor did matters improve for France in the following year: July and August 1630 may be regarded as one of the most critical periods in Richelieu's career. Mantua itself fell to the Imperial army on 18th July, and Casale seemed about to suffer the same fate; the king abandoned the campaign in Piedmont, and on 22nd August recalled Richelieu to Lyon; it became clear, with the continuing influx of Imperial and Spanish troops into North Italy, that an entirely new French army would have to be raised to maintain a hold over Piedmont, although France was already rebellious and Richelieu's opponents had grown dangerously powerful once again.[96] France appeared poised upon the brink of humiliating and total defeat over Mantua. From this Richelieu was saved, not by French arms, but by the rebellion of the German Electoral princes against the Emperor at the Diet of Regensburg. For reasons which remain unclear in objective political terms, the Emperor allowed himself to be taken in by the promises and threats of the princes, although the presence of his army across Germany gave him an overwhelming military advantage. This Imperial surrender, on 14 August 1630, aptly termed 'the Habsburgs' Day of Dupes' by one historian,[97] overturned the political and military situation. The chief concession granted by the Emperor was the dismissal of his military enterpriser and Commander-in-Chief, Wallenstein, and the disbandment of most of the Imperial army. The landing of Swedish troops under Gustavus Adolphus on the Pomeranian coast, which had hitherto appeared a significant but low-priority threat, now became very serious indeed. The Electors, having destroyed the Emperor's military power, proved predictably unwilling to carry out any of their reciprocal obligations for the defence of Germany.[98]

Thus, just at the moment when it appeared that Spanish/Austrian cooperation was about to receive its triumphant vindication in North Italy, this entire campaign theatre became a dangerous burden on Habsburg resources. It became apparent that any gains to be made here would be disproportionate to the price of allowing the situation in Germany to deteriorate further. Not merely would no more Imperial troops be committed to Italy, but those there at present would have to be drawn back as quickly as possible to face the threat on the Baltic. But the Habsburgs' problem in Italy was that the injustice of their cause — the attempt to deprive the legitimate Duc de Nevers of his Duchy of Mantua — ensured that any peace settlement not dictated from a position of outright military predominance would be very favourable to France. Nonetheless, a settlement was pushed through. The first attempt, which sought to tie the Spanish climbdown in Italy to the settlement in Germany,[99] failed: Richelieu had no intention of abandoning support for all the Habsburgs' enemies as the price of a general peace. Negotiations continued in a situation which grew progressively more favourable to France as the Swedish threat to Germany increased. When finally Spain accepted the Treaty of Cherasco in June 1631, it reflected a set of political and military circumstances wholly different from those of the war itself.

In the light of this, the Mantuan war and its settlement may be suggested to have had a very mixed effect upon Richelieu. Certainly the treaty was a total vindication of his belligerent foreign policy and a pattern for further assertiveness. Equally, however, the war left him in no doubt about the formidable military power of the Habsburgs, and the very narrow margin of his success. One of the fundamental concerns of Richelieu's foreign policy now became to avoid any possibility that France might find herself facing the combined forces of Spain and Austria without the support of her allies; this was the 'worst possible situation that could arise'.[100] But at the same time that Richelieu was learning a harsh lesson about the military realities of challenging his enemies, he had also acquired a high estimation of the value of his allies as a means to ensure that Habsburg power was not brought to bear upon France. The combination of Sweden, Holland and the German Protestant princes appeared effective as a check upon Imperial and Spanish forces. Richelieu and his agents also made efforts to create alliances with the Catholic German princes, and with the independent Italian states;[101] but it was upon the Protestant powers that France's support consistently depended. In 1631/2 the power of France's main allies was indisputable: Gustavus Adolphus had, if anything, disconcerted Richelieu by his progress across Germany. Meanwhile, the Dutch had assumed the offensive, capturing s'Hertogenbosch in September 1629, and seizing Maastricht in August 1632.[102] After the death of Gustavus Adolphus at Lützen (November 1632), the Heilbronn League of German Protestant states under the leadership of Sweden still seemed able to block Habsburg progress in Germany.[103] Not merely did these allies appear capable of tying down Habsburg forces, but — as had been demonstrated in late 1630/early 1631 — they had the ability to place pressure upon the crucial points in the Habsburg 'system', drawing resources away from other theatres which might be more dangerous to French interests.

It was the assumption of the effectiveness of these allies which underpinned Richelieu's policies from 1631. For their pressure upon the Habsburgs allowed the Cardinal to pursue aggressive measures of confrontation and territorial annexation, with reasonable confidence that they would not provoke war. Spain, France's main rival, simply could not afford to add another major power to her enemies, and so would not respond to French assertiveness with measures leading towards war. Evidence from Spain indicates that Richelieu was perfectly correct in making this assumption. While some advisers — Oñate and Cordoba — sought an immediate break with France, Olivares, despite his characteristic belligerence, held back; Richelieu's assertiveness might appear intolerable, but Spain was in no position to retaliate decisively.[104]

Yet why did Richelieu take the risk of pursuing such provocative policies? Given the character of his personal authority and its assertion, discussed at the end of the second section, it was something of a foregone conclusion. It may not have suited Richelieu to involve France in open warfare, with its burdens and risk of defeat, but it was essential to the maintenance of his power for France to pursue belligerent policies that led to confrontation with her rivals. If France was not actually at war, then her government was to be organised upon a war footing: unprecedented armies were being maintained and deployed;[105] the military budget remained at the levels supported during the Mantuan war.[106] Richelieu could consolidate his own power in government, together with that of his *créatures*, and eliminate his rivals, justifying his government monopoly and harsh measures on the grounds of an 'absolute necessity' created by the foreign situation.

The pursuit of the policy after the success of Cherasco seems inevitable; no documents survive in which Richelieu counsels any general principle of moderation in France's foreign objectives. If open war was to be avoided, this by no means implied passivity or conciliation towards the Habsburgs. On the contrary, the overwhelming impression given in policy documents is that France should not go to war because she can gain as much or more by exploiting the existing situation of 'warlike peace'. The aims of Richelieu's belligerence reflected an expanding notion of France's 'vital interests'; the all-embracing concept of 'long-term security' appears in various seventeenth-century guises. France wished to gain the greatest possible territorial and strategic advantages from the present favourable situation. In part the areas which she sought to occupy were those which might facilitate an invasion by enemy forces in the future. The threat of invasion across the eastern frontier was one which, quite correctly, preoccupied Richelieu's government. During the Mantuan war, significant forces had been committed to the frontiers of Champagne to guard against the rumours of such an attack by Imperial forces.[107] In the event that the position of France's allies deteriorated, frontier territory was equally essential for the establishment of military communications — Richelieu's celebrated 'gates': points of secure entry and exit for troops operating in Germany. In the existing circumstances, occupation of territory was seen as a means to assist France's allies without going to war on their behalf; advancing beyond the eastern frontier offered the chance to disrupt the tenuous line of Habsburg communications which ran up from North Italy, through the Alpine passes into the Tyrol, then doubled back across Catholic South Germany into Franche-Comté and up along the Rhine.[108] The more effectively that France could obstruct this route, the weaker would become the position of the Spanish in the Low Countries and on the Rhine.

Yet beneath the concern for 'long-term security' was a more straightforward wish to achieve territorial expansion for its own sake. Serving as a means to persuade the king of the success of the foreign policy, it would both provide vistas of dynastic aggrandisement, and help overcome any scruples felt by Louis about his failure to support fellow Catholic princes. The view that France was consciously expanding to fill some set of 'natural frontiers' is no longer accepted; after all, Louis XIII's highest ambition was to make good his claim to Lombardy and Naples. Equally unacceptable is the opinion that Richelieu regarded the Rhine as the border of a 'greater France'.[109] It is recognised that the process of expansion was more pragmatic, while its gains were to be open to subsequent negotiations. Nonetheless, merely because many of the territories occupied were held as 'protectorates', and because Richelieu — aware of the hatred for any foreign presence within Germany — made great play upon the idea that France's sole aim was the preservation of German 'liberties',[110] there is no reason to see French policies in reality as a totally disinterested bid for general security.

Circumstances could dictate the permanent occupation of territories *precisely* as a guarantee against an uncertain political future — as the towns of Alsace discovered after the treaty of Westphalia. The conventions of dynastic legitimacy determined the use of 'protection'. Louis had no family claim to the overlordship of most of the German towns and fortresses occupied by France; adopting the concept of 'protection' went some way to shield France from the reputation of Sweden and other powers, who had simply claimed territory by right of conquest. In a political environment which, despite the reality depicted by Grotius and others, was characterised by an obsessive concern about legitimacy and 'just' war, it was a means to clothe the aggressiveness of French policy in some rags of kingly duty and legal justification.

The real nature of 'protection' is perhaps more obvious in the subsequent harsh treatment of territories such as the Electorate of Trier, subjected to military taxation and administration, and a complete disregard, in practice, for its 'liberties'.[111] While this treatment was typical in occupied territory throughout Germany, at least Wallenstein did not claim to be 'protecting' Saxony when his army occupied it in late 1632. When the French king *did* claim a legitimate title to the territory which he occupied, as in the case of Lorraine or the bishopric of Metz, concern for the rights of subjects was even more attenuated. The *protection souveraine* accorded to Metz, which had been claimed by French kings since 1552, amounted to an assertion of full royal authority. In 1633 a *Parlement* was introduced into Metz, as both a means to profit from the sale of office and to establish outside officials in the territory. In 1637 the *Parlement* was transferred to Toul, and replaced by an intendant in Metz; the crown's intention of integrating the bishopric into France was evident.[112]

The issue of French intentions concerning these territories in the period up to 1635 is of limited importance. The crucial factor is the way in which French foreign policy was perceived by the Spanish, and there can be no doubt that it was seen as an unrelenting assault upon interests perceived as equally 'vital'. Rightly or wrongly, 'protection' was regarded by the Spanish as nothing but a cynical means to engage in territorial expansion without offering a direct challenge to the Habsburgs.

The circumstances which led up to the outbreak of the war deserve brief analysis; they demonstrate more clearly than any theoretical discussion how a series of actions and decisions contributed to the development of a critical level of political tension, and how this rapidly turned to open war in the changed circumstances after September 1634.

French concern to sever Spanish communications with the Low Countries by occupying territory along the Rhine had been matched by an equally strong Habsburg determination to do whatever seemed necessary to maintain or strengthen their hold on these territories. The main Spanish preoccupation remained the occupation of Alsace, already promised to her by a secret treaty with the Emperor in 1617, although these terms had never been enforced.[113] It was predictable that the highpoint of Habsburg success in the later 1620s should have been accompanied by a bid to consolidate a position that had already been greatly strengthened by the Spanish occupation of the Rhine Palatinate after 1621. In 1629/30 part of the Imperial army crossed the Rhine and occupied strategically important points in Alsace. In February 1630, taking advantage of France's preoccupation with the Italian conflict, these troops seized the fortresses of Vic and Moyenvic, within the bishopric of Metz.[114] At this point it was the French who felt unable to take the risk of confrontation: Metz itself was fortified, but no attempt was made to drive the Imperial troops out of their new conquests.[115]

Yet as we have seen, circumstances were quickly turned against the Habsburgs. Throughout 1631 they were on the defensive, and with the shattering defeat suffered by the Imperialists and their Catholic allies at Breitenfeld (17 September 1631) their fortunes reached a nadir. Richelieu remained cautious about exploiting this situation in 1631. The opportunity was used to abrogate the treaty with Savoy-Piedmont over Pinerolo, and to ensure that the fortress would remain permanently in French hands. The 'handing-over' of Casale to the French Duke of Mantua was accomplished by an agreement which left it garrisoned by French troops and those of her Swiss allies.[116] Perhaps most significant for the future, Richelieu began to put pressure upon the Duke of Lorraine, eventually forcing him to accept the treaty of Vic in January 1632 under threat of military intervention. On this occasion the pressure seems to have been aimed at discouraging the Duke from giving open support to the Emperor, and asserting the principle of his allegiance to the crown of France. Nonetheless the Duke was obliged to surrender the town of Marsal to the French for three years, as a guarantee of his 'good behaviour'.[117] By late 1631, Richelieu had become restive at the continued presence of Habsburg forces on the Rhine. On 9 December the King ordered the retaking of Vic and Moyenvic, and both had surrendered to France by 27 December.[118] In the same month Louis issued his declaration offering 'protection' to all German princes who requested French support. As the fate of Bavaria in Spring 1632 was to reveal, France had no intention of going to war with Sweden on behalf of her German allies,[119] but the opportunity for a *fait accompli*, by which France could occupy the Catholic Rhine principalities of Cologne, Trier and Mainz, was immensely enticing. In fact, only the archbishop of Trier was in a position to ask for French protection, finally agreed by a treaty in April 1632.[120] Mainz had fallen to Gustavus Adolphus by Christmas 1631, while Cologne was too close to the border with Spanish Flanders for the Elector to be prepared to link himself firmly to France. Had either of these latter accepted French protection, it would have created severe diplomatic — and probably military — complications both with the Habsburgs, whose territories would be directly threatened by French troops in Cologne, and with Gustavus Adolphus, who had fixed upon Mainz as the operational centre for his German campaign.

This over-ambitiousness in French policy extended beyond the question of protection. Taking advantage of the discomfiture of the Habsburgs, Richelieu pushed a proposal through the Council on 6th January 1632 for a series of pre-emptive French military strikes, aimed at the occupation of most of Alsace. Haguenau and Saverne were to be besieged, while claims to be 'protecting' the

Duke of Württemburg and the Marquis of Baden could be used to justify the occupation of Strasbourg and Kehl. He was discouraged from this plan by Père Joseph, who argued that such nakedly ambitious French intervention would threaten to draw the German states, including the Protestants, back towards the Emperor, as well as causing difficulties with Sweden.[121]

Moreover, while the Elector of Trier appealed to France for support, this did not lead to any quick and diplomatically neat French occupation. Richelieu was expecting to occupy the Elector's strategically important Rhine fortresses at Philippsburg, Coblenz and Ehrenbreitstein. The Elector gave France the right to garrison these places, but this permission was contrasted with the lack of enthusiasm amongst his subjects for the occupation. Ehrenbreitstein was duly garrisoned by the French, such that one royal administrator could celebrate:

> La félicité de la France par ... victoires obtenues ... principalement en Allemagne, qui ont porté les bornes de la France jusqu'au Rhin.[122]

But at this point the Spanish reacted with their first open challenge to the eastward advance of France's armies. The population of Trier, antagonised by the Elector's pro-French policy, drove him out of the city and accepted a Spanish garrison. The Spanish, concerned at the threat posed by the French possession of Ehrenbreitstein, took the opportunity to occupy Coblenz, on the west bank of the Rhine and directly opposite Ehrenbreitstein. For several weeks French and Spanish troops skirmished in the area around the two fortresses.[123] Meanwhile the governor of Philippsburg, encouraged by the presence of Spanish troops in the electorate, refused to open the gates to the French troops who had come to relieve him. Richelieu's response to these events was overtly belligerent: relying upon the Imperialist' total commitment to the struggle with Gustavus Adolphus in Bavaria, he despatched marshal d'Effiat, at the head of an army of some 20,000 troops, to drive the Spanish out of the Electorate of Trier.[124] The Spanish resisted, and indeed d'Effiat was killed at Lützelstein on 27 July, when his forces engaged with the Spanish.[125] But Olivares had no wish to see this confrontation develop into general war; Spain had enough difficulties with her desperate attempt to raise the siege of Maastricht. The Spanish did not match the French commitment, and abandoned Trier and Coblenz in August, although Philippsburg continued to resist French occupation.[126]

This episode characterises Richelieu's handling of foreign policy. French interests were to be defended with whatever force was required short of open war. That the French response was not even more rigorous reflects, not a concern at the Habsburg response, but the consideration that France was already committed to a military assault upon Lorraine. The Duke's support for Bavaria against the Swedes had provided Richelieu with a suitable excuse; the Duke could be said to have broken the Treaty of Vic, and this time France intended to intervene militarily to extract a more favourable treaty from Charles. The French employed troops that had apparently been raised to ensure the protection of Trier, and launched them in a surprise attack on Lorraine.[127] Faced with overwhelming French superiority, Duke Charles had no choice but to negotiate, ceding

Clermont, Dun, Stenay and Jametz to the French by the Treaty of Liverdun (26 June 1632).[128] France now had a foothold in Lorraine, which both facilitated the overrunning of the rest of the Duchy should it prove necessary, and offered more scope for intervention in Alsace. It did not, however, produce a more amenable Duke. Charles IV, far from placing his army at the disposal of Louis, continued to intrigue with the Habsburgs. With a fatal disregard for the survival of his own Duchy, he accepted and garrisoned two key fortresses in Alsace, Haguenau and Saverne, granted him by the Count of Salm with the consent of the Emperor.[129]

The situation in Alsace by late 1632 was totally confused: Spanish, Imperial and Swedish forces, together with troops from Lorraine, all held positions within the territory, while France angled for the opportunity to confer protection. The death of Gustavus Adolphus and the relative weakening of the Swedish forces after Lützen (16 November) gave Richelieu the opportunity to extend a French military presence into Alsace without a serious political confrontation with the Swedes. France's renewal of subsidies to the Swedish/Protestant Heilbronn League was conditional upon an acceptance of the principle that the French should establish a military presence on the left bank of the Rhine and in certain key fortresses on the right. Indeed, the French understanding of the agreement was that if any of these key places should fall to the Swedes (particularly Philippsburg and Breisach), they should be handed over for garrisoning by France.[130] Richelieu's primary concern remained the annexation of Lorraine, but the opportunity presented by the confusion in Alsace could also be exploited to French advantage. Making the assumption that France would receive the right to garrison the place subsequently, Richelieu persuaded the Swedes to lay siege to Haguenau. The Duke of Lorraine, anxious to protect this fortress granted him in Alsace, engaged the Swedish forces, and suffered a severe defeat at Pfaffenhoffen (10 August 1633). Once again, without any formal declaration of hostilities, French troops rolled into Lorraine, overrunning the Duchy of Bar, for which it was claimed that the Duke had failed to render homage to Louis XIII.[131] Strategically, this offered France great advantages: domination of the territory just below the diocese of Metz, greater access into Alsace, and a position from which she could move against Charles' capital, Nancy. The opportunity presented by this success proved irresistible; Richelieu began operations to overrun the rest of Lorraine, beginning with the siege of Nancy, which capitulated on 20 September 1633. By the Treaty of Charmes, Charles was forced to accept French occupation of Nancy for 30 years.[132]

This is not the appropriate place to discuss the French miscalculation in attempting to seize Lorraine, imposing on herself a lengthy and inconclusive series of military campaigns, and a territory which remained consistently hostile to French occupation down to 1648, when it regained its semi-independent status. The significance for the situation in 1633 was that France now held a major fortress, Nancy, and a strategically crucial territory, from which she could assume a predominant role in Alsace.[133] French offers of protection, which hitherto had seemed distant and uncertain, were now entertained with greater seriousness — not least because they might be preferable to a French occupation carried out without invitation. This reconsideration was further stimulated by Spanish action. Greatly concerned at both the French movements in Lorraine and Alsace, and the Swedes' siege of Breisach, the Spanish put together a small force of Spanish veterans in North Italy. In the summer of 1633 they were led into Alsace by the Duke of Feria, who proved able to relieve Breisach.[134] Spanish troops were in dangerous proximity to French forces. Richelieu was prepared to contemplate active intervention to prevent the relief of Breisach. When this proved impractical, he still favoured the presence of strong French forces in Alsace to block any further Spanish progress.[135] Olivares and Philip IV had strongly opposed an original proposal that Feria should move up into Germany through Swiss territory sympathetic to France — the Grisons — on the grounds that it might provoke too aggressive a French response.[136] However, concern at the deteriorating situation in Alsace and Lorraine persuaded them that Feria should move west in a bid to lift the siege of Nancy.[137] The fall of Nancy and the lateness of the season discouraged Feria from launching this operation, which would probably have brought the opening of the war forward by eighteen months.[138] But even without the feared military confrontation, Feria's campaign had greatly intensified tensions between the two powers. The threat of Spanish forces operating across large areas of western Germany, together with the consolidation of the Spanish military base in the Sundgau region of Alsace, drove a number of princes to request French protection and to hand over their key fortresses to French garrisons. In October 1633, the Duke of Württemburg placed Montbéliard in French hands. He was followed in December by the Count of Hanau, who opened the towns of Bischweiler, Ingwiller and Neuwiller in Lower Alsace to French troops. In January 1634, the Count of Salm, whose 'protection' by the Duke of Lorraine had proved so ill-fated, switched across to the French, who gained Haguenau, Saverne and Hohbar without firing a shot. The Bishop of Basle followed the example a few weeks later.[139] By military means France was in the process of overrunning Lorraine; by forceful diplomacy — and the fear of other powers — she now held a significant proportion of the major Rhine fortifications from Ehrenbreitstein and Coblenz down to Basle. One setback was Philippsburg; it had been captured by the Swedes during 1633, who proved unwilling to accept the implicit agreement that it should be passed across to France as the protector of the Archbishop of Trier.

To Olivares, the situation was disconcerting; Spain's armies had done no more than shore up a deteriorating situation. Meanwhile France, taking advantage of the other powers' struggles, had immensely enhanced her position and influence with almost no hindrance. Whereas in 1632 Richelieu's initial advances had been blocked or resisted by the Habsburgs (and the Swedes) so far as possible, in the few months since August 1633 her progress had been uninterrupted. It was at this point, in Spring 1634, that Stradling suggests that Olivares' 'patience snapped'.[140] Or rather it was at this stage that the policy of avoiding direct confrontation with France appeared a greater threat to Spanish security and communications than a more recalcitrant stand. But despite indications that Olivares' attitude had now changed in principle, it is clear that did not alter Spain's practical inability to act effectively against France. On 13 April 1634, the Spanish council of state resolved against a declaration of war.[141]

In the same month Richelieu accepted terms for a renewal of the alliance with the Dutch. A proposal that it should be extended to a full offensive treaty, aimed at the partitioning of the Spanish Netherlands, was rejected by Richelieu at this stage. The Dutch required from France an open and immediate break with Spain, while Richelieu was unprepared to sacrifice France's present favourable situation on the sidelines.[142] However, Richelieu had made it clear as early as 1633 that he was prepared to commit troops instead of, or in addition to, financial subsidies to prop up the present alliance. The 1633 instructions to Charnacé, French ambassador to the United Provinces, had permitted him to offer up to 12,000 foot and 2,000 horse from France if this should prove necessary to keep the Dutch in the war.[143] Perhaps fortunately for the international situation, the Dutch preferred cash to ill-disciplined French troops, and in 1634 the subsidy was simply increased.[144] But even without French troops in Dutch service, the alliance appeared suspect to the Spanish. The difference between this 'defensive' support for Holland, and a full offensive agreement, aimed at conquering the Spanish Netherlands, was probably not apparent. Equally, when Feuquières, the French ambassador in Germany, presented terms for a general peace in early 1634, they proved harsher than those actually accepted by the Emperor at Westphalia in 1648.[145] France was using the success of her allies and her own position to try to achieve predominance over the Habsburgs without actually going to war. Richelieu was emphasising that France was 'winning the peace', and that without a settlement another round of political and military assertiveness could be expected.

Unable to act directly against France with military force, Olivares resorted to an attempt to bind Spain and Austria together more closely. Although France was now indisputably the gravest threat to both branches of the family, she could only be tackled when a degree of control had been enforced upon events in Germany. In early 1634, Habsburg fortunes here seemed far from assured. However the Duke of Feria's campaign had provided evidence of what could be achieved by even a small high-quality field army. Straining resources to the utmost, a new Spanish army was raised in the Milanese during the first half of 1634. Marching through the Valtelline and into Bavaria, it joined up with the elite of the Imperial army, which had just recaptured Regensburg from the Swedes. Moving slowly west towards the Rhine, the combined forces laid siege to Nördlingen. The main Swedish and Protestant armies attempted to relieve the place, were drawn into battle and wiped out on 6 September. In a few hours the existing political situation had been overturned.

During the first half of 1634 Richelieu had deployed most of France's military resources in an attempt to bring the remaining strongholds in Lorraine under French control. The protracted siege of La Mothe did not end until 26 June, while Wildenstein, the last major fortified town, held out until 5 August.[146] Only then was the main part of the French army pushed forward onto the Rhine, where it was maintained between Coblenz and Breisach awaiting further instructions.[147] But despite this limited activity, France's position was still apparently very powerful in early September. Moreover, the immediate effects of the Habsburg victory at

Nördlingen were paradoxical: if Richelieu had feared an immediate attack upon French possessions, it was soon clear that this would not occur. Spain's priority was to march its part of the army up into the Spanish Netherlands without further interruption. The Imperialists were more anxious to root Protestant forces out of Franconia and Württemburg than to cross the Rhine into Alsace.[148] The first consequences of the Habsburg revival were beneficial for France: the Swedes, who had placed obstacles in the way of handing over Philippsburg to the French ever since its capture in 1633, accepted its transfer to a French garrison on 26th August, after the fall of Regensburg.[149] Nördlingen produced another call for protection, this time from the Rhinegrave, the most significant German ruler in Alsace. Fearing the advance of the Imperialists, he offered Colmar, Schlettstadt and the other significant towns in Upper Alsace to France. By mid-October these strongpoints had been garrisoned by French troops.[150] Richelieu began another round of negotiations to persuade his shattered allies of the Heilbronn League to continue the struggle, but still without guaranteeing an open declaration of war by France.[151] Indeed, France's only real 'concession' was to relieve the burden on Swedish forces by taking a much larger military role in the defence of the Palatinate — on both sides of the Rhine.

Yet even as the French advance eastwards progressed, the general situation had turned against Richelieu. The destruction of the Swedish/Protestant army had represented the first stage of the Habsburgs' programme. Halting the remorseless progress of French aggrandisement now become the primary objective of the war effort. Dr Stradling demonstrates how Olivares, forced to cancel his plans for a triple assault on France in later 1634, spent the winter in frantic preparations to ensure that the attack should be fully prepared for 1635.[152] Further events on the Rhine served only to confirm the Conde-Duque's resolution. For although Richelieu appears to have realised that the situation had shifted against France, he was unable, or unwilling, to check the momentum which his policies had acquired. The attempt to subsidise Sweden to continue the war without any firm commitment to French involvement had antagonised Oxenstierna, who refused to ratify the agreement. It was not until 30 April 1635, when it was obvious that France would go to war, that Sweden finally accepted the terms.[153] Meanwhile Richelieu was left to pursue his policies without the full cooperation of the Swedes. His principal concern was the proximity of Imperial troops on the right bank of the Rhine to French positions in Alsace and the Palatinate. The Imperial invasion of the Upper Palatinate and the siege of the capital, Heidelberg, in November/December was regarded as a challenge to French interests in Germany — now extending to the east of the Rhine. Richelieu's first expedient was to encourage the Protestant German *condottiere*, Bernhard of Saxe-Weimar, to act as a French proxy. He was offered 6,000 troops to move against the Imperialists in the Upper Palatinate and along the Main. Recognising that it was now France whose bargaining position was weak, Saxe-Weimar demanded an entire French army for the operation, and threatened to abandon the defence of the Rhine to the French by moving his troops up into North Germany.[154] These threats simply strengthened the demand of Richelieu's generals to despatch the main French army across the Rhine. Richelieu hesistated, then accepted this proposal. The French army relieved Heidelberg on 4 December.[155] This move inevitably led to large-scale clashes with Imperial troops. Spain had already resolved upon war with France, and this confrontation convinced Vienna that nothing was to be gained by further conciliation.

The Imperial response was the surprise attack and capture of Philippsburg on the night of 23/24 January 1635, followed a few weeks later by the taking of Sierck, another French-held fortification on the Moselle. Carrying the assault across the Rhine, Imperial troops had simultaneously seized Speyer.[156] These moves provoked consternation in the French council. Richelieu had consistently aimed to acquire his 'glacis' — territory beyond the French frontier which would serve for defence or the deployment of French armies — without provoking a major war. But as is so frequently the case, the concept of 'vital interests' proved infinitely extensible; what had originally been launched as a pragmatic exploitation of favourable circumstances had yielded territory that France was now prepared to risk war to retain. Richelieu began to formalise France's offensive alliances; now that war seemed unavoidable, the terms which she had hitherto rejected seemed more acceptable. On 8 February 1635, Richelieu negotiated a full offensive alliance with Holland, by which both powers agreed to invade the Spanish Netherlands with armies of 30,000 troops before the end of March.[157]

In March it was the Spanish who finally gave notice of their belligerent intentions, with the abduction of the Archbishop of Trier and the occupation of his territory. This was to be cited as the *casus belli* in the French declaration of war, delivered against Spain on 19 May. In fact, it was merely one incident among many: the declaration also followed upon what had become a state of open warfare in Lorraine between the Duke, his Imperialist supporters, and the French,[158] while French military support for the Protestants was now overt. Spanish preparations for the strike against France were unambiguous by the first months of 1635; the Spanish ambassador was recalled from Paris in late April.[159] Above all, French military cooperation with the Dutch had been undisguised since March. French forces had already crossed the border into the Netherlands before 19 May; three days after the declaration, they surprised and defeated a small force of Spanish troops at Aveins.[160]

Why did Richelieu trouble with the formality of the declaration? War had been inevitable since March, and it was merely the slowness with which seventeenth-century armies prepared themselves for campaigning which produced the delay. It was both a gesture of good faith to the Dutch and the Swedes, and a statement to the German Protestant princes negotiating the Peace of Prague with the Emperor. Although in the campaign theatres it was perfectly clear that French forces were engaged against both Spanish and Imperial troops, it was diplomatically desirable for France not to admit to hostilities with the Emperor. The creation of a clear-cut choice between an Imperial and a French alliance, together with the implications of a declaration of war for French intentions in Germany, would simply drive the Protestants more readily into their negotiations with a conciliatory Emperor. Richelieu gambled that by declaring war only upon Spain, he would be able to persuade some of the great Protestant princes to abandon their negotiations with the Emperor and assume a French-sponsored neutrality. The success of the Prague negotiations over the summer of 1635 proved him over-optimistic; both Saxony and Brandenburg accepted the proferred Imperial peace and alliance. Crucially, this had not been apparent when Richelieu had formulated the declaration of war.

Richelieu's concern at the military capacity of the Habsburgs proved all too well-founded. He had blurred the issue of respective military power throughout the early 1630s by relying upon the apparent strength of France's allies. Yet the power of Sweden and the German Protestants had been gravely weakened by the events of 1634–5. (Indeed, Saxony and Brandenburg were to fight as Imperial allies in the following years.) Richelieu now relied upon the Dutch to absorb a large part of the Spanish war effort, but did not allow that the Dutch envisaged the French as occupying the same role.[161] After the dismal Franco-Dutch campaign of 1635, practical military cooperation was minimal. Relying upon depleted or undependable allies, Richelieu was prepared to take the risk of going to war in 1635. In fact in the first few weeks of the war, he expressed optimism about a successful outcome, writing that the Conde-Duque could not long delay negotiations.[162]

On the other side, this optimism was matched, perhaps with more reason, by Olivares. Convinced that France lacked the military experience and internal cohesion to withstand the battering of veteran Habsburg armies, open war appeared to him to promise a quick and decisive solution to Spain's problems: the destruction of France's capacity to meddle beyond her frontiers, and the firm establishment of a European *Pax Austriaca*.

Both statesmen had finally come to see war simply as a means to force intolerable political tensions to a resolution. France now defended her 'vital interests' in terms of a glacis extending beyond the Rhine. While Spain and Austria had been forced to acquiesce in France's expansion to the Rhine over the preceding three years, it was a situation which they were now prepared to reject — a threat to lines of communication, an annexation of Habsburg fiefs, and a challenge to the principle of Imperial suzerainty. When combined with the consolidation of the French position in Piedmont and Montferrat, and the existence of an offensive alliance with Spain's hereditary enemies, the Dutch, it was inevitable that greater force would now be committed to an attempt to roll back the French advance and prevent its recurrence. Here we have a clear case of unpremeditated war. Wanted by neither side in 1631, war finally appears as the only possible direction for two powers whose political difficulties have progressively become irreconcilable. Aggressive and expansionist French policies, matched by deliberately ambiguous and threatening Habsburg responses, created a situation where the only alternative to taking the final steps into conflict would be an unconditional surrender of 'vital interests'. Both sides, over-optimistic about their military capacities, preferred to take the much shorter route into open warfare.

The result was the inconclusive conflict which dragged through to 1659. Olivares' plans for a pre-emptive strike in 1635 misfired. They were finally implemented on a much smaller scale in 1636, when the Spanish/Imperial invasions did threaten the possibility of a permanent enemy presence in Picardy and Champagne, and the deposition of Richelieu. But the gamble failed, and Olivares found himself involved in a war which Spain could not win. Although her armies remained consistently superior to those of France, winning the great majority of engagements down to 1656, Spain was unable to deploy the men, finance and *matériel* required to turn these victories to political advantage. She had to fight on, amidst internal disruption of her own, until France could finally mobilise her own resources and allies in sufficient strength finally to force the Austrians out of the war in 1648, and the Spanish in 1659 (the Treaties of Westphalia and the Pyrenees).

Spain won victories without being able to exploit them. France under Richelieu poured resources into a massive war effort which finally yielded a number of strong-points (Breisach, Arras, Perpignan) amidst an uninterrupted sequence of setbacks and defeats in the field. Only after Richelieu's death, with the battle of Rocroi in 1643, did it seem conceivable that a French army could prove equal to a Spanish force. For French contemporaries, the war was a highly unpopular and risky gamble, which probably had more to do with Richelieu's own hold upon power than with any general perception of French interests. France survived, but only just; the price of failure would have been a collapse into internal anarchy, and the end of any prospect of challenging a Habsburg settlement in Europe.

It might have been expected that twenty-four years of war would have resolved the political issues that had precipitated the conflict. With hindsight, historians have considered that the 1659 Peace of the Pyrenees embodied a decisive new European ranking, dominated by France. By the 1667/8 War of Devolution, this domination was evident; French armies, which had made such limited progress on the Flanders frontier before 1659, now sliced through enfeebled Spanish resistance. At the time, however, the Peace of the Pyrenees appeared a far from decisive verdict on the international hierarchy. Richelieu's successor, Mazarin, was aware that he had taken advantage of a sudden and severe downturn in Spanish fortunes to gain a favourable peace; the first years of Louis XIV's reign were dominated by the concern that Spanish 'decline' might prove temporary, and that measures should be taken to guard France against this threat.[163] The causes of Louis XIV's first wars might in turn be sought in the failure of this earlier conflict to resolve the issues which had originally provoked its outbreak in 1635.

NOTES

I would like to thank both my Oxford supervisor, Robin Briggs, and Robert Stradling, whose ideas and conversation have proved invaluable in developing my own views about this subject.

1. G. Blainey, *The Causes of War* (1973), surveys most major wars since 1700; B. Brodie, *War and Politics* (1974) and R. Aron, *Peace and War. A Theory of International Relations* (Eng. trans., 1966), restrict themselves to post-1800, and in most cases take examples after 1860. Although Q. Wright, *A Study of War* (abridged ed., 1964) establishes 'modern war' as conflict since the Renaissance (p. 50), his examples are also taken predominantly from the period after 1700. Even Clausewitz, *On War*, ed. M. Howard, P. Paret (Princeton, 1976), draws almost all his examples from 18th and early 19th-century warfare, or from antiquity.

2. Wright, *op. cit.*, p. 56, quotes figures drawn up by P. Sorokin which examine the intensity of warfare from century to century, and proposes that the 17th century was only surpassed in this respect by the 20th.

3. For this brief survey, I found the works of Blainey, *op. cit.*, pp. 127–174, and Brodie, *op. cit.*, pp. 276–340, particularly useful, as also the reasoned scepticism of M. Howard's article, 'The Causes of Wars', in his volume of essays of the same title: (1983) pp. 7–22. A much fuller and more satisfactory discussion than can be provided here has just appeared as the first chapter of T. C. W. Blanning, *The Causes of the French Revolutionary Wars* (1986).

4. J. Scarisbrick, *Henry VIII* (1968), pp. 574–81, 654.

5. R. J. Knecht, *Francis I* (Cambridge, 1982), p. 33; D. Bitton, *The French Nobility in Crisis, 1560–1640* (Stanford, 1969), pp. 2–3.

6. T. Hobbes, *Leviathan*, ed. C. B. Macpherson (1968), p. 162.

7. R. J. Wernham, 'English Policy and the Revolt of the Netherlands', in *Britain and the Netherlands*, ed. J. S. Bromley, E. H. Kossmann (1960), pp. 29–40.

8. J. Israel, *The Dutch Republic and the Hispanic World, 1606–61* (Oxford, 1982), pp. 33–4, 70–71.

9. J. H. Elliott, *Imperial Spain* (1963), pp. 130–5.

10. See *passim* P. Dukes, *The Making of Russian Absolutism, 1613–1801* (1982).

11. Hobbes, *Leviathan*, p. 161.

12. H. Grotius, *De Jure Belli et Pacis*, ed. W. Whewell (Cambridge, 1853), 3 vols., i. viii.

13. *The New Cambridge Modern History* (Cambridge, 1957), i. 353; See also the scathing comments of Machiavelli on the 'Holy League' and its failure: *The Discourses*, ed. B. Crick (1970), pp. 437–40.

14. P. Goubert, *Louis XIV and 20 million Frenchmen* (Eng. trans., 1970), pp. 233–8.

15. S. Lundkvist, 'The Experience of Empire: Sweden as a Great Power', in *Sweden's Age of Greatness, 1632–1718*, ed. M. Roberts (1973), 20–57, pp. 38–9.

16. Clausewitz, *On War* (Princeton, 1976), p. 605; the more familiar variant is on p. 87.

17. *Ibid.*, p. 149.

18. *Ibid.*, pp. 605–9.

19. A case well made by Blainey, *The Causes of War*, pp. 164–74.

20. Aron, *Peace and War*, pp. 162–7.

21. J. H. Elliott, *Richelieu and Olivares* (Cambridge, 1984), pp. 118–9.

22. A. Van Der Essen, *Le Cardinal-Infant et le Politique Européenne de L'Espagne, 1609–41* (Louvain, 1944), pp. 23–5.

23. G. Ramsay, 'The Foreign Policy of Elizabeth I', in *The Reign of Elizabeth I*, ed. C. Haigh (1984), 147–168: pp. 164–5.

24. J. Michael Hayden, *France and the Estates General of 1614* (Cambridge, 1974), pp. 43–9.

25. W. MacCaffrey, *The Shaping of the Elizabethan Regime* (1969), pp. 57–66.

26. See Brodie's criticism of this fallacy: *War and Politics*, p. 342.

27. R. Lockyer, *Buckingham* (1981), pp. 180–4; C. Hill, *God's Englishman* (1970), pp. 157–64.

28. Aron, *Peace and War*, pp. 72–4; Brodie, *War and Politics*, pp. 343–9.

29. A. Corvisier, *Louvois* (Paris, 1981), pp. 435–44.

30. G. Parker, *The Thirty Years' War* (1984), pp. 127–8.

31. J. B. Wolf, *Louis XIV* (1968), pp. 223–4.

32. Aron, *Peace and War*, p. 53; Blainey, *The Causes of War*, pp. 108–24.

33. D. Buisseret, *Henry IV* (1984), pp. 57–68.

34. *Ibid.*, pp. 79–86; G. Parker, *Europe in Crisis, 1598–1648* (1979), p. 122.

35. Blainey, *The Causes of War*, p. 247, and pp. 115–9.

36. H. G. Koenigsberger, *The Habsburgs and Europe, 1516–1660* (1971), p. 199.

37. See *passim* F. Redlich, *The German Military Enterpriser and his Work Force* (Wiesbaden, 1964–5: Vierteljahrschrift für Sozial- und Wirtschafts-geschichte, Beihefte 47–8), 2 vols; Redlich, 'Contributions in the Thirty Years' War', *Economic History Review*, xii (1959–60), 247–54.

38. M. Roberts, *The Swedish Imperial Experience* (Cambridge, 1979), p. 52.

39. G. Mann, *Wallenstein, His Life Narrated.* (Eng. trans., 1976), pp. 513–25.

40. G. Parker, *The Thirty Years' War*, pp. 182–3, 186.

41. Roberts, *The Swedish Imperial Experience*, pp. 53–5.

42. I. A. A. Thompson, *War and Government in Habsburg Spain, 1560–1620* (1976), is concerned specifically with the decentralisation that took place in the Spanish armed forces after 1580.

43. R. Stradling, *Europe and the Decline of Spain* (1981), pp. 88–9.

44. [A. J. du Plessis] Richelieu, *Lettres, [Instructions Diplomatiques et Papiers d'Etat du Cardinal de Richelieu]*, (ed. G. d'Avenel, Paris 1853–77), 8 volumes, iv. 790, [2 December 1634].

45. G. Hanotaux, Duc de La Force, [*Histoire du Cardinal de*] *Richelieu* (Paris, 1893–1947), 6 vols. iv. 434–75.

46. R. Stradling, 'Olivares and the Origins of the Franco-Spanish War 1627–35', *English Historical Review*, ci (1986), 68–94, p. 75.

47. D. Dessert, 'Le 'laquais-financier' au Grand Siècle: mythe ou réalité?', *XVIIe Siècle*, cxxii (1979), 21–36; J. F. Bosher ' 'Chambres de Justice' in the French Monarchy', in *French government and Society 1500–1850. Essays in Honour of A. Cobban*, ed. J. F. Bosher (1973), pp. 19–40.

48. J. Dent, *Crisis in Finance: Crown, Financiers and Society in Seventeenth-Century France* (Newton Abbot, 1973), pp. 132–63.

49. J. Israel, *The Dutch Republic and the Hispanic World*, pp. 68, 72–3.

50. R. Bonney, *The King's Debts* (Oxford, 1981), p. 169.

51. An argument convincingly developed over a longer timespan by M. Howard, 'The British Way in Warfare: a Reappraisal', in *The Causes of Wars*, 189–207, pp. 200–1.

52. G. Lacour Gayet, *La Marine Militaire de la France sous les Règnes de Louis XIII et Louis XIV* (Paris, 1911), i. 124–6.

53. Stradling, 'Olivares and the Origins', p. 92.

54. C. J. Burckhardt, *Richelieu and his Age* (Eng. trans., 1970), 3 vols. ii. 384–92. The period is covered in exhaustive detail by D. Albrecht: *Die Auswärtige Politik Maximilians von Bayern, 1618–35* (Göttingen, 1962: Schriftenreihe der Historischen Kommission bei der Bayerischen Akademie der Wissenschaften, Schrift 6), pp. 211–348.

55. Sully, quoted in D. Buisseret, *Sully and the Growth of Centralized Monarchy in France, 1598–1610* (1968), p. 177.

56. Michael-Haydn, *France and the Estates General of 1614*, p. 45.

57. [A. J. du Plessis] Richelieu, *Les Papiers de Richelieu* (ed. P. Grillon, Paris, 1975–), 6 vols, v. 208, [13 April 1630].

58. V. L. Tapié, *La Politique Etrangère de la France et le Début de la Guerre de Trente Ans (1616–21)* (Paris, 1934), pp. 27–30.

59. *Ibid.*, pp. 222–3; 233–40.

60. *Ibid.*, pp. 431–4.

61. *Ibid.*, pp. 509–13.

62. Stradling, 'Olivares and the Origins', p. 73.

63. Hanotaux/de La Force, *Richelieu*, ii. 185–99, 266–354; M. Carmona, *Marie de Medicis* (Paris, 1981), pp. 325–44, 369–397.

64. Accounts of this episode in: Hanotaux/de La Force, *Richelieu*, ii, 547-52; P. Chevallier, *Louis XIII* (Paris, 1979), pp. 272-4; Burckhardt, *op.cit.*, i. 152-7.

65. A. D. Lublinskaja, *French Absolutism: the Crucial Phase, 1620-29* (Eng. ed., Cambridge, 1968), pp. 263-4.

66. Hanotaux/de La Force, *Richelieu*, ii. 547 ['Capturing his imagination with ideas of the glory and the grandeur that could be achieved by the crown'].

67. *Ibid.* iii. 6; Tapié, *France in the Age of Louis XIII and Richelieu* (Eng. ed., 1974), pp. 127-30; Lublinskaja, *op cit.*, pp. 263-8.

68. H. Weber, *Frankreich, Kurtrier, der Rhein und das Reich, 1623-35* (Bonn, 1969), pp. 32-3.

69. Richelieu, *Les Papiers de Richelieu* (ed. Grillon), v. 208, [13 April 1630] ['If the King resolves upon war, it is necessary to abandon all thought of respite, of retrenchment and of good order within the realm. If, on the other hand, he wishes for peace, then he should abandon all thought of Italy for the future . . .'].

70. [A. J. du Plessis] Richelieu, *Testament Politique* (ed. L. André, Paris, 1947), pp. 231-5: indicates Richelieu's scepticism about any reform of the system of venal office-holding in France.

71. The best account of Richelieu's 'personal' government is in O. Ranum, *Richelieu and the Councillors of Louis XIII* (Oxford, 1963), esp. pp. 27-44.

72. Elliott, *Richelieu and Olivares*, p. 146 & n. 16; Marquis de Puységur, *Les Guerres de Louis XIII et Louis XIV (Memoirs)*, (Paris, 1883), 2 vols. i. 250; R. Mousnier, 'Histoire et Mythe', in *Richelieuu81, Collection Génies et Réalités (Paris, 1972), 239-52*, pp. 241-2.

73. See the comments of Elliott, *Richelieu and Olivares*, p. 147.

74. Elliott, *Richelieu and Olivares*, p. 101; Israel, *Dutch Republic and the Hispanic World*, pp. 313-4.

75. Elliott, *Richelieu and Olivares*, pp. 151-2.

76. R. Stradling, *Europe and the Decline of Spain*, pp. 69-70; P. Brightwell, 'The Spanish Origins of the Thirty Years' War', *European Studies Review*, ix (1979), 409-31.

77. Elliott, *Richelieu and Olivares*, pp. 36, 38-41.

78. *Ibid.*, pp. 138-9.

79. R. Stradling, 'A Spanish Statesman of Appeasement: Medina de Las Torres and Spanish Policy, 1639-70', *Historical Journal*, xix (1976), 1-31, p. 2.

80. G. Pagès, *La Guerre de Trente Ans* (Paris, 1939), pp. 204-7; Tapié, 'Echec aux Habsburg', in *Richelieu*, Collection Génies et Réalités, 109-129, pp. 123-4.

81. Weber, *Frankreich, Kurtrier*, pp. 147-50; Pagès, *La Guerre de Trente Ans*, pp. 160-3.

82. M. Roberts, *Gustavus Adolphus. A History of Sweden, 1611-32* (1955-8), 2 vols. ii. 594-5.

83. Pagès, *La Guerre de Trente Ans*, p. 202.

84. Bonney, *The King's Debts*, pp. 159-92.

85. *Ibid.*, pp. 165-8.

86. G. Mongrédien, *La Journée des Dupes* (Paris, 1961), pp. 129-49.

87. Hanotaux/de La Force, *Richelieu*, v. 147-52; Burckhardt, *Richelieu and his Age*, iii. 181-2.

88. Stradling, 'Olivares and the Origins', p. 85 & n. 3.

89. *Ibid.*, p. 71.

90. *Ibid.*, pp. 78-9.

91. *Ibid.*, pp. 86-90; Richelieu, *Lettres* (ed. Avenel), iv. 612-3 [22 September 1634], iv. 642 [16 November 1634].

92. Stradling, 'Olivares and the Origins', p. 86.

93. Elliott, *Richelieu and Olivares*, p. 112.

94. H. G. Koenigsberger, *The Habsburgs and Europe, 1516-1660*, p. 243; G. Parker, *Europe in Crisis*, pp. 201-5. These and other contributors to the debate are cited in Dr. Stradling's article: 'Olivares and the Origins', p. 69 & n. 4.

95. E. Straub, *Pax et Imperium. Spaniens Kampf um seine Friedensordnung in Europa zwischen 1617 und 1635* (Paderborn, 1980), p. 367.

96. Burckhardt, *Richelieu and his Age*, i. 359–62; Straub, *Pax et Imperium*, p. 406.

97. Straub, *Pax et Imperium*, p. 429.

98. Parker, *The Thirty Years' War*, pp. 111–3.

99. *Ibid.*, pp. 113–4.

100. [Paris: Archives des] A[ffaires] E[trangères], C[orrespondance] P[olitique], Suède, vol. 3, fo. 265, [11 September 1634] — cited in Pagès, *op. cit.*, p. 204.

101. G. Fagniez, *Le Père Joseph et Richelieu* (Paris, 1894), 2 vols. ii. 132.

102. *Israel, Dutch Republic and the Hispanic World*, pp. 176–87.

103. Fagniez, *Père Joseph*, ii. 141: letter of Père Joseph to Richelieu, 9 April 1633.

104. Straub, *Pax et Imperium*, p. 452.

105. Fagniez, *Père Joseph*, ii. 150, cites Père Joseph's boast in 1633 that France had 60,000 foot and 20,000 horse under arms. This is an exaggeration, and more appropriate to the *real* French armies maintained after 1635. Nonetheless, it is reasonable to assume that forces did not fall much below the 40,000 troops supported in 1630. By 1634, the evidence from musters and *revues* provides a conservative indication that France had some 48,000 men under arms.

106. Bonney's figures for military expenditure from 1629–34 show (approximate totals, in millions of *livres*): 18.3; 23; 15; 18.5; 16.8; 24.8 [*King's Debts*, pp. 306–7: figures taken from Mallet's accounts].

107. Richelieu, *Lettres* (ed. Avenel), iii. 453, [15 October 1629]; *Papiers de Richelieu* (ed. Grillon), iv. 697, [September 1629]; v. 153, 170 etc. [March/April 1630]; Weber, *Frankreich, Kurtrier*, p. 84.

108. The much-diverted alternative to the 16th-century 'Spanish Road': G. Parker, *The Army of Flanders and the Spanish Road, 1567–1659* (Cambridge, 1972), pp. 70–77.

109. H. Weber, 'Richelieu et le Rhin', *Revue Historique*, ccxxxix (1968), 265–80, pp. 268–70.

110. Richelieu, *Lettres* (ed. Avenel), iii. 878, [24 August 1630]; Fagniez, *Père Joseph*, ii. 149.

111. Weber, 'Richelieu et le Rhin', p. 275: details of the maltreatment of the Elector of Trier and his subjects by French forces of occupation.

112. G. Zeller, *La Réunion de Metz à la France, 1552–1648* (Paris, 1926), 2 vols. ii. 267–93.

113. Brightwell, 'Spain, Bohemia and Europe, 1619–21', *European Studies Review*, xii (1982), 371–99, pp. 374–6.

114. Zeller, *La Réunion de Metz*, ii. 237–8: the two fortresses were subsequently garrisoned by troops of the Duke of Lorraine in the name of the Emperor.

115. *Ibid.*, ii. 240.

116. Hanotaux/de La Force, *Richelieuu81, ii. 420*–1; Straub, *Pax et Imperium*, p. 449.

117. Burckhardt, *Richelieu and his Age*, iii. 24.

118. Weber, 'Richelieu et le Rhin', p. 273.

119. Albrecht, *Die Auswärtige Politik Maximilians von Bayern*, pp. 320–1, 343–5; Weber, *Frankreich, Kurtrier, der Rhein und das Reich*, pp. 170ff.

120. Weber, 'Richelieu et le Rhin', p. 274.

121. Hanotaux/de La Force, *Richelieu*, iii. 429–30; Weber, *Frankreich, Kurtrier*, pp. 148–50.

122. Weber, 'Richelieu et le Rhin', pp. 274–5 ['The felicity of France, gained through her victories, principally in Germany, that have carried her frontiers up to the Rhine'].

123. Weber, *Frankreich, Kurtrier*, pp. 207–8.

124. Pagès, *La Guerre de Trente Ans*, p. 167.

125. Bonney, *King's Debts*, p. 159.

126. Weber, *Frankreich, Kurtrier . . .*, pp. 225–30.

127. Richelieu, *Lettres* (ed. Avenel), iv. 269–73 [*Advis* to the King from end-March 1632].

128. Burckhardt, *Richelieu and his Age*, iii. 26.

129. Pagès, *La Guerre de Trent Ans*, pp. 195–6.

130. Hanotaux/de La Force, *Richelieu*, iii, 433–4.

131. Burckhardt, *Richelieu and his Age*, iii. 27–8.

132. *Ibid.*, iii. 30.

133. Weber, *Frankreich, Kurtrier*, p. 314.

134. Parker, *The Thirty Years' War*, p. 132.

135. Hanotaux/de La Force, *Richelieu*, iv, 490–3.

136. Van Der Essen, *Le Cardinal-Infant*, pp. 158–63.

137. *Ibid.*, pp. 164ff.

138. Parker, *The Thirty Years' War*, p. 132.

139. Pagès, *La Guerre de Trente Ans*, p. 198.

140. Stradling, 'Olivares and the Origins', p. 88.

141. Parker, *The Thirty Years' War*, p. 144.

142. Pagès, *La Guerre de Trente Ans*, p. 201.

143. Richelieu, *Lettres* (ed. Avenel), iv. 421–5 [*Instructions à M. de Charnacé*, 13 January 1633].

144. Bonney, *The King's Debts*, p. 163.

145. Fagniez, *Père Joseph*, ii. 169–70.

146. Hanotaux/de La Force, *Richelieu*, v, 41–5.

147. *Ibid.*, v. 46; Fagniez, *Père Joseph*, ii. 179, who suggests, reasonably, that the army was of 29,000 men.

148. Burckhardt, *Richelieu and his Age*, iii. 49–50.

149. Hanotaux/de La Force, *Richelieu*, v. 89–90.

150. Burckhardt, *Richelieu and his Age*, iii. 51–2.

151. Hanotaux/de La Force, *Richelieu*, v. 91–2.

152. Stradling, 'Olivares and the Origins', pp. 89–91.

153. Hanotaux/de La Force, *Richelieu*, v. 91–2.

154. Burckhardt, *Richelieu and his Age*, iii. 54–5.

155. *Ibid.*, iii. 56, and see note 43.

156. *Ibid.*, iii. 57; Hanotaux/de La Force, *Richelieu*, v. 92.

157. Fagniez, *Père Joseph*, ii. 207; Richelieu, *Lettres* (ed. Avenel), iv. 651, [17 January 1635], for details of negotiations.

158. Pagès, *La Guerre de Trente Ans*, p. 220.

159. Stradling, 'Olivares and the Origins', p. 93.

160. A. E. Mémoires et Documents, France 814, fo. 115 [late May 1635].

161. Israel, *Dutch Republic and the Hispanic World*, pp. 256ff., 300–1.

162. A. E. Mémoires et Documents, France 814, fo. 157, [11 June 1635].

163. Goubert, *Louis XIV and 20 Million Frenchmen*, pp. 72–3; H. Méthivier, *Le Siècle de Louis XIV* (Paris, 1950), p. 71.

4

THE ORIGINS OF LOUIS XIV'S WARS

Paul Sonnino

Whatever else the Kings of France may have been noted to be, they could never quite escape a certain reputation for frivolity. John the Good contributed mightily to it when, in the midst of the disastrous war against England, he rewarded his younger son with the Duchy of Burgundy, afflicting the French monarchy with a perpetual thorn on its eastern frontier. Barely had France recovered from this Hundred Years' War than a succession of French Kings, Charles VIII, Louis XII and Francis I, began their cavalcades into Italy, brilliant flashes of impetuosity which merely lighted the way for Ferdinand of Aragon to entrench himself on the peninsula. These combined actions of the Kings of France appeared all the more irresponsible in retrospect as the house of Burgundy blended by marriage into the Habsburg house of Austria, and this virile Imperial house, in turn, collected the crowns of Aragon and Castile. Before he could realize what was happening, Francis I found himself confronted with Charles V, and a chivalric excursion at the expense of the Italians became a grim struggle for dynastic independence. But the sixteenth century had even greater surprises in store, in the form of mute forces of nature rising from the dust and expressing themselves through human voices: an expanding population, economy, and geographical horizon; greater social mobility, a sense of instability, and the emergence of new classes; a grassroots religious movement among both Protestants and Catholics, fueling and being fueled by economic, social, and political tensions. Wars, by virtue of the larger armies, new firearms, and new fortifications, were more expensive though no more decisive, and the original dynastic struggle had to accommodate itself to the behests of two international religious conspiracies, each claiming direct authority from the Almighty. Europe became acquainted with the phenomenon of the ideological conflict, which set brother against brother and united total strangers according to their formula for salvation. The authority of the neo-feudal state, limited at the best of times, disintegrated. France was torn by religious wars, with only a minority of French Catholics being prepared to accept Henry of Navarre, the Protestant claimant to the throne. English Catholics plotted against their queen. Only in the Spanish portion of the Habsburg possessions, inherited by Philip II, did the interest of the state and that of the Church march in unison, and even he was unable to prevent the revolt of his subjects in the Low Countries and the adhesion of the northern provinces to the Protestant cause. The first Bourbon King of France barely eked out a compromise by becoming a Catholic himself, granting his armed Protestant supporters a measure of toleration by the Edict of Nantes, and permitting any *bourgeois* who had crashed the nobility by purchasing a judicial office to keep it within his family by paying the *paulette*, this limited restoration of order by Henry IV being interrupted by his assassination in 1610.[1]

The seventeenth century, therefore, began with an intermission. Every individual, group or institution which had been deprived of its rights during the previous century was firmly determined to regain them at the first opportunity. Every individual, group, or institution which had extracted some rights out of the previous century was equally determined to augment them if it could. In France the nine-year old Louis XIII, a foreign queen-regent and her Italian favorites were easy prey for the new nobility of the robe and the leaders of the Huguenot party. In England James I theorized wildly about the Divine Right of kings, while the most Puritan among his subjects agitated for a saintly commonwealth. And yet, the new century had a few surprises in store of its own. The rates of growth of the population and the economy began to slow down, and the chances for social advancement became more rare. The dust, in other words, was beginning to settle, and as it did, so also the struggle for power became less international and more localized, with the economic, social, and religious groupings concentrating first and foremost on entrenching their political position at home even if this meant sacrificing their ideological allies abroad. The big issue was one of whether and on what political terms the new nobility of the robe and the Huguenots could make a place for themselves in France, whether the fresher elements of the gentry and of the clergy could be mollified in England, or whether the great merchant oligarchs who had risen to power in the Dutch Republic, more interested in commerce than in religion, could shake off their military dependance on the house of Orange, which thrived on the conflict against Catholic Spain.[2]

The career of Armand du Plessis epitomizes the prevailing trends of his time. As a member of the old aristocracy of the sword, he was infuriated that the pristine purity of his class had been soiled by the 'nobility' of the robe. It was their function, in his view of the natural order, to engage in commerce, not to clutter up the courts with their insolent pedantry. As a Catholic bishop, he shared in the passion of his Church to re-establish religious unity. Heresy was to him an anomaly. There was no place for it in an orderly society. Finally, as an advisor to the queen-regent and subsequently as prime minister to the king, the now Cardinal Richelieu set about achieving these goals under the aegis of royal authority. It was, he had no doubt, divinely established, and with good reason, to maintain discipline throughout the state and to defend it from its enemies abroad. The first matters which invited his attention were domestic: the restoration of the natural social hierarchy, the stimulation of trade, and the reimposition of religious orthodoxy. But the great war, destined to last for thirty years, broke out in the Holy Roman Empire. The Spanish Habsburgs resumed their efforts to reconquer their rebellious provinces, combining with the Austrian Habsburgs in their efforts to dominate the German princes. Aware of a divergence between the interest of the dynasty and religious solidarity, Louis XIII and the cardinal both concluded that the Kings of France could not possibly perform their duty toward God if they sacrificed the political independence of their state. In 1625, therefore, the king proceeded to send military support to the Protestant Grisons against the

Habsburgs. Likewise, when the Huguenots of France were touched by this same dilemma, they came to a similar conclusion. They revolted against Louis XIII, forcing Richelieu to abandon their co-religionists. He returned to his original priorities, managing by 1629 to deprive the Huguenots of their military bases. But once again, before he could push forward with his domestic program, other imperatives imposed themselves upon him. The Habsburgs by their victories were coming closer than ever before to the achievement of universal monarchy, giving him, according to his lights, no alternative but to subsidize Protestant Sweden and later to enter the war on the side of both the Dutch Republic and the Swedes. These were agonizing decisions. In order to maintain an army of 130,000 men, he had to leave the judges in possession of their offices, the Huguenots in the practice of their religion, and the peasantry at the mercy of the tax collectors. Still, by the time of his death in 1642 and that of the king the following year, the French monarchy had beaten back, even if it had not eliminated, its challengers at home, and with such generals as the Prince de Condé, emerged victorious abroad.[3]

The minority of Louis XIV, the regency of the foreign Anne of Austria, and the prime ministry of her ingratiating Italian advisor Cardinal Mazarin seemed to presage a repetition of the bad old days. England too was approaching the climax of its political confrontation. The Spanish Habsburgs under Philip IV and his Austrian cousin Emperor Ferdinand III were in the final stages of exhaustion, many of their possessions such as Portugal were in open revolt, and France's steady progress in the Low Countries was beginning to worry her Dutch allies so much that they were preparing to abandon her in return for Spanish recognition of their independence. This is what they did in 1648 at the Treaty of Westphalia, leaving the French regency with the limited option of making its peace with the emperor and fighting on alone against Spain. Nevertheless, as Europe approached the mid-century mark, the mute forces of nature were operating powerfully toward the preservation of the *status quo*. They reverted to a kind of endemic harshness, resulting in a population which neither grew nor diminished, an economy in which gains and losses balanced each other, a society in which the former parvenus were becoming fixtures. Not that this emerging stability was immediately evident. In France the regency government, pressing its people to the limit, did not fail to arouse its own revolt of nobles and judges, the *Fronde*. But this revolt, as its name suggests, was a pale imitation of its forerunners. Its instigators were divided, its religious overtones were restricted to a few scheming Jansenists, its social rumblings never got off the ground. The well-to-do were simply too haunted by the recollection of past troubles and by the frightening stories coming from England to tamper violently with the Richelieuan compromise. The little king observed the collapse of the revolt with a mixture of caution and conceit that became the hallmark of his personality. He clung to Mazarin like a son, while concluding that revolutions were perfectly avoidable if a monarch ran his own government with a modicum of good sense. Once order was restored, Louis' able general, Marshal de Turenne, resumed the conquest of the Spanish portion of the Low Countries. The young king sat silently by, however, as the cardinal decided that there was nothing to be gained by it. There was no reason to alarm the Dutch, who were performing the service of holding off Cromwellian England, there was no reason to alienate the princes of Germany, who had even toyed with the idea of electing Louis emperor and had joined him in forming a defensive alliance, the League of the Rhine, there was no reason to stir up more popular discontent everywhere. Mazarin, through the dim haze, perceived the emergence of a new system of Europe, highly advantageous to France and detrimental to her enemies. Thus in 1659 he concluded the Peace of the Pyrenees with Spain, obtaining territorial concessions, a Spanish *infanta* as a wife for his king, and leaving Spain in possession of a large buffer zone between France and the Dutch Republic. When the cardinal died in 1661, Louis shed copious tears of affection and appreciation, but he also recalled in his *Mémoires* for the Dauphin that 'his ideas were naturally quite different from mine . . . his maxim being to provide for the present at any cost and to let the future take care of itself'.[4]

Fortune may not have been smiling upon Europe in 1661, condemned as it was to several decades of economic stagnation, but she was certainly smiling on the King of France as he began his personal reign. The crises of the sixteenth and early seventeenth centuries were horrors of the past, yet they were vivid enough in everyone's imagination for no one to desire their recurrence. By the same token, there was very little to do abroad: a barely restored Charles II in England banking exclusively on the good will of his subjects; the Spanish Habsburgs under Philip IV still contending with the Portuguese rebellion; the Austrian Habsburgs under the young Emperor Leopold kept in line by the princes of Germany; and the Dutch Republic, led by that quintessential merchant oligarch Johan de Witt, interested above all in maintaining the *status quo*. Louis too was disposed to watch his step, choosing as his ministers, or members of his *conseil d'en haut*, Michel Le Tellier, the secretary for war, Nicolas Fouquet, superintendant of the finances (quickly replaced by Jean-Baptiste Colbert as intendant and then controller-general), and Hugues de Lionne, secretary for foreign affairs. These men were all creatures of Cardinal Mazarin, advocates of domestic consolidation, and, as long as England or the Habsburgs did not rise again, of international peace. It was a policy of which Colbert, likewise in the best tradition of Cardinal Richelieu, became the acknowledged champion. One of Colbert's primary objectives was to balance the budget and get the monarchy out of debt, another to stimulate commerce and industry, a third to erect high tariffs against foreign imports, a fourth to augment foreign trade, a fifth to lighten the burden on the peasantry. In relation to these benefits, war had a purely ornamental role. It was, ideally speaking, a luxury, like building palaces or having a magnificent court, which could be undertaken as a result, not to the detriment, of the general economic prosperity. Nor was the king unresponsive to his ministers' urgings. He asserted in no uncertain terms that he was committed to 'restoring all things to their natural order', and his early foreign policy was indeed a combination of adhering to the established system, for example renewing his alliance with the Dutch; and inexpensive sabre rattling, for example avenging insults to his ambassadors. He also learned how to combine self-interest with displays of public spiritedness, as when in 1664 he joined his allies of the League of the Rhine and sent 6000 men to the aid of the emperor against the Turks.[5]

The cautious young Louis who could sit in council day in and day out listening to one dispatch after the other, however, was in constant contention with another king who 'wished for more external affairs' and who would have reproached himself for failing to make his mark in military history. But if he was smitten by the same fancy as Charles VIII, Louis XII and Francis I, he could not go off to war with their same insouciance. He was well aware of the criticisms which had been levelled at his predecessors. Moreover, he was of a type whose belligerence needed some link with utility, some philosophical cover, some political reason in order to feel respectable, and, needless to say, he found it. He discovered it in the principle that 'the state of the two crowns of France and of Spain is such today and has been such for a long time in the world that it is impossible to raise one without humbling the other'. Thereby, he had come up with a complete transfiguration of the ideas of Richelieu and Mazarin into the thesis, not that the Kings of France had to preserve their independence when it was threatened, not that they had to participate in sustaining the new system of Europe, but rather that it was their sacred duty to keep on kicking the Habsburgs when they were down. One wonders whether, as he dictated these ominous lines, he had any notion that this was not at all why his allies had joined him and that, if he persisted in such a policy, he was committing himself to losing them one by one. A pretext for beginning this process would soon be at hand: a *private* law of devolution in the Spanish Low Countries according to which a daughter by a first marriage (his queen Maria Theresa) stood to inherit *property* prior to a son by a second marriage (Philip IV's son Carlos). The ministers were quite prepared to exploit this claim up to a certain point, but they were faced with competition from someone whose attitude was much closer to the king's. This was the legendary Marshal de Turenne, eager to resume the French advance into the Spanish Low Countries, and whenever he was called into the council, he was almost invariably inciting Louis to keep his adversaries off balance. Still, the position of the French monarchy was enviable. In 1665 a new naval war broke out between England and the Dutch Republic. The King of France found himself courted by both sides. There was an election coming up in Poland at which he was advancing the candidacy of his cousin the Prince de Condé. It would have been very difficult for Louis to feel threatened by anyone.[6]

The year 1665 constitutes a quiet and largely unobserved turning point in the personal reign. At that time Colbert, aggressively pursuing his program of domestic reform, was beginning to push for a reform of justice, involving a possible unification of the laws and the fulfilment of Richelieu's dream, the elimination of the *paulette*. Colbert was well aware of the economic, social, and political implications of these changes, and particularly of doing away with the inheritance of judicial offices, but he felt that the king was in a position to impose his will even if he subsequently found himself embroiled in a war. That Colbert, however, was thinking only of a limited war for the maintenance of the system of Europe is illustrated by a *mémoire* which he composed at that same time on the war between England and the Dutch. His principal fear was that it would end up by increasing the power of England. Thus he advised that as long as Johan de Witt and his party of merchants did not lose heart, France should remain neutral. If, on the other hand, they were in danger of succumbing in their own country to the English-related house of Orange, then France should intervene to redress the balance. This was the comfortable fence being straddled by Louis XIV and his ministers when, on September 17, 1665, Philip IV of Spain died, leaving his monarchy in the hands of the Queen-regent Mariana and their four-year old son Carlos II. The King of France was now presented with the more absorbing dilemma of whether he should pursue his domestic reform or interrupt it in the interest of annexing the greater part of the Spanish Low Countries. Superficially, it was the same dilemma which had tormented Cardinal Richelieu in 1629. On even mild reflection, it emerges as a dilemma of an entirely different order and provides us with a keen insight into the origins of Louis XIV's early wars. He himself would have been the first to admit that his situation was in no way comparable to Richelieu's. Yet on the eventual possibility that a sickly child's descendants might some day revive the empire of Charles V, the king was prepared to jeopardize his relations with England, with the Dutch, with the Germans, and to accept the judicial officials as part of the natural order. It was as if he had reversed Mazarin's maxim into 'provide for the future at any cost and let the present take care of itself'.[7]

Even so, Louis was not about to dash lightly into the fray. His call to easy glory was complicated by the continuing Anglo-Dutch War, which confronted him with two interrelated questions: should he declare war upon England in support of his Dutch allies, and if so, should he engage in one war at a time or simultaneously press his demands upon the Spanish? After much thought, and in keeping with the preferences of his *conseil d'en haut*, he decided to go to the aid of his allies, but on the more ambitious option, in spite of his passion 'to fulfil the great expectations that I had for some time inspired in the public', he concluded that 'the greatness of our courage must not make us neglect the aid of our reason' and settled for doing first things first. While participating in this peripheral war, however, he prepared for the primordial one, and here we can observe him extending his methodological spirit to his quest for military fame: counting and recounting his handsome troops in a series of parade-ground reviews, building up stocks of provisions in a number of frontier strongholds, and basing his campaign plan on the dazzling execution of a few perfect sieges. Let us not be too impressed! Once his troops grew weary, his supplies ran out, and the initial strongholds were taken, he fully intended to huddle with his generals and decide what to do next. Still, he thought farther ahead than most seventeenth-century strategists. He had two principal collaborators in these endeavors: Turenne, to the consternation of all the ministers, and Le Tellier's 24-year old son and fellow-secretary Louvois, to the consternation of Colbert and Lionne. As a result of this new preoccupation, Turenne was also being called with greater frequency to the meetings of the *conseil d'en haut*, where he began to advocate a major shift in foreign policy: reconciliation with the English, hostility toward the Dutch. It was an unsettling portent of things to come.[8]

The king began his War of Devolution in 1667 without even declaring it, merely announcing that he was going to march in and take possession of Maria Theresa's rights. The campaign was, just as he had planned it, an unqualified success. He had an army of 85,000 men, all the instruments of siegecraft, and the enemy was too weak to interfere. The problems arose elsewhere. The ministers were terrified at Turenne's growing prestige, even Le Tellier, in spite of the fact that Louvois was also gaining in influence through the war. Colbert, complaining bitterly about its costs, rushed back to Paris to collect more money, and Lionne's health failing, he left the army permanently. He spent the rest of the campaign advising Louis by long distance *mémoire* to offer compromise terms and to impose them upon the Spanish in collaboration with the Dutch Republic. The English and the Dutch were already coming to terms with each other at Breda, but Turenne, who had the advantage of being at the king's side, was urging an alliance with the same English against Spain and the Dutch in an explosive merger of both wars. Meanwhile, the entire French network of alliances, so laboriously built up by Richelieu and Mazarin, was collapsing. The Spanish were making peace with Portugal, the princes of Germany refused to renew the League of the Rhine, Sweden was wavering. The *conseil d'en haut* had to wait until the campaign was over to impress Louis with the seriousness of the situation, but he was ultimately induced to offer some more precise and moderate peace terms. Lionne's particular drive, moreover, gained impetus from an unexpected quarter. Leopold of Austria, unable to assist his Spanish nephew militarily, offered the King of France a secret treaty for the partition of the entire Spanish monarchy in case Carlos II died without issue. It was concluded in Vienna on January 19, 1668. On the other hand, soon thereafter England, the Dutch Republic and Sweden patched together a Triple Alliance, which, as tactfully as was possible, threatened the French with a general war if they did not bring their conquests to a halt. Louis blustered and threatened to turn all his forces, now approaching 130,000 men, against the insolent De Witt, but in the end, the king displayed another characteristic of his unfolding personality, a definite loss of inclination, when the going got rough, to stick by his guns. He suddenly felt sufficiently satiated by his military victories and inspired by the prospect of soon obtaining large portions of the Spanish succession. Thus he hearkened to the advice of his ministers, and notably of Lionne, over the counsels of Turenne, and accepted the compromise Treaty of Aix-La-Chapelle in 1668.[9]

Since Louis had shown himself susceptible to their urgings, the regulars of the *conseil d'en haut* looked forward after the war to the re-establishment of their credit. But the obvious need to quench his thirst for glory was beginning to divide them among themselves. Each was attempting to devise his own method and had his own schedule for satisfying the king. Le Tellier was the most confident in the future. He desired for the peace to last only until such time as his son would be in a better position to counteract the influence of Turenne. Colbert was the most demanding in his expectations. He presumed to expect a perpetual peace so that he could carry out an economic policy which would eventually make France the mistress of Europe. Lionne hoped for an indeterminate period of calm in which to dissolve the Triple Alliance and pave the way for the implementation of the secret treaty of partition. Before they could reach their destinations, however, the ministers had a number of immediate challenges to overcome. Every seventeenth-century peace was followed by complicated disputes over the dependencies of the territories which had been ceded. Louis' lawyers did not fail to discover that a few additional Spanish strongholds should also belong to him. The *conseil* got him to approve the creation of a bilateral limits commission, thus postponing the issue. Then there was the angry Turenne. He was now pressing for an alliance pure and simple with England against the Dutch. The ministers got Jean-Baptiste Colbert's brother, Colbert de Croissy, appointed ambassador to England, hardly the most supple man for this delicate negotiation. They also enticed the king to endorse a peace with the Jansenists, convincing him that patience was the best means to dispose of the Jansenist heresy, and that he should appoint the leading Jansenist's nephew, the brilliant Arnauld de Pomponne, as ambassador to the Dutch Republic. Although these were favorable signs, the regulars of the *conseil* were not at the end of their trials. The longer the peace lasted, the more impatient Louis became. Held back from exploiting his claims in the dependencies dispute and finding that the negotiation in England was not progressing, he, in collaboration with the like-minded Louvois, came up with his own crude, direct and infallible formula for resuming the conquest of the Spanish Low Countries, namely to bully the Spanish as much as possible and provoke them into declaring war. It was also, of course, a crude, direct, and infallible formula for isolating France in Europe.[10]

The king was aiming to get himself into a great deal of trouble. He was only diverted by a combination of chance and skill. Who could have predicted that in restoration England, a country gushing with royalist Anglican sentiment, its king should have set his heart on restoring Catholicism? This proposition was so outlandish that he could not even present it to his full council. And yet, early in 1669, he sent the Earl of Arundel on a secret mission to France, seeking first and foremost support for a declaration of Catholicity. It was Louis who replied that restoring Catholicism was all well and good, but that he would not subsidize it unless Charles II also consented to attack the Dutch. But why the Dutch? True, the Dutch had insolently participated in forcing the French to put a stop to their conquests in the War of Devolution. True, the Dutch had made a shambles out of the English navy in their previous war. But, by the same token, this constituted at least one valuable service to each monarchy. The only consistent explanation for the decision to attack the Dutch rests on the individual reasoning of the plotters. The King of France knew perfectly well that the English would never consent to a common war against Spain. His only hope was to begin with the Dutch in the expectation that Spain would be obliged to rush to their assistance. His ministers considered that a negotiation with England would draw his attentions from his confrontations with Spain, be useful in undermining the Triple Alliance, and ultimately come to nothing. The King of England concluded that agreeing to attack the Dutch was the only means to advance his declaration of Catholicity. The decision, therefore, was a typical compromise decision, not entirely satisfactory to anyone, except perhaps to Turenne, and based on conflicting assumptions.[11]

The conscientious young Louis also attempted to impose some extraordinary restrictions upon himself. He still intended to wage his wars without in the least disturbing his subjects, either through the depredations of his troops or through the imposition of new taxes. This bore testimony to the continuing influence of Colbert, and Turenne, who formulated the initial strategy, had to adapt it to these new-fangled ideals. Thus his plan called for an army of 100,000 troops, not even as many as had been collected for the second year of the War of Devolution. The French agent, Prince Wilhelm von Fürstenberg, was to procure a number of German allies, the Catholic Archbishop-Elector of Cologne and the Bishop of Münster, Catholic and Protestant princes of the house of Brunswick, and the Protestant Elector of Brandenburg, seasoning the righteous indignation with an inter-denominational flavor. Indeed, it was the opinion of the ministers that the war was not feasible without the participation of the Elector of Brandenburg. As to the campaign, it was to be as straightforward as usual. The king and Turenne would besiege the Dutch stronghold of Maastricht, an Anglo–French fleet would take control of the seas, and the German allies would create a pesky diversion. There was no thought of taking Amsterdam, not even Utrecht, all the more proof that Louis had other destinations in mind. So did the regulars of the *conseil*. They continued to hope that the entire elaborate project would fall of its own weight, and we may imagine their surprise when they found themselves witnessing the secret Treaty of Dover with England in June of 1670. But still, the plan was miscarrying. The indispensable Elector of Brandenburg, far from joining in, seemed inclined to assist the Dutch. The king, moreover, displayed another facet of his long-range perfectionism, his predilection for the preemptive strike. On the vague rumor that the neighboring Duke of Lorraine was seeking to join the Triple Alliance, Louis, without even consulting his ministers, occupied Lorraine, creating fear and hesitation all over Germany. Lionne had to resort to all sorts of diplomatic expedients, like an effort to replace the German princes with the alliance of Sweden. On Lionne's death in September 1671, Louvois entered the *conseil d'en haut*. The upshot of this vacillation and change of personnel was that the less the king felt he could rely on his allies, the more he felt compelled to strain his own resources. He decided to bypass Maastricht and march directly to the Dutch outposts on the Rhine. He tried to bully Spain into the war unceremoniously and was forced to relent by the cries of consternation in England. He resolved to increase the size of his army to 144,000 men and, in the process, came to a showdown with Colbert, who had to be threatened with dismissal if he did not produce the necessary funds. In order to obtain his substitute war against the Dutch, therefore, Louis ended up by mortgaging his own principles and corrupting those of his old ministers, soon to be joined by the new secretary for foreign affairs, Arnauld de Pomponne.[12]

While the aggressors were free to bargain among themselves, it is very hard to imagine what the Dutch could have done to avoid their fate. The urban patriciate, or 'states' party, which dominated the politics of the republic, harbored an inveterate distrust of the house of Orange, which they had deprived of its influential military offices, and which the young William III aspired to regain.

The patricians were the commercial rivals of England, and the political rivals too since William's uncle had been restored to the English throne. They preferred to rely for their security on a strong navy rather than on an obtrusive army which only served as a refuge for William's sympathisers. Johan de Witt, the chief spokesman for the patriciate, was prepared to appease France as much as he could, short of putting her in possession of the Spanish Low Countries. His political critic from the same party, Coenraad van Beuningen, was much more open in publicizing the French threat, but his solution was not much more effective. He was a kind of Colbert in reverse, believing that a peaceful tariff war would bring the French to their senses. The Dutch knew perfectly well that the King of France was trying to form a German alliance against them, although they did not have the slightest suspicion about the Treaty of Dover. They had every reason to expect, however, that their outlying strongholds of Maastricht, Wesel, Orsoy, and Rheinberg should have been able to occupy an invader and their navy strong enough to stymie the English until such time as the system of Europe could be brought into play. The Spanish and the emperor were precisely of the same opinion. As soon as they saw that Louis' vengeance was directed against the Dutch, they breathed a sigh of relief. The Spanish concluded an alliance with the Dutch, agreeing to aid them as 'auxiliaries' while refusing to enter the war directly, and Leopold actually made a treaty with the king, virtually inviting him to try his hand against the Dutch as long as he did not threaten either the Spanish or the Empire. It would be incorrect to assume that either the Spanish or the emperor came to this decision easily, but, as it turned out for them, the decision proved to be infinitely wise. They would neither play into the hands of the French nor exempt the Dutch from absorbing the first blow.[13]

If we keep in mind that the war in conjunction with England against the Dutch in 1672 was not quite the one the Louis would have preferred, its bizarre twists and turns will become more comprehensible. Let us take the first campaign. It was, to all appearances, an astonishing success. The decision to bypass Maastricht took the Dutch entirely by surprise, and within a month over forty of their strongholds fell into his hands. The Dutch hurried to his camp with offers of humiliating concessions, but the story of Louvois advising the king to reject them and Pomponne, who emerged as a skilful diplomat of the Mazarin persuasion, advising the contrary, does not seem to fit the facts. The Dutch were merely stalling for time and so was Louis. He did not have the capability, by his own plodding standards, to advance into the heart of their country. He also knew that he had to eliminate the possibility of the Elector of Brandenburg coming to their aid before they could negotiate seriously or before the Spanish would return to intervening. This is why the king alluded cagily in his *Mémoires* on the Dutch War to his self-fullfilling 'premonition that the war would fall upon the Spanish Low Countries'. It was not quite that simple. The lynching of De Witt in The Hague opened the way for William of Orange to become stadholder, and Turenne, marching into Westphalia against the relieving forces of the Elector of Brandenburg and Leopold of Austria, forced the former to make peace and the latter to withdraw. But at this critical juncture in 1673 came another instructive example of Louis' fatal predilection for the preemptive strike. Rather than withdrawing his troops from Germany as everyone expected him to do, he ordered Turenne to advance further into the country, simply to insure that the emperor would not come out again. Pomponne was scandalized by the move. He did not share his king's faith that a force of 24,000 men could undermine the system of Europe, and Pomponne proved to be right. In spite of Louis' taking Maastricht, Turenne was outmanouvered by Leopold's forces, and the king, with the examples of his frivolous predecessors no doubt in mind, was forced to abandon most of his Dutch conquests. The war on which he had staked so much of his reputation became grim, Colbert having to resort to all sorts of financial expedients in order to pay for it. When Louis finally did get Spain into it, Charles II of England pulled out, reverting to a posture of diffident neutrality. Too little attention has been paid to the domestic revolts and the revival of Jansenism in France during the middle years of the war. By 1676 the king, his people supporting an army of 240,000 men, was again on the verge of conquering the entire Spanish Low Countries, but he was now faced with the specter of revolt at home, a puritanical pope, Innocent XI, who seemed ready to make common cause with the Jansenists, and the possibility that England would ally herself with the Dutch. Once more Louis had to convince himself that a war which had originally been intended for the conquest of the Spanish Low Countries had nevertheless been a great success, in this case a masterpiece of opportunism against a host of jealous enemies. Once more he had to rely upon a moderate minister to procure an advantageous compromise peace, in this case Pomponne to procure the Treaty of Nijmegen in 1678.[14]

By now some of the recurring patterns in the king's conduct ought to be emerging. We might expect, for example, that the qualified success of the war would be followed by the usual reassessment. What we might not suspect, however, would be its quickness and violence. Fondly reminiscing about his great victories and no longer having to repeat them in the field, it suddenly dawned upon him that he had won the war and lost the peace. His rage found its first victim in Arnauld de Pomponne. It was he who had consistently urged moderation. It was he who had masterminded the Treaty of Nijmegen. It was he who was sounding more and more like his sanctimonious Jansenist relatives. On the flimsiest of pretexts, Louis dismissed Pomponne, ridding the *conseil d'en haut* of its last open dissenter. It was now made up of Le Tellier, who was glad to remain silent, Louvois, who ruled the roost, Jean-Baptiste Colbert, who had learned how to behave, and Pomponne's replacement, Colbert de Croissy, who always did as he was told. The king could give his longstanding confidence in the efficacy of brute force its greatest opportunity to vindicate itself. He maintained the peacetime army at 140,000, treated his neighbors like puppets, and offered Croissy virtually no support in his efforts to reconstruct the alliance system. It is interesting to compare the way in which Louis had allowed himself to be guided by his ministers in 1668 with the way in which he brooked no restraint after 1679. In 1668 he had allowed his *conseil d'en haut* to defuse the dependencies dispute. Neither compromise nor indirection, however, had lived up to its promises and he was tired of feeling cheated by the peace. Thus he and Louvois, with little resistance from Croissy, launched their policy of reunions, peacetime armed annexations, culminating in the reunion of Strasbourg and the blockade of Luxembourg. In 1668 the king had been willing to temporize with heresy. Neither the Huguenots nor the Jansenists, however, had obligingly receded into the woodwork, and never again did he intend to adjourn a war out of fear of rebellion at home. The result was Louvois' dragonnades and the renewed persecution of the Jansenists.[15]

However much resentment Louis' policies may have been stimulating in every corner of Europe, his last round of violence seemed to be working remarkably well. There was still in the early 1680s no power or combination of powers that could equal his. The secretly Catholic King of England was preoccupied with assuring the English succession to his openly Catholic brother, the Spanish monarchy was at its lowest ebb, the emperor was menaced by the most terrifying Turkish invasion of all time, the princes of Germany were as divided as ever, and the merchants of the Dutch Republic were once more at odds with William of Orange. Accordingly, early in 1682, the King of France and Louvois were pursuing their blockade of Luxembourg without opposition. But this was also an excellent moment for Michel Le Tellier and the two Colberts to encourage a faint revival of the Mazarin tradition. Why not lift the blockade temporarily and make an offer, as in 1664, to help Leopold against the Turks? It would, if accepted, again invite French armies into the Empire and, if rejected, improve their moral claim to pick up the pieces. Louis went along. He offered the emperor 30,000 troops, which were defiantly refused, and while the Turkish armies were besieging Vienna in 1683 the king resumed his pressures on Luxembourg. It was a disturbing year in many ways. Maria Theresa died, Jean Baptiste Colbert died, to be replaced by a Louvois man, Claude Le Peletier, and the Turks were repulsed, but Louis and Louvois, under less restraint than ever, did accomplish one of their favorite peacetime objectives, namely to provoke the Spanish into a declaration of war. As a result, in 1684 the king's armies besieged and took Luxembourg. There was still no one to stop him. That same year the Spanish and the emperor agreed to the Truce of Regensburg, which accepted all of Louis' reunions temporarily and postponed a final decision until 1704. He had, like so many aging men before him, been unable to fulfil all of his youthful dreams. He had not suppressed the heredity of judicial offices, he had not kept his budgets balanced, and he had not overthrown the system of Europe, but he had re-established religious uniformity, and no previous King of France had ever extended her frontiers so widely.[16]

The king had grown so accustomed to a certain level of population, a certain order of society, and a certain dominance of Europe that he almost considered himself as the arbiter of events. He was hoping, in that capacity, for a period of serenity, enjoying the company of Mme. de Maintenon, remodeling Versailles, and watching for the opportunity to pick up the entire Spanish succession. He did not sense that the stagnation of the mid-century was turning into a decline, nor did he sense that his subjects who had experienced no cataclysms for several generations were becoming less fearful of each other and more critical of him. What he did sense was the deterioration of his position in Europe, all the more unsettling since this was precisely what he had specialized in preventing. France was still the leading power, but suddenly his petty larcenies upon his neighbors took on a particularly villainous look in contrast to what Leopold and his allies were undertaking in the East, a great crusade against the Turks which was dramatically expanding his domains and reversing 300 years of Christian retreat. This unaccountable loss of grip was enough to restore Louis' confrontational philosophy to its fullest vigor. He had no doubt that his jealous enemies would soon be out to get him and that the slightest hint of concession on his part would be interpreted as a sign of weakness. He had by now deprived himself of any ministers who would help him to distinguish between efforts to maintain the *status quo* and imminent threats to his security. When the new King of England, James II, made a tenuous alliance with the Dutch merchant oligarchs for the mere defense of the Truce of Regensburg, the King of France took great umbrage. His new claims upon the Palatinate in 1685 seemed to presage a new round of violence just as the official revocation of the Edict of Nantes closed an old one. Le Tellier, the last of the original triumvirate, died, and when, the following year, the emperor, still engaged in fighting the Turks, Spain, caught up in her anxieties over a childless king, Sweden, always unreliable, and a number of German princes formed the League of Augsburg in the hope of collecting some 60,000 troops for the defense of the truce, Louis was visibly shaken. He not only wanted to dominate Europe. He expected an ironclad guarantee from all of his victims that they acquiesced in his right to do so. That same year, largely on the initiative of Croissy, the king began to press for the transformation of the truce into a permanent peace. A prince confident in his own strength was in no need of such paper guarantees. This was a loss of nerve and no one failed to observe it.[17]

Fortune may not have been smiling on Europe in 1687, condemned as it was to several decades of economic decline, but it was smirking at Louis XIV. Gone was his former flair for directing events. He employed a large part of his infantry in diverting waters to Versailles. The soldiers deserted or got sick. He hoped that the campaign in Hungary would go badly for the emperor. It went splendidly. But the straw that broke the king's back was about to be wafted from the Electorate of Cologne. His old client, the archbishop-elector, was approaching the end of his life, and there were two candidates for his succession, his long-time advisor and instrument of Louis' policy, the now Cardinal Wilhelm von Fürstenberg, and the elector's nephew, young Joseph Clement of Bavaria. Max Henry was for Cardinal Wilhelm rather than for Joseph Clement, and it seemed as if there would be no trouble at all in retaining the electorate in the French orbit. In January of 1688 the cathedral chapter elected Fürstenberg as coadjutor by an overwhelming majority, and there was every indication that on the elector's death, which occurred on June 3, Cardinal Wilhelm would be elevated to the electoral dignity by the necessary two-thirds vote. Instead, by another startling turn of events, he did not receive it. The choice of a successor now fell to none other than the king's bitter antagonist, Pope Innocent XI, and it is amusing to observe even Louvois at this point frantically attempting to work his charm upon the pope, who, of course, would have nothing of it and took the greatest of pleasure in postulating Joseph Clement. How critical, however, was this setback to the French monarchy? It was a question of perspective. Although the house of Bavaria was at that moment on good terms with Leopold, it seldom remained that way with the house of Habsburg for very long. The Electorate of Cologne was not exactly a dagger aimed at the heart of France, and, particularly in view of the latest turn of events, the burghers of Amsterdam had less reason than ever to subsidize William III, either in a war against Louis or in an attempt to dethrone the King of England. Yet the King of France seemed incapable of doing precisely what his enemies had done in 1672, namely wait and see. He could already visualize the emperor making peace with the Turks, William of Orange seducing the Dutch oligarchs, and the army of the League of Augsburg pounding at the gates of Paris. The solution that Louis applied in the shadow of his dilemma could not have been more predictable: a preemptive strike aimed at taking Philippsburg, immobilizing William III, and setting up one more impregnable line of defense. In October the French armies, preceded only by a self-righteous manifesto, invaded the Holy Roman Empire.[18]

While none of Louis' preemptive strikes had ever come close to their promises, his invasion of 1688 proved his most counter-productive. The military part did do its job of taking Philippsburg along with some other German strongholds on both sides of the Rhine. The problem was again one of disparity between physical power and its intended psychological effects. Rather than immobilizing William of Orange, the attack merely tipped the wavering Dutch into supporting his invasion of England, which, contrary to the King of France's second line of expectations, was an immediate success. He and his minister of war found that they had brought upon themselves precisely what they had been warned against over the years by Lionne and Pomponne: the union of England, the Dutch Republic, Leopold and the Empire into a permanent coalition against France. Never particularly rich in imagination, Louis was running out of alternatives and, most of all, of self-confidence. Confronted with the very war which he had sought to avoid, he and Louvois had no choice for the year 1689 but to stand on the defensive. Their best efforts at carrying out a scorched earth policy in the Palatinate, however, did not prevent the emperor and his allies, in the course of the same year, from recovering the key stronghold of Mainz. The king had neither the courage nor the gall to disgrace his indispensable minister of war, but it is clear that, in more rapid succession than ever before, he was revising his views and casting about for a scapegoat. The changes in the composition of the *conseil d'en haut* which occurred toward the end of the year indicated his search for more independent ministers. Le Peletier, for one thing, gave way to Pontchartrain. In 1690, as the league against France expanded to include Spain and Savoy, Louvois again managed to revive the fortunes of war, but when he died of a heart attack in June of 1691, Louis manifested how far he wished to go in emancipating himself from the ideas of his late all-powerful minister. The king immediately summoned to the *conseil d'en haut* the disgraced weakling who had gotten France out of the Dutch War, Arnauld de Pomponne, and if this display of contrition were not enough, Louis also called in an aristocratic model of pacifist piety, the Duke de Beauvillier. It was this ministry, led by Pomponne, which went back to the time-tested formulas for getting France out of a war: diplomatic concessions aimed at the weakest link in the opposition. But even though France returned to the defensive, the war bore frightfully on a declining population forced to support an army of over 300,000 men, and cries of discontent drifted up from the peasantry, through the *bourgeoisie*, to the nobility. The king knew he had contravened his own commandments. He would not have gone so far as to accept the platitudinous scoldings of the abbé de Fénelon, which Mme. de Maintenon was too shrewd to forward, but the work which does express Louis' official sentiments, Chamlay's *Mémoire historique*, shows the king prepared to admit some excesses: unjustified reunions, overly zealous dragonnades, wasteful use of troops on building projects, the very things which his new entourage could lay at the feet of the late Louvois. Pomponne, working first through Croissy and after his death in 1696 through his son and successor Torcy, finally broke the coalition by detaching the Duke of Savoy. By the time the Treaty of Ryswick was signed and the Nine Years' War was over, Louis had been taught a little respect for the system of Mazarin.[19]

The king had still another reason to regret his past impetuosity. No sooner had the war blessedly ended than the fading health of the King of Spain faced Europe with the issue of the Spanish succession. It is interesting to observe how Louis' perception of it had changed over the years. In his youth he had been more than willing to partition the Spanish monarchy for the benefit of his own. In his old age, he seemed less interested in the expansion of his own state than in securing the entire succession for his younger grandson, the Duke d'Anjou, this in spite of the historical lesson that the family bond would weaken over the generations. Had the king been able to cultivate his own garden between 1688 and 1697, he would have been in an excellent position to enforce his rights as he pleased. Now he was constrained to make the best possible settlement under the circumstances. He was not entirely without resources. He still had, through his wife and progeny, the most direct claims, followed by the Elector of Bavaria, whose son was a great grandchild of Philip IV, and by the emperor, whose male offsprings were merely descendants of Philip III. It seemed, moreover, as if popular and aristocratic opinion in Spain favored the French candidacy, the Spanish feeling that only Louis' protection could keep their monarchy intact. The problem was that the Queen of Spain, Maria Anna of Neuburg, controlled Carlos II dictatorially and would most certainly direct him to bequeath his monarchy to Leopold's younger son, the Archduke Charles. But the King of France had at his disposal the old Pomponne, who was an expert at navigating the system of Europe, and his new son-in-law Torcy, eager to be trained in the same tradition. The emperor's recent gains in the East permitted these ministers to revive the specter of Charles V. Their first effort was to approach Louis' old enemy William III, who had pushed his own Dutch and English constituencies to the limit during the war, on whether he would consent to the entire succession going to a Bourbon heir, with the exception of the Spanish Low Countries for the Elector of Bavaria. The king-stadholder said no. To him the establishment of a Bourbon dynasty in Spain was far more upsetting than the re-establishment of a Habsburg one. He suggested, however, that the entire succession be transferred to the young son of the Elector of Bavaria. Emotionally, this involved an immense sacrifice for the King of

France, and we may well imagine Pomponne, supported by Torcy, Beauvillier, and even Pontchartrain, reminding Louis that since the King of Spain intended to deliver his entire monarchy to the Archduke Charles, William's suggestion, if it were accompanied by some territorial compensation, would be infinitely more advantageous than placing a Bourbon on the throne of Spain. In the end it was arranged that the King of France would receive Naples and Sicily, the *presidi* of Tuscany, Finale, and the Spanish province of Guipuzcoa. Thus was concluded the secret partition treaty of 1698. It was a great *tour de force* by Pomponne and Torcy, but at the same time it required an extraordinary degree of unity between France and her new-found allies and an extraordinary display of passivity by her enemies in order to succeed.[20]

This desperate effort to recapture control of events, however, did not even get an opportunity to prove itself. In February of 1699 the agreed heir to the Spanish monarchy, the Electoral Prince Joseph Ferdinand, fell ill and died, thus reopening the entire question of the Spanish succession. We must now imagine Pomponne and Torcy trying to convince the king that since Carlos II was bound to bequeath his monarchy to the Archduke Charles, it might be just as well to accept the inevitable in return for adding Lorraine (whose duke would be transferred to Milan) to the French portion. It is a measure of the extent to which Louis was still caught up in the throes of repentance that he accepted this reasoning, and it is a measure of the extent to which the King of England felt unsure of his subjects that, by an agreement signed in June, he went along with it as well. In September Arnauld de Pomponne died, depriving the King of France of his most expert negotiator, and it was not until March of 1700 that the Dutch also affixed their signatures to the second partition treaty. Clearly, it was just as fragile as the first, if not more so, and as the moment of truth approached, the demeanor of France's new allies was hardly such as to inspire much confidence in their fidelity. Still, if the King of Spain had performed as expected and bequeathed his possessions to the archduke, Louis would probably have adhered to the treaty. He had no other choice, unless he wished to combat all of Europe. But neither he, nor the great Pomponne, nor any of the ministers had counted on the unpredictability of events in Spain. There the rumors of the partition treaties had confirmed the highest councillors in the view that only the protection of the King of France could maintain the territorial integrity of the Spanish monarchy. They convinced Carlos on his deathbed that he should make a will bequeathing the entire monarchy to the Duke d'Anjou, and if he refused, to the Archduke Charles.[21]

The courier from the French resident in Madrid reached Fontainebleau on the morning of 9th November, 1700, and once again Louis was presented with an eventuality for which he had been completely unprepared. That very afternoon he assembled a council in the apartment of Mme. de Maintenon. In attendance were the Dauphin, Pontchartrain, Beauvillier, and Torcy. Torcy had the first word, and it is hardly surprising that he was embarrassed. Upon him, since the death of Pomponne, fell the entire responsibility for having underestimated the surge of Spanish opinion. He had little choice but to continue discounting it. He emphasized the superiority of a unitary state and the value of adjoining provinces.

If the king accepted the testament, the ensuing war would be ruinous. He could expect little help from Spain, no sympathy from the rest of Europe, and after all his sacrifices, the Spanish Bourbons would eventually develop their own interests. But Louis did not seem to like what he was hearing, and the flustered Torcy refrained from concluding one way or the other. His arguments were strongly supported by the inflexible and principled Beauvillier. Pontchartrain, on the other hand, could afford to sound very different. He evoked the busy ghost of Charles V, counted all the economic advantages of a Spanish connection, and ended up with the homely reflection that even when families fought, they eventually kissed and made up. But Torcy and Beauvillier had already done the damage, and Pontchartrain did not conclude either, although his arguments were strongly supported by the uncharacteristically spirited Dauphin. The king, dissatisfied, undecided, or both, asked everyone to sleep on it and meet again the following day. Torcy was by this time desperately seeking to avert an acceptance. One sign of it was the letter which he wrote for Louis on the morning of the 10th begging Leopold to accept the partition treaty without delay. But that very afternoon a courier from the interim Spanish regency arrived, bearing the actual testament and preparing, if it were rejected, to move on to Vienna. This threat produced a dramatic shift of opinions in the council held that evening. Torcy was again the first to speak, but although he carefully recapitulated the arguments in favor of rejecting the testament, he also began to repeat many of Pontchartrain's arguments for accepting it, adding to them this one capital point: that the ill will of William III would make the war inevitable in any case. This time Torcy concluded in favor of accepting the testament, and Beauvillier was left alone. It was Pontchartrain who retreated a bit and left the final decision to the king, but the Dauphin held steadfastly for acceptance, and Louis felt sufficiently confident to make the most daring decision of his life.[22]

Although the reasoning which took place at Fontainebleau on 9th and 10th November, 1700 has been the subject of many reconsiderations, it may not be amiss to attempt a few more within the perspective of this essay. It is not at all apparent at first sight, but one of the most common features of both councils is the complete lack of consensus as to the guiding principles of the policy to be followed. Three years of debate over the merits of the partition treaties, the resilience of France, and the reliability of Spain were suddenly transformed by the news of the testament into mere accompaniments to meandering rhetoric. It is as if the ministers, sensing that the king had already settled the issues emotionally, became extremely reluctant to address them in detail. This also helps to explain the most striking difference between the two councils, namely the shift by Torcy from advocating one set of propositions passionately but inconclusively to supporting their opposite half-heartedly but definitively. His behavior may seem a bit peculiar, but then, what 35-year old minister who had been brought up on the story of Pomponne's fall was going to assume responsibility for the consequences of a moderate policy? The very nature of the point which Torcy adopted as conclusive — that the infidelity of the allies made the war inevitable — marks his abject surrender to the principle of the preemptive strike, for he could easily, before a different tribunal, have carried his argument one step further. It is true that some kind of war may have been inevitable, but only against the emperor and his son. All Louis had to do in case the allies did not cooperate was to order his troops into Guipuzcoa, Catalonia, and Navarre, announcing that he would withdraw the moment the new King of Spain accepted the partition treaty or its equivalent. If it is agreed that the king-stadholder could never have roused the English and Dutch into a war which would have violated his own treaty arrangements, this leads us into the last and perhaps most revealing feature of the two councils, namely that they show the King of France casting off his penitential robes and reverting to his old self. It was the same man who had invaded the Spanish Low Countries in 1667, the Dutch Republic in 1672, and the Holy Roman Empire in 1688 who accepted the will of the late King of Spain in November of 1700.

If Louis' preemptive action of 1688 was his most disastrous of this kind, his bold stroke of 1700 was his most successful. William III could only rage impotently. The worldwide Spanish monarchy greeted Philip V as its rightful ruler. Leopold moved menacingly but in isolation. The curse lay in the King of France's fatal flaw, his utter inability to leave well alone. Having liberated himself from his self-imposed restraints, he resumed his perennial quest for one more advanced position, one more demonstration of his power, one more acknowledgment by his enemies of his right to feel secure. Even as the King of England and the Dutch Republic were reluctantly recognizing the new King of Spain, Louis proceeded, at the behest of the Spanish government, to send his troops into the Spanish Low Countries and to expel the Dutch contingents stationed there. If this were not enough by way of provocation, French companies immediately obtained new trading privileges in the Spanish colonies. What it had taken him and Louvois nine years to bring about between 1679 and 1688, it took the king by himself nine months to conjure up in 1701, a grand alliance of continental and naval powers against France. And still he did not stop. There was his recognition on the death of James II of his son as King of England, just what was needed to coalesce English support behind William III. Nor did Louis drastically alter his prescriptions for waging war. In 1702, at the age of 64, he still felt he could demoralize his enemies by personally besieging Maastricht, the very extravaganza which had failed to conclude the Dutch War in 1673. It took the terrible defeats at Blenheim, Ramillies and Oudenarde, and the dreadful winter of 1709, to recall him to his mood of 1691, and the perspectives of his deathbed to convince him, before he could change his mind again, that he had loved war too much.[23]

NOTES

1. Fernand Braudel, *La Méditerranée et le monde méditerranéen à l'époque de Philippe II* (Paris, 1949); Immanuel Wallerstein, *The Modern World System* (New York, 1974), I; Michael Roberts, *The Military Revolution: 1560-1660* (Belfast, 1956); Roland Mousnier, *La Venalité des offices sous Henry IV et Louis XIII* (Rouen, 1945).

2. Wallerstein, II, Chs. 1-2; Mousnier, *passim*: R. H. Tawney, 'The Rise of the Gentry: 1558-1640', *Economic History Review*, XI (1941), pp. 1-58, Hugh Trevor-Roper, 'The

Gentry: 1540-1640', *Economic History Review*, Supplement 1 (1953); Lawrence Stone, *The Crisis of the Aristocracy: 1558-1641* (Oxford, 1965); Pieter Geyl, *Geschiedenis van de Nederlandse stam* (Amsterdam, 1948-58), I.

3. Georges d'Avenel, *Richelieu et la monarchie absolue* (Paris, 1884-95), 4 vols; Gabriel Hanotaux and Auguste de La Force, *Histoire du Cardinal de Richelieu* (Paris, 1896-1947), 6 vols; Henri Hauser, *La Pensée et l'action économiques du Cardinal de Richelieu* (Paris, 1952); C. V. Wedgwood, *The Thirty Years War* (1938).

4. Pierre Adolphe Chéruel, *Historie de France pendant la minorité de Louis XIV* (Paris, 1879-80), 4 vols; Pierre Goubert, *Louis XIV et vingt millions de Français (Paris, 1966);* Boris F. Porshnev, Frantsiia, angliskaia revoliutsiia, i evropeiskaia politika v seredine XVII veka (Moscow, 1970); John B. Wolf, *Louis XIV* (New York, 1968), Chs. 1-10; Andrew Lossky, 'France and the System of Europe in the Seventeenth Century', *Proceedings of the Western Society for French History*, I (1974), pp. 32-48; Louis XIV, *Mémoires for the Instruction of the Dauphin*, ed. Paul Sonnino (New York and London, 1970), pp. 23, 91.

5. Wolf, Chs. 11-4; Colbert's *Mémoires sur les affaires des finances de France pour servir à l'histoire*, published in *Lettres, instructions et mémoires de Colbert*, ed. Pierre Clément (Paris, 1861-82), II, pp. 17-68; Louis XIV, *Mémoires*, p. 43; Camille Rousset, *Histoire de Louvois* (Paris, 1862-3), I, pp. 34-68.

6. Louis XIV, *Mémoires*, pp. 28, 53, 46; Herbert H. Rowen, *The King's State* (New Brunswick, 1980), pp. 93-107.

7. *Avis sur l'annuel, Mémoire sur la reformation de justice …15 may 1665, Mémoire sur la guerre entre l'Angleterre et la Hollande*, published in *Lettres …de Colbert*, VI, pp. 247-9, 5-12, 244-7; Louis XIV, *Mémoires*, pp. 116-7, 41-4; Albert N. Hamscher, *The Parlement of Paris after the Fronde* (Pittsburgh, 1976), pp. 11-3, 190-1.

8. Louis XIV, *Mémoires*, pp. 122-4, 148-55, 180, 218-20; Rousset, I, pp. 82-98; *Avis du Vicomte de Turenne sur les affaires d'Angleterre & de Hollande, Instruction dressée par le Vicomte de Turenne pour le Marquis de Ruvigni, Projet de lettre du Roi d'Angleterre au Roi de France, redigé par le Vicomte de Turenne*, and *Mémoire sur les affaires d'Angleterre & de Hollande*, published in *Collection des lettres et mémoires trouvées dans les portefeuilles du maréchal de Turenne*, ed. Philippe Grimoard (Paris, 1782), I. pp. 663-6.

9. Paul Sonnino 'Louis XIV's *Mémoires pour l'histoire de la guerre de Hollande*', *French Historical Studies*, VIII, 1 (Spring, 1973), pp. 29-50, 'Hugues de Lionne and the Origins of the Dutch War', *Proceedings of the Western Society for French History*, III (1975), pp. 68-78, 'Louis XIV and the Dutch War', in *Louis XIV and Europe*, ed. R. M. Hatton (1976), pp. 153-78, 'Jean-Baptiste Colbert and the Origins of the Dutch War', *European Studies Review*, XIII (1983) pp. 1-11, 'The Marshal de Turenne and the Origins of the Dutch War', *Studies in History and Politics*, IV (1985), pp. 125-36.

10. *Ibid.*

11. *Ibid.*, as well as Cyril Hartmann, *Charles II and Madame* (1934), Ch. XIII.

12. See articles cited in note 9. For the initial strategy, see also the *mémoire* published by Georges Pagès in his *Contributions à l'histoire de la politique française en Allemagne sous Louis XIV* (Paris, 1905), pp. 35-41.

13. Simon Elzinga, *Het Voorspel van den Oorlog van 1672: De economisch-politieke betrekkingen tusschen Frankrijk en Nederland in de jaren 1660-1672* (Haarlem, 1926), Ch. IX; Herbert H. Rowen, *John de Witt, Grand Pensionary of Holland: 1625-1672* (Princeton, 1979), Chs. XXXV-VI; Haus-Hof-und Staatsarchiv *Friedensakten* 110, Konvolut 1670/71, fols. 4-9, *Gutachten*, August 8, 1670, *Frankreich Varia* 6, fols. (pt. 3) pp. 85-8, *Protocollum über den Foedus cum Gallo*, September 23, 1671, excerpted in Alfred Pribram, *Franz Paul Freiherr von Lisola: 1613-1674 und die Politik seiner Zeit* (Leipzig, 1894), pp. 502-3 and 527-9.

14. See articles cited in note 9 as well as Sonnino, 'Arnauld de Pomponne, Louis XIV's Minister for Foreign Affairs during the Dutch War', *Proceedings of the Western Society for French History*, I (1974), pp. 49-60. See also Armand de Feuquières, *Mémoires* (1775), pp. 36-7; Rousset, I, p. 532; Carl J. Ekberg, *The Failure of Louis XIV's Dutch War* (Chapel Hill,

1979); and Leon Bernard, 'French Society and Popular Uprisings under Louis XIV', *French Historical Studies*, III, 4 (1964), pp. 454–74.

15. See articles cited in notes 9 and 14. See also Gaston Zeller, 'Louvois, Colbert de Croissy et les réunions de Metz', *Revue historique*, CXXXI (1919), pp. 267–75, and Jean Orcibal, *Louis XIV et les Protestants* (Paris, 1951).

16. Bertrand Auerbach, *La France et le Saint-Empire romain germanique* (Paris, 1912), Ch. IV; Wolf, Ch. 25; Andrew Lossky, 'Maxims of State in Louis XIV's Foreign Policy in the 1680's', in R. M. Hatton and J. S. Bromley (eds.), *William III and Louis XIV: Essays 1680–1720 by and for Mark A. Thomson* (Toronto, 1968), pp. 7–23, as well as Lossky's 'The General European Crisis of the 1680's', *European Studies Review*, X (1980), pp. 177–97. See also Sonnino, 'Jean Racine and the *Eloge historique de Louis XIV*', *Canadian Journal of History*, VIII (1973), pp. 185–94.

17. Rousset, III, Ch. IV, and IV, Ch. VIII; Auerbach, Ch. IV; Richard Place, French Policy and the Turkish War: 1679–1688, (University of Minnesota Ph.D thesis, 1966).

18. Rousset, IV, Ch. IX; Richard Place, 'The Self Deception of the Strong: France on the Eve of the War of the League of Augsburg', *French Historical Studies*, VI, 4 (1970), pp. 459–73; Geoffrey Symcox, 'Louis XIV and the Outbreak of the Nine Years War', in *Louis XIV and Europe*, pp. 179–212; Richard Bingham, Louis XIV and the War for Peace: The Genesis of a Peace Offensive: 1686–1690, (University of Illinois at Chicago Circle Ph.D thesis, 1972).

19. Rousset, IV, Chs. IX–XIV; Wolf, Chs. 27–8; Bingham, *passim*; Heinrich Ritter von Srbik, *Wien und Versailles 1692–1697: Zur Geschichte von Strassburg, Elsass und Lothringen* (Munich, 1944); François de Fénelon, *Oeuvres* (Paris, 1850), III, pp. 425–9. See also Sonnino article cited in note 16 as well as Ronald Martin's 'The Authorship of 'Racine's' *Relation de ce qui s'est passé au siège de Namur*', in the same journal, pp. 195–200. Both suggest that the piece found in Archives de la Guerre *Série A*[1] 1183, Chamlay's *Mémoire historique de ce qui s'est passé depuis 1678 jusqu'à l'an 1688*, was written for Racine's use in the king's official history. Excerpts from this *mémoire* are published in Rousset, III, pp. 227, 233, 414, 432–3.

20. Arsène Legrelle, *La Diplomatie française et la succession d'Espagne* (Paris, 1888–92), 4 vols.

21. *Ibid.*

22. Compare the account of the first council in the *Mémoires de Saint-Simon*, ed. Alexandre de Boislisle (Paris, 1879–1930), VII, pp. 293–310, the project of Louis' letter to Villars, published in Legrelle, IV, pp. 466–7, and the account of the second council in the *Mémoires du Marquis de Torcy*, pp. 95–9, *Collection des mémoires relatifs a l'histoire de France*, ed. Petitot et Monmerqué, LXVII. Legrelle, IV, pp. 156–9, jumbles the accounts of the two councils together, leading him to conclude that one contradicts the other.

23. Legrelle, IV, Chs. VII–VIII; Wolf, Chs. 30–4. See the king's own *mémoire* in *A*[1] 1639, fols. 88–91, 92–102 (copy in Chamillart's hand on fols. 82–5), and 103–5, the last titled, *2e memoire pour 1703*.

5

ORIGINS OF WARS IN THE BALKANS, 1660–1792

Karl Roider

Before discussing the origins of wars in the Balkan Peninsula in the early modern period, one must take a step usually not needed in discussing wars in the remainder of Europe: one must define war itself. If war is identified as armed conflict between sovereign states, then twelve wars took place in the Balkans between 1660 and 1792, wars that covered 45 of those 132 years. These included five between the Ottoman Empire and the Habsburg Monarchy (1663–1664, 1683–1699, 1716–1718, 1737–1739, and 1788–1791), three between the Ottoman Empire and the declining power of Venice (1645–1669, 1684–1699, and 1715–1718), and four between the Ottoman Empire and the rising power of Russia (1710–1711, 1736–1739, 1769–1774, and 1787–1792).[1] War, however, is not always defined as armed conflict between sovereign states; it can include various forms of civil strife, religious conflict, and armed rebellion. If one accepts a broad definition of war, then it is possible to describe the early modern Balkans as being in a state of perpetual conflict. The American scholar Peter Sugar has written of the seventeenth and eighteenth centuries: if war denotes 'any armed action or conflict that either by its scope or . . . nature influences the lives of more people than those who took part in it, . . . we wind up with a picture of two hundred years of endemic war in the Balkans'.[2]

The fundamental cause of the ongoing hostilities was the decline of the Ottoman Empire in every phase of its existence: politically, militarily, socially, economically, and demographically. This decline gave rise to wars of all kinds. Heavy taxation by officials no longer concerned about administrative or judicial supervision inspired armed rebellion in many provinces; Ottoman troops, removed from Constantinople owing to the central government's fear of mutiny, introduced reigns of terror in outlying provinces against both the local population and the legally constituted authorities; and provincial governors, sometimes dispatched from Constantinople and sometimes locally selected, established semi-independent power bases from which they made war on neighboring provinces or even on the sultan himself. Adding to the general turmoil were the international wars as the surrounding powers took advantage of Turkey's increasingly miserable internal situation to lop off some of the sultan's territories.[3]

Given such troubles, in order to understand the causes of war in the early modern Balkans one must first appreciate the reasons for and the consequences of Ottoman decline. Traditionally, the primary reason cited by scholars for that decline was the desperately poor quality of the ruling sultans following the death of Suleiman the Magnificent in 1566. The rapid degeneration of the dynasty is usually attributed to two family policies introduced in the early decades of the seventeenth century. The first ended the custom of a sultan arranging for the murder of all the ruling family's other male members (except his own sons) upon his securing the throne. The males could now live, but, in order to make certain that none would become a rival to the reigning sultan, all of them were confined to special quarters in the palace and allowed no communication with the world outside. The second policy, introduced in 1617, arranged for the succession to pass not to the eldest son but to the oldest male of the ruling family. That meant that, from then on, the office of sultan would not pass to the last sultan's male offspring, who had been raised under fairly normal circumstances, but to his oldest living relative, who had spent his entire life in the luxury and dissipation of the palace. A state ruled by such men could not survive the vicissitudes of great power confrontations and could not resist the deterioration of central authority within the empire itself.[4]

Scholars have recently tended to minimize, although not to rule out, the role of the sultans as a cause of Ottoman decline. They have instead identified as the main cause what Peter Sugar has labeled the 'long war', a series of seemingly endless struggles that began in 1593 and lasted until 1702.[5] These wars included far more than just Ottoman conflicts in the Balkans against western European foes; they included hostilities against Poland and Russia in the Ukraine and against Persia in Mesopotamia and eastern Anatolia. These wars demanded ever-increasing numbers of men and amounts of money, both provided in the past primarily by the same system, that of the *timars*. As the Ottoman Empire had expanded in its early days, the sultan awarded to their warriors *timars*, grants of land that provided their proprietors (*timarlis*) with income so that they could continue to fight in the armies of the sultan. A *timar* was not private property; it remained in the hands of the *timarli* only so long as he provided military service. When he died, it passed back to the sultan for distribution to another warrior. Aside from providing the bulk of the armed forces of the empire at low cost to the central government, the *timar* system also provided an inexpensive administration, for the *timarlis* fulfilled the functions of government at the local level, especially in dealing with the Christian serfs who made up the work force on the *timars*.

The 'long war' dealt a devastating blow to the *timar* system. It did so first by causing the deaths of many *timarlis* in battle. While some historians have argued that the Ottoman Empire declined because it could not conquer any more land to give to its warriors, in fact by 1650 there was a surplus of *timars* and a shortage of warriors available to acquire them. This decline in the number of *timarlis* compelled the sultans to find other sources of manpower to compose their armies, and they did so generally by hiring mercenaries or at least by employing soldiers paid with cash and not with land. But here a second problem arose that contributed to the decline of the *timars*. To pay for such men and for the other expenses of ongoing war, the central government required ever-larger amounts of revenue, much of which had traditionally been collected by the *timarlis* from the peasant population. As the number of *timarlis* declined, tax collection at the local level became ever more uncertain. Consequently, the central government relied increasingly upon tax farmers, who paid to Constantinople a specified annual sum for the right to gather revenue for themselves from certain areas. But this method posed problems as well. While it provided money for the central government, tax farming for the investor was often a risky business. A tax farmer purchased his privilege for ready cash, but he was never certain if he could recoup his payment plus the anticipated profit before either his privilege expired or some unforeseen event in the capital city caused the central authorities to revoke his contract. Tax farmers therefore insisted upon some security for their investment, which the government often provided by granting to them full, private ownership of the lands they tax-farmed. In Ottoman terminology, that meant turning *timars*, traditional lands owned by the sultan and given only in exchange for military service, into *chiftliks*, lands privately owned by whoever could buy them.

The transformation of *timars* into *chiftliks* became increasingly widespread during the seventeenth and eighteenth centuries, and with it came fundamental changes in the relationship of all levels of society to each other and to the sultan. As the tax-farmers gained full possession of their properties and the security that accompanied it, other elements of Ottoman society demanded and received the right to do the same. Ottoman administrators, Moslem officials, well-to-do Christians, and even *timarlis* purchased landed property from the central government. Especially favored officials were awarded not only personal ownership of land but often as tax-free holdings, which removed at times sources of considerable revenue from the tax rolls. The best example was the city of Athens, awarded as personal property to the *kizlar aga*, the chief of the black eunuchs of the harem, who from then on collected for his personal use the revenue that formerly went to the sultan.[6]

The spread of the *chiftliks* meant more than just the expansion of private landholding in the Ottoman Empire. It also meant the forfeiture by the central government of much of its authority in the countryside, and that was especially hard on the peasants who worked the land. Under the *timarlis*, the peasants not only enjoyed specific rights protected by Moslem laws but also the presence of nearby Moslem judicial and administrative officials to enforce those laws. In the *chiftlik* system, those protections vanished. The peasant was reduced to the status of property along with the land he worked. To make matters worse, in many cases the owner of the *chiftlik* was an absentee, interested only in the amount he could extract from his new lands and not at all in the wellbeing of the people on them. In other words, most peasants now faced the increasing exploitation of their labor and produce with decreasing opportunities to appeal to governmental authority for relief.

Many Balkan peasants did not accept this change in conditions peacefully. Those who resisted resorted either to migration into nearby mountains, to the protection of a local strong man who might offer better conditions under which they could work, or, if they were hardy and belligerent, to the formation of bandit groups. It was the increasing number of bandit groups that brought about the prevalence of violence in the Balkans, a violence that often took on the characteristics of civil war. The fury of these bands was directed largely at the *chiftliks* and their owners or managers. They stormed manor houses, murdered the occupants, set fire to barns and storehouses, and stole food and goods. They struck particularly at the possessions of prominent men such as Ottoman viziers and the sultan's favorites. *Chiftliks* were not, however, the only targets; the bandits attacked the property of prosperous merchants, trading convoys, treasure trains, town markets, and rich bazaars. They especially sought out tax collectors whom they robbed and killed.[7] While too much has been made of the proto-nationalist or Robin Hood-like character of these people, it is true that they envisioned themselves as fighting against the oppression of their fellow peasants and for Christianity — Orthodox Christianity — against Islam. The peasants understood and appreciated what these men were doing; they often hid the bandits, gave them food and supplies, refused to identify them for the authorities, and obstructed the authorities in their searches for them. They also encouraged the anti-Islamic nature of the resistance, providing the bandits with striking articles of clothing such as brightly colored shirts or feathers for their hats so that they could openly defy the Ottoman law that prohibited Christians from wearing ostentatious or bold dress.[8]

Lest the reader get the impression that the internal warfare that plagued the Ottoman Empire consisted solely of Christian bandits attacking Moslem property owners, it must be noted that a number of offices in the Ottoman military establishment were held by Christians, and Christian forces often joined in the suppression of Christian bandits.[9] Moreover, Christian bandits by no means confined their attacks to Moslems only; they often robbed wealthy Christians, and, at times when food was scarce or honor at stake, they battled with each other. There even existed Moslem bandit groups, but in insignificant numbers compared to the Christian bands.[10]

The prevalence of banditry and its accompanying violence increased markedly in the late seventeenth and eighteenth centuries. It did so not only because of the spread of *chiftliks*, but also as a direct consequence of the military campaigns that made up the period of the 'long war'. The international wars transformed in some provinces what was traditional banditry into full-scale revolt against the Ottoman state. The Candian War, fought between the Ottoman Empire and Venice from 1645 to 1669, and the Ottoman–Habsburg war of 1683–1699 gave rise in Montenegro to a movement for independence that featured bandit groups led by Orthodox clergymen. Montenegro had always been one of the most difficult of the Balkan provinces for the Ottomans to subdue and an area where banditry was a particularly honored way of life. As the Ottomans struggled against the Venetians and the Austrians, the Montenegrins first refused to pay tribute and then attacked and robbed Turkish Officials and Moslem residents. In response, the Turks seized Christian property, burned villages, held hostages, and displaced Christian clans, all of which led only to greater resistance. On the nature of this strife, Wayne Vucinich has written: 'The Turks initially viewed their armed encounters with the Montenegrins as punitive expeditions, but for the Montenegrins every encounter with the Turks was a war, even though some Turkish armed forays against them were not ordered by the sultan but were the work of unruly local chiefs'.[11] The high point in this struggle — according to Montenegrin tradition — came in 1711 when Peter I of Russia, as part of his appeal for a general rising of the Balkan Christians against the Turks, dispatched money and two Russian officers to the Montenegrins to assist their armed resistance. The money and officers did not lead to a Montenegrin victory, but from then on the Montenegrins looked upon Russia as the great savior who would some day assist them in a successful war of liberation.[12] While some historians have dismissed the Montenegrin trouble as not a full-scale civil war but only more evidence of Ottoman difficulty in controlling their provinces, the Montenegrins themselves had no doubt that they were fighting a major conflict against Turkish tyranny.

The Montenegrin experience was not the only one that turned from localized banditry into widespread revolt in the wake of an international war. In the Serbian lands in the mid-seventeenth century, bandit activity had likewise intensified as the *chiftlik* system became the common form of property-holding and social control. Then in the 1680s this banditry took the form of a liberation movement in response to the great victories achieved by the Holy League — an alliance of Austria, Venice, Poland, and the Papacy — against the Turkish armies first in Hungary and then in Serbia proper. Assisting the forces of the Christian powers were Serbian bandit groups that ranged far and wide as scouts, raiders, guides, skirmishers, and foragers. In 1690 the withdrawal of many Habsburg troops for duty against the armies of Louis XIV and a successful Ottoman counter-offensive exposed many of these men and their families to reprisals as the Ottomans reasserted their control over Serbia. To escape Turkish vengeance and in response to Habsburg promises of religious toleration and economic wellbeing, about 200,000 Serbs under the leadership of Arsenije III Crnojevich, metropolitan bishop of Peć, crossed the Danube and Sava rivers into Austrian-held territory, where they established a Serbian society of some significance and reinforced the Serbs of the Military Border, the official Habsburg institution in the Balkans to protect the monarchy's lands from Turkish raids.[13]

As banditry and incipient civil war spread throughout their Balkan provinces, the Ottomans set out to quell them, but they did so in ways that usually stimulated rather than diminished the growing violence. A truly calamitous decision reached by Constantinople was to send the janissaries into the countryside to impose order. When organized initially in the fourteenth century, the janissaries were a small, elite fighting force recruited from slaves who had been gathered as small boys, converted to Islam, and trained as soldiers. They became the backbone of the Ottoman army, so proficient in arms that it was said that in battle the sultan was safer among his janissaries than inside a stone fortress. By the mid-seventeenth century the janissaries had deteriorated dramatically. Initially a group of celibate, dedicated soldiers, in the early 1500's they had won the right to marry, followed shortly thereafter by the right to engage in trade and manufacturing, and then by the right to enroll their sons in the corps. By 1650 they constituted no longer an elite fighting force but a huge, hereditary interest group intent on protecting its real and perceived privileges — by violence if necessary. Because the central government now feared the janissaries, it began sending them into the provinces both to put down bandits and other threats to Ottoman authority and to prevent mutinies by them in the capital.

The arrival of the janissaries in a province usually meant not the restoration of order but its further deterioration. Generally a small group of military janissaries (of the 400,000 janissaries enrolled in 1800, approximately 20,000 could still provide effective military service[14]) would gather about them armed bands of auxiliaries and descend upon the countryside where they exploited peasants and landlords alike. They forced peasants to pay added taxes, tribute, and protection money, murdered local leaders, confiscated manor houses, defied authorities, and sometimes simply took effective control of whole provinces. Since the central government could not subdue these men, local popular forces rose to do so, sometimes in alliance with the legally constituted officials and sometimes not; in any case, the violence in those areas intensified.

All of these intertwined developments — the 'long war', the weakening of central authority, the spread of the *chiftlik* system, the upsurge in banditry, and the terror perpetrated by the janissaries and their cohorts — had a profound impact on Balkan society. The most pronounced result was a decline in population. International war, a lower birthrate, the destruction that accompanied the lawlessness, and continuing plague had such an impact upon the population of the Balkans that some areas became totally empty. Besides simple population loss, this period also witnessed considerable population movement. As the Serbs involved in the war of 1683–1699 fled Serbia for southern Hungary — thus making that region primarily Slavic — the land they left behind, notably the epic Serbian heartland of Kosovo-Metohija, became peopled by Albanians. Bulgarians moved southward from their traditional areas into the depopulated lands of Macedonia, while many urban Jews, fearful of the growing religious intolerance fueled by the prevailing anarchy, left Ottoman cities altogether to take up residence in western Europe.[15] Accompanying the decline in population came a decline in economic productivity, which meant of course less revenue for the central government. That in its turn encouraged the sale of more land as *chiftliks*, thus exacerbating the conditions that led to the violence and loss of population in the first place.

The degeneration of the Ottoman Empire would have been unfortunate for its government and society at any time, but it happened to occur when two of its enemies, Austria and Russia, were undergoing a centralization and military strengthening that made them more than ever a threat to Turkey's existence. It is the wars between the Ottoman Empire on the one hand and the Habsburg Monarchy and Russia on the other that command the Balkan international scene in the early modern era. These were not wars that simply repeated one another in the similarity of their causes, progress, and effects. The last wars of the seventeenth century resembled the many previous wars fought between the Ottoman Empire and various Christian powers. They were generally incited by struggles for influence along ill-defined borders and usually featured an invasion of Christian lands by Ottoman armies of considerable size. A major element in these wars was always religious enthusiasm, as the leaders and people on both sides participated in prayers and ceremonies exhorting the Almighty to inflict the greatest possible harm upon the unbelievers of the opposing side.[16] In contrast, the religious element faded in the wars of the eighteenth century. In western Europe religion itself lost considerable influence as the men of the Enlightenment labeled all faiths as encouraging ignorance, superstition, and intolerance — the very qualities that had for centuries encouraged the especially vicious warfare between Moslem and Christian in the Balkans. But the more important reason for the decline of religious enthusiasm in the international wars in the Balkans was the decline of the Ottoman Empire itself. As the empire's internal affairs grew increasingly chaotic, whipping up fervor for a Moslem war against a Christian great power was lost in the social, religious, and political struggles within the empire itself. And as the western powers saw more and more evidence of Ottoman decline, defending Christianity against oncoming Moslem hordes became an idea of the past. European statesmen in the eighteenth century came to view the Ottoman Empire no longer as the arch enemy of Christendom but as one of the players — and increasingly as one of the spoils — in the great game of war and diplomacy.

The first complete, international Balkan war to occur in the period from 1660 to 1792 was that between the Habsburg Monarchy and the Ottoman Empire in 1663-1664. Its cause was meddling by Austria in the autonomous principality of Transylvania, formally a tributary state of the sultan but for much of the early seventeenth century a state that had become practically independent. Transylvanian independence and Austrian meddling were nothing new in Balkan politics, but what made them a cause for war at this time was a temporary revival of Ottoman power carried out by the first two of the Köprülü grand viziers, members of the Köprülü family that dominated politics in Constantinople between 1656 and 1702. These two grand viziers, Mehmed (1656-1661) and his son Ahmed (1661-1676), were determined to reassert the sultan's authority over areas where it had grown lax, and one of those areas was Transylvania. Since 1648 Prince George II Rákóczy, the ruler of that land albeit at the sultan's discretion, had carried on as if he were the sovereign of a considerable power, even entering a war between Sweden and Poland (1655-1660) in hopes of becoming the latter country's king. Displays of such independence by an Ottoman vassal were too much for Mehmed Köprülü, who sent a military expedition to Transylvania, deposed Rákóczi, and established a more compliant prince on the throne, but one whom the Habsburgs refused to recognize and conspired to overthrow.

This Habsburg interference in Transylvania led Ahmed Köprülü (who had become grand vizier following his father's death in 1661) to organize an army of approximately 120,000 men and march into Austrian territory. The ensuing campaign had all of the features of the old wars of Christendom versus Islam. The Ottoman army had its usual array of Moslem troops including the dreaded Crimean Tartars while the Habsburg army consisted not only of Austrians but of volunteers from all over Christian Europe including full contingents from various German states and even a French regiment sent by Louis XIV. These two armies collided in August, 1664 at St. Gotthard on the Raab River in western Hungary, where the Christian forces inflicted a significant defeat upon the Ottomans.

Fearful, however, of potential trouble with France in the west, Vienna did not pursue the victory but concluded an immediate peace, a peace both beneficial to and welcomed by the Turks, who had been surprised by their unexpected defeat.[17]

In terms of international warfare, the Balkans remained peaceful for almost twenty years thereafter, as the Ottomans conducted campaigns against the Russians and the Poles in the Ukraine and the Habsburgs focused their attention on the French. In 1683, however, there erupted a Habsburg–Ottoman war with causes similar to those in 1663 but with far more significant results. The issue this time was not Transylvania and its Ottoman overlords but ongoing trouble between the independent-minded nobility of Habsburg Hungary and their sovereign in Vienna (at this time Hungary was divided into Habsburg and Ottoman Hungary, the larger part being the latter). Throughout the 1670s the Hungarian nobles and the Habsburgs had engaged in growing animosity over the monarchy's religious and constitutional policies. In the course of this trouble, some Hungarian noblemen appealed to the sultan for help in resisting what they believed were Habsburg encroachments upon their rights. This appeal was welcomed by Ahmed Köprülü's successor as grand vizier, Kara Mustafa Köprülü, a man both less talented and less successful than the first two Köprülüs. Why he chose to assist the Hungarian insurgents is still unclear, but two likely reasons were the insecurity he felt because he was not a direct descendent of the first two Köprülüs and the unfortunate result of his first military effort as grand vizier in which he had been defeated by the Russians and forced in 1681 to cede to them the western Ukraine, a land that his predecessor had wrested from Poland in 1676. His eagerness to make war on the Habsburgs may have stemmed from his desire to achieve a spectacular success so that his humiliation at Russian hands would be forgotten.[18]

Whatever motivated Kara Mustapha to begin this war, the Austrians clearly wished to avoid it. Between 1678 and 1681 Vienna sent a number of diplomatic delegations to Constantinople to renew past peace settlements, but all were unsuccessful. In fact, all were greatly impressed by the growing martial spirit among Ottoman officials and warned Vienna that the viziers were contemplating an invasion of Austria. While still hoping to avoid hostilities, Vienna in 1681 decided that war seemed likely and began to seek monetary and military aid from other European sources. As in 1663 the preparations for war at this time took on the spirit of a crusade. Again volunteers and contingents from western Europe — and an army from Poland — marched to help the Austrians, while clerics and popularizers issued ringing appeals to all Christians to strike down the infidels. Again the Turkish leaders marched up the military road from Constantinople with a huge army — possibly 200,000 men — the Tartars in front spreading mayhem and destruction as they advanced into Christian territory. The objective this time was Vienna itself, which the Turks reached in July 1683. A siege ensued that lasted for two months, until 12 September when a multi-national force of Austrians, German imperial troops, European volunteers and Poles poured from the Vienna woods and utterly routed the besieging Turks. The Ottoman troops fled before the oncoming Christians, abandoning weapons, stores, vehicles and treasures in their frantic rush to escape.

The victory was a resounding one for the Habsburgs and their allies, but in the long view of history what made this event truly remarkable was not the victory itself but the war that followed it, a war that lasted until 1699 and in its progress not only won for Austria possession of most of Ottoman Hungary and Transylvania but revealed those defects in the Ottoman system that were rotting its economic, social, and political structure. The great war that resulted from the relief of Vienna can be traced to the Austrians' decision to pursue their victory, remarkable in itself since the Austrians were notorious for failing to take advantage of their successes. The reason offered for this unusual decision and the doggedness with which the Austrians pursued it was the triumph of the 'eastern party' over the 'western party' among the advisers of Emperor Leopold I. In the autumn of 1683 the core of the eastern party, consisting of the papal nuncio, the Venetian ambassador, and the commander of the Habsburg forces, persuaded Leopold that the time had come for the Austrians to remove once and for all time the Ottoman threat to central Europe and, in doing so, to add territory to the monarchy that would give the emperor sufficient resources to deal effectively with his enemies in the west.[19]

Undoubtedly these arguments were persuasive, but one must not overlook at this time the religious appeal of such a campaign, especially for a man as devout as Leopold I. It provided more than an opportunity to conquer territory and to confound his western enemies; it offered the opportunity to strike a lasting blow for the true faith. For these reasons Leopold accepted the advice of his easterners. He formed an impressive anti-Ottoman coalition with Poland, Venice, the Papacy, and later Russia, and waged generally successful war against the Turks for the next sixteen years. The crowning blow came in 1697 when forces commanded by the young Prince Eugene of Savoy destroyed an entire Ottoman army at the battle of Zenta, killing in the mêlée the grand vizier and many prominent Turkish officials. The result was the Treaty of Carlowitz in 1699 that formally ceded to the Habsburgs most of Ottoman Hungary (except an area in the south known as the Banat of Temesvar) and Transylvania.[20]

As mentioned earlier, the causes of international war in the early modern Balkans prior to 1699 had been like those of centuries before: resistance to Ottoman expansionism, Moslem-Christian antagonism, and disputes along the borderlands and in the tributary states separating the great powers. Surrounding all of these causes was the general acknowledgment of Ottoman military superiority. After 1699 the causes of war in the Balkans reflected in one way or another the acknowledgment of Ottoman decline. In fact, in the 1690s Austria had not been the only power to inflict serious losses on the Turks; Russia had done so as well. Although one might imagine Russo-Turkish hostilities to be a product of the distant past, in fact the initial encounter between Russian and Ottoman regular troops (except for a brief skirmish that occurred during the reign of Ivan the Terrible) came in 1677 at the beginning of the first Russo-Turkish war. From then on, however, Russo-Turkish conflicts were frequent and bloody. In 1695 they reached a milestone, when a Russian army under the command of Tsar Peter I besieged the fortress of Azov on the Sea of Azov, the first time the Russians seriously threatened to reach the Black Sea. The following year Azov fell to the

Russians, and in 1697 the tsar concluded with Austria a formal anti-Ottoman alliance, the first of many to come. This alliance lasted only until the Treaty of Carlowitz in 1699, but it prophesied the appearance of Russia as a force to contend with in south-eastern Europe.

The recognition of Ottoman decline meant different things to the different powers interested in the Balkans. For Russia Ottoman decline offered opportunity for expansion, either in the form of direct conquest of territory or in the guise of liberator of the Balkan Orthodox Christians from Ottoman rule. Indeed, when he marched southward in 1711, Peter issued proclamations to the Serbs, Greeks, Montenegrins, Wallachians, and Moldavians announcing his eagerness to free them from the Turkish yoke in the name of Orthodoxy. As we have seen, these proclamations inspired some of the Balkan peoples to rise up, and the memories of the proclamations and the risings certainly contributed for the remainder of the century to the ongoing turmoil in the Balkan provinces of the Ottoman Empire. Regardless of the form it took, however, the Russians' gaining influence in the Balkans would likely lead to their acquiring control in some way of Constantinople and the Straits, which would represent not only a religious triumph in the return to Orthodoxy of its holiest city but also a strategic and economic bonanza in Russia's gaining access to the Aegean and Mediterranean seas.

For Austria Ottoman decline also offered opportunity for expansion, but the Austrians were not so certain that they wished to take advantage of it. In the eighteenth century, loyalty to a state or to a sovereign was not seen in Vienna as being predicated on nationalism or regionalism but on religion. Habsburg officials assumed that Roman Catholics would be loyal to the emperor, Protestants to the king of Prussia, Jews and Moslems to the sultan, and Orthodox Christians to the tsar. The conquest of additional Balkan lands would thus bring under the Habsburg sceptre large numbers of Orthodox, whose loyalty to the monarchy might be questionable at best. Besides, whereas Russian expansion into the Balkans could lead to the conquest of Constantinople and the Straits and the achievement of clearly defined religious, strategic and economic gains, the geography of the area dictated that Austrian expansion south-eastward would add to the monarchy little more than thousands of square miles of underpopulated, impoverished and unpromising lands that would require enormous investment both to protect and develop with no guarantee that such an investment would ever bring adequate returns. Indeed, the decades-long Habsburg effort to populate and to improve the relatively small Banat of Temesvar (annexed by Austria in 1718) brought such meager advantages that the government must have paled at the thought of trying to bring the same progress to territory vastly greater in area. Perhaps Maria Theresa in 1777 summarized best the reasons why conquering the Balkans would bring little benefit to the monarchy: 'What can we gain from such conquests, even to the gates of Constantinople? Provinces unhealthy, depopulated, or inhabited by treacherous and ill-intentioned Greeks [Orthodox] — they would not strengthen the monarchy but weaken it'.[21]

For the Ottomans the decline of their own empire was expressed in frustration, anxiety, and wonder, feelings that at times brought surges of westernizing reform and just as often the reassertion of traditional Islamic practices, especially when the Moslem establishment blamed the empire's degeneration on Allah's anger at seeing too great a western influence on Ottoman politics and society. The ensuing struggles between reformers and traditionalists contributed not to Ottoman resurgence but to its continuing decay. One might imagine that, given Ottoman weakness and Austrian and Russian strength, the relations among these powers would be characterized by Austrian and Russian aggressiveness and Ottoman conciliation. In fact, of the five wars fought in the eighteenth century, the Turks declared war first in four of them. Lest the reader wonder at what seems to be remarkable Turkish recklessness, he should be assured that such declarations were expressions of Turkish anxiety rather than confidence, reflecting both a fear of growing debility and a wish to belie that fear by an act of aggression.

Given these assumptions, it is possible to identify at this time the beginnings of what diplomats and historians would later call the Eastern Question, loosely defined as the worry that inevitable Ottoman collapse would lead to a vacuum in the south-east, a vacuum that the Russians would seek to fill in order to become a significant power not only in the Balkans but in the Aegean and Mediterranean seas as well. The first state to appreciate that emerging problem and to express concern about it as a matter of policy was Austria. In 1709, as part of the Great Northern War between Russia and Sweden, the Russians under Peter I crushed the Swedish army of King Charles XII at the Battle of Poltava in the southern Ukraine. At the battle's end Charles fled to Ottoman territory, where the sultan granted him asylum and where he began to lobby vigorously for an Ottoman declaration of war on Russia. At the same time but for different reasons, Vienna was concerned that the sultan might declare war on Austria. Since Austria and Russia both seemed threatened by Turkey, the question arose among the emperor's advisers as to whether Vienna should seek a formal, anti-Ottoman alliance with Russia for their mutual defense. It was in the debate over this question that an awareness of what would become the Eastern Question appeared. All of the advisers agreed that the Russians might aid Austria significantly should Turkey attack, but they also wondered as to what might happen in the ensuing war if the Russians emerged victorious over the Turks. If they did, the Russians might extend their influence into the Balkan Peninsula and perhaps right to the Austrian border. Indeed, the advisers counselled the emperor, 'If the tsar is victorious, he could throw himself into Turkish territory as far as the Danube and possibly force his way to Constantinople'.[22] And that, they agreed, could be more dangerous for Austria's future than keeping the Ottoman Empire as master of the Balkan Peninsula. That sounded a theme that would later be repeated often in Austrian foreign policy circles: it was better to have a weak Turkey as a neighbor than a strong Russia.

Implicit in these expressions was the perception that Turkey was becoming too weak to defend itself. That perception was underscored in 1711 when, at the outbreak of another Russo-Turkish war, many European diplomats and even newspapers predicted certain Russian victory.[23] This war was begun by the Turks, who had succumbed to the pleas of Charles XII and of the khan of the Crimea to drive the Russians back from the Ukraine. It was the Russians, however, who took the initiative, their army marching southward under Peter's personal command as far as the Pruth River and thus entering the Balkans in force for the first time. To the surprise of everyone concerned, the Russians achieved not victory but defeat. At Stănilesti on the Pruth, Peter found himself and his army surrounded by Turks, and he was able to escape only by offering considerable concessions and distributing generous bribes to the Ottoman leaders.[24]

This Turkish victory did not, however, spark any significant reappraisal of the balance of power in south-eastern Europe. Most observers regarded the Ottoman success as little more than an interlude in its decline. Four years later, as the Austrians were contemplating another war against the Turks, the Habsburg envoy in Constantinople advised Vienna: 'Now exists the opportunity not only to defeat the Turks, who, in the opinion of knowledgable and experienced people, are in a very wretched state, but also, God willing, to throw them completely out of Europe'. The Ottoman army, he continued, was 'more accustomed to flight than to victory' and could not stand up to even '30,000 well-led Germans'.[25]

An opportunity to test this assessment came in 1715 when the sultan declared war on Venice. The formal reasons were Turkish anger at Venetian support for the Montenegrins during their rising in 1711 and the seizure of an Ottoman ship carrying the harem of a high-ranking official.[26] In fact, the war was an act of revenge against Venice for its participation in the war of 1683–1699 and its annexation of the Morea (Peloponessus) at Ottoman expense. Ottoman leadership could accept defeat at the hands of a great power like Austria, but losing to Venice, not only a lesser power but an increasingly weaker one, was difficult for Constantinople to stomach. European envoys at the Ottoman capital had reported throughout the first decade of the eighteenth century that, of the territory lost in the recent war, the Turks resented most the loss of the Morea.[27] In the spring of 1715 Ottoman troops invaded that land.

The question asked by all sides at the invasion's opening was whether Austria would come to Venice's aid. After all, Austria and Venice had together fought against the Turks in the war of 1683–1699, and Venice appealed to Vienna to do so again in the name of the Holy League. Since 1700, however, Venice and Austria had not been on the best of terms; the two powers had been at times hostile during the War of the Spanish Succession, and Vienna had been particularly angered by Venetian efforts to keep the Adriatic Sea closed to Habsburg shipping. Yet, Vienna also had no desire to see the Turks reassert their authority over any previously lost territory, because it might give them the confidence to resume the contest for control of Hungary. Moreover, Vienna — in this case particularly Prince Eugene, now the monarchy's premier military figure — saw the war as an opportunity to secure Austria's new Hungarian possessions, particularly by conquering the Banat of Temesvar, the last Ottoman holding in Hungary, and the fortress-city of Belgrade, the defensive bastion straddling both the middle Danube and the great military road between Constantinople and Vienna.[28]

At Prince Eugene's urging, Emperor Charles VI declared his support for Venice in May, 1716, and in the summer and autumn of that year the Habsburg army under the prince's command crushed a major Turkish field force and conquered the Banat, thus achieving one of Vienna's goals. The following year the prince enjoyed more success, routing yet another Turkish army and capturing Belgrade and its surroundings.[29] These victories seemed to portend the end of the Ottoman Empire in Europe, for, after the destruction of two of his armies in two years, the sultan could scarcely prevent the Austrians from marching to the walls of Constantinople if they chose to do so. But the Austrians advanced no farther, in part because of a Spanish invasion of the then Habsburg island of Sardinia but also because they already questioned the advisability of bringing so much of the Balkans into the monarchy. Prince Eugene in particular believed that there was little point in annexing more Balkan land. In mid-1718, when queried as to whether Vienna should demand further territories east of Belgrade as part of the peace settlement, he remarked in terms that others would repeat later: 'I do not find that Your Majesty would be well served by these faraway places because their distance and difficult communication would cause more problems than advantages and their situation would demand half again as many obligations'.[30]

As Austrian enthusiasm for Balkan acquisitions declined, Russian enthusiasm rose. As a consequence of the defeat in 1711, Peter had given up the lands that he had acquired from the Turks in the 1690s, including Azov, and had undertaken no additional campaigns to retake them or to gain other territory that might give Russia access to the Black Sea. Following Peter's death in 1725, foreign policy in Russia became the province of a man who had served as one of his advisers and who had shared his ambitions, Count Heinrich Ostermann, a Westphalian by birth. Ostermann dreamed of realizing the one goal that had eluded Peter: securing the northern coast of the Black Sea for Russia. By the early 1730s conditions seemed favorable for achieving that goal. Internally Russia was enjoying stability under Tsarina Anne; the Ottoman Empire was weakened even more by a war with Persia; Sweden and Poland, two potentially hostile neighbors, were reasonably friendly; and Austria was an ally dating from a treaty signed in 1726. In 1735 Ostermann seized upon a Tartar incursion into Russian territory as an excuse to declare war, and in the autumn of that year Russian troops marched toward the Black Sea.

As this war began there seemed again little doubt that Russia would inflict a serious defeat upon the Turks. The commander of the Russian army, Burchard Münnich, confidently proclaimed that he would overrun the Crimea, seize the Black Sea coast, occupy the Romanian principalities of Moldavia and Wallachia, cross the Danube, and finally march on the Ottoman capital itself. To Anne he wrote, 'The banners and standards of the tsarina will be erected, where? ... In Constantinople! The tsarina will be crowned empress of the Greeks in the oldest Greek church, in the renowned cathedral of Santa Sophia, and will bring peace — to whom? ... to the whole world'.[31] These words might sound like so much bravado, but, given Turkish weakness, many Europeans thought them by no means empty boasts. In Vienna especially, the emperor's ministers echoed the concerns expressed in 1710 that a Russo-Turkish war would result in the Russian acquisition of much of the Balkans and a neighbor on Austria's border considerably more dangerous than a declining Turkey. Yet the Austrians certainly could not assist the Ottoman Empire in resisting Russian aggression. Not only was Russia an ally but it had done Austria good service in the recently concluded War of the Polish Succession. Moreover, Austria could not very well come to Turkey's aid directly, for the old Austro-Turkish antagonism had by no means disappeared; Turkey was still spoken of publicly as the arch enemy of Christendom.

Austria, then, had to compose a policy that would both maintain the Austro-Russian alliance and concurrently restrict Russian conquests at Ottoman expense. To achieve these apparently contrary goals, the Austrian policy-makers decided to declare war on the Ottoman Empire as Russia's ally and then to keep a close watch (and presumably act as a brake) on Russian military advances.[32] It was a complex, some might say silly, policy, but it was never properly tested because the very premise upon which it was based, Russian victory, did not come to pass. In three years of fighting, the Austrians and Russians suffered disappointment after disappointment, mostly because of their own foolishness rather than a resurgence of Turkish military might. The end came in fitting fashion: a series of misinterpreted communications, faulty assessments, and unverified rumors seduced an Austrian soldier/diplomat into concluding the Treaty of Belgrade, by which Austria surrendered to Turkey all of Serbia including mighty Belgrade itself. Although the Russians howled at what they labeled Austrian cowardice, they quickly agreed to the treaty's provisions, which for Russia meant the restoration of the *status quo ante bellum* and continued exclusion from the Black Sea.

The war of 1737–1739 was a Turkish victory. Yet, like their victory in 1711, it neither halted Ottoman decline nor altered the perception of that decline in the west. Even as the Austrian ministers were debating whether to sacrifice Belgrade to restore peace, one minister remarked that such a concession would be temporary because chronic Turkish debility would allow the Austrians to retake it very soon.[33] But Belgrade was not retaken quickly, for in 1740 Frederick II of Prussia invaded Silesia, an event that turned the attention of all the European great powers away from the Balkans for almost three decades.

Not until 1768 was there another international war in the Balkans, again between Russia and the Ottoman Empire. The underlying cause rested in events in Poland. If the Ottoman Empire were declining steadily in the eighteenth century, Poland was declining precipitously. A victim of its own constitution which effectively prevented it from defending itself, Poland as a state had been reduced by the mid-eighteenth century to virtual impotence. This impotence was particularly evident in 1763 when the Polish nobility elected as the country's king Stanislaus Poniatowsky, a protégé of the newly crowned Catherine II of Russia. The election promised stability in Poland but a stability based on Russian enforcement rather than on Polish contentment. The promise was unrealized. Growing restrictions on the Orthodox and Protestant minorities in Poland by the Roman Catholic majority led first to warnings on behalf of the minorities from Orthodox Russia and Protestant Prussia and then in 1767 to armed Russian intervention. This time, however, the Poles did not accept Russian interference peaceably; they resisted it, and by 1768 virtually all of Poland was beset by armed conflict.

Most of the great powers were uneasy about growing Russian involvement in Poland, the Ottoman Empire especially so. The sultan and his advisers feared that soon Poland would submit completely to the Russians and thus free them to focus their aggressive policies exclusively on Turkey. Still, the Ottoman viziers were reluctant to come to the aid of the Polish insurgents, because they worried that a war with Russia might lead to Turkey's defeat. In July, 1768, however, an overly zealous Russian army officer, chasing some Polish patriots, led his men into Ottoman territory and razed the town of Balta, massacring a number of the inhabitants. The sultan found the cries of outrage among the people and religious leaders in the Ottoman capital irresistible, and he declared war on Russia.

In light of what happened later, the Ottoman decision to go to war in 1768 bordered on the suicidal. Despite the years of international peace in the Balkans between 1739 and 1768, Turkey had by no means slowed its growing chaos. Internally the disorder in various provinces continued, and the central government, despite some efforts at reform in the 1750s, could not quell it. In contrast, Russia in the 1760s was embarking on one of its proudest periods in terms of territorial expansion. Catherine II would oversee the acquisition of the northern coast of the Black Sea, the Crimean Peninsula, and much of Poland, and she would dream of placing her grandson on the throne of a restored Greek kingdom with his capital a Constantinople draped again in Orthodox splendor.

At the time, however, the Turkish decision to go to war did not seem outrageous. Russia was deeply involved in Poland and would have difficulty turning the full weight of its military might upon the Turks. Moreover, France seemed to have renewed an old interest in eastern Europe and was vigorously encouraging the sultan to break the Russian grip on Poland by armed force if necessary. The French were a bit callous about the whole affair, the French foreign minister remarking that the Turkish effort to defeat Russia 'will probably be fatal to them', but in fact Versailles did not at this stage believe the Russians significantly stronger than the Turks.[34] Not even the Austrians considered the result of the war a foregone conclusion. The great Austrian chancellor Wenzel Anton Kaunitz believed Turkey and Russia evenly matched and expressed the hope that each would fight the other to exhaustion, thus keeping the scales of power between them even while weakening both relative to Austria.[35]

The war was disastrous for the Turks. Fighting at first primarily in the Romanian principalities and then in the Crimea, the Russian army inflicted defeat after defeat upon the Turks. Moreover, to encourage revolution among the sultan's Orthodox subjects, Catherine sent a fleet from the Baltic to the Aegean so that Russian sailors and marines could join local bandits and Christian militias in spreading havoc among the Turks. While the presence of the Russian navy generated considerable enthusiasm and some guerilla activity, its great achievement came on 6/7 July, 1770, when it destroyed the entire Ottoman fleet at Cesme with only minor losses on the Russian side. These Russian victories seemed the harbinger of the long-prophesied dissolution of the Ottoman Empire.

But the Ottoman Empire did not disappear in this war either; it was saved by its old arch enemy, Austria. For the previous sixty years, Austrian statesmen had voiced concern about Russia becoming an Austrian neighbor, and the Russian victories, especially those in Moldavia and Wallachia, seemed likely to make that a reality. Consequently, Vienna undertook a vigorous campaign to persuade the Russians to withdraw from those provinces and return them to Ottoman rule. It reinforced the Habsburg army as if preparing to attack the Russian forces; it concluded a concert with Turkey — the first of its kind between the two states — by which the Ottomans would help pay for Austria's military posturing; and it hinted strongly to foreign capitals that it would rather fight than allow the Romanian principalities to pass permanently into Russian possession.[36] These threats and poses were all an elaborate bluff, but they worked. The result was the First Partition of Poland as that pathetic state and not the Ottoman Empire was sacrificed for what most believed was the sake of peace in eastern Europe. Part of the agreement provided for the Russian evacuation of Moldavia and Wallachia and their restoration to Turkey; thus, no Austro–Russian border came to pass.

After each of the previous wars in the eighteenth-century Balkans, most observers wondered if the Ottoman Empire could ever defend itself again; after the Russo–Turkish war of 1768–1774, everyone was certain that it could not. The treaty ending the war, that of Kuchuk-Kainarji, established the Russian presence firmly on the northern coast of the Black Sea, created an independent Crimea that most assumed (correctly) would soon be annexed by the Russians, and contained a provision granting Russia the right to protect an Orthodox church in Constantinople but containing wording sufficiently vague so that it could be interpreted to allow the Russians to claim that they were protectors of all the Orthodox Christians in the Ottoman Empire.[37] Upon reading the treaty, the Austrian envoy in Constantinople wrote, 'From now on, [Turkey] falls into the category of being a Russian province . . . . Never was a nation at its destruction less worthy of condolences than this one'.[38]

In the years following 1774 events inside the Ottoman Empire seemed to affirm the Austrian's assessment. A Turkish reform effort of some vigor began in the late 1770s, but it seemed unable to overcome the anarchy in the provinces or to resist continuing pressures from the great powers. In 1777 a dispute among members of the ruling family in the supposedly independent Crimea led to Russian interference there that the Ottoman Empire was powerless to oppose; six years later Russia simply annexed that peninsula amidst ineffectual Turkish protests. Indeed, the Russians in general displayed nothing but contempt for the Ottoman Empire after 1774, and it was evident that Catherine considered it only a matter of time and opportunity before she dissolved it altogether.

The opportunity presented itself in 1787. In the summer of that year Catherine undertook a pompous and gaudy tour of her newly won southern provinces in the company of her favorite, Prince Gregor Potemkin, and the Austrian emperor, Joseph II. Although the intention of the visit was not to threaten Turkey, the sultan and his advisers assumed that it included preparations for an Austro-Russian invasion of their land. In hopes of anticipating such an invasion, the sultan in the autumn of 1787 declared war on Russia. Both the Russians and the Austrians were caught unaware, especially the Austrians who thought Catherine's ostentatious journey to be a lot of nonsense anyway. But the Austrians had concluded a defensive alliance with Russia and the sultan was formally the aggressor, so for the second time in the century Austria joined Russia in a war against the Turks.[39] Once again the Ottomans seemed destined for defeat and once again — for the first year at least — they did better than expected. But in 1789 the Turks suffered reversals on every front, and the army melted away. Describing the campaign as one of the most unfortunate in Ottoman history, the historian Stanford Shaw summarized its result succinctly: 'as the winter [of 1789-1790] began, the Ottoman Empire was on the brink of disaster'.[40]

Again, however, the empire survived, this time in novel fashion. Prussia and Great Britain, two countries previously little concerned about Turkey's fate, put sufficient diplomatic pressure on Austria to restore the *status quo ante bellum* (the Treaty of Sistova, 1791) and on Russia to be content with limited gains (the Treaty of Jassy, 1792). The Prusso-British effort was less important for what it achieved than what it portended. The Eastern Question and thus the future of the Balkans were no longer issues to be resolved among the immediately interested powers of Russia, Austria and the Ottoman Empire; they were becoming European problems, with previously distant powers convinced that the fate of the Ottoman Empire was becoming part and parcel of their national interests.[41]

The war had a great impact upon Turkish internal affairs as well. It witnessed the emergence of Selim III, the first sultan fully intent upon instituting wholesale reforms in the Ottoman Empire to cure those ills that had reduced it to impotence. But the rot had now spread far and deep. As he introduced his reforms, the violence and disorder increased; bandits resisted efforts to quell their raids, janissaries fought against troops sent to restrict their depredations, and autonomous pashas defended their satraps from Constantinople's efforts to curb their independence. As these forms of violence expanded, they began to take on a new aura, that of nationalism. The bandit warriors, janissary leaders and local pashas slowly became national heroes and national villains, and a whole new motive for warfare spread its shadow over the Balkans. These two trends, national rebellion and growing involvement by all the European great powers in Balkan affairs, would provide the causes for war in the Balkans of the nineteenth century.

NOTES

1. Two other wars between Russia and the Ottoman Empire were fought in the early modern period, those of 1677-1681 and 1695-1700, but the fighting occurred in the area north of the Black Sea, not in the Balkans.

2. Peter Sugar, 'Conclusions', in Béla K. Király and Gunther E. Rothenberg, eds., *War and Society in East Central Europe* (New York, 1979), p. 349. The best studies on war and society in the Balkans are the book just cited and its companion volume, Gunther E. Rothenberg, Béla K. Király, and Peter Sugar, eds., *East Central European Society and War in the Pre-Revolutionary Eighteenth Century* (Boulder, Colorado, 1982).

3. The best recent studies of the Ottoman Empire and its decline include Stanford J. Shaw, *History of the Ottoman Empire and Modern Turkey, Volume I: Empire of the Gazis: The Rise and Decline of the Ottoman Empire, 1280–1808* (Cambridge, 1976); Peter Sugar, *Southeastern Europe under Ottoman Rule, 1354–1804* (Seattle, 1977); and Barbara Jelavich, *History of the Balkans, Volume I: Eighteenth and Nineteenth Centuries* (Cambridge, 1983).

4. For the best exposition of this view see L. S. Stavrianos, *The Balkans Since 1453* (New York, 1958).

5. Sugar, *Southeastern Europe*, pp. 195–202

6. *Ibid.*, p. 213.

7. Bistra Cvetkova, 'The Bulgarian Haiduk Movement in the 15th–18th Centuries,' in Rothenberg, Király, and Sugar, eds., *East Central European Society and War*, p. 324.

8. *Ibid.*, pp. 326–27.

9. A list of such offices can be found in Wayne S. Vucinich, 'Serbian Military Tradition,' in Király and Rothenberg, eds., *War and Society*, p. 293.

10. Cvetkova, 'The Bulgarian Haiduk Movement,' p. 327.

11. Wayne S. Vucinich, 'Prince-Bishop Danilo and His Place in Montenegro's History,' in Rothenberg, Király, and Sugar, eds., *East Central European Society and War*, p. 276.

12. B. H. Sumner, *Peter the Great and the Ottoman Empire* (1949), pp. 45–49.

13. For the Military Border see primarily the works of Gunther Rothenberg, *The Austrian Military Border in Croatia, 1522–1747* (Urbana, Illinois, 1960); *The Military Border in Croatia, 1740–1881* (Chicago, 1966); and 'The Habsburg Military Border System: Some Reconsiderations,' in Király and Rothenberg, eds., *War and Society*, pp. 361–392.

14. Sugar, *Southeastern Europe*, p. 193.

15. *Ibid.*, pp. 222–23.

16. For an excellent example of the religious enthusiasm of the time see Robert Kann's discussion of Abraham a Sancta Clara in *A Study in Austrian Intellectual History: from late Baroque to Romanticism* (New York, 1960).

17. John P. Spielman, *Leopold I of Austria* (New Brunswick, N. J., 1977), pp. 50–51.

18. Thomas M. Barker, *Double Eagle and Crescent: Vienna's Second Turkish Siege and its Historical Setting* (Albany, N. Y., 1967), pp. 68–72. There is considerable literature in many languages on the siege of Vienna in 1683. The best studies in English are Barker's work just cited and John Stoye, *The Siege of Vienna* (New Yorks, 1964). The war archives in Vienna sponsored the publication of a brief study by Guenter Dueriegel entitled *Wien 1683* (Vienna, 1981) that contains some references to newer materials. Felix Czeike, *Die Türkenkriege in der historischen Forschung* (Vienna, 1983) reviews scholarship being done in Yugoslavia, Poland, Romania, Czechoslovakia, Turkey, Hungary, and Austria on many Turkish wars including this one. The Inner Asian and Uralic National Research Center at Indiana University and the Center for Austrian Studies at the University of Minnesota sponsored an international conference on the siege of Vienna in the autumn of 1983; the papers delivered at that conference are to be published, but as of this writing have not appeared.

19. Barker, *Double Eagle and Crescent*, pp. 368–69.

20. The best study in English of Prince Eugene is Derek McKay, *Prince Eugene of Savoy* (1977), but one must not overlook Max Braubach's monumental *Prinz Eugen von Savoyen*, 5 volumes (Vienna, 1963–1965).

21. Quoted in Karl A. Roider, Jr., *Austria's Eastern Question, 1700–1790* (Princeton, 1982), pp. 156–57.

22. Conference Protocol, 23 February 1711, Vienna, Haus- Hof- und Staatsarchiv, *Vortrage*, p. 16.

23. Radu Florescu, 'Contemporary Western Reaction to the Battle of Stănilesti', in Rothenberg, Király, and Sugar, eds., *East Central European Society and War*, pp. 415–29.

24. Sumner, *Peter the Great and the Ottoman Empire*, pp. 37–44; J. Black, 'Russia's Rise as a European Power', *History Today* 36 (Aug. 1986), pp. 26–7.

25. [Anslem] Fleischmann to the War Ministry, 25 October 1715, Vienna, *HHSA, SK, Türkei,* I, p. 180.

26. Francesco Pometti, 'Studi sul pontificato di Clemento XI, 1700–1721', *Archivio della R. Societa Romana di Storia Patria,* XXII (1899), p. 122.

27. Ekkehard Eickhoff, *Venedig, Wien und die Osmanen: Umbruch in Südosteuropa* (Munich, 1970), pp. 432–34.

28. Roider, *Austria's Eastern Question,* pp. 41–44.

29. See Braubach, *Prinz Eugen,* III, pp. 311–64; McKay, *Prince Eugene,* pp. 158–68.

30. Eugene to Emperor Charles VI, 20 June 1718 in *Feldzüge des Prinzen Eugen von Savoyen* (Vienna, 1891), XVII, supplement, p. 238. This is a 20-volume work containing text and documents published by the Austrian war ministry in the late nineteenth century.

31. Quoted in Lavender Cassels, *The Struggle for the Ottoman Empire* (London, 1966), p. 100.

32. Karl A. Roider, Jr., *The Reluctant Ally: Austria's Policy in the Austro-Turkish War, 1737–1739* (Baton Rouge, La., 1972), pp. 54–67.

33. *Ibid.,* p. 179.

34. J. A. R. Marriott, *The Eastern Question* (Oxford, 1917), p. 146.

35. Roider, *Austria's Eastern Question,* p. 111.

36. *Ibid.,* pp. 109–30.

37. M. S. Anderson, *The Eastern Question, 1774–1923* (London, 1966), pp. 2–9.

38. Thugut to Kaunitz, 17 August 1774, Vienna, HHStA. Sk, *Türkei,* II, 63.

39. Karl A. Roider, Jr., 'Kaunitz, Joseph II, and the Turkish War', *Slavonic and East European Review,* LIV (1976), pp. 538–56; J. Black, 'Sir Robert Ainslie: His Majesty's Agent-provocateur? British Foreign Poilicy and the International Crisis of 1787, *European History Quarterly,* 14 (1984), pp. 253–83.

40. Stanford Shaw, *Between Old and New: The Ottoman Empire under Sultan Selim III, 1789–1807* (Cambridge, Mass., 1971), p. 40.

41. Anderson, *Eastern Question,* pp. 17–21.

6

THE ORIGINS OF THE WAR OF THE SPANISH SUCCESSION

William Roosen

When King Carlos II finally died on All Saints Day in 1700, the Spanish government acted with uncharacteristic speed. The last testament of the defunct king was opened and read; a regency government was formed; and a courier was sent to France to offer the Spanish Empire to Philip of Anjou, the second grandson of Louis XIV. The absence of lethargy testifies to the importance of the problems raised by the death of the last male Spanish Habsburg. Although Carlos II's death had long been expected, decision-makers were still faced with the problem of what to do next. The story of the ensuing moves, counter-moves, and counter-counter-moves is inherently interesting and dramatic, especially since the events of the next few months culminated in the outbreak of a war which was to be the longest and in many ways the most difficult of Louis XIV's long reign.

Generations of researchers have ransacked archives in their search for evidence about the origins of the War of the Spanish Succession. The results of their efforts have been published in massive, often multi-volume works printing the letters, orders, and memoirs of everyone involved.[1] It is unlikely that even the most assiduous and imaginative researcher today will discover any documents which will substantially change the story as it is already known. But how has this mass of material been used? Most scholars have either just narrated events or they have taken a conventional historical approach to discuss the 'cause' or 'causes' of the war.

It is appropriate, however, to use these materials in a different way. Some years ago David Pinkney suggested that the most valuable contribution historians living west of the Atlantic can make to European history is to 'write works of synthesis and interpretation'.[2] Following his advice, this study neither attempts to present new documents nor to supplant the work of such excellent scholars as Mark Thomson and Ragnhild Hatton.[3] Rather, it approaches the subject from a different perspective in hope of achieving a better understanding of both the origins of war and early modern international relations in general.

We can start with the traditional question — why did the War of the Spanish Succession occur? Most answers have focused on the goals and actions of leaders. Scholars frequently have been primarily concerned with assigning blame for the war, especially to Louis XIV.[4] Since most historians emphasize the uniqueness of historical events, they usually find such answers satisfactory.

Many social scientists, however, think that explanations based on the behaviour of individuals are too limited. Believing that the answer one finds to a question

151

depends on where one looks, they are reminded of the joke about a man looking at the ground under a street light. A second man approaches and asks: 'What are you doing'? 'Looking for some money I dropped'. 'Where did you drop it'? 'Over there by that tree'. 'Then why are you looking here'? 'Because I can see better here under the light'. Scholars who look at individuals and/or events in western Europe for the origins of the War of the Spanish Succession are better off then the man who lost money because they can indeed find some answers. However, explanations today can take advantage of twentieth-century knowledge of the social and behavioural sciences, especially of international relations, to find better answers. This approach shows that there was not a single cause or even a number of causes of the War of the Spanish Succession. Rather, the structure and inherent characteristics of the international system itself brought on the war.

The best way to demonstrate this proposition is to examine the structure of the international system around 1700, first from a geographical perspective, then from the levels of analysis approach, and finally by an examination of the process by which relations between states change from peace to war. Next a look at the background of the Spanish succession issue will focus on those aspects which contemporaries thought most important, especially the legal or hereditary rights of succession. A brief narrative of some relevant events of diplomatic history will be followed by an examination of the *weltanschauung* or mind set of decision-makers, their fears and misunderstandings of other participants in the international arena, their fears of universal monarchy and of threats to the equilibrium of Europe (balance of power), and the participants' conflicting goals.

I will argue that all these combined to make armed conflict between states inevitable from the moment Joseph Ferdinand of Bavaria died on 6 February 1699 (barring some truly miraculous events). The accuracy of this thesis will be tested by examining potentially different patterns of events to see if any of them could have produced a plausible alternative to the outbreak of the War of the Spanish Succession.

How could such a disastrous war start? Earlier in the seventeenth century many rulers and their advisers believed that war was an acceptable and perhaps even desirable activity. After the Peace of Ryswick in 1697, however, most decision-makers in the important western European states would have preferred to settle the issue of the Spanish succession without fighting.[5]

Many of the rulers of minor states also would have preferred peace, but their hopes and needs were essentially irrelevant. Unlike the early twentieth century when a conflict involving a very minor state escalated into World War I, the smaller states were not in a position either to start or prevent a general European war around 1700.[6] By focusing their attention almost entirely on the most important western states — France and Britain — most scholars implicitly recognize small states' lack of importance. The role of the United Provinces (the Netherlands) is often subsumed under the heading of the Maritime Powers — which accurately reflects the power situation. Until recently, the goals and behaviour of the other two states which in fact had important roles, the Austrian

Habsburgs and Spain itself, have often been considered only in passing.

This focus on north-western Europe reflects the orientation of the rulers whose archives have been most carefully searched. It also satisfies those who presume that the British role must have been predominant immediately after Ryswick since it was so important later. Finally, that focus is appropriate for those who believe that the actions of Louis XIV were of primary importance. Now, however, a number of twentieth-century historians, especially Ragnhild Hatton, have demonstrated the importance of southern and eastern Europe.

Even more important than the geographical focus of those who study the origins of the War of the Spanish Succession is the level at which they perform their analysis. Twentieth-century social scientists have long recognized the value of studying international relations on three levels: 'within man, within the structure of the separate states, [and] within the state system'.[7] Although the terminology of levels of analysis may not be familiar to historians, the fundamental concepts are. In keeping with traditional historical practice, however, historians often do not clearly distinguish which of these levels is most important or even which they are discussing at any given moment. Rather, information and interpretation on all the levels are usually mixed with little or no regard for the resulting confusion.

Most accounts of the origins of the War of the Spanish Succession are primarily descriptive and narrative rather than analytical.[8] This is typical in

> diplomatic history [which] has been indifferent to the problems of methodology and conventionally narrative. In any traditional textbook or study, for example, we could readily find the relatively simple facts of each historical case .... We would find it much more difficult to discover an explicit treatment of the influence of stress or organizational process upon decision making, the characteristics of alliance politics, or the diplomatic system as a whole, or upon the dynamics of bargaining with threats of force and escalation during intense international crises .... 'The general reaction of most diplomatic historians to these innovative efforts,' writes one observer, 'has been akin to the papal response to Galileo.'[9]

In effect, authors of traditional diplomatic history often just rummage around in the past picking out interesting facts and interpretations without any theoretical framework for judging importance other than their own feelings or intuitions.[10]

Most diplomatic historians find explanation based on the first level of analysis — that of individual human beings — convincing because of their special interest in the actions of people.[11] Like politicians, they find the world more acceptable if historical events can be explained on the basis of individual actions. Furthermore, many historians are convinced of the importance of unique events. They are part of a longstanding tradition which sees wars as arising 'from the wilful machinations of statesmen and soldiers, princes and diplomats ...'[12] This is a variation on the Great Man theory of history — which most analyses of the origins of the War of the Spanish Succession honour in practice if not consciously. In effect, diplomatic historians adopt the perspective of early modern chancelleries with their assumption that relations between states depended especially on the personalities, characters, knowledge, and errors of statesmen.[13]

This is why so many historians ultimately blame one individual, Louis XIV, for the outbreak of the War of the Spanish Succession. For example, Stephen Baxter, a biographer of William III, states flatly that Louis XIV's conduct made war over the Spanish inheritance inevitable.[14] After the Second World War, French historians concerned with diplomatic history also thought in terms of the individual level of analysis, usually blaming Louis XIV (or sometimes his ministers and advisers) for the outbreak of his wars.[15] Mark Thomson closes his very knowledgeable discussion of the start of the War of the Spanish Succession by claiming that Louis XIV 'had made inevitable the very war he dreaded'.[16] Paul Langford agrees, expressing astonishment at 'why Louis XIV wilfully provoked a war in the course of 1701 ...'[17] Even Ragnhild Hatton, whose knowledge of the subject is unsurpassed, seems ultimately to place responsibility on Louis XIV: 'That Louis did not enjoy the peaceful possession of the Spanish succession was in part due to the accidents of history, ... But it was also due to Louis's own mistakes ...'[18] The authors of the most recent general study of early modern diplomacy argue that 'within a year of Philip V's accession Louis had made general war inevitable'.[19] The idea that Louis XIV himself caused the War of the Spanish Succession because of his mistakes or 'blunders' is obviously still widely accepted.

When they are not focusing on individuals, historians tend to focus on the role of states — in Waltz's words, 'within the structure of the separate states'. This is the level of analysis used in studies of the role of Parliament, the States General, and Louis XIV's council meeting with his heirs and ministers which discussed whether to accept the testament of Carlos II. Somehow it is believed that the war started because of differences between the various states involved. Changes in British or Dutch public opinion, for example, are seen as having made war either possible or necessary. The problem with these two approaches so far as the War of the Spanish Succession is concerned is that they lead to the fundamental misconception that the war resulted from the behaviour of individuals or individual states rather than from the structure of international relations.

Few historians have paid much attention to the third level of analysis — the international state system itself. The idea that there may have been something about the very structure of interstate relations which led to the War of the Spanish Succession is almost unknown.

In the following discussion, my goal is not to claim that individuals had no importance. Rather, it is to show the tremendous importance of the context in which individuals behaved, a context which was the primary 'cause' of the war. The reader should constantly remember the importance of the different levels of analysis in this discussion. At the same time, an organizing principle will be the distinction between developments which occurred as a result of behaviour of various decision-makers and those which resulted from the conditions which predetermined or at least strongly predisposed them to make certain decisions and/or behave in certain ways. In *Power and the Pursuit of Peace*, F. H. Hinsley sees an important distinction in the causes of wars

> between the given conditions and the policy of statesmen, between the profound
> causes of war and the decisions that lead to war .... One war may be almost entirely

due to the given conditions and hardly at all the consequence of the conduct of the men involved. Another war may be almost entirely due to that conduct and hardly at all the consequence of the given conditions.[20]

The weight of the evidence shows that the War of the Spanish Succession was the former type. With the death of the electoral prince in February 1699, events escaped the control of human beings, and Europe was set on a course in which only a miracle could have prevented the outbreak of war.

Most early modern rulers and ministers recognized that relationships between states were much more complex than a simple distinction between peace and war. They 'realized that relations between states were not a dichotomy of either peace or war but rather that such relations lay along a continuum ranging from all-out enmity to all-out friendship'.[21] Just like today it was possible in Early Modern Europe for relations between two states to move rapidly from one end of the continuum to the other. For example, Britain and the Netherlands went quickly from fighting each other in the Third Anglo–Dutch War to cooperation. Toward the end of the Nine Years' War the duke of Savoy deserted the Allied side and made peace with Louis XIV. A few years later, near the beginning of the War of the Spanish Succession, he reversed the process and rapidly changed from a French ally to an opponent. Relations between states usually changed more slowly, however.

Changes in relations between western European states after the Peace of Ryswick can be compared to the behaviour of children on a playground without adult supervision. To a distant observer the children appear to be peacefully playing together. Suddenly, one child hits another and a general fight erupts. An adult who intervenes is beset by various children claiming that someone else 'started it'. For practical reasons the adult may decide to blame one of the children for starting the fight, especially if the adult can determine who did hit first. That kind of decision is not very helpful, however, if one wishes to understand the process which led to open conflict.

The process is basically the same as occurs in other interpersonal conflicts:

When one observes an interaction carefully ... he often notes that a kinesic interchange gradually and subtly escalates until one participant's contribution passes a threshold of awareness and becomes evident to the others. The others then jump to the conclusion that the now-conspicuous partner started the whole thing. This kind of blame-fixing fits in with the Western notion that social processes are set in motion by heroic or guilty parties [rather than by broader contextual forces].[22]

This is what happened on the playground. All or many of the children were engaging in subtle name-calling, slight pushes and shoves, and increasingly vehement competition to use the play equipment. The process may not have been obvious to the participants or the observing adult. Only the first punch, the contribution which passed the threshold of awareness, is noted and the puncher blamed for starting the fight even though any fairminded observer would apportion responsibility among all those who participated in the hidden struggle or place responsibility on the situation in which the children were playing. Any parent will recognize this scenario.

It is foolish and inaccurate to place blame for the playground fight on the child who hit first. So too is it foolish to blame Louis XIV or any other decision-maker for the outbreak of the War of the Spanish Succession — at least in the sense of thinking the war started because of an individual's internal qualities or free will actions. A systems or holistic way of thinking requires one to realize that in such a situation there is not just one cause or one villain. Social structures, communication systems, cultural norms and the like all play a role and they must be considered if we are to overcome the 'notion that broad social processes can be explained by small ones'.[23]

Because of the seriousness of the issues and consequences, most people hesitate to compare the behaviour of statesmen to that of children. Nevertheless, the coming of the War of the Spanish Succession was essentially the same as the coming of the playground fight except that it took longer to happen and the pushes and shoves were over more important matters than who gets to play where. As is always the case in diplomacy, the pushes and shoves took such forms as 'promises, appeals to interest, attempts at striking a bargain, devices of cajolery', taunts, bullying, blackmail, and impudent bluff.[24]

> The portion of the communications spectrum which embraces political events is composed of units of much longer duration. Meanings must be found in the context of hundreds of years of history . . . a message that has been building up for years. The message is composed of numerous situations and acts — something which is understood by any political scientist or statesman. Diplomacy and political strategy can be seen as a kind of debate where the words cover years.[25]

One must avoid reading too much into the overt act which indicates that the relationship between states has changed from peace to war since 'such an act may merely be the first visible sign of an interaction which has already been developing without observers being aware of it'.[26]

Few scholars would claim that the War of the Spanish Succession really started with the formal declarations of war by the Allies in May 1702 or by the French declaration in July. Clearly the conflict had begun earlier, at least with the Austrian incursion into Italy the previous year. In fact, the relations between states which would lead to war were started decades earlier by the marriages and births which created conflicting claims to the Spanish succession.

It is very tempting for modern scholars, especially those with a realistic bent, to downgrade or even ignore the question of hereditary claims to the Spanish succession. At the end of the seventeenth century, decision-makers certainly did not allow legal considerations to take precedence over political realities. In fact, such attitudes already existed earlier when pragmatic politicians like Richelieu and Mazarin knew that legal rights to crowns 'were not incontrovertible but rather subject to compromise in the diplomatic process'.[27]

The inheritance rules of all early modern states were a combination of practice, positive law, age-old traditions, and declarations or testaments of monarchs. No state had clear-cut rules for all possible eventualities. Before 1700 successions were occasionally determined pragmatically — for example, Henry VII's acquisition of the crown of England despite his illegitimate descent or the Valois dynasty's success in France which established the Salic Law as one of the kingdom's fundamental rules. The Portuguese crown had been gained by Philip II and then lost by Philip IV. Pragmatism, as opposed to legality, was well established long before the death of Carlos II once again brought the issue to the fore.

Nevertheless, arguments based on legalities were taken into consideration when decisions were made, even if other factors were more important. In a sense, dynastic and legal claims played a role analogous to religion. Rulers might follow a policy contrary to their religious beliefs (like Leopold's allying himself with the Protestant Maritime Powers in the Nine Years' War), but it was a relief when policy could coincide with religion. So too was it a relief when policy could coincide with perceived legal rights. A decision-maker could ignore his or someone else's claims and/or push them into the background when other factors were predominant. But the claims would still give psychological and emotional support or pain, and they were always there to be drawn upon during a debate over policy.[28]

The claims to the Spanish succession were complex. Since there was no international supreme court to judge the relative value of the claims, a decision-maker could almost always find an argument based on heredity to support whatever policy he wished to follow. This is why each of the decision-makers involved could honestly feel that whatever action he took regarding the Spanish succession enjoyed the support of tradition and law despite the equally strong feelings of others that he was acting illegally. Such contrary opinions are, of course, a continual problem inherent in the structure of international relations.[29]

The possibility that the Spanish monarchy might pass out of the Habsburg dynasty was recognized in the early seventeenth century when Anne of Austria, the elder daughter of Philip III, married Louis XIII. Anne was required to renounce her rights of succession both for herself and her heirs. It may be that the Spanish were attempting to establish a kind of reciprocity between France and Spain since the Salic Law prevented women from inheriting or passing on a claim to the French throne. Nevertheless, a renunciation could never be as strong as the Salic Law since it was a clear deviation from the established Spanish order of succession and also because no one knew if the rights of unborn heirs could be renounced.[30] The marriage of Anne's younger sister to the Austrian Habsburg emperor produced Leopold I. At the end of the seventeenth century, he was the closest heir whose claim was not clouded by some kind of renunciation.

The Spanish male succession was not secure in 1660 when Maria Teresa, Philip IV's daughter, married Louis XIV. Her marriage and renunciation could have had more immediate repercussions except for the birth of her half-brother, Carlos II, the next year. Many modern scholars repeat the old story that Louis XIV claimed his wife's renunciation was invalid because her dowry was never paid.[31] They overlook the key point that any renunciation was suspect because of its questionable legality according to Spanish custom and law. Arguments like those

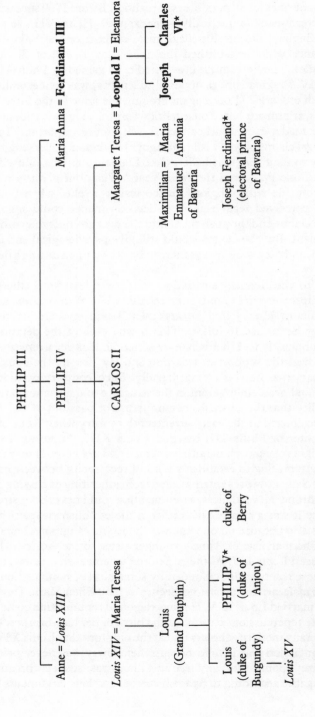

GENEALOGICAL CHART OF THE SPANISH SUCCESSION

NAMES IN CAPITALS = Kings of Spain
Names in Italics = Kings of France
Names in Boldface = Austrian Habsburg Emperors
*People designated at some time as the heir of Carlos II

made in a book published in 1699 defending the rights of Maria Teresa and her Bourbon heirs were more important.[32] On the other hand, the legal arguments in favor of the Austrian Habsburgs could be presented just as strongly.[33]

The last dynasty which had a substantial claim to the Spanish inheritance was the Bavarian Wittelsbachs. Maximilian Emmanuel married Leopold's daughter by his first wife who was the younger daughter of Philip IV. Before the marriage Leopold had insisted that his daughter renounce in his own favor all the rights which she held from her mother and through the will of Philip IV. Max Emmanuel had agreed to the renunciation, but it had never been recognized in Spain. The claim of their son Joseph Ferdinand, commonly called the electoral prince of Bavaria, was thus fairly strong.

In order to understand the role of these conflicting claims in the outbreak of war, we need to recognize that all the decision-makers could easily believe in their own rights and at the same time discount the claims of others. Furthermore, any claimant who agreed to accept less than the whole of the Spanish Empire (which he believed to be legitimately his) could easily believe that he was giving up so much that his other requests should certainly be recognized as legitimate. Such a mind set was a key part of the *weltanschauung* which ultimately led to the outbreak of the war.

Another part of decision-makers' mind set was their memory and understanding of earlier events related to the Spanish succession. It is not appropriate here to retrace the history of international relations and diplomacy in the seventeenth century. Rather we can just examine those developments which influenced decision-makers' thinking as the problem became more critical.[34] After making peace at Ryswick, they were well aware of the Spanish succession's potential for plunging Europe back into the maelstrom of war. Unlike some military men and young hotheads, however, none of the important rulers actually wanted war over the issue.[35]

The British and the Dutch faced a special difficulty when Louis XIV raised the issue in March 1698. During the Nine Years' War the Maritime Powers had agreed that Leopold's second son would mount the Spanish throne after the death of Carlos II; it was debatable whether they were still bound by that promise. Furthermore, just by agreeing to negotiate about the future of the Spanish Empire they were giving up one of their strongest bargaining points — the idea that the renunciations by the dauphin's mother were valid; if the dauphin had a right to part of the Spanish inheritance, he clearly had a right to the whole.[36] There was also the danger that even discussing partition would make enemies of both the Austrians and the Spaniards.

The Maritime Powers eventually agreed to negotiate with Louis XIV because there was no realistic alternative. The Spaniards refused to admit that the Maritime Powers had any right to discuss what they claimed was an internal Spanish question. Leopold did not wish to discuss partition while Carlos II still lived and argued that the earlier Anglo-Dutch promise to support his son's claim to the whole inheritance still applied.[37] William and Heinsius could either negotiate with France or do nothing. Doing nothing seemed like a sure way of starting another war. Seeing the partition treaty of 1668 in which Emperor Leopold had agreed to divide the Spanish Empire with Louis XIV may have helped them overcome their qualms.[38] Negotiations continued through the spring and summer of 1698. A fundamental difficulty was that William and Heinsius did not really want France to gain anything at all from the Spanish succession. Louis XIV proposed one alternative after another, gradually relinquishing more and more of 'his legitimate expectations'. The First Partition Treaty, signed by Louis XIV, William III, and the Dutch in the autumn of 1698, recognized Joseph Ferdinand, the electoral prince of Bavaria, as main heir; parts of the Spanish possessions, mainly in Italy, were divided between the Grand Dauphin and the second son of Leopold I.[39] When they learned of the treaty, Leopold fumed and the queen of Spain rampaged around, breaking the furniture in her room.

The First Partition Treaty had a very important effect whose significance has often been overlooked. It prompted Carlos II to make a will leaving his entire empire to Joseph Ferdinand. Had Carlos died immediately, the Spaniards and the rest of Europe would probably have welcomed the accession of the electoral prince as the solution to the problem. Since he was a prince of a minor dynasty who nevertheless had a good hereditary claim, Louis XIV, Leopold I, and other rulers could have accepted him as king of Spain without doing too much damage to their own sense of rightfulness and legitimacy. Even more important, such a new dynasty in Spain would not substantially change the status quo. Unfortunately, just a few months after the First Partition Treaty and the will of Carlos II were made, the young prince suddenly died. There were, of course, the rumours of poison which usually accompanied the sudden deaths of prominent persons in Early Modern Europe, and the prince's father suspected an Austrian plot.[40] Poor, sickly Carlos II may even have felt some satisfaction at having outlived the child who was to be his heir.

The real importance of Joseph Ferdinand's death was that it made war inevitable by removing the last viable candidate who was not a Bourbon or an Austrian Habsburg. The hereditary claims of the king of Portugal, the duke of Savoy, and several Spanish nobles were so tenuous that neither of the major claimants could conceivably accept one of them as an alternate.

Upon learning of the electoral prince's death, Louis XIV immediately started negotiating a Second Partition Treaty. It was signed in March 1700 although ratification came much later. The emperor's younger son, Archduke Charles, was to receive the portions originally intended for the electoral prince (Spain, the southern Netherlands, and the overseas possessions) except Milan which was to be added to the dauphin's portion. According to a secret clause certain territories given to France were to be exchanged, if possible, with the duke of Lorraine and/or the duke of Savoy. Once again, the emperor was called upon simply to accept a *fait accompli*.[41]

Meanwhile, the situation in Spain was becoming desperate as it became even more obvious that Carlos II would neither father an heir nor live much longer. His family ties, the Austrian ambassador, and possibly his German-born second wife all pressured him to make a will leaving his empire to the Austrian Habsburgs. But an ever-growing number of Spaniards, especially the powerful Cardinal Portocarrero, were becoming convinced that the only way to maintain the empire intact was to pass it to one of Louis XIV's grandsons. At Portocarrero's suggestion, Carlos II asked Rome for advice. Nothing was certain, however, even when Carlos had a will drawn up in the form used by Philip IV but with the main names left blank. On 3 October 1700 the key clause was written in — leaving the entire Spanish inheritance to Louis XIV's second grandson, Philip of Anjou, or to Philip's younger brother. If Louis did not accept, the whole undivided empire was to be offered to Archduke Charles.[42] Perhaps as a sop to the Habsburgs or even to his own family feelings, Carlos suggested that the Bourbon successor could marry an Austrian archduchess. After a brief interlude of slightly improved health, Carlos II, the last Habsburg king of Spain, expired on November 1st.

In theory, the will neither strengthened nor weakened Philip of Anjou's claim to the Spanish Empire; it merely recognized that the fundamental law of succession and the renunciations by his father and elder brother made Philip the legitimate king.[43]

In fact, the will of Carlos II presented Louis XIV with a dilemma he had not expected; he had never believed that Carlos II would name a Bourbon as his heir. The will posed both a moral and a political dilemma. If Louis accepted the inheritance for his grandson, he would be breaking the pledged word he had just given in the Second Partition Treaty. If he refused, the same courier would carry the offer to Leopold who would definitely accept. After deliberation with his heirs and ministers, Louis accepted the will and presented his grandson to the assembled courtiers as the 'king of Spain' on 16 November 1700.

The next few months saw a rush of events. Although Philip left Versailles fairly soon, he was not allowed to cross into Spain until after the final date which had been set for Leopold to accept the Second Partition Treaty. A number of rulers including those of Bavaria, Poland, and Savoy recognized Philip as king of Spain even before he left Versailles. The British and the Dutch also recognized him later in the spring although Louis XIV's official recognition of Philip's place in the line of succession to the French throne caused concern. In February, officially at the request of Spain, French troops occupied the Barrier fortresses in the Spanish Netherlands which had been established to protect the Dutch against a French attack. France also acquired from a Portuguese company the unexpired portion of the *asiento* which the British had hoped to have for themselves.

Open military conflict began in spring 1701 when Austrian troops under the command of Prince Eugene moved into Italy. There was soon fighting in the duchy of Milan whose Spanish governor had already recognized Philip V. Negotiations between the western powers came to naught. On 7 September 1701 the old anti-French alliance of Britain, the Netherlands and Austria was recreated, except this time Spain was on the same side as Louis XIV. This so-called Grand Alliance of The Hague was already in existence before James II died and Louis XIV recognized his son as king of England — an act which undoubtedly made the Grand Alliance more popular than it would otherwise have been. Despite the death of William III in March 1702, the Maritime Powers began military operations. The Allies soon formally declared war, but France did not do so until July. The war which so many rulers had hoped to avoid was in full swing.

As these events took place, rulers were making decisions according to assumptions and attitudes which reflected their experience and backgrounds. These attitudes often led them to attribute certain kinds of goals to the others which affected how and what kinds of actions they took.[44] Fears, misunderstandings, and mistrust of each other played a major role in the outbreak of the war.

In the nineteenth century it was often thought that during his whole reign Louis pursued some 'consistent program such as the Spanish succession or the attainment of France's natural boundaries . . .'[45] After it was demonstrated that he followed no such program,[46] French scholars since the Second World War have clung to the idea that his avid desire for glory and predominance in Europe were the most important factors in his conduct of foreign affairs. British and American scholars have tended to look for more rational explanations and to downgrade emotional and ideological motives.[47] One of the valuable results of this work is that it helps us understand better the context in which Louis XIV and his fellow rulers operated.

First, Louis XIV was very much a man of his time, and his goals and motives were very similar if not identical to those of his fellow rulers.[48] Although they all believed resorting to war was an acceptable way to settle an issue, at the end of the seventeenth century Louis and most of the others no longer looked upon warfare simply as an ordinary royal activity like building and hunting. The heavy tolls exacted by Louis XIV's Dutch War and the Nine Years' War made that impossible.

Second, no early modern decision-maker had well-planned and thought-out grand strategies for conducting foreign relations. Most were pragmatically willing to take advantage of developments to achieve whatever gains were possible. They might have a specific goal like trying to acquire a certain territory or a more general one like increasing their security against invasion. Louis XIV's continuing concern about the defense of his northern and eastern frontiers was matched, for instance, by the Dutch desire to protect their southern frontiers. The issue of what would happen to the Spanish succession, of course, became more and more important as time passed, but no European leader had a definite plan to achieve his end.[49]

Like many politicians, the rulers of the major powers shared a distrust or at least a healthy scepticism of the motives of their fellows. William III seems not to have trusted anyone fully, not even Englishmen or his Dutch friends.[50] Is it surprising then that William was extremely suspicious of Louis XIV and Emperor Leopold? As practical politicians, these rulers recognized that deception and hypocrisy are natural behaviours which are found in all human relationships. The level of deception differs in various societies, but it is often quite high in diplomatic relations, despite the frequent calls for honesty found in manuals dealing with the topic.[51]

This is not to say that rulers felt no responsibility to act honestly. Louis XIV and most of his fellow monarchs tried to act according to the precepts of international law and their own pledged word insofar as they could, both because it was a potential blot on their own *gloire* to do otherwise and because they knew it was necessary if their fellow rulers were to have confidence in them.[52] It is often argued that Louis XIV's decision to break the word he had given in the Second Partition Treaty by accepting the will of Carlos II had the effect of making other rulers distrust him more than they would have otherwise. This is very questionable. Most early modern rulers were realistic enough not to be surprised or to put too much weight on such an act. 'Failure to observe treaties was not so rare as to excite surprise or great ill-feeling between sovereigns.'[53] The generalized mistrust of other rulers was in existence long before the issue of the Spanish succession became critical.

One important result of this distrust was a characteristic which is almost a constant in international relations — the inability of decision-makers to accept that others were really serious about wanting to avoid war. Diplomatic contacts around 1700 are replete with protestations of peaceful intentions by statesmen, yet few of them were taken seriously. The problem was raised by William III in 1697. Even though the British and French agreed on all essential points, it was still difficult to make peace because of mutual suspicion that neither side was in earnest.[54] This generalized distrust was not the fault of any individual ruler or even all of them; it was a result of their common experience in international affairs. This is a system level problem even though its effect is felt by individual decision-makers.

Any message of peaceful intent was automatically discounted. This was even the fate of actions which the 'sender' may have intended to be peaceful or conciliatory. By most ordinary criteria, for example, the recognition of Philip of Anjou as king of Spain by the British and Dutch in 1701 would appear to be conciliatory. So too was Philip's delay in crossing into Spain until after the deadline for the emperor's accepting the Second Partition Treaty had passed. Such 'peaceful' acts may not have been taken seriously because it was all too easy to misinterpret the meaning of the action. All behaviour is multiple — that is, all acts may have a variety of different meanings at the same time, and it is often not clear which meaning is intended at any given moment.[55] Indeed the actor himself might not know the 'true' meaning of his action. Such ambiguity is often valuable in diplomacy because ambiguity may 'facilitate changes in policy to accord with whatever opportunities may arise or to retreat when necessary without seeming to do so'.[56]

A problem arises, however, because decision-makers need to interpret or judge the meaning of the action in order to know if and how to respond. What usually happens is that, of the many potential interpretations, the decision-maker chooses the one which most accurately reflects his own hopes and/or fears. In other words, 'both sides remain alert to seize upon whatever formulation of meaning most nearly correlates with their own policies'.[57] The response of a decision-maker who misinterprets an opponent's action may well be that which happens in ordinary human intercourse; he may feel that he has 'been intentionally cheated or wronged'.[58]

On the international scene, such a situation causes problems because bargainers are likely to engage in costly and destructive retaliation if they feel they have been publicly exploited or made to look foolish or weak. Such retaliation will often be undertaken even if the bargainer knows that it will be costly.[59] For example, Louis XIV might have interpreted Anglo–Dutch recognition of Philip V in a favourable way, as a message that the Maritime Powers had accepted his setting aside the Partition Treaty. If it later appeared that their recognition of Philip was only a way of gaining time to prepare their armed forces, the misinterpretation could lead to greater mistrust and conflict since Louis XIV could honestly feel the Maritime Powers had dealt falsely with him.

It was quite normal around 1700 for statesmen to misinterpret each other's words and actions; this was not because they were evil or stupid. Rather it was inherent in the early modern system, just as it still is today, for decision-makers to have substantially different perceptions of reality. This unfortunate characteristic must be recognized and understood when considering the origins of the War of the Spanish Succession because it is well-established that 'differing perceptions of reality are one of the causes of conflict'.[60] By themselves the differing perceptions would not have brought about open fighting, but they played a substantial role in setting the stage for war.

Two different perceptions of the international system were a fundamental part of the background which made the War of the Spanish Succession inevitable long before the actual fighting started. Fear of universal monarchy was very old while the concept of balance of power was more recent.

One of the Roman Empire's many heritages was the idea of universal monarchy. Although independent states had become political realities before 1700, the idea that all of Christendom should be unified under one ruler was still widespread.[61] According to a 'framework of existing fact and inherited thought . . . it was natural for one Power to be rated above the rest and . . . while they had always been resisted by other states, it was impossible for that Power's pretensions to stop short of the control and protection of Christendom'.[62] By the early years of Louis XIV's personal reign, France had replaced Spain as the state which appeared to aspire to universal dominion.[63] Although it is clear in retrospect that after the Peace of Ryswick Louis XIV could no longer hope to dominate Europe (if he ever did entertain such an idea), fear of the Sun King remained a given for much of Europe. In some ways the fear itself, when added to the greater fear which arose when Louis XIV's grandson mounted the Spanish throne, was sufficient cause for the outbreak of war.[64]

The situation was virtually identical to a pattern which has occurred again and again from ancient times until the present. Thucydides explained the Peloponnesian War centuries ago: 'What made war inevitable was the growth of Athenian power and the fear this caused in Sparta'.[65] If one replaces the name Athenians with Bourbons, and Sparta with the Grand Alliance, the model describes the origins of the War of the Spanish Succession. A problem with the model is that, from the Bourbon point of view, it was the Maritime Powers and more especially the Austrian Habsburgs who played the role of the Athenians since their power was growing as they expanded into the Balkans.[66]

The newer perception of the international system which was becoming ever more widespread around 1700 was the equilibrium of Europe, or, in modern terms, the balance of power.[67] Earlier the idea of balance had primarily been seen as a way of avoiding the hegemony of one power.[68] This was the sense in which it was usually used by the enemies of Louis XIV although the sense of one power or group of powers balancing another was certainly known.[69] Louis XIV himself referred to the idea of France and Austria counter-balancing each other; he thought that his power should increase if the emperor's did 'que la mienne soit toujours en état de lui faire contre-poids'.[70]

Louis seems to have worked in favour of a balance of power in the early eighteenth century,[71] but other rulers did not necessarily see his actions in that light. Louis may even have thought his accepting the entire Spanish inheritance for his grandson was maintaining a balance since nothing was added to the crown of France. Other rulers, however, perceived it as a substantial threat to the balance since the House of Bourbon was aggrandized. The Maritime Powers were less concerned with developments in central Europe than with western Europe; they were thus less capable of appreciating Louis XIV's perception that, in view of the great successes of the Austrian Habsburgs against the Turks, any aggrandizement of the House of Bourbon was not really a threat to the balance of power.[72]

One should not presume, however, that the War of the Spanish Succession would somehow have been avoided if all the decision-makers had fully understood the presuppositions, viewpoints, positions, interpretations, and arguments of the others. As is always the case in international relations, there was more involved than just differences of opinion and understanding or failing to understand someone else's point of view. The war eventually started because the various participants had opposing interests which were important enough to fight for — their bottom lines.[73]

All decision-makers had such bottom lines. When the leaders of at least two states reached theirs, fighting began. The best way to understand these basic positions is to abandon the traditional emphasis on France and the Maritime Powers and look at Spain and the Austrian Habsburgs.[74]

Before the Act of Union, England and Scotland shared a common monarch but were still separate kingdoms with separate laws, traditions, and representative bodies. The situation in the Iberian peninsula was similar but more complicated. 'As a state structure Spain did not exist until the eighteenth century. Official terminology used the term only sparingly and it echoes popular usage.' The idea of Spain and of a Spanish Empire had, however, long been established in the consciousness of the Spanish elites.[75]

Traditionally, however, such consciousness had little significance in early modern international relations. Territories were frequently shifted among rulers without regard for the wishes of the inhabitants, most recently at the Peace of Ryswick. Daniel Defoe, for example, reflected this view when he assumed that

Britain, the Netherlands and France could do what they wished with the Spanish territories without paying any attention to the desires of the populace.[76]

Nevertheless, the Spaniards who belonged to the social groups which benefited from the empire's existence felt very strongly that the whole inheritance should be transmitted intact to a single successor after Carlos II's death. Despite their long allegiance to the Habsburgs, their desire to avoid partition took precedence over loyalty to the House of Austria. Had the electoral prince of Bavaria outlived Carlos II, they would have accepted him as their king in order to maintain the integrity of the empire. After the death of the young Bavarian, the Spanish elites would probably have accepted any candidate whose accession would prevent partition. The fundamental fact remains that any attempt to partition the Spanish Empire would have led to armed resistance by at least some Spaniards, even if there were no real hope of success.[77]

For many years scholars paid little or no attention to what Emperor Leopold wanted or to how important his actions were. It is only within the last few decades that more scholars are recognizing his importance.

In particular, more attention is now being paid to Italy.[78] The peninsula's importance in European politics at the end of the Renaissance as well as its departure from centre stage during much of the seventeenth century are well known. As late as the Nine Years' War, Italy had not 'represented a very high priority for the Austrians'.[79] It was only the prospect of acquiring territory in Italy after the death of Carlos II and the fear of danger if Italy should fall to the Bourbons which prompted a dramatic shift in Austrian attitudes after the Peace of Ryswick.[80] They could not let the French establish themselves in the peninsula, especially in Milan, either directly by the Grand Dauphin's inheriting the territories or indirectly (as they saw it) by Philip of Anjou's controlling the Spanish territories.

Louis XIV, already concerned by Leopold's successes in the Balkans, could not allow the Austrians to establish themselves in Italy either. Louis correctly recognized that Italy (especially Milan) was the key to preventing the communication and cooperation between Spain and Austria which would be such a terrible danger to his own realm.[81]

In any case, Louis had agreed in the Partition Treaties to take his share of the Spanish inheritance mainly in Italy because of the position of the Maritime Powers. They opposed Louis XIV's getting any benefits from the Spanish succession, but they realized that they had to agree that he receive something. In that case, so far as the British and Dutch were concerned, it was preferable that any French gains be as far away from their own borders as possible — hence the decision that Louis XIV's gains would be in Italy.[82]

In view of these assumptions and conflicting goals, what conclusions must be drawn about the origins of the War of the Spanish Succession? First, the view that traditional, political factors were more important than other kinds — economic, for example — is correct. But, it is necessary to place politics in a wider perspective than is ordinarily done.

Second, the situation between 1697 and 1702 must be examined on the level of the international system itself. We need to see the context in which individuals acted rather than focus on the personalities of the decision-makers.

Third, the outbreak of war was part of a process, essentially the same process which led to the fight on the playground discussed earlier. The direction of events was set in February 1699 when the death of the electoral prince of Bavaria removed the last possibility that the Spanish succession could be resolved peacefully. War was inevitable. No human being could stop relations between the major powers from deteriorating into war. It was only a question of when they would start fighting.

Use of a word like 'inevitable' raised hackles. What proof is there that an event was inevitable other than the tautology that it was inevitable because it happened? Since historians and social scientists do not enjoy the luxury of a laboratory in which to test their theories by replaying events, we must use reason and historical common sense to see whether there were any plausible alternatives which could have resolved the Spanish succession without war. A number of scenarios have been proposed.

Some suggestions can only be classed as miraculous. If Carlos II had somehow gained the health he never had and lived many more years, some unforeseeable solution might have developed. Similarly, if Carlos and his second queen had somehow conceived and delivered a living heir, the problem would have been resolved as long as the heir lived. A birth at such a late date would have been a true miracle, however, or at least the result of an incredibly unlikely indiscretion on the part of the queen.

A more likely act of God was the death of one of the other key figures in the drama. Would the death of Leopold I, Louis XIV or William III have created a situation in which their successors would have been either forced or able to avoid war? Leopold's heir, Joseph, was such a warhawk that he would certainly have taken stands which were at least as forceful as anything his cautious father did. The Grand Dauphin felt so strongly about the Spanish succession that he roused himself from his usual lethargy to argue forcefully in favour of accepting the will of Carlos II. It is unlikely that he would have given up without a fight had he become king of France before Carlos died. If both William III and/or his sister-in-law Anne had died before Carlos, there are a number of possible consequences. Many of them would have led to conflict at home and abroad. Such a conflict might have been settled peacefully, but it would have been much more likely to merge with a European-wide war. In sum, it is most unlikely that the death of any of the other major rulers would have led to a substantially different course of events, especially not one which meant peace in Europe.

Another scenario suggests that either Louis XIV or Leopold I might have abandoned all his claims and allowed a prince of the other dynasty to acquire all of Carlos II's territories. This idea is utterly implausible; it disregards everything we know about the assumptions and behaviour of early modern rulers. Completely ignoring, for example, Louis XIV's belief that the Bourbons were the legitimate successors of Carlos II, neither he nor any other French monarch could have seriously considered such an act: 'that would mean — in view of Leopold's refusal to give an undertaking that the empire of Charles V should not be restored — the certainty of encirclement, the probable loss of the gains of his own reign ... and the possibility of losing even the gains of 1648 and 1659'.[83] Leopold had equally good reasons not even to consider the possibility of abandoning the whole succession.

Furthermore, 'the other European powers looked with horror at the prospect of the entire Spanish empire passing into either French or Austrian hands'.[84] While the Bavarian electoral prince still lived, Louis and Leopold might have renounced their dynastic claims in his favour as a way of avoiding war. After Joseph Ferdinand died, however, there was no alternative candidate with hereditary claims strong enough to allow both Louis and Leopold to accept him. The idea that either Louis or Leopold could have totally renounced his claims in favour of the other is absurd. No early modern monarch could have done that.

Another scenario for avoiding war is that Leopold might have accepted the Second Partition Treaty — the one which gave so much of the Spanish inheritance to his own house in the person of his second son, Archduke Charles. If Leopold had accepted the treaty and if the other signatories had all acted in concert, Spanish opposition to partition might have been overcome. Such a suggestion ignores the deep-seated mistrust which decision-makers had of each other and assumes the very unlikely possibility that none of the major powers would try to take advantage of Spanish unrest or revolt in order to defend or increase its own share and thereby provoke a war.

More importantly, this scenario ignores the fact that the Second Partition Treaty did not come close to recognizing, much less satisfying, the most basic Austrian interests. True, the House of Austria would receive the lion's share of the Spanish monarchy, but this would go to a cadet line whereas the portion assigned the Bourbons would go to the Grand Dauphin and eventually be joined with the French royal patrimony.[85] Furthermore, since the division of territory envisioned by the Second Partition Treaty had been decided primarily to satisfy the desire of the Maritime Powers to keep any gains Louis XIV made as far away from themselves as possible, the portions assigned to the Habsburgs were not those which Leopold wanted. In particular, the Habsburgs were not to have Milan, and the state which possessed that would be a constant threat to the nearby Austrian hereditary lands. The Austrians also recognized that their exclusion from Italy was designed to limit their communications with Spain itself.[86] It is difficult if not impossible to believe that any early modern ruler in Leopold's place, no matter what his personality, could have accepted the *fait accompli* which the Second Partition Treaty offered him.

If not by the Second Partition Treaty, could war have been avoided by some other division of the Spanish inheritance? After all, Leopold had made a partition treaty with Louis XIV in 1668 in which he yielded much more than the Second Partition Treaty required him to give up. It has been argued that 'Leopold was prepared, despite his strong dynastic feelings, to contemplate a partition of the inheritance, though he refused to discuss one while Charles II was alive'.[87] Also:

'Leopold might have been willing to listen to French offers after the publication of Carlos' will, but his pride forbade him to make the first step'.[88] Others believe that, before Carlos II died, Leopold 'would probably have accepted a partition, had his share of the succession included the whole of Spanish Italy'.[89]

This analysis runs into several problems. Louis XIV would certainly have discussed a partition with the Austrians, but they simply would not negotiate at a time when something positive might have been accomplished. Furthermore, it is impossible to imagine a partition treaty giving all of Spanish Italy to the Habsburgs which would also have been acceptable to Louis XIV and the Maritime Powers. The British and the Dutch did not want Louis XIV to gain benefits on the northern or north-eastern frontiers of his kingdom which threatened them; neither would they have agreed to give large portions of the Iberian peninsula or the Spanish colonies to him, even if he wanted them. Louis could hardly have accepted the great increase in Austrian power which owning Italy would give them without some substantial compensation elsewhere. But there was nothing else he could be offered which would have been acceptable to the other powers.

What if Louis XIV had decided differently when presented with the will of Carlos II? What if he had stood by the Second Partition Treaty instead of accepting the inheritance for his grandson? Insofar as the outbreak of hostilities was concerned, there was really no alternative. Upon Louis XIV's refusal, the same offer of 'Spain entire' would have been made to Leopold's second son and the emperor would unquestionably have accepted. Louis would then have been forced to fight not only the Austrians but the Spaniards in order to get his son's portion. As William said, the Maritime Powers had made the Partition Treaty to avoid a war, not to fight one; they would not fight on the Sun King's behalf. Whichever way Louis decided when presented with the will of Carlos II, there would still have been war unless Louis simply abandoned his son's claim to any portion of the Spanish inheritance, a scenario which has already been rebutted.

In his biography of William III, Stephen B. Baxter presents yet another possibility:

> Louis XIV seems to have hoped that he would be allowed to take the whole of the Spanish inheritance without a war. And well he might have, if he had played his cards better. They were excellent cards. If he had been willing to offer the maritime powers some assurances as to their trade and their barrier in the Netherlands; if he had coupled this with some negligible offer of satisfaction for Leopold such as Milan ... ; then it might well have been impossible for William to reform the Grand Alliance. But Louis would not offer any reasonable satisfaction to the English or the Dutch or the Emperor. Perhaps the French thought they could keep everything. More likely they felt war to be inevitable, and by their conduct they made it so.[90]

There are a number of major problems with these suggestions. Baxter assumes that Louis had enough control over his grandson to force Philip to sacrifice Spanish territories and interests. Even if he did have such control over Philip himself, Louis could scarcely have dared to weaken the new king's position with the Spaniards as much as such sacrifices would have entailed. Second, no king of France could have offered enough concessions in the Spanish Netherlands to satisfy the Dutch without creating an intolerable danger to the already questionable security of France's northern frontier, especially given the climate of mistrust which reigned in those years.

Finally, even if Louis could have insisted that Milan be turned over to Leopold despite the opposition of the Spaniards, is it realistic to think that the Austrians would have been satisfied with such a negligible offer? Would they not have insisted on most if not all of the Spanish possessions in Italy?

After all, Leopold believed that he could afford a war with the Bourbons because he was certain that the Maritime Powers would be forced to join him in any conflict. Upon learning that Louis XIV had accepted the will of Carlos II, Leopold declared: 'France has pushed the Maritime Powers over to my side; she cannot go back to the Partition Treaty, and Europe will join with me to prevent her having the [Spanish] monarchy'.[91] Although his opinion appeared overly optimistic at that moment, time would prove Leopold correct. Within a year Britain and the Netherlands had joined him in the struggle against the Bourbons. As Ragnhild Hatton says, in any conflict over the Spanish succession the Dutch and the British 'would eventually be drawn to the side that fought against Louis XIV'.[92] Although she does not press the point, this is one of the key reasons that a widescale European war was inevitable. Leopold was wrong, however, in saying that Louis XIV had pushed the Maritime Powers to his side. Once the inevitable conflict between Leopold and Louis began, the Maritime Powers could not stand aside because they essentially shared the belief expressed by Daniel Defoe: 'Let our Measures be what they will, if we do not keep the Enemy, the French I mean, out of *Spain*, we are undone'.[93] The entry of other lesser powers was just a matter of time and their interest, but not of great importance.

Other potential scenarios could be suggested. Defoe at one time claimed that Louis XIV's acceptance of Carlos II's testament was simply a ploy to see what the other European powers would do and that he would back down if they resented it too much.[94] In 1701 the duke of Savoy seemed very concerned that Philip V would marry an Austrian archduchess as Carlos II suggested in his will.[95] But even if such ideas were accurate, it is difficult to see how they would have prevented the outbreak of war. Other scenarios are even more far-fetched.

The conclusion is clear. The military men who rejoiced at the death of the electoral prince of Bavaria in February 1699 because it was 'an inevitable cause of war'[96] were right. When the Peace of Ryswick was made in 1697 before the death of Carlos II, thereby excluding the question of the Spanish succession from settlement at the same time as the other issues of the Nine Years' War, the likelihood of war over the Spanish succession was greatly increased. After the death of Joseph Ferdinand of Bavaria, the only realistically possible compromise candidate for the Spanish throne, war became inevitable. The conflicting goals and interests of the major states and princes could not have been peacefully resolved without abandonments of claims and rights which were unthinkable in the early modern period.

Just as statesmen could not control the events in 1914 which led to the First World War, neither could statesmen living around 1700 control events leading to the War of the Spanish Succession. The situation on the system level of international relations was beyond the control of any individual acting alone or even with a few others. Only a comprehensive effort by all the major rulers to work in concert could have avoided the catastrophe, but the mutual mistrust and conflicting interests inherent in the international system made such cooperation impossible.

There is no plausible scenario for a course of international relations around 1700 which would not have led to war. Once fighting started between some of the states (especially between France and Austria), there was no plausible way it could have remained limited. The war was determined at the level of the international system itself.

NOTES

The author wishes to thank Northern Arizona University for a sabbatical leave and the University Organized Research Committee for summer support which made completion of this article possible. Thanks also to the staffs of the Newberry Library, the Huntington Library, the British Library, the British Museum, the Public Record Office, the Bibliothèque Nationale, and the Archives of the Ministère des Affaires Etrangères. Suzanne, Andrew, and Laura Roosen have all helped on this project in many ways.

1. Examples include C. Hippeau, *Avèrement des Bourbons au trone d'Espagne* (2 vols., Paris, 1875); A[rsène] Legrelle, *La Diplomatie française et la succession d'Espagne* 2d ed. (6 vols., Braine-le Comte, 1895-99); Hermile Reynald, *Succession d'Espagne, Louis XIV et Guillaume III, Histoire des deux traités de partage et du testament de Charles II d'après la correspondance inédite de Louis XIV* (2 vols., Paris, 1883).

2. David H. Pinkney, 'The Pinkney Thesis Reconsidered', *Proceedings of the Annual Meeting of the Western Society for French History* 2 (1975), p. 410. Pinkney writes specifically about French history, but the idea applies to all European history. See also his 'The Dilemma of the American Historian of Modern France', *French Historical Studies* 1 (1958), pp. 11-25, and 'The Dilemma of the American Historian of Modern France Reconsidered', *French Historical Studies* 9 (1975), pp. 170-81.

3. Especially Mark A. Thomson, 'Louis XIV and the Origins of the War of the Spanish Succession', reprinted in Ragnhild Hatton and J. S. Bromley, eds., *William III and Louis XIV, Essays 1680-1720* (Liverpool, 1968) pp. 140-61. Ragnhild Hatton's many works are included in appropriate notes below.

4. See, for example, William F. Church, *Louis XIV in Historical Thought from Voltaire to the Annales School* (New York, 1976), or almost any biography of Louis XIV.

5. Derek McKay, *Prince Eugene of Savoy* (London, 1977), p. 55.

6. See the comments on the role of small states in Richard H. Thompson, *Lothar Franz von Schönborn and the Diplomacy of the Electorate of Mainz from the Treaty of Ryswick to the Outbreak of the War of the Spanish Succession* (The Hague, 1973), pp. 112-13.

7. Kenneth N. Waltz, *Man, the State and War: A Theoretical Analysis* (New York, 1959), p. 12.

8. See, for example, Gaston Zeller, *Les Temps modernes, II, de Louis XIV à 1789*, vol. 3 of *Histoire des relations internationales* (Paris, 1955), pp. 81-86, or Geoffrey Treasure, *The Making of Modern Europe, 1648-1780* (1985), pp. 274-78.

9. Paul Gordon Lauren, 'Diplomacy: History, Theory, and Policy', in his *Diplomacy: New Approaches in History, Theory, and Policy* (1979), p. 6.

10. *Ibid.*

11. Norbert Elias, *The Court Society*, trans. Edmund Jephcott (New York, 1983), pp. 1–3.

12. Michael Howard, *War and the Liberal Conscience* (Oxford, 1981), p. 23.

13. J.-B. Duroselle, 'De l'"Histoire diplomatique" à l'"histoire des relations internationales"', in *Mélanges Pierre Renouvin* (Paris, 1966); J. M. Black, 'The theory of the balance of power in the first half of the eighteenth century: a note on sources', *Review of International Studies* 9 (1983); Albert E. Scheflen, *Body Language and the Social Order: Communication as Behavioral Control* (Englewood Cliffs, New Jersey, 1972), p. 201.

14. Stephen B. Baxter, *William III and the Defense of European Liberty, 1650–1702* (New York, 1966), p. 388; Church, *Louis XIV in Historical Thought*, p. 88.

15. Zeller, *Temps modernes*, pp. 81–86; Church, *Louis XIV in Historical Thought*, pp. 85–86.

16. Thomson, 'Louis XIV and the Origins', p. 161.

17. Paul Langford, *The Eighteenth Century, 1688–1815*, Modern British Foreign Policy Series (New York, 1976), p. 54.

18. Ragnhild Hatton, 'Louis XIV and His Fellow Monarchs', in John Rule, ed., *Louis XIV and the Craft of Kingship* (Columbus, Ohio, 1969), pp. 178–79; Church, *Louis XIV in Historical Thought*, pp. 90–91.

19. Derek McKay and H. M. Scott, *The Rise of the Great Powers, 1648–1815* (1983), p. 57.

20. F. H. Hinsley, *Power and the Pursuit of Peace: Theory and Practice in the History of Relations between States* (New York, 1963), pp. 331–32.

21. William Roosen, 'Early Modern Diplomatic Ceremonial: A Systems Approach', *Journal of Modern History* 52 (1980), pp. 470–71; Andrew Lossky, 'France in the System of Europe in the Seventeenth Century', *Proceedings of the Annual Meeting of the Western Society for French History* 1 (1974), p. 33.

22. Scheflen, *Body Language*, p. 83.

23. *Ibid.*, p. 201; see also pp. 130 and 202.

24. Herbert Butterfield, 'Diplomacy', in Ragnhild Hatton and M. S. Anderson, eds., *Studies in Diplomatic History: Essays in Memory of David Bayne Horn* (1970), p. 361; see also Robert T. Oliver, *Culture and Communication: The Problem of Penetrating National and Cultural Boundaries* (Springfield, Illinois, 1962), pp. 12–13.

25. Edward T. Hall, *The Silent Language* (Garden City, New York, 1959), p. 122.

26. Geoffrey Blainey, *The Causes of War* (New York, 1973), pp. 157–59.

27. Paul D. Solon, 'From the Justice of War to the Law of Conquest: An Essay on the Relationship between International Law and French Historiography in the Seventeenth Century', *Proceedings of the Annual Meeting of the Western Society for French History* 8 (1981), p. 109.

28. William Roosen, *The Age of Louis XIV: The Rise of Modern Diplomacy* (Cambridge, Mass., 1976), p. 54.

29. Herbert Butterfield, 'The New Diplomacy and Historical Diplomacy', in H. Butterfield and M. Wight, eds., *Diplomatic Investigations* (Cambridge, Mass., 1966), p. 188.

30. Sirtema de Grovestins, *Guillaume III et Louis XIV*, new ed. (8 vols., Paris, 1868) 7, pp. 52–54.

31. For example, W. E. Brown, *The First Bourbon Century in France* (London, 1971), p. 162; Robert A. Kann, *A History of the Habsburg Empire, 1526–1918* (Berkeley and Los Angeles, 1974), p. 83; Thompson, *Lothar Franz von Schönborn*, p. 148, n. 67.

32. George d'Aubusson, *La Défense du droit de Marie-Thérèse d'Austriche, reine de France, à la succession des couronnes d'Espagne* (Paris, 1699).

33. Paris. AE. CP Espagne vol. 57, fols. 250–250v, 'Question problématique: Qui est-ce qui sera le successeur du Roy Charles d'Espagne, s'il n'avoit point d'enfans'.

34. Lauren, 'Diplomacy', 9.

35. London. BM. Add. MSS. 34335, fols. 69–70; Louis André, *Louis XIV et l'Europe* (Paris, 1950), p. 285; Ragnhild Hatton, 'Louis XIV et l'Europe: Eléments d'une révision historiographique', *XVIIe siècle*, no. 123 (1979), pp. 128–32; Comte d'Haussonville, 'La

Reprise des relations diplomatiques entre la France et la Savoie au moment de la paix de Ryswick', *Revue d'histoire diplomatique* 13 (1899), pp. 362–63.

36. Grovestins, *Guillaume III et Louis XIV*, vol. 7, pp. 145–46; Henry Kissinger made the point 'that *the way* negotiations are carried out is almost as important as *what* is negotiated. The choreography of how one enters negotiations, what is settled first, and in what manner is inseparable from the substance of the issues'. *American Foreign Policy*, expanded ed. (New York, 1974), pp. 110–111.

37. McKay, *Prince Eugene of Savoy*, p. 55; Reynald, *Succession d'Espagne*, vol. 1, p. 33.

38. Grovestins, *Guillaume III et Louis XIV*, vol 7, p. 137.

39. London. PRO. SP 108/68.

40. Count Merode-Westerloo, *Mémoires*, as quoted in R. B. Mowat, *A History of European Diplomacy, 1451–1789* (1928 [reprinted 1971]), pp. 159–60.

41. London. PRO. SP 108/69.

42. An English translation of the will is in Geoffrey Symcox, *War, Diplomacy, and Imperialism, 1618–1763* (New York, 1974), pp. 62–74.

43. Paris. AE. Mém et doc, fonds divers. Espagne, vol. 88, fol. 39ff.

44. Daniel Druckman, *Human Factors in International Negotiations: Social-Psychological Aspects of International Conflict* (Beverly Hills, 1973), pp. 62–63; Saul Friedländer and Miklos Molnar, 'Histoire nouvelle et histoire des relations internationales', in Saul Friedländer and others, eds., *L'Historien et les relations internationales* (Geneva, 1981), p. 84; Dean G. Pruitt, 'Definition of the Situation as a Determinant of International Action', in Herbert C. Kelman, ed., *International Behavior: A Social-Psychological Analysis* (New York, 1965), p. 394.

45. Church, *Louis XIV in Historical Thought*, pp. 85–86.

46. Gaston Zeller, 'Politique extérieure et diplomatie sous Louis XIV,' *Revue d'histoire moderne* 6 (1931), p. 131.

47. Church, *Louis XIV in Historical Thought*, p. 73; Zeller, *Temps modernes*, 9.

48. Hatton, 'Louis XIV et l'Europe', p. 116.

49. *Ibid.*, pp. 126–32.

50. Baxter, *William III*, pp. 274–75.

51. Edward O. Wilson, *Sociobiology: The New Synthesis* (Cambridge, Mass., 1975), p. 553; François de Callières, *The Art of Diplomacy*, ed. H. M. A. Keens-Soper and Karl W. Schweizer (New York, 1983), p. 83; [Antoine] Pecquet, *Discours sur l'art de negocier* (Paris, 1737), pp. 6–8.

52. Hatton, 'Louis XIV et l'Europe', p. 118.

53. Mark A. Thomson, 'Parliament and Foreign Policy, 1689–1714', in Ragnhild Hatton and J. S. Bromley, eds., *William III and Louis XIV, Essays 1680–1720* (Liverpool, 1968), p. 131.

54. Ragnhild Hatton, *War and Peace, 1680–1720* (1969), p. 6; for a sample peaceful protestation, see d'Avaux's instruction in February 1701, *Recueil des instructions données aux ambassadeurs . . . Hollande*, vol. 22 (Paris, 1923), p. 110.

55. The comment by Steven Lukes in 'Political Ritual and Social Integration', *Sociology* 9 (1975), p. 305, refers to rituals but the statement applies more broadly. See also Erving Goffman, *The Presentation of Self in Everyday Life* (Woodstock, New York, 1973), p. 51, and Hall, *Silent Language*, p. 121.

56. Oliver, *Culture and Communication*, p. 65.

57. *Ibid*; Humphrey Trevelyan, *Diplomatic Channels* (Boston, 1973), p. 68.

58. Konrad Lorenz, *On Aggression*, trans. Marjorie Kerr Wilson (New York, 1966), p. 82.

59. Bert A. Brown, 'The Effects of Need to Maintain Face on Interpersonal Bargaining', *Journal of Experimental Social Psychology* 4 (1968), pp. 108–109 and 119–121.

60. Chadwick F. Alger, 'Personal Contact in Governmental Organizations', in Herbert C. Kelman, ed., *International Behavior: A Social-Psychological Analysis* (New York, 1965), p. 532.

61. Charlie R. Steen, 'Christendom as a Representation of Belief in European Unity at

the Time of Louis XIV', *Proceedings of the Annual Meeting of the Western Society for French History* 2 (1975), pp. 48–58; Hinsley, *Power and the Pursuit of Peace*, p. 18.

62. F. H. Hinsley, 'The Development of the European States System since the Eighteenth Century', *Transactions of the Royal Historical Society*, 5th ser., 2 (1961), p. 70.

63. Joseph Klaits, *Printed Propaganda under Louis XIV: Absolute Monarchy and Public Opinion* (Princeton, 1976), p. 23.

64. Matthew Prior, *The History of His Own Time*, 2nd ed., ed. J. Bancks (London, 1740), p. 102.

65. As quoted in M. E. Howard, *The Causes of Wars*, The Creighton Trust Lecture 1981 (London, n.d.), p. 9.

66. McKay, *Prince Eugene of Savoy*, p. 53.

67. Butterfield, 'Diplomacy', pp. 367–70; Hinsley, *Power and the Pursuit of Peace*, pp. 27–29; Gaston Zeller, 'Le Principe d'équilibre dans la politique internationale avant 1789', *Revue historique* 215 (1956), pp. 25–26.

68. Hinsley, 'Development of the European States System', p. 73.

69. See William Roosen, *Daniel Defoe and Diplomacy*, forthcoming.

70. Louis XIV to Tallard, 13 Feb. 1699, Grovestins, *Guillaume III et Louis XIV*, vol. 7, p. 222.

71. Church, *Louis XIV in Historical Thought*, pp. 88–89.

72. Charles W. Ingrao, *In Quest and Crisis: Emperor Joseph I and the Habsburg Monarchy* (West Lafayette, Ind., 1979), p. 1.

73. Butterfield, 'Diplomacy', pp. 360–61.

74. Hatton, *War and Peace*, pp. 18–19.

75. Antonio Dominguez Ortiz, *The Golden Age of Spain, 1516–1659*, trans. James Casey (New York, 1971), pp. 1–2.

76. Daniel Defoe, *The Two Great Questions Consider'd. I. What the French King will Do, with Respect to the Spanish Monarchy. II. What Measures the English ought to Take* (London, 1700), 28 pp. , reprinted in his *A True Collection of the Writings of the Author of the True Born English-Man* (London, 1703), pp. 345–63.

77. Linda and Marsha Frey, *A Question of Empire: Leopold I and the War of Spanish Succession, 1701–1705* (Boulder, 1983), p. 11.

78. Andrew Lossky has noted Italy's importance at many historical meetings. See also Jean Bérenger, 'Louis XIV, l'Empereur et l'Europe de l'Est', *XVIIe siècle* (31 (1979), pp. 173–94; Hatton, *War and Peace*, p. 18; Guido Quazza, 'Italy's Role in the European Problems of the First Half of the Eighteenth Century', in Hatton and Anderson, eds., *Studies in Diplomatic History*, p. 140.

79. McKay, *Prince Eugene of Savoy*, p. 37.

80. *Ibid*; Frey, *A Question of Empire*, pp. 1–2; Ingrao, *In Quest and Crisis*, p. 5.

81. Louis XIV to Tallard, 13 Feb. 1699, Grovestins, *Guillaume III et Louis XIV*, vol. 7, pp. 222–23; Hatton, *War and Peace*, pp. 18–19; Prior, *History of His Own Time*, p. 100; McKay, *Prince Eugene of Savoy*, p. 54.

82. Vauban to Puyzieulx, 22 Aug. 1700, *Lettres intimes (inédites) addressées au marquis de Puyzieulx, 1699–1705*, ed. Hyrvoix de Landosle (Paris, 1924) pp. 95–97; McKay, *Prince Eugene of Savoy*, pp. 55–56.

83. Hatton, 'Louis XIV and His Fellow Monarchs', p. 178.

84. McKay, *Prince Eugene of Savoy*, p. 55; Daniel Defoe, *The Interests of the Several Princes and States of Europe Consider'd, with respect to the Succession of the Crown of Spain* (London, 1698), pp. 29 & 32, and also his *Two Great Questions Consider'd*, p. 358; Manchester to Vernon, 9 Nov. 1700, *Court and Society from Elizabeth to Anne* (London, 1864), vol. 2, p. 172; Ludwig von Pastor, *The History of the Popes from the Close of the Middle Ages*, trans. Dom Ernest Graf (London, 1940 [reprinted 1957]), vol. 32, pp. 681–82; Kann, *History of the Habsburg Empire*, pp. 77–78.

85. See, for example, Prior, *History of His Own Time*, pp. 97–101; Paris. AE. Mém et doc, fonds divers. Espagne, vol. 88, fol. 28v.

86. McKay, *Prince Eugene of Savoy*, pp. 55–56; Ingrao, *In Quest and Crisis*, p. 5.

87. McKay, *Prince Eugene of Savoy*, p. 55. This argument may be doubted. When the French envoy extraordinary in Vienna notified Leopold about the Second Partition Treaty on 18 May 1700, the Imperials suggested other divisions. Extract from negotiations of Villars, Paris. AE. Mém et doc, fonds divers. Autriche, vol. 3, fols. 31–32.

88. Hatton, 'Louis XIV and His Fellow Monarchs', p. 194, n. 144.

89. Ingrao, *In Quest and Crisis*, p. 79.

90. Baxter, *William III*, p. 388.

91. André, *Louis XIV et l'Europe*, p. 303.

92. Hatton, 'Louis XIV and His Fellow Monarchs', p. 176.

93. Defoe, *Two Great Questions Consider'd*, p. 362.

94. *Ibid.*, p. 345.

95. Paris. AE. Mém et doc, fonds divers. Sardaigne, vol. 7.

96. André, *Louis XIV et l'Europe*, p. 288.

7

FROM UTRECHT TO THE LITTLE WAR WITH SPAIN: PEACE AT ALMOST ANY PRICE HAD TO BE THE CASE

Claude Sturgill

In the early modern European world, war was the trade of kings, and life was short, brutal, and nasty as John Dryden knew only too well.[1] Yet by the Treaty of the Pyrenees between France and Spain of 1659 the settled, established states, especially in western Europe, had realized that a conquered territory denuded of crops, working mines and people was at worst a pyrrhic victory and at best a constant drain on the treasury for some generations to come. Just short of a century later Lord Chesterfield could write in one of his famous letters, 'War is pusillanimously carried out in this degenerate age; quarter is given; towns are taken and the people spared; even in a storm, a woman can hardly hope for the benefit of a rape'.[2] During this century discipline had come to the armies. At least in western Europe soldiers were now better fed, paid, and cared for than had been the sorry lot of their ancestors during the bloody and seemingly constantly recurring wars of the Reformation era from 1520 until 1659.

Wars were not to be fought now for religious reasons although religion could, from time to time, still be a very convenient excuse for butchering a few Turks here and there. Wars were now to be fought for limited dynastic gains. At the conclusion of this type of conflict some territory was expected to change hands but the national integrity of each of the recognized European powers such as Britain, France, Spain, Prussia, and Austria was, beyond question, always allowed to continue. The western European balance of power, if not founded by the Wars of Louis XIV from 1666–1715, had certainly come to be an established fact in the minds of all the diplomats by the end of the War of the Spanish Succession in 1714.

The cost of this single war, fought over the last will of Charles II of Spain, had left all of the European governments in an unsettled financial and political situation. New dynasties seemed to be the order of the day. The Hanoverians arrived in Britain, the Bourbons were established in Spain, and France entered another of her regency periods which, at least in French history, always seem to signify a period of national weakness and irresolution at the very pinnacle of that state.

The great colonial wars were still in the future. What was needed after 1715 was a long period of peace. It is not at all surprising that the type of international diplomacy practised in this short period is analogous to that of the United States of America in the very short period between the Spanish American War of 1898 and their entry into World War I in 1917. During this brief period Elihu Root wrote as the motto of the United States Army War college, 'Make Peace, Not War!'[3] A few years later, while serving in a different capacity as the American Secretary of State, Root wrote, 'The main object of diplomacy [is] to keep the country out of trouble!'[4] When nations need a period of peace they only very regretfully engage in warfare. The obverse is also true. When nations have enjoyed a long period of peace, for a generation or so, they become fearful of other nations for any reason that just happens to be around, be it dynastic, economic, colonial, or just a matter of national pride and honour. The eighteenth century would see many wars fought over trade, colonies, and pride but not in the years immediately following the conclusion of the War of the Spanish Succession. What was needed was peace and not war.

For thirty years after Utrecht the greatest maritime power, Britain, and the greatest land power, France, remained at peace with each other. As long as this condition continued a general European war, such as those in the age of Louis XIV, could not begin. Neither kingdom could afford to continue the long period of warfare that had really stretched from the 1680s until 1715. It was not really a question of either country being satisfied with the Treaty of Utrecht but rather a matter of finance and hereditary monarchy. France and Britain were both on the verge of economic collapse or at least in a state of semi-bankruptcy. This grave problem was exacerbated by another set of circumstances surrounding the successions to their thrones: Louis XIV was about to die without any adult male heir and the Hanoverians were to inherit Britain.

A long period of peace could only come about if the successions to the thrones of Britain and France were rigidly maintained. According to the Treaty of Utrecht Britain had to be Protestant and Hanoverian. The Stuart Pretender James III and his followers the Jacobites threatened the Hanoverian succession.[5] Until the birth of a dauphin in September 1729 the succession to the young Louis XV, the infant great-grandson of Louis XIV, was also very uncertain. As part of the Utrecht settlement Louis XV's uncle Philip V of Spain, a grandson of Louis XIV, had renounced his right of succession to the French throne, leaving as the next in line Louis XIV's nephew, Philip II, Duke of Orléans. Philip V doubted the validity of the Utrecht renunciation and maintained links with a formidable 'Spanish' party in France.[6]

These insecure successions were the crucial element in international relations from Utrecht to the Quintuple Alliance of 1720. Other international problems, such as the Great Northern War, paled in comparison to the fearful thought that the western European powers would once more engage in a world war. Both the diplomatic and warfare sides of this era have been exceedingly well researched and possibly written to death with the display of every type of specific detail that lies withering in deadly wait for the historian's pen. What has not been done with this subject is to marry political necessity with not only the diplomatic manoeuvring but also with the hard and often harsh military facts that were only too well known to the French Regent, Philip of Orléans, and the advisers of George I of Britain.

Immediately after the end of hostilities at the conclusion of the War of the Spanish Succession, both Britain and France began to reduce their imposing military forces by land and by sea. By the opening of 1717 France had reduced her standing army from some 400,000 men under arms to a force little more than 140,000 and had virtually drydocked her fleet. The British had reduced the standing establishment to less than 30,000 which would soon drop another 10,000. Thus both kingdoms in a real sense were down to garrison strength, maintaining only enough military forces to provide for the police of their respective kingdoms and colonies. In contrast the period witnessed a substantial growth in Spanish forces, one made necessary by the aggressive plans of Philip V, his second wife Elisabeth Farnese, and his leading minister Cardinal Alberoni. They sought a reversal of the pro-Austrian diplomatic settlement of Italy at Utrecht, a reversal that the Austrian ruler, the Emperor Charles VI, was determined to resist. Technically Spain and Austria were still in a state of war, although both were enjoying a protracted cessation of hostilities. War was prevented by Charles' Turkish commitments and the Spanish need for a breathing space. Charles VI did not have the resources to fight a two-front war and the Spanish economy had been badly mauled during the War of the Spanish Succession, a major part of which had been fought in Spain. Though Philip V, thanks to Cardinal Alberoni, was prepared to strike before Charles VI could finish off the Turks in and around Belgrade and then shift enough troops to Italy to make any real difference, the threat of war was always there and it was really up to the French and the British to preserve the peace, the Dutch being largely out of the picture in any active diplomatic and military sense.

It was not at all surprising to the French when Lord Stair, the British ambassador in Paris, made the first overtures for a special Anglo-French alliance, in which both countries would agree to respect and enforce the provisions of Utrecht.[7] This was done not long before the death of Louis XIV in 1715, at a time when it was still uncertain just exactly what the provisions of that king's last will and testament would be. Stair had received instructions to cultivate the prospective French regent and even to go as far as offering to help Philip of Orléans secure a complete regency and even, one step further, to promise the regent that in the event of Louis XV's death he would have full British support to ascend the French throne. In return it was expected that Orléans would not only oppose James III but he would also drive him from France, and that the other provisions of the Treaty of Utrecht, such as the total destruction of the port of Dunkirk, on which Louis XIV was dragging his feet, would quickly be accomplished.

There is not any hard evidence to support the impression that Orléans paid any attention to what he was being offered by the British. Undoubtedly his mind was preoccupied with the thought that he might not be Regent at all or with very reduced powers. Yet when it was learned that Orléans had been named Regent, the British ministry was delighted. The news was better received in London than in Paris. The British ministers saw their chance to forge an alliance between the two monarchs. George I was threatened with possible problems from James III, Orléans from Philip V. The pro-Spanish party at the French court was led by such notables as the Duke and Duchess of Maine and Marshal Huxelles, the chief of the French ministry of foreign affairs. Among the French military leaders such marshals as Villeroy, Berwick, and Villars preferred Philip V of Spain as the king of France. Many members of the Parlement of Paris and the provincial nobility, especially in Brittany, resented the increasing centralization of authority in the person of the Regent as it was quickly applied in the space of three years, from 1715 to 1718. A small group of men philosophically in tune with Orléans, such as Abbé Dubois, John Law, and Claude le Blanc, who were three notable examples of the Regent's coterie, applied their common definition of Cartesianism to all aspects of the French state.[8] Simply put, Orléans insisted that it was the duty of the Crown to regulate all aspects of life in order to protect France and her people. Possibly the Duke of Orléans would have been more receptive to a British alliance much earlier but for the fact that he was not absolute, even in the sense of Louis XIV, even after the Parlement set aside the will of the latter. Given the weakness of his position Orléans was not in any position to make any decision that might entail a major shift in French foreign policy, at least not until he had some three years to gradually work his will using the very loyal royal bureaucracy and military forces. Nothing was going to deter the British ministers and their agent Lord Stair. Lord Stair understood that the Regent had first to establish control within France by reducing the indebtedness of the state, assuring the loyalty of key civil and military figures, and providing for the education and protection of the young Louis XV. Stair's method was to keep up a running dialogue with the Duke of Orléans but in such a way as to charm and cajole while never seemingly to push or anger.

Orléans continued his policy of trying to please everyone when it came time to support James III's invasion of Scotland in late 1715. He went as far as to have some vessels loaded with arms and ammunition but just as quickly had them unloaded on the proper British diplomatic protest. Of course Lord Stair was outspoken in his complaint but not to the point of angering beyond recall. Stair had the key to the character of Orléans, which was simply to stay alert and active around a man who was not looking for any form of trouble. The great difference in the handling of the French Regent between London and Madrid was that the Spanish, using their ambassador in Paris, Cellamare, plotted a *coup d'état* against Orléans, while the British at least appeared to be helpful in the form of letting the French diplomatic service know of the plot. The British diplomats had correctly reasoned that the key to their sought-after long period of peace was firm cooperation with the French and not with the Spanish.

After the failure of the '15, which proved the pro-Stuart party in the French court wrong, Orléans was more free to pursue a pro-British policy. After all the regent was not a dolt. He could see that to unite the first sea and the first land powers was the only viable way to ensure the continuance of the Treaty of Utrecht. And that, of course, meant that the peace would be kept.

The failure of the Pretender's descent somewhat changed the tone of the British offer to France; Lord Stair could now be just a shade firmer in his negotiations. Obviously George I was secure on his throne, despite any misgivings and fears still expressed in the Parliament and elsewhere. Stair could now begin to demand the permanent expulsion of the Pretender and his friends from France, the complete and total ruin of the port of Dunkirk, and that all of the provisions of the Treaty of

Utrecht be enforced in the most rigid manner possible. At this moment the cause came near to being lost. A backdoor soon opened that led to the long sought-for conclusion of a Franco-British Alliance. The Abbé Dubois, the old tutor of Philip of Orléans and possibly his oldest confidant, was sent on a secret diplomatic mission. Marshal Huxelles, chief of the French committee on foreign affairs, was aware of this mission at which he hotly protested as he was a leading member of the pro-Spanish party at the French court. On 2 July, 1716 Dubois left Paris disguised as a used book merchant. At The Hague he met George I's minister and these two strong-minded diplomats resolved to make the necessary treaty despite any misgivings on both sides of the channel. Dubois and Stanhope emerged from this meeting convinced that the other had opened negotiations in good faith. From this meeting on it was only a matter of working out enough compromises so that each could justify his actions at home.

Events also came to quicken the pace of the diplomacy. George I, as Elector of Hanover, was fearful of the renewed warfare between the contending parties in the Baltic region.[9] Orléans was aware that his troubles in Brittany, Languedoc and Paris were being manipulated by the Spanish. Both parties became eager to agree. To avoid the appearance in each of their countries that either head of state had sacrificed anything at all, they finally agreed in their formal treaty to guarantee only those parts of the Treaty of Utrecht that regulated the successions to their respective thrones. The implications were obvious. Much more had been discussed and agreed to. George I and Orléans had become partners in a European-wide peacekeeping operation. They would consult when their common interests were threatened and they would assist each other with military muscle when needed. These arrangements were settled in October, 1716 and formally agreed on 28 November 1716. The United Provinces acceded to the alliance on 4 January, 1717, and thus the Triple Alliance came into being. For all practical purposes the Triple Alliance remained the Dual Alliance, as the Dutch rarely ever actively participated save for a few combined fleet operations in the Baltic and some regiments on loan to George I. It appears that the Dutch were only consulted when it was convenient to London and/or Paris. By the Triple Alliance all three states agreed to come to the aid of their partners if one was attacked by any outside power. James III could not live in France, Lorraine, or Avignon and none of the allied powers would furnish any assistance to him or his followers. The deep water canals at Mardyke, which were under construction near the destroyed port of Dunkirk, would be filled in. Yet all of these detailed provisions required consultation prior to any action. The usual diplomatic loopholes were available.

This was a diplomatic revolution in the true sense of that often bandied-about phrase. Within two years France and Britain would be at war, in league with Charles VI and Victor Amadeus II, the Savoyard King of Sicily, against the grandson of Louis XIV, Philip V of Spain. This grand accomplishment proved the correctness and the perseverance of the most astute diplomatic advisers of George I. What France and Britain needed most was peace. Neither nation had any interest that would be served by another general war. Had this treaty not come along when it did, the likelihood would have been that both nations would have become involved in another Spanish Succession war. This Triple Alliance would prove strong enough to enforce the peace of western Europe[10] and to punish any warmonger who would try to disrupt this precious tranquillity.

In the eyes of France, Spain, by the time of the formal signing of the Triple Alliance, had already taken the first steps toward war. She was preparing for military conquest. Fortunately for the Anglo-French Alliance, Elisabeth Farnese forced Alberoni into military action long before the Spanish were ready. In August 1717 Spanish naval units landed some 9,000 troops on the island of Sardinia. The very weak Austrian garrisons quickly fell.[11] Spain had to be dealt with. A diplomatic solution would have been nice, but both London and Paris knew that a solution would have to be found on the battlefield. The trick would be to keep all military operations on the smallest possible scale. Really the idea was not to make war but to make peace. The diplomats had to remain in control and they had to keep the military on a short leash. Diplomatic exchanges were stepped up. Both the British and the French ambassadors tried to negotiate with Madrid. Abbé Dubois was sent to London and the British embassy in Paris became a clearing house for the protracted negotiations with Charles VI who remained the stumbling block to effective action, due to his Balkan war. Finally a pact was hammered out that all parties could live with. The terms of the Quadruple Alliance were not only realistic but even reasonable: Charles VI agreed to the Treaty of Utrecht, the Duchies of Parma and Tuscany were reserved for the sons of Elisabeth Farnese, Philip V would have to agree to the Treaty of Utrecht, Sicily would be ceded to the Emperor, Sardinia would go to the Duke of Savoy.[12] The Quadruple Alliance, signed in July 1718, did not represent a complete rejection of Spanish interests in Italy.

It was useless for Spain to oppose the military might aligned against her. Any further military actions on her part would require landings on both Sicily and mainland Italy. A complete mastery of the western Mediterranean would have to be maintained as well as very strong garrisons on her common frontier with France.

However, on 18 June 1718 the Spanish fleet left Barcelona, and on 3 July the Spaniards landed at Palermo, capturing the fortress there eleven days later. The weak Savoyard garrisons could do little more than shut themselves up in their citadels which fell with rather monotonous regularity until the Spanish controlled the island.[13] The invasion of Sicily drove the Duke of Savoy into the Quadruple Alliance. To exchange Sicily for Sardinia was a bad bargain but at least it was something.

The invasion of Sicily left the allied powers with but two choices, diplomatically speaking: Elisabeth Farnese could be permitted to do as she pleased or sufficient military force could be applied to convince her of the error of her ways. Yet the latter was a very hard choice, for it meant that the normal diplomatic routines had failed. In this era failed diplomacy meant that it was time to declare war. That could mean that all of the laborious diplomatic manoeuvring stretching back to at least the spring of 1715 would be for naught. What had to be done was to fight a little, carefully contained war, a war in which Spain would be put in her place but not really hurt. Diplomats and not generals had to maintain control. The only possible viable diplomatic–military strategy was to force the Spanish ships and men back within Spanish frontiers.

The allied diplomats, who directed the battleplan, kept all of these things in mind in their plans. A British fleet was needed to cut off the Spanish troops on Sardinia and Sicily. An Austrian major land force was to clear Sicily of Spanish troops. A strong diversion was necessary along the Pyrenees to prove that France was in earnest. France and Britain would carry out combined operations on Spanish seaports that were possible bases for a Jacobite invasion. All of these things and some other lesser ones proved that the diplomats still ruled the Quadruple Alliance and were working very hard to keep the peace of Europe.

The blows began to fall on Spain as, one by one, the fantasies of the Spanish Queen and her husband were punctured by the realities of sound international diplomacy and effective military cooperation. Admiral Byng sent the covering Spanish naval force to the bottom during the Battle of Cape Passaro off Syracuse on 18 August 1718. Spanish troops were now isolated on both Sicily and Sardinia. Negotiations were again opened with Madrid. A somewhat more rational Spanish royal pair would have realized that the game was up and agreed to the terms of the Quadruple Alliance. The other Spanish schemes came to light one by one as they completely failed in their execution. Alberoni had tried to obtain an agreement whereby Charles XII of Sweden would attack Britain in conjunction with a Spanish-led Stuart descent. Even when Charles XII was killed in Norway on 30 November 1718, the Spaniards determined to invade Britain. A fleet of some twenty-four ships, mostly transports, were sent on 15 March 1719, only to have many of them lost off Cape Finisterre during a hurricane.

Spain would not negotiate. Britain and France formally declared war on Spain in the winter of 1718–19. While both countries had declared war in what they considered to be a case of extremis, this was a particularly hard thing for Orléans. This meant that he would be sending French troops to shoot at the grandson of Louis XIV, hardly the most popular cause in France. What Philip V of Spain did not realize or could not accept was that by 1719 Orléans's authority was firmly established in France. The French army, save for a few personal exceptions, fought the Spanish. Officers and men did their duty with firmness and dispatch but not with very much enthusiasm. Orléans had to place the Duke and Duchess of Maine under a very light house arrest. He did arrest the Spanish ambassador and escort him out of the country. A few Breton noblemen lost their heads, others were fined, and several fled into exile during the Spanish-backed Pontcallec conspiracy of 1719. But all of these schemes just proved to be more failures.

All wars that are fought other than to the point of annihilation of one side or the other have been difficult to bring to a conclusion, any conclusion. In the eighteenth century balance of power era, an enemy of today's war could be tomorrow's friend. Our little war with Spain had been fought under the tight control of the diplomats, for a very limited objective. Spain had lost, but the diplomatic trick was to get her to make peace before it was necessary to begin the campaigning season of 1720 and do her even more injury. It was not at all unusual during this period of early modern European history to deliberately limit one's gains in a victorious war and to offer genuinely generous peace terms. Yet the factor that was keeping Europe under arms was the same stubborn refusal of the Spanish royal pair to admit their mistake even when offered a way out. The door to peace had been open all along. All that Philip V had to do was to accept the terms of the Treaty of Utrecht and join the Quadruple Alliance. The sons of Elisabeth Farnese had an absolute guarantee of the Italian Duchies of Parma and Tuscany. Some brilliant diplomatic compromise had to be arranged by which Philip V could agree to all of this, but most of all a ploy had to be devised by which the Spanish royal pair could keep their sense of honour. The removal of Alberoni, blamed for the conflict, was the solution. The war with Spain illustrated the ability of the international system to limit conflict, itself an explanation of the willingness of some powers to consider war. The war, like the peace, showed the capacity of the system to prevent substantial shifts of power.

NOTES

1. John Dryden, *King Arthur*, II ii. Van Roy Baker, Dryden's Military Images (unpublished PhD thesis, Columbia University, 1971), p. 211.

2. Lord Chesterfield, *Letters*, 12 January 1757.

3. Logo of the United States Army War College. Root Hall, Carlisle Barracks, Pennsylvania.

4. Richard W. Leopold, *Elihu Root and the Conservative Tradition* (Boston, 1954), p. 50.

5. J. Black (ed.), *Britain in the Age of Walpole* (1984), pp. 2–4.

6. A. Baudrillart, 'Les prétensions de Philippe V à la couronne de France', *Séances et travaux de l'Académie des sciences, morales et politiques* 127 (1887).

7. E. Bourgeois, *Le Secret du Régent et la Politique de l'Abbé Dubois* (Paris, 1892).

8. C. Sturgill, 'The Spirit of the Enlightenment and the Enlightened Self-Interest Among the Regent's Men: The Mind-Set of 1717–1723', *Acta No. 7*, International Commission of Military History, 1984, pp. 171–180; J. H. Shennan, *Philippe, Duke of Orléans* (1979).

9. J. Black, 'The Anglo-French Alliance: 1716–31', *Francia* 13 (1986).

10. For a different view, J. Black, 'Parliament and the Political and Diplomatic Crisis of 1717–18', *Parliamentary History* III (1984), p. 88.

11. On the significance of Italy in early eighteenth-century international relations, G. Quazza, *Il Problema Italiano e L'Equilibrio Europeo, 1720–1738* (Turin, 1965); G. Quazza, 'Italy's role in the European problems of the first half of the eighteenth century', in R. M. Hatton and M. S. Anderson, eds., *Studies in Diplomatic History* (1970); M. Martin, 'The secret clause: Britain and Spanish ambitions in Italy, 1712–31', *European Studies Review* 6 (1976).

12. O. Weber, *Die Quadrupel-Allianz vom Jahre 1718* (Vienna, 1887).

13. Accounts of the war and diplomacy in Sicily are plentiful: Raimund Gerba, *Die Kämpfe der Kaiserlichen in Sicilien und Corsica, 1717–1720 und 1730–1732*, 1891: J. L. Cranmer-Byng, ed., *Pattee Byng's Journal, 1718–1720*, 1950; V. E. Stellardi, *Il Regno di Vittorio Amadeo de Savoia in Sicilia dal 1713 al 1719*, 1866; and Jaime Miguel Guzán, *Memorias Militaires sobre La Guerra de Cerdeña y Sicilia*, 1898. Among the diplomatic archives I found the following to be the more helpful: Great Britain. Public Record Office. State Papers. Foreign, 78 (France), 161–165; France. Archives des Affaires Etrangères. Angleterre 277, 317–326 and Mémoires et Documents. Espagne, 141–143; Italy. Archivio di Stato di Torino. Lettere di S.A.R. Sezione Guerra e Marina. Volume 12–13 for 1717 and

Azienda Generale di Guerra. Ordini Generali Misti, Sezione Guerra e Marina, Volume 25 for 1717–1720; Spain. Archivio Histórico Nacional. Secretaria des Despacho de Estado. Año 1719, Leg. 1418 et Año 1720, Leg. 2556.20. The French account of this little campaign has yet to be published although it now exists as part of a typescript of my own, The Quadruple Alliance's Little War With Spain, 1717–1720. Primary source materials for this campaign are located in the French military archives at the Chateau de Vincennes in Series A[1] 2544, 2548–2555, 2557–2564, 2573–2574, 2618–2619, 2630 and Series A[4] 10–11.

8

THE ANGLO-SPANISH WAR OF 1739

Philip Woodfine

'Let us exert the Courage that our Wrongs have inspired us with: In short, let us tread in the Steps of former Ages.'
  William Pulteney

'War is called for without Doors, it is called for within Doors; but Gentlemen don't consider how little you can gain by War.'
  Henry Pelham[1]

Discussions of the war between Britain and Spain which began in 1739 have conventionally attributed primary importance to British aims, and stressed particularly the impact on decision-making of merchant lobbying and clamour from the public. At the simplest, the causes of the war are reduced to British decisions made in response to the alleged popular outcry when Spanish coastguards cut off the ear of Captain Robert Jenkins. Other eighteenth-century wars involving, as this did, great colonial stakes, might require careful explanation in terms of the international rivalries involved, but the 'War of Jenkins' Ear' can be dismissed with a brevity bordering on facetiousness:

> The main outline of the story is familiar enough. Britain had gone to war with Spain in 1739 ostensibly, as tradition has it, over a crude bit of auricular surgery performed without benefit of either clergy or anesthesia.[2]

Implicit in such views is the belief that the war was the outcome solely of British domestic politics, though on the face of it one would expect that the Spanish side of the dispute, and the ambitions and expectations of Spain's policymakers, would receive at least some attention. There is no very satisfactory schema available from the history of that country which might provoke second thoughts about the Spanish share in the war, since the period between the end of Habsburg Spain and the beginning of the reign of Carlos III has been rather neglected. Spanish historians are content to subscribe to the one-sided view that the 'guerra de la Oreja de Jenkins' was caused by British domestic policy.[3] This belief in the primacy of the domestic policy of one participant as a cause of war is one which has found many adherents, especially in Germany, where the debate between domestic and foreign policy models of causation has been prolonged. The polarisation of these two alternatives is artificial: it has been forcefully pointed out that an ideal, or fully free domestic policy could exist in any case only in total isolation, as in some island utopia, or at least in the absence of any foreign menace.[4] In the late 1730s British domestic policymakers were far from enjoying such isolation, and were in fact acting in an unstable condition of European rivalries in the Caribbean, and shifting diplomatic relations between France and Spain, the major catholic powers whose active alliance would also threaten an invasion to restore the Pretender to the British throne. Domestic pressures, even those coming from without the doors of parliament, cannot be understood in isolation from the wider international situation to which they were a response. Domestic policy decisions, though partly made under home political pressures, were also made in the context of an international diplomacy which had its own pressures and pace, and were influenced by a range of calculations as to national advantage which, to some extent at least, transcended the narrow sphere of party contention.

At the broadest level of explanation, it might even be contended that the outbreak of war between Britain and Spain over the colonies was intrinsically likely at any point after the Utrecht settlement brought about an indecisive end to the War of Spanish Succession. Geoffrey Blainey has argued that decisive wars tend to guarantee a long period of peace, and vice versa, an argument familiar to the combatants in 1739. Leading opposition whig spokesman William Pulteney declared himself for war on just those grounds: '... a vigorous war is the only means of obtaining a lasting Peace'.[5] The war might plausibly also be described principally in terms of the influence of colonial rivalries in drawing European powers into war, a pattern of events which was to be a prominent feature of the conflicts of the rest of the eighteenth century. The belief that the war of 1739 introduced major changes in the stakes for which eighteenth-century wars were fought was put forward by Harold Temperly in an essay which has had considerable influence on historians writing in English since his day:

> ... the year 1739 was a turning point of history. It was, perhaps, the first of English wars in the which the trade interest absolutely predominated, in which the war was waged solely for balance of trade rather than for balance of power.[6]

This aspect of the war inspired a considerable body of scholarly work in the interwar period, much of which concentrated on the South Sea Company's commercial activities and relations with Spain, and on the extensive British illicit trade to the Spanish Caribbean. Viewed from that perspective, the responsibility for the rupture with Spain was usually laid firmly at the door of the South Sea Company, whose actions, direct and indirect, led the Spanish crown to repudiate the provisions of the Convention agreed at the Pardo, near Madrid, on 14 January 1739.[7] This is a useful emphasis in the sense that the direct cause of the war certainly was the breakdown of this agreement, rather than any immediate impact of popular or opposition opinion at home. However, in recent times such concerns have been subordinated to the stress upon the primacy of internal pressures.

This emphasis springs in part from the abundant comment of contemporaries, such as ministry supporter Henry Etough, who blamed the war on the agitation of a '... mad and vain nation ... warmed and hardened by pride and prejudice'.[8] This was a natural interpretation for those who were embroiled in the struggles of domestic politics, and who felt the force and malignancy of the opposition campaign to unseat leading minister Sir Robert Walpole. Walpole's brother Horatio, himself a diplomat influential in the ministry, was emphatic at the height of the debate over the Pardo convention that the mischievous opposition leaders would end their agitation at once ' . . . if the Clamour they have raised for a War will but help them to put an End to the present Administration and let those in who have been so long excluded from a share in it'.[9] It is tempting to adopt the interpretative lines so confidently drawn by the circle of those who knew affairs in this period, lines which follow the interest of modern historians in the extra-parliamentary workings of British politics. In a political system characterised by aristocratic dominance and, at least in most boroughs, a restricted electorate, the agitation for war in 1738 and 1739 provides a rare glimpse of the power which popular opinion could exercise over ministerial decisions. This dimension has therefore loomed large, even in the best of modern accounts of the war.[10] To stress popular opinion, though, as the main component in the causes of the war, is to rely on something which is in itself incompletely known, since the term 'the nation without doors' as used at the time seems often to have been synonymous with agitation in London and one or two major seaports and provincial towns. If the reality is a petitioning and press campaign led mainly by London's commercial classes, then it would be instructive to know more about the level of concern — and indifference — in the provinces.[11] Furthermore, the impact of this undoubted clamour upon specific stages of the decision-making process is not easy to define. A great discussion in parliament about Spanish depredations and merchant grievances was held in March 1738, yet the ministry was not forced into precipitate action at that time, despite the voting by Parliament of extra supplies intended to equip a fleet against Spain. There was an outcry against the January 1739 Convention with Spain, yet the Convention passed safely, though narrowly, through Parliament, in March of that year. Despite the most vigorous press and political campaign, the probability was that the Walpole ministry would recoup its forces, while the Opposition languished for want of a similar specific issue to oppose. It must also be borne in mind that between the March 1738 debates and the actual declaration of war in October 1739 lay eighteen months of peace and discussions. The difficulties of explaining the timing of the war, faced with such facts, are often resolved by appeal to ideas of a 'mounting wave of national indignation', but the wave was not single, and not continuously swelling. When war came, it was not because the Opposition attacked the Convention, but because the terms of that agreement were infringed — broken by the Spanish Crown, and by the South Sea Company. As one scholar recently remarked; 'It is all too easy for historians to use public opinion as an explanatory device where it is difficult to find evidence for other influences'.[12]

Other influences are certainly to hand, in this case, and most obviously that of the South Sea Company, which refused to pay the sum agreed as due to the Crown of Spain, and more than any other body precipitated the ensuing war. The South Sea Directors were involved in the details of negotiations for a number of years, in ways often hard to distinguish from those of national diplomacy.[13] The leading foreign minister, Secretary of State for the South the Duke of Newcastle, was anxious at an early stage of the tensions with Spain to regulate the disputes between that country and the Company, encouraging the appointment of

Geraldino as the Spanish ambassador to London in the vain hope of furthering that end. When the company's claims were finally settled, though very little to their satisfaction, after the close of the War of Austrian Succession, Lord Chancellor Hardwicke, an influential policy adviser, gave trenchant expression to the resentment of ministers:

> We have tried Negociation for above Twenty Years, two references to Commissaries, & a War, partly on their account, & all in vain. And I suppose no Man in his Sences will think of Entering into another War to prove the pretended Ballance of their Accounts.[14]

The negotiating position of the Spanish crown is also of great importance in assessing responsibility for the war. Philip V and his advisers, especially Patiño (until his death in November 1736) but even the more humdrum administrator La Quadra who succeeded him, wanted fairer trading, and larger profits for Spain, part of a long-standing though ineffectual policy in the Americas. The mercantilist stress upon imports of treasure, and the failure to develop an adequate manufacturing base upon which to build a mutual trade with its colonies, were fatal inconsistencies in Spain's plans for colonial aggrandisement, opening the way to the poaching of this trade by outsiders.[15] At the same time, ministers faced with interloping trade did not wish to repudiate existing treaties unless they could be sure that their European interest lay in acting with France and making a break with Britain. Hence the long-continued Spanish policy of allowing checks upon and punishments of smugglers by their local agents in the Caribbean, with the second line of defence, or of reparation, provided by cumbersome enquiries and judicial process in Spain. Importantly also, Philip and Queen Elizabeth, and a growing number of their advisers, placed a high value on nationalist considerations, and could not brook the loss of face involved in giving up Spanish claims to supremacy and to administrative control in the Americas. Caribbean profits were only part of an important attempt to build up Spanish effectiveness and prestige, goals which could not be met by a tame submission to the demands of the British King or of a chartered trading company.

The internal debate of the late 1730s, in the British Parliament and in the press, about the rights and wrongs of a punitive war against Spain is therefore not the central issue, though important in domestic politics, and even instructive as a case study of how decisions about wars are made. Certainly a large share of the responsibility for the war must rest with Britain, and clearly the major internal pressure for the warlike course of policy came from the Opposition groupings who were united on the need to overthrow Walpole, if on little else. Politicians as diverse as the eloquent and individualistic William Pulteney, and William Wyndham, the inveterate Jacobite tory leader, had been united for several years as the 'patriot' opposition, whose central aim was the overthrow of the long-standing leading minister, Sir Robert Walpole. The 'patriots' used and fomented a vociferous merchant lobby, part of the increasing independence of City of London politics, and they enjoyed the aid of 'the numerous tribe of malignant writers' in the periodical press and in a busy pamphlet war.[16]

These same critics, however, were noted for their hostility to government expenditure, especially on defence, and the years before the war were certainly not characterised by an arms race, or naval build-up, on the British side. In Spain, too, the readiness for war could not be attributed to an increase in armed strength: there had been consistent attempts to finance and revive the navy, but the general condition of the Spanish marine was poor.[17] At the best, Spanish ministers could feel that they were better prepared for defence, if need be, than they had been a decade before. Spanish naval and military weakness was notorious, even exaggerated, and so the opponents of Walpole confidently believed that Spain could be brought to heel by a relatively inexpensive policy of naval deployment. A move of this kind would bring a decisive change in colonial power relationships, since it must lead to territorial gains in the Caribbean on easy terms, probably for Britain and possibly also for France and the United Provinces, if war became general. 'Spain knows the Consequence of a War in America; whoever gains, it must prove fatal to her . . .', argued William Pitt in a striking intervention in the Convention debate of 8 March (o.s.) 1739. The reason why Spain must in any circumstances lose had been explained by Lord Bathurst on 1 March in the Lords debate, and lay in the absolute necessity of that country's being supplied with treasure:

> In a War with *Spain*, if we judge from Experience, we have more to hope than to fear. We may do them great Damage, and gain considerable Advantages to our selves, even by Privateering, or seizing their Ships at Sea.[18]

Positive gains of colonial territory and markets were hoped for, and the least favourable outcome anticipated was the crippling of rival Spanish commerce, while few politicians were willing to promote the military and naval strength necessary to achieve either. This confusion was not at all untypical of the conflicting objectives of the period, both in England and Spain. What both sides wanted in the 1730s was access to the rich profits of colonial trade in the Caribbean. But the Spanish government wanted colonial wealth mainly as part of a revival of the finances and the international strength of the country. Underpinning this aim was a set of values which were firmly Catholic, and potentially French-oriented. An alliance of Spain and France, to promote a reconquest of Britain by its rightful catholic monarch, was an attractive objective to Philip V of Spain, and was lacking only in tactical appeal to his Italian-born wife, Queen Elizabeth (Farnese). By contrast, an alliance with a Protestant trading country ruled by an interloper was, at least emotionally, less appealing. When Spain's Caribbean interests and ambitions were to be saved only at the expense of the country's pride and European standing, the two sets of national objectives came into conflict, and Spanish ministers were likely to give freer rein to the long-held belief that their commerce languished in British chains, and give fresh ear to proposals from France. This natural effect of Spanish diplomatic priorities could be disguised from contemporary commentators by the strange character of the King and Queen. Philip V was mentally unstable, a sufferer from melancholia and an excess of religious scruple. Elizabeth's great care in life was to distract her husband, who had already once abdicated, and in endeavouring to prevent his thoughts returning into that quarter the queen built the life and amusements of the court around his eccentric timetable of sleeping and eating hours. Her own two children, giving place to Philip's son by a former marriage, had little to expect from a change of reign, and she herself would be powerless in retirement, whereas by careful management Elizabeth hoped to bring her consort to pursue the policies which she favoured, especially in regard to providing Italian territories for her sons.[19] This was a *menage* unprecedented in Europe among the courts which generated the vital flows of diplomatic intercourse. Because of its peculiarities, the policy stance of the King and Queen of Spain could easily be presented as eccentric, as it was by the British envoy in Madrid, Benjamin Keene, in April 1737:

> These People are certainly not content with what passes in America, neither are they in a condition to support an expensive Engagement; but considerations of this sort do not always hinder them from precipitating themselves into it; and notions of Injustices done them will make stronger impressions upon minds like these than the bad state of their Finances.

At the sensitive highpoint of discussion of the Convention, the influence of particular ministers within the court, too, was blamed for the pursuit of rival policies to that of accommodation with Britain:

> La Quadra is more dull and stubborn than I could well conceive. He lets himself be entirely guided by Don Casimiro Ustaritz, first Commis in the War Office: And these two together have so filled their heads with the *Grandeur* of the Spanish Monarchy, the injury it receives from Foreigners and Foreign Commerce, and how much it has been trickt in former Negociations, with such like Common Place, that this Court is much more Intractable than in any other period of time that I have known it.[20]

The Spanish court always had the choice of a humble and conciliatory approach, and yet the decision instead was made to pursue the larger national interests, or consult national pride, even at the expense of war. The immediate occasion of war was the breakdown of the Convention of the Pardo, due to a Spanish refusal to pay the £95,000 then agreed as compensation, and also to the suspension of the Asiento or slave supply contract. The timing of that choice was partly conditioned by the British opposition clamour, as seen from Madrid, and by what was seen as a provocative choice by the Duke of Newcastle, to keep a British fleet cruising on Spanish coasts, but it was also undoubtedly influenced by the improving prospects of assistance from France from the summer of 1738 onwards.[21] For the first time since the signing of the secret Bourbon family compact in 1733, these two powers came close enough together to create a real possibility of a new colonial situation, one in which the largest and most advanced catholic power in Europe could form a partnership with the largest catholic empire overseas. Perhaps Walpole focused his attention rather narrowly on the Jacobite invasion threat, but that too was a likely outcome of this major diplomatic change.[22]

In the choices facing Britain, the desired wealth of the West Indies could be tapped in three main forms: by the existing trade, much of it illicit commerce by

British colonial interlopers; by an enlarged cooperation with Spain, driving a wedge between Spanish and French commerce, which was the ministry's preference; or by a policy of war with Spain, to make conquests and force a complete freedom of trade in the Caribbean. All were ways of exploiting colonial opportunities, but each faced difficulties. Trade of the irregular kind that existed paid a sort of implicit tax by virtue of the searches and seizures imposed by Spanish agents in the Americas. This may have been moderate in the context of the total gains: a ministry pamphlet of 1739 calculated it at some £5000 a year, or around two and a half per cent on the whole trade to the Spanish West Indies, while Horatio Walpole in a later private memoir estimated, on the merchants' own inflated figures, an average loss of around £8000.[23] The tax represented by Spanish colonial justice, though, was an irregular and uncertain levy, and one which could be almost entirely eliminated by insisting on freedom from search and seizure, when vessels were once away from Spanish ports. In the attempt to guarantee this freedom, serious discussions were entered into by the British ministry so as to produce a more cordial and violation-proof commercial relationship. Many traders and politicians, though, came to believe that only force would bring success, and so the alternative of war, and with it the alluring prospect of conquests, took hold among ministry opponents. Not only the parliamentary opposition saw the matter in this light. Horatio Walpole put the matter succinctly in a cabinet paper of January 1738:

> ... I do not see any effectual way to be revenged on the Spaniards, if they continue their unjust Depredations, but coming to an open War with them. And there is no doubt but the English might in such a Case, undertake some Enterprise on the Spanish Settlements, as might be of infinite prejudice to them, provided we were sure of having a war with Spain only, and that we should not be engaged immediately with other Nations at the same time.[24]

This position was heavily modified, for the ministry, by the ever-present danger of a French entry into such a war, and opposition groups were freer to take a more vociferous line, not least because of the admixture of other important political effects which would follow from it, chiefly the downfall of Sir Robert Walpole.

In both Britain and Spain, then, the specific war which took place in 1739 was envisaged as a possibility for some time beforehand, both as a matter of danger and of opportunity. It was obvious that war would follow the breakdown of diplomacy, and that it would take the form, in the first instance, of a colonial war. In both countries, strenuous official attempts were made to avert such a war, and yet, in both, the effective political nation (minute as this perhaps was in the Spanish case) cherished objectives which were preferred to peace. Explanations of the war which began in 1739 would therefore be satisfactory to the degree that they took account of these objectives, and the respective sticking points of both sides. The current more one-sided accounts are generally skewed by the need to accommodate the name usually given to the conflict; if this is the War of Jenkins' Ear, then a place must be found for Jenkins and his aural sufferings, even if the resulting explanation becomes improbable. Most accounts find a place for

> ... the famous appearance of Captain Jenkins at the bar of the Commons, with his severed ear in a jar of pickle as evidence of Spanish atrocities.[25]

Jenkins' appearance is even made to seem the high point of the anti-Spanish campaign:

> Then, as a capstone to the frenzy caused by the memorials, came the testimony before the Commons of the celebrated Captain Jenkins ... As dramatic proof of all his charges, he displayed his bottled ear, severed from his head, he said, by a Spanish blade on that infamous day.[26]

Not only is this a war caused by internal pressure, then, but an important part of that pressure derived from the horror engendered by the story of Jenkins of the *Rebecca*, and his ill usage by Spanish coastguards. The timescale involved causes immediate difficulties, since Jenkins lost his ear in an incident in April 1731, the enraged Commons debates took place in March 1738, and war was finally declared in October 1739. What perhaps really needs to be emphasised is the Peace of Jenkins' Ear, a long though uneasy period of peace which endured despite numerous depredations committed by both sides in the Caribbean, and occasional affronts to British shipping in the Mediterranean. When war came to the West Indies in 1739, it was no decisive rupture with a long and stable period of good relations, but an intensification of hostilities which had been rumbling for many years. Perhaps partly for that very reason the war there proved indecisive, with the eventual postwar settlement leaving the situation much as before. The war which the British opposition had so much desired proved to be as indecisive and frustrating as the peace had been. The case of Jenkins was not a singular one in the years of troubled relations and mutual transgression, except in that his vessel does really appear to have been a fair trader when taken by the Spanish coastguards. It is puzzling, then, that it should have been considered so important as to give Captain Jenkins' name to the later war, especially since, following a comment of Burke's in 1796, the whole story was generally considered a fable until the late nineteenth century.[27]

Attention could better be given more generally to the complex commercial and colonial ties of the two countries, which were always potential sources of conflict. The Spanish Crown retained all the formal administrative power over its own colonies, and maintained its ancient claim to sovereignty in the seas of that part of the world, yet after 1713 could not directly manage the valuable commerce of its own colonies. The South Sea Company, whose Governor was the British King, was the official beneficiary of the arrangements agreed to in the treaties concluded at the end of the War of Spanish Succession: the Asiento concession of 1713, confirmed in 1716, and the provisions of the Treaty of Utrecht. Under these arrangements, a possible growth of Spanish merchant enterprise and wealth was hampered by the franchised British trade of the South Sea company, with its concession of the exclusive supply of negroes to the Spanish colonies, and also the annual ship allowed to trade to the Central American fairs. The harm done to the trade of the Spanish merchants was revealed in the way in which the sailings of the annual great fleet, the *Flota*, were often put off, and the privilege of the Company's annual ship also held back, for the simple reason that the colonial markets were already saturated with European goods.[28] Only seven of the 'annual' ships ever actually sailed between 1713 and 1739, and the regular sailings of the negro ships were the real source of company profits, and the illicit fringe dealings of its servants. By the late 1720s there was much friction between the Company and the colonial authorities, who did what they could to hamper it, while the Company in turn successfully frustrated Spanish attempts to supervise its business.[29] It was a very watchful care which led Patiño, the chief minister in the mid-1730s, to denounce '... the illicit Trade which they have carried on incessantly to the prejudice of His Catholic Majesty's Treasury ...'[30] By and large, however, there was little actual interference with the ships of the official trader. More worrying was the much larger volume of illicit trade carried out by British seamen both home and colonial, especially those of Jamaica and Rhode Island. These were pure interlopers in the Spanish commerce, 'moonlighting' at the expense of a foreign economy, supplying the Spanish colonists so that they did not have the inconvenience and cost of buying their imports from centres such as Portobello, Vera Cruz or Cartagena.

The seizures which were publicised by the British opposition stemmed from the difficult sailing waters in which both these ships and legitimate traders ventured, in the Caribbean and the Gulf of Mexico. While trade homeward-bound for Europe was safe in the vast Atlantic, the chances of interception were much greater before clearing the Bahamas. The prevailing winds penned sailing ships into restricted routes, so that ships' masters had to stand in close inshore, and could not avoid seeming to lie upon the Spanish coast.[31] Once a ship had put in close to Spanish colonial coasts, it came under suspicion of being an illegal trader to settlements there, and became liable to investigation by the *guarda costas* who were commissioned to search and, where necessary, to seize, vessels carrying contraband cargo. Ship and crew in such cases were conveyed to a nearby colonial port, where an enquiry, and often seizure, followed. It was enough to have aboard the smallest quantity of Spanish colonial produce, or the Spanish coin of 8 *Reales*, the 'pieces of eight' which were the common currency of the whole Caribbean. The *Betty* and *Anne* galleys were taken in 1727 and 1728 on such evidence, if the masters are to be believed, and in the latter year there was taken the *Robert* whose master, Story King, was tortured for three days with lighted matches between the fingers, and thumbscrews. Not all such sailors, though, were peaceful traders, and atrocities were committed by Dutch and English crews, regularly so by those operating out of Jamaica. Rear-Admiral Stewart wrote to Newcastle in 1731 that '... the sloops that sail from this island, manned and armed on that illicit trade, has (sic) more than once bragged to me of their having murdered 7 or 8 Spaniards on their own shore'.[32]

It was this general situation which Jenkins, and his ship the *Rebecca*, have come to epitomise. On the 9th of April 1731, bound from Jamaica for London with a cargo of sugar, the *Rebecca* lay caught in one of the regular calms off Havana, and was boarded by an oared *guarda costa*, the crew of which could not at first find on board any Spanish coin, still less other colonial produce. To persuade him to talk,

Jenkins was hoisted up the mast by his neck three times, and thrown down the forehatch, according to the fullest reports later published. His personal money was stolen, and the Lieutenant of the *guarda costa* then

> ... took hold of his left Ear, and with his Cutlass slit it down, and then another of the *Spaniards* took hold of it and tore it off, but gave him the Piece of his Ear again, bidding him carry it to his Master King George.[33]

The affair was a passing curiosity in the press in 1731, mentioned only briefly in the *Gentleman's Magazine*, for instance, along with the details of other captures, such as that of the sloop *Runslet*, whose men, like Story King, had their fingers tortured with gunlock screws and lighted matches, to reveal where their money was.[34] Neither Jenkins's case nor even his mutilation was entirely unprecedented. In the same month as his news arrived home, all the periodical press carried a rather fuller account of Japhet Crook, alias Sir Peter Stranger, who in front of a large crowd lost both his ears to the hangman's pruning knife, and had both nostrils cut with scissors, one of them seared with a hot iron, on the pillory at Charing Cross. Crook had the misfortune to be a forger, when a recent Act had made the crime a felony.[35] Stomachs were strong enough to accept quite violent abuses of the person, but for all that the assault upon Jenkins, and the recent spate of such incidents, was taken seriously. The Duke of Newcastle protested at Spanish dilatoriness in redress, '... especially in Cases that cry aloud for Justice, such as that of Jenkins ...'[36]

The case of the *Rebecca*, however, after an early memorial to the King, seems to have been laid aside fairly quickly, and was not one of those for which compensation was being actively sought in the late 1730s. In this sense, Jenkins and his owners did not have a particular stake in the war which was given his name. Numerous others did, and received publicity accordingly, including captures even earlier than his. The case of the *Anne* galley resulted in 1737 in a printed pamphlet in which Samuel Bonham, one of the *Anne*'s owners, provided a tart reminder of the ministerial attitude of seven years earlier. Newcastle had replied to one petition, in words perhaps more suited to a non-representative system of government, '... that it was a Matter of State, and Merchants had no Business to meddle therewith, those Things being out of their Province'.[37] These older incidents might have been jostled aside by more newsworthy depredations, especially given the dramatic nature of some of them. One such was the murder of Captain Thomas Weir, a man 'Maim'd of both Arms', and confined to his bed when he was betrayed, and murdered, with eight of his crew, not by raffish and uncontrollable *guarda costas*, but by Spanish colonial officials.[38]

The earlier stories, though, contributed in three ways to the debates of 1738–9. First, the older grievances served to swell out the list of such newer offences. This can be seen in a printed list of autumn 1737, accompanying a petition to the King signed by 149 merchants, as part of their campaign for government action. Perhaps because the King took a personal interest, or because ministers were wary at his being involved in this unusual way, the petition, and the grievances listed in it, caused a considerable flurry of activity within the ministry. When the merchants had been examined by a committee of Privy Councillors, Newcastle declared that 'His Majesty was so sensibly touched with the losses and sufferings of His Trading Subjects, that he was pleased immediately to direct a Memorial to be prepared'.[39] The convention in ministerial writing that the king does all, and the lack of an archive of George II's correspondence, makes it difficult to estimate what share the king really had in the matter, but the flustered tone of those close to the throne makes it seem not unlikely that he did intervene personally. The grievances of the merchants do appear in this case to have helped to trigger off the firm Memorandum sent by Newcastle to Madrid, beginning a new and more intense phase of negotiation. And the grievances were filled out with old histories: the printed list gives details of 52 ships attacked or seized, of which only one fifth were recent.[40]

Such older depredations were of use, in the second place, since they showed the long delays which could be expected from Spanish justice, and increased the level of impatience over more recent captures. A third contribution was a corollary of this, in a technical legal sense: the possibility that these delays in satisfaction would justify the outmoded device of issuing Letters of Reprisal with which owners and merchants could redress their wrongs by seizing Spanish vessels and goods of equivalent value. Horatio Walpole wrote an important 'position paper' in January 1738, in which he laid out with great care the position of the treaties between Britain and Spain, and among other concerns, he dealt at some length with the issue of reprisals. Like the rest of the memoir, internal evidence indicates that he was addressing specific issues raised by the inner circle of ministers. Walpole gave it as his opinion that the new captures of 1737, since the Spanish court had promised further enquiry and justice, did not create a case for reprisals. The older instances might: '... this may be such an Unreasonable delay of Justice as to fall under the Rules of Reprisals ...' Rightly, however, Walpole drew back from giving full support to a remedy born in an earlier age, of less professional naval force, and he feared that sanctions,

> ... if granted in this last case, may be the cause of such a Retalliation on the side of Spain, as to occasion Hostilities in the W. Indies equal to War.[41]

Furthermore, the event even of successful reprisals would be equivalent to war in Europe also, with unforeseen consequences, to guard against which the navy would need to be deployed in the Mediterranean. These were solid misgivings:

> But yet if the Merchants will accept Letters of Reprisal, They cannot be refused them, the Cases of doing ourself Justice are so flagrant, & have subsisted so long, that such a refusal would make us appear a most Contemptible Nation, with all our Maritime Power.[42]

In the event, when Letters of Reprisal were offered in March 1738, the merchant community realistically showed no interest; only in time of war, and with the backing of naval force, could such a step be feasible when Spanish men of war could cruise in defence of their own shipping. Even so, the lobby power of merchants, in such a sensitive area of national prestige, could hardly be more clearly stated. The demands of the traders had sufficient force to make the administration permit a step which would have led to almost certain conflict and which, even though not taken, was seen by Spanish diplomats as a menace of war.[43] For this very reason, it should be stressed again that the authorisation of reprisals in fact led to no specific actions and did little to bring war closer: merchant lobby power can be seen in the making of particular decisions, but its more general impact can easily be exaggerated, with an implicit assumption that the merchants were a consistent force having a major effect on government policy. One succinct textbook treatment enshrines this conventional view, linked as usual to Jenkins:

> The merchants, illicit and legitimate, . . . began a furious campaign for government action in 1737, and this rose in intensity over the next two years . . .
> The political temperature was considerably raised in March 1738 when a Captain Jenkins showed a suitably horrified House of Commons his unfortunate ear, which he claimed had been lopped off by a *guarda-costa* captain and which Jenkins had kept pickled in a jar. There were immediate demands for war.[44]

The logical difficulties in the way of accepting the timescale implied in such accounts have already been mentioned, but a further problem deserves to be emphasised: 'the famous appearance of Captain Jenkins at the Bar of the Commons' never took place. The loss of Jenkins' ear may have been no fable, but his dramatic appearance before the House was; a fact that has been in the public domain for over half a century, but which historians have been reluctant to acknowledge. The story of the dramatic Commons appearance was given authoritative sanction by Archdeacon Coxe's biography of Walpole written in 1798:

> According to contemporary accounts, he related the transaction, with many additional circumstances of insult and barbarity, and displayed the ear, which he had preserved, as some assert in a box, and others in a bottle . . .[45]

This meticulous archival scholar was obviously unhappy, though, with what he twice describes as 'this ridiculous story', particularly since he could find no positive proof of Jenkins' testimony before the House, and Coxe implied that the story was at least embellished by the *Gentleman's Magazine* article which first printed it.[46]

Despite Coxe's unease over the story, the next century and more saw a continuation of his basic attitude among other historians: a disinclination to believe in the actual atrocity visited upon Jenkins, a belief in his Commons appearance, and a reluctance to abandon a good story. In 1936, however, William Thomas Laprade, in the course of his researches into the press in the early eighteenth century, discovered that, though summoned to give evidence, 'Jenkins was otherwhere engaged and did not go'. The story was a product of the recent ban on the customary printing, during the parliamentary recess, of the debates. The *London Magazine*, to circumvent the ruling, launched its disguised debates of a 'learned and political club', with speakers given Roman names, and so the *Gentleman's Magazine* came out in the next month, June 1738, with its famous 'Debates in the Senate of Magna Lilliputia'. The fictionalised account of the March debates was the result of a struggle for readers. 'Some license, even fiction,' concluded Laprade, 'was permissible when a periodical was in a pinch.'[47] Laprade's richly informed, but laconic and ill-referenced, work may have failed to carry conviction, but ten years later A. J. Henderson followed up this lead, to provide fuller details of what occurred:

> The truth is that Jenkins was not in London nor even in England at the time of the investigation (March, 1738). He was aboard his ship, the *Harrington*, homeward bound from a voyage to the West Indies; and he did not arrive in London until May 25, which was five days after Parliament had been prorogued for the summer.[48]

Though the episode of Jenkins' ear was an old one, not unique in its cruelty, not refreshed by any recent publication, and not supported by any appearance before the House, it could still be argued that politicians made such striking use of his tale in 1738 and 1739 as to arouse the nation. However, this does not at all appear to be the case, though the opposition campaign upon the subject of the plundered merchants and the proud and insolent Spaniards was certainly a vigorous and successful one. It appealed to national sentiment and commercial interest alike, and called for strong action, decrying the motives and spirit of an administration engaged in unwieldy and time-consuming series of negotiations, which were always likely to be prejudiced by the domestic clamour against them. Such negotiations were not a parliamentary but a ministerial process, and parliament in any case had been in recess for eight months during the long and sensitive discussions, so leading Opposition politicians felt all the frustration of exclusion, and the tide of their criticism grew more swollen and irresponsible. No single case could expand to these dimensions, and appeals were increasingly made instead to historical examples of British daring, and to the ease of enforcing the country's will upon the haughty and cruel, but cowardly, Spaniards. A pro-ministerial writer of 1739 summarised, in lamenting, the position:

> Why the Enemies of the Government have made so much Noise in the World, its Friends so little by their Writings, is because the one have had the labouring Oar, the *defensive* and *argumentative* Part, which few understand, and fewer attend to: the other the declamatory, satirical and defamatory Part, which all have a Taste for.[49]

The specific charges embedded in this declamatory onslaught had very little to do with Jenkins. Much more successful use was made of the Spanish practice of putting their prisoners to work in labour gangs. A month before the agitated Commons debates of March 1738, the *Craftsman* prepared the ground with a story of sailors 'enslaved' in this way, and imprisoned in Havana, ragged, meagre, and half-starved:

> Are *our brave English Mariners* to be thus abused, who have committed no Crime, and whom the *Spaniards* durst not look in the face upon equal Terms, were their Hands unty'd?[50]

Two of their ships, the *Loyal Charles* and the *Dispatch* were well known to the London commerce, and the West India merchants there almost at once launched a petition to the House of Commons, soon to be supported by others. This grievance, not Jenkins' ear, helped to precipitate a distinct stage in the domestic pressure for an aggressive posture towards Spain.[51]

The popular appeal of this, reflected in contemporary prints, lay in the picture of British seamen in chains, but the need to be free of searches upon the high seas was the key issue, and already to the fore in the wording of the commercial petitions.

This incident furnishes a good example of the two sides to the problem of disputes with Spain, since Cayley, the British Consul in Cadiz, where the prisoners were from January, soon provided evidence of the exaggeration of the prisoners' complaints, and of legal obstacles to the immediate release of some of them.[52] In any event, there was a significant disparity between the way in which such pressures of opinion were felt in a representative system such as Britain's, and in personal monarchies such as those of France and Spain. It was taken for granted by Keene that '. . . as the French Ministry can stop the Cryes of the Merchants when they think fitting, they never fail to do so when they contradict any private view they may have to sooth this Court'.[53] In Spain, the merchants were often uncooperative and stubborn, but were ultimately subjected to the royal will. The levels of taxation levied on them could be sharply and retrospectively raised as in 1731 and 1737, an arbitrary regulation which was publicly celebrated as promoting the interests of British colonial smugglers.[54] In this very different atmosphere of Spain, the leading minister La Quadra was calmly dismissive of merchant opinion in London, and even Benjamin Keene seems to have been rather offhand about the charges — which were in fact by no means unprecedented. Even when Keene was roused to stronger protest, the Spanish court remained persuaded that the noisy resolve of the nation was a temporary effect of lies by the captured sailors, fomented, as their London ambassador Geraldino informed them, by '. . . the Malice of those who oppose the Administration, joyned by what that Minister calls the Prince's Party'.[55] Diplomats engaged in negotiating over such issues could in any case hardly expect a sovereign country to give an undiscriminating compliance with their requests: while public opinion, fired about Spanish slaves on a scanty foreign diet, could expect nothing less.

Even the grievance of the 'enslaved' British seamen, together with other depredations, could not make an entire platform of opposition. In fact, if one were to go upon explicit published references, then Walpole's abortive Excise scheme of 1733, a novel fiscal measure overthrown in a highly emotional campaign 'without doors', would seem to be an integral part of the depredations crisis. Each issue of the *Craftsman* in 1738–9 was full of indirect assaults on Walpole's tyrannical and dishonest regime, and as in the pamphlets and speeches of the Opposition, the attack on corruption was embedded in appeals to history. Freedom of the seas, as a cry of immediate policy, was made to rest on a great fabric of past national achievement, a tradition of seafaring toughness and daring rooted in the Elizabethan past, but vigorously pursued even under Cromwell. Along with this firmly, and repetitively, historical approach, went a strong suggestion that the freedom of the seas was somehow intimately involved with liberties at home. The Excise, a wash of placemen, and a great surge of growth in the standing army, were threats of immediate moment if the country bowed its head before the Spanish enemy whom — there was much insistence on this point — the British had so regularly and so disdainfully beaten in the past.[56]

Growing within this forcing frame was also a more positive conviction that the time was ripe to assert British naval strength in order to make important gains from Spain. In June 1738 the *Craftsman* was propounding a plan of campaign. Land attacks against Spain were dismissed as unlikely to succeed, while the Spanish *flotas* upon the ocean had proved elusive. Captures in America, accordingly, were to be the aim of naval force, beginning if possible with the capture of Havana, to give a stronghold on Cuba. The pseudonymous editor 'Caleb d'Anvers' allowed himself a certain vagueness about particular objectives, but averred that many places held by Spain in the Americas were 'more healthy and less strong' than such fortified towns as la Cruz and Portobello. A notable weakness of these plans was the difficulty by naval force alone of keeping such conquests — no increase in the army list was likely to be supported — but the *Craftsman*'s answer to this lay in the scheme of bringing liberation to the subject peoples of Spain, offering them the benefits of a free system of government.[57] This was the happy frame of mind in which the crisis over depredations was approached, and great results were expected from a 'blue water' naval strategy, supported by the force of private enterprise in reprisals, and rendered ultimately invincible by the successful export of the Revolution Settlement.

These expectations came out more fully in the crucial year ending in the early summer of 1739. The domestic political struggles had by then resulted in a precarious but distinct victory for the administration, and the final resolution of the crisis lay largely in Spanish hands, though those hands were closely tied by the non-cooperation of the South Sea Company and by the form and vigour of the British uproar. Opposition protests were directed, oddly enough, most vehemently against the most comprehensive attempts ever made to resolve differences with Spain, and prevent future depredations. The reason is clear: if both Britain and Spain were to be satisfied, each must abate some part of their claims, whether of finance or of principle, in a genuine compromise. Such agreements lack glamour, and could easily be portrayed as an inglorious abandonment of the national interest, even where the discussions succeeded. Unlike opposition politicians, ministers had a duty to attempt such a reconciliation, however complex, and especially so where commercial interests pointed the way, as did the rich trade with old Spain. In doing so, much importance necessarily attached to conventional diplomatic considerations, with which popular spokesmen did not need to concern themselves. When the depredations issue flared up again in 1737, the prospects for a closer understanding with Spain had actually looked good. Calm and optimism prevailed, and the diplomatic correspondence of that year was characterised by a light-hearted diversity born of free hours, and driven out only by the death of George II's wife Queen Caroline in November. In March, Keene was confident, despite rumours of an impending conflict in North America, that Spain had no intention of giving uneasiness to Britain, and had no power to do it.[58] At this point, the way was clear for a peaceable diplomatic initiative, and the ministry in Britain was very alert to the changes in personnel at the Spanish court which followed the death of Don Jose Patiño, the architect of financial and naval recovery, in November 1736. Newcastle, and particularly Sir Robert Walpole, agreed well with Don Thomas Geraldino, the Spanish representative in London of the South Sea Company, and wished to see him fixed there as ambassador, as he soon after was. At the same time, the ministers hoped to see 'the calm, & composed Temper' of Don Sebastian de la Quadra in charge of affairs in Spain, rather than the more abrasive and energetic contender, the Marquis of Montemar, advised by such nationalists as Uztariz. With Geraldino performing fair offices from England, and la Quadra as Secretary of State in Spain, a visible change took place, as Keene reported:

> I do not perceive that there is half that prejudice and violence in their Counsels and Proceedings, which reigned but too visibly in them for several years last past.[59]

These expectations were thwarted, by the winter of that year, when the rising flood of grievances revealed the difficulties of dealing with a ministerial system which, though now less hostile, was also weaker and more divided than before. La Quadra, without active ill will, behaved more like a clerk than a secretary, and remitted all affairs possible to their separate departments. The Secretary of the Marine and the Indies, Torrenueva, was easily swayed by those around him, and Montijo, in the overlapping, key, post of President of the Council of the Indies was ambitious and unlikely to risk much in the cause of peace with Britain, besides having personal grievances against the Directors of the South Sea Company. Internal pressures, and simple muddle, were likely to shape Spanish diplomatic responses, and Keene reported that:

> ... we who are employed at this Court, are obliged to transact great part of our affairs with those who are only the Canals thro' which they pass; and that the authors of the reports that are made upon our Instances, remain, and I may say, fight under cover.[60]

This changed diplomatic situation must be stressed, because the strongly-worded memorial sent by Newcastle to the Spanish court in November 1737 had a greater and more harmful effect there than it might previously have done. Historians have tended to view the memorial as a deliberate departure in British policy, attributable to Newcastle's own designs and impatience. From this point the undoubted rift between Walpole and Newcastle is usually seen as widening significantly, and the intemperate demands of the Secretary of State are put forward as reasons for the breakdown of Anglo-Spanish relations.[61] Newcastle's views and hopes of gain did come to approach those of the Opposition, but the disparity between his and Walpole's ideas was not yet so great. Walpole's brother and confidant Horatio endorsed what he called '... ye strong, well reason'd and becoming Memorial relating to the Spanish depredations', and had earlier interfered, as was his way, urging Keene to much more emphatic action, and denouncing Spanish lethargy.[62] Sir Robert Walpole is usually credited with toning down the memorial by sending private instructions to Keene, which is extremely likely, though the destruction of the ambassador's papers makes this hearsay. It is not pointed out that Newcastle himself also accompanied the Memorial with a private letter urging accommodation, insisting to Keene that:

> His Majesty is far from being desirous of quarrelling with the Court of Spain; On the contrary, the King would do every Thing that he could, consistent with His own Honour, and the Interest of His Subjects, to avoid it . . .

His reading of the diplomatic situation gave him confidence that Patiño's legacy of assertiveness over the West Indies trade was the only obstacle to an understanding:

> The present Situation of the court of Spain with other Powers, the cool Foot they are upon with France, and the secret Enmity that they have towards the Court of Vienna . . . makes it impossible, that they should have any Designs at present to quarrel with us . . .[63]

What Keene feared, as he told Horace Walpole, was not design, but the mere remissness which could cause a rupture, and the possibilities for offence grew as months of waiting were spent in increasing irritation on the British side at what Newcastle termed 'the roundabout way, which has hitherto been so ineffectually practised'.[64]

Fears of a breakdown intrinsic to the negotiating process were not removed even by the plan for a financial settlement which was first proposed to Geraldino by M. P. Arthur Stert, a Spanish specialist and intimate of Walpole, from whom the scheme is assumed to have emanated. Stert's plan calculated the total of British claims at over £343,000, and the Spanish total (mainly for warships destroyed in the Mediterranean in 1718) at £180,000. The compromise proposal was for Spain to make over some £200,000, in various forms, of which £60,000 would be returned to satisfy Spanish claims. At a meeting between Stert, Geraldino, and Sir Robert Walpole, it was made clear that the ministry were willing to compromise on the details of payment.[65] The fear of loss of face was uppermost in the minds of Spanish negotiators, Keene perforce responding to irate charges that Spanish claims had been much reduced, and England's left intact, by reducing the £140,000 effectively demanded by Stert to a new figure of £95,000.[66]

This proportionate reduction was accepted, though it was later to provide easy ammunition for opponents, and the ministry seems to have been relatively harmonious in pursuing the new initiative, which soon became mainly a matter of pinning down suitable forms of words. Newcastle's account of one particular conference certainly contradicts the generally held view of a hawkish Secretary of State, held back by the pacific Walpole. Sir Robert, 'with all ye firmness imaginable', told Geraldino that the negotiations were over unless freedom from search on the high seas were acknowledged:

> Sr. R. is very positive, not to yeild, & sd. very rightly, yt if we did, all ye World would say, we had given up our Rights for 95 th[ousand], When we were in a Condition to force them to admitt them.[67]

Further, Newcastle was at this time making serious plans to build a good relationship with Spain, including a proposed complete new treaty of commerce:

good relations with Spain, indeed, were consistently seen as desirable by Newcastle, not least because of the adverse effects upon his bugbear, the French.[68] The ministry, though no doubt riven by personality divisions, was more agreed as to policy at this point than has been usually argued, and than was believed by the Opposition at the time, who blamed Walpole alone for the whole train of compensation discussions.

Neither Newcastle nor Walpole could be held accountable for the destructive involvement of the South Sea Company directors, who had agreed to pay the £95,000 in London on behalf of Spain. Since the Asiento treaty the Company was accustomed to making payments on behalf of the Spanish Crown, as the Catholic King's share of the annual ship, and the negro duties payable to him upon the slave trade, lay in the company's vaults. Now, however, the Asientists dug in their heels, hoping to use the leverage of their position to secure long-delayed compensation for the loss of Company goods in 1718 and 1727, when war had broken out between Britain and Spain.[69] Not only was this a private grievance of the company, it was one which might well have been more easily resolved after the conclusion of a peace convention between the two nations: yet the directors instead saw in the negotiations a chance to improve their own affairs. A still more threatening intrusion into international relations was the prolonged dispute over the money owed by the Company to the Spanish crown, which had been agreed in 1737 to amount to £68,000. At this delicate juncture in the negotiations, when the reduction in the sum to be paid in compensation to British merchants had been accepted only in return for a prompt payment, the company's directors made it a great point of condescension to accept an adjustment of disputes over the exchange rate of the colonial dollar, and insisted that they would act as the Spanish king's bankers, and pay what they themselves owed, only when *cédulas* (warrants) were made out for the effects lost ten and fifteen years earlier.[70] The striking thing is that this intransigence did not immediately cause a rupture. So seriously was the diplomatic accommodation taken in Spain that, not without much distress and anger in Madrid, la Quadra remitted the *cédulas* required.[71] This concession represented a serious erosion of the bargaining flexibility available from the Spanish ministers, and even so brought affairs only to the first stage of the convention process. After the mutual payments came disputed matters such as rights of search and freedom of navigation, which were to be referred to plenipotentiaries. Even the first step proved to be a stumble, however, when the company refused to accept the conditions which were attached to the *cedulas*, and would not act to furnish payment on behalf of Spain. This decision by the asientists was critical, since a condition of la Quadra's signing the convention had been that the South Sea Company should pay over the £95,000, failing which Spain would be free to cancel the Asiento. A private commercial transaction now seemed likely to result in a unilateral breach, by Spain, of an international treaty: though the convention would go ahead, and Spain pay the £95,000, it would be almost impossible to avert a war. British diplomats were not blind to the danger. An anxious inner circle of ministers met at Sir Robert Walpole's in mid-October, with the annulling of the asiento prominent on their agenda.[72] A sticking point internal to the diplomatic process of discussion was firmly embedded before ever parliament had the chance to debate the matter. No subsequent negotiation proved entirely capable of separating in Spanish minds the issues of reparations, freedom from search, and the other substantive matters as seen from Britain on the one hand, and the particular grievances against the asiento company on the other. Such a confusion of private and national business was all the more natural because the envoy in Madrid, Benjamin Keene, was also the South Sea Company representative there. Keene himself admitted that his was an ambiguous role: '. . . it has not been possible for me to put the Affairs depending between Spain and the Company in the situation I could wish, nor adjust them at the same time with those of the Nation in general'.[73]

The confusion of interests was accepted as perilous, and Walpole launched efforts to secure a second agreement, the eventual convention of the Pardo, which would skirt around the delicate issue of making payment through the Company. Even as Keene and others laboured to produce it, changes were taking place in the readiness of the Spanish court to enter into compromise. One reason for the change was the dispute between the two nations over the respective boundaries of their territories in North America. Spain's ancient claims to hegemony of the whole of the Americas had been moderated in the treaty with Britain of 1670, to allow Britain secure possession of all her then North American colonies, including the Carolinas. During the 1730s, however, a body of trustees led by James Oglethorpe was creating the separate colony of Georgia, which led to disputes over whether or not this territory fell within the old boundaries of south Carolina. This dispute, which had flared up in the autumn of 1737, so as to create a scare of a planned Spanish invasion, blew now hot and now cold, but the erosion of Spain's land empire in America did nothing to help along a general accommodation.[74] More immediately, a new resolve was becoming apparent among the Spanish ministers, sharply altering the optimistic British diplomatic assessments of 1737. One factor at work in this, though not the most critical, was undoubtedly the pressure of British public opinion, which did become a component in decision-making in Spain as well as at home. If a confrontation seemed likely to be forced upon a popular government, Spanish ministers might be more inclined to enter into closer links with France as a matter of urgency. As early as May 1738 the impression made by the British memorial, and firmness, had been effaced by the Spanish reaction to the parliamentary and popular clamour, and Keene reported that encouragements had been sent from France to Madrid.[75] This gloomy assessment, however, was inconclusive, and the part of British opposition cries in driving Spain into the arms of France is hard to guess at. When the discussion over the first convention had reached its height, Keene was inclined to attribute Spanish inflexibility rather to considerations purely internal to the Spanish court. With King Philip in a parlous mental condition, Queen Elizabeth ran more risks with international security than she would if she had been less alone, or with more enterprising and independent judgements around her. Certainly a critical change in the nature of diplomatic interchange took place within the Spanish court, and with no obvious connection with British domestic politics. From early December

1738, la Quadra desired all foreign ministers, but especially the key British, French and Papal envoys, to submit in writing the substance of all important matters to be brought to him. As Keene had long complained, la Quadra was the only Secretary through whom the king could be approached, and from his hands all business went off along a maze of diplomatic channels. Now this traffic was to be put in the constricting form of written memoranda, in which it was far harder not to offend '. . . the superstitious delicacy of this Court'.[76]

This change in tone and in method was not purely dictated by the capacities of ministers, or the arrangement of responsibilities, but represented an attempt to control the fluid diplomatic relations of the major powers. A year earlier, the possibility had existed of a real coming together of Britain and Spain, linked as they were by substantial trading ties, and such a union would have served to check the power of France. The leading French minister, Cardinal Fleury, was anxiously making proposals for closer links with Britain to preserve 'a just Balance of Power in Europe', and the choice of partnership with one or the other of the Bourbon powers in the enjoyment of colonial dominion seemed open to British diplomats, given sufficient care. A year later, after so many months of disputes, and facing the prospect of conflict without the necessary armed force to sustain it, the Spanish court was inclined to infuse warmth into the chill body of the Bourbon family compact. Too late, Newcastle pushed forward again with his long-desired scheme of a 'strict Union with the King of Spain for the mutual Benefit of both Crowns, as well as for the general Good of Europe'.[77] The time had been missed, for the Spanish and French courts were negotiating a royal wedding which would bring them closer, and intransigence was the mood in Madrid, as Keene reported:

> Their party is taken; they think the honour of their Crown would be sullyed, and that it would be buying a Peace if They did not act as they have done.[78]

Important steps in the direction of war were taken far away from the coffee houses of London, and the margin for manoeuvre was much reduced before ever the Convention was laid before the British parliament.

The debates on the Convention were long and vehement, giving a temporary boost to the momentum of the anti-Walpole campaign; but they did not cause the war with Spain. The bellicosity and vigour of the opposition perhaps made it more likely that the ministry would face a major challenge at the next election, but the immediate effect was that the ministry secured majorities of around thirty votes in two crucial divisions, after which many of the leaders of the opposition embarked on an ill-judged secession from parliament. Without a proper opposition, and in recess from mid-June until mid-November 1739, the palace of Westminster was not the place in which the crucial steps in the path to war were taken. It would be foolish to suggest that ministers, least of all Newcastle, were insulated from clamorous outside opinion, but only one important action can be traced to this cause. After the Convention debates, in March 1739, Newcastle decided to countermand the recall of Admiral Haddock's provocatively stationed Mediterranean fleet, a move which certainly caused a stiffening of attitudes at the Spanish court, and accounted for the fact that the rupture, when it came, was made in

Madrid, and without French diplomats even being informed.[79] In May the asiento contract was suspended, and in June came the outright refusal to pay the sums agreed in the Convention, after which war was overwhelmingly likely. A refusal by the 'insolent' Spanish king to pay the agreed sum was an issue which could not easily be contained in British domestic politics, and which also involved crucially the prestige of the Hanoverian monarchy.

Spanish intransigence was the cause of this breakdown, though certainly the outcry in Britain affected the negotiations at some crucial points. The underlying problems were far more deep-seated, and the issues not immediate ones of individual outrages, but concerns such as the vast object of colonial empire, the inescapable pressure of national esteem, and underlying ambitions for change in the balance of European diplomatic power. The rhythms of depredations, in any case, followed closely the general diplomatic situation, moderating at times when Spanish ministers and colonial governors alike judged that they needed British goodwill, as during the War of Polish Succession, and increasing when that need diminished. Though the prospect of assistance for Spain from France came to little at first, it may still have been far more important in leading to hostilities than the cries of 'your people in coffee houses', as La Quadra dismissively called them. The Dutch example shows how this kind of outcry could be contained, public opinion there being outraged over a series of depredations by the Spanish, including the captain who lost not an ear only but his hand, lopped off and boiled before his eyes, and which he was made to eat. Yet the United Provinces, after angry early preparations, settled down to the pragmatic course of commercial profit rather than national revenge.[80] That Britain took a different course may have much to do with the forms of diplomatic intercourse which existed between monarchies, aggravated by the cumbersome structure of the Spanish colonial administration. The need to involve the respective crowns, and the multitudinous causes of delay and therefore of offence built into the system, made the conventions of diplomacy ill suited to deal with such complex commercial and colonial issues, and still maintain the jealously guarded dignity of both catholic and protestant monarchs. Within these conventions, the Spanish crown could not ignore the deliberate obstruction of the South Sea Company, and the British crown could not ignore the breakdown of the Convention agreement, so that without actively wishing war, but cherishing objectives important to national prestige, both sides were led to accept a war for which neither was at all well prepared. Since colonial disputes were to dominate the rest of the century, this immaturity in diplomatic forms, and the far from one-sided origins of the war, deserve greater stress than they have received. To attribute the war only to British public opinion is a disservice to the study of international relations, stemming from an often unconscious adoption of an 'innenpolitik' model of explanation. In reality, the domestic campaign set the limits within which the British ministry had to work, but foreign concerns, and the particularly complex network of negotiations, were at least equally important. The causes of the war of 1739 are not to be found solely in Britain, much less in the cries of parliament and press, and not at all in the ear, left or right, boxed or bottled, of Captain Robert Jenkins.

NOTES

I am grateful for support provided by the research and staff development funds of Huddersfield Polytechnic. Jeremy Black gave valuable comment on an earlier draft of this paper. Dates are given in New Style unless otherwise indicated.

1. William Pulteney, opposition whig leader, and Henry Pelham, the ministry's deputy leader in the Commons, debate on the Convention of Pardo, 8 Mar. (o.s.) 1739; R. Chandler (ed.), *History and Proceedings of the House of Commons* Vol. XI, London (1743), pp. 64–5.

2. D. E. Leach, 'The Cartagena Expedition, 1740–1742, and Anglo-American Relations', in M. Ultee (ed.), *Adapting to Conditions. War and Society in the Eighteenth Century* (Alabama 1986), p. 44.

3. The consensus view is summarised in V. Palacio Atard, *El Siglo de las Reformas* (Madrid 1978), p. 28.

4. R. L. Bindschedler, 'Zum Primat der Aussenpolitik', in U. Altermatt & J. Garamvolgyi (eds.), *Innen- und Aussenpolitik. Primat oder Interdependenz?* (Bern & Stuttgart 1980), p. 33. See discussion in T. C. W. Blanning, *The Origins of the French Revolutionary Wars* (1986), pp. 19–23.

5. G. Blainey, *The Causes of War* (Melbourne, 2nd. ed. 1976), pp. 17, 271; Pulteney, speech 6 Mar. (o.s.) 1739, Chandler, *Commons Proceedings*, p. 64.

6. H. W. V. Temperley, 'The Causes of the War of Jenkins' Ear, 1739', *Royal Historical Society Transactions*, 3rd. Series, III, 1909, p. 197.

7. R. Pares, *War and Trade in the West Indies 1739–1763* (1936); E. G. Hildner, 'The Role of the South Sea Company in the Diplomacy leading to the War of Jenkins' Ear 1729–1739', *Hispanic American Historical Review*, 18, 1938, pp. 322–41; J. O. McLachlan, *Trade and Peace with Old Spain 1667–1750* (Cambridge 1940); G. H. Nelson, 'Contraband Trade under the Asiento 1730–1739' *American Historical Review*, 51, 1945–6, pp. 55–67.

8. Rev. Henry Etough Journal, B.L. Add. 9200, f. 67.

9. [H. Walpole], *The Grand Question, Whether War, or no War, with Spain . . .* (1739), p. 24.

10. This emphasis seems to affect the shrewd and convincing discussion in H. T. Dickinson, *Walpole and the Whig Supremacy* (1973), pp. 136–7, and the otherwise thorough and balanced account in D. Marshall, *Eighteenth Century England* (2nd. ed. 1974), pp. 176–183.

11. For the limited interest of one West Riding apothecary, see C. E. Whiting (ed.), *Two Yorkshire Diaries*, Yks. Archaeol. Soc. Record Series Vol. CXVII (Leeds 1952), pp. 57–61. The campaign is summarised in H. T. Dickinson, 'Popular Politics in the Age of Walpole', in J. Black (ed.), *Britain in the Age of Walpole* (1984), pp. 47–8.

12. J. Black, *British Foreign Policy in the Age of Walpole* (Edinburgh 1985), p. 182.

13. See for instance 'The Royal Assiento Company's Reply to the answer given by His Catholick Majesty's late Minister M. Patino to their Complaint of Grievances', 24 Feb. (o.s.) 1737, B.L. Add. 33032, ff. 185–199.

14. Newcastle to Keene, 3 Mar. 1737, P.R.O. 98/125., Hardwicke to H. Walpole, 13 Dec. 1750, B.L. Add. 9132.

15. G. J. Walker, *Spanish Politics and Imperial Trade 1700–1789* (1979), pp. 11–15, 159–192; M. Grice-Hutchinson, *Early Economic Thought in Spain, 1177–1740* (1978), pp. 137–168.

16. For the opposition see L. Colley, *In Defiance of Oligarchy: the Tory Party 1714–1760* (Cambridge 1982), pp. 77–84, 221–235; R. Browning, *Political and Constitutional Ideas of the Court Whigs* (Baton Rouge, La., 1982), pp. 21–31; quotation Etough Journal, B.L. Add. 9200, f. 62.

17. Keene to Newcastle, 18 Mar., 16 Sept., 28 Oct. 1737, B.L. Add. 32794, 32795, 32796.

18. Chandler, *Commons Proceedings* p. 32; E. Timberland (ed.), *The History and Proceedings of the House of Lords* (1742), Vol. VI, p. 154. The elder Pitt first came to prominence in these debates; Bathurst was a tory stalwart.

19. W. Coxe, *Memoirs of the Kings of Spain of the House of Bourbon* (5 Vols. 1815), III, pp. 225-30, 249-55; E. Armstrong, *Elisabeth Farnese* (1892), pp. 337-44; Waldegrave (envoy in Paris) to Newcastle, 29 May 1737, Keene to H. Walpole, 19 Aug. 1737, Keene to Newcastle, 13 Dec. 1737, B.L. Add. 32795, 32796.

20. Keene to Newcastle, 2 Apr. 1737, Keene to Newcastle, 13 Jan. 1739, B.L. Add. 32794, 32800.

21. Keene to Newcastle, 29 May 1738, Waldegrave to Newcastle, 29 Jan. 1739, Newcastle to Waldegrave, 1 Feb. (o.s.) 1739, B.L. Add. 32798, 32800.

22. Waldegrave to Keene, 5 Feb. 1737, Waldegrave to Keene, 3 Feb. 1739, Keene to Newcastle, 16 Feb. 1739, B.L. Add. 32794, 32800; [H. Walpole], *The Grand Question*, p. 15; *The Original Series of Wisdom and Policy* (1739), pp. 23-5.

23. *The Original Series*, p. 50; 'Mr. Walpole's Apology', B.L. Add. 9132, f. 99v. The average annual credit balance of the official South Sea Company alone in the late 1730s was some £600,000, though Spanish seizures and also excessive dividend declarations by the Company brought profits down; A. S. Aiton, 'The Asiento Treaty as Reflected in the Papers of Lord Shelburne', *Hispanic American Historical Review*, 8, 1928, p. 175.

24. H. Walpole, 'Points, to be Consider'd with Regard to the Depredations of Spain', B.L. Add. 9131, f. 271.

25. J. R. Jones, *Britain and the World 1649-1815*, (1980), p. 199. Similar summaries may be found in W. A. Speck, *Stability and Strife. England 1714-1760* (1977), p. 234; J. H. Parry, 'Rivalries in America: the Caribbean', *New Cambridge Modern History*, Vol. VII (Cambridge 1970), p. 518; J. H. Parry & P. M. Sherlock, *A Short History of the British West Indies* (1956), p. 105; Sir A. Burns, *History of the British West Indies (2nd. ed. 1965), p. 474.*

26. R. Browning, *The Duke of Newcastle* (1975), p. 91. This view of events has a long pedigree: see the similar account by J. R. Green, *History of the English People*, Vol. IV (1880), p. 154.

27. E. Burke, *Thoughts on the Prospect of a Regicide Peace* (1796), p. 25; for a typically dismissive treatment see W. E. H. Lecky, *History of England in the Eighteenth Century* (1883), pp. 384-5. Evidence for the episode from Admiralty records was first published by J. K. Laughton in 'Jenkins's Ear', *English Historical Review*, 4 Oct. 1889, pp. 741-749.

28. See for instance Stanhope to Newcastle, 15 Nov. (o.s.) 1724, B.L. Add. 9152.

29. 'Heads of Sundry Matters necessary to the Establishment of the Assiento Trade' c.1729, B.L. Add. 33032, f. 41; G. H. Nelson, 'Contraband Trade under the Asiento, 1730-1739', *American Historical Review*, 51, 1945-6, pp. 55-6.

30. Quoted in 'The Royal Assiento Company's Reply ...', B.L. Add. 33032, f. 189.

31. See R. Pares, *War and Trade*, pp. 23-4.

32. Affidavit of May 15, 1731, P.R.O. 94/129; memorial B.L. Add. 32774, ff. 118-20; Laughton, 'Jenkins' Ear', p. 742.

33. [A. Boyer], *The Political State of Great Britain*, Vol. XLI (1731), p. 11.

34. *The Gentleman's Magazine*, Vol. 1, no. VI, June 1731, p. 265.

35. See for instance the account in *The Historical Register*, XVI, 1731, p. 29.

36. Newcastle to Keene, 30 Sept. 1737, B.L. Add. 32774.

37. *The Case of Samuel Bonham ...* (1737), p. 1. Another early case, the seizure of the *Betty* galley in 1727, made a stir in 1739; *The Case of Richard Copithorne ...* (1739); *Craftsman*, 24 Feb. (o.s.) 1739. There was no similar revival of the *Rebecca* case.

38. Account of an inhabitant ... 21 Dec. 1736, P.R.O. 98/129; Newcastle to Keene, 13 Jan. (o.s.) 1737, B.L. Add. 32794. Another tale of cruelty was that of the sloop *Fanny*: Information of Wm. Fisher [passenger], in Newcastle to Keene, 24 Mar. 1737, P.R.O. 98/129.

39. Newcastle to Keene, 4 Nov. (o.s.) 1737; see also H. Walpole to Keene, 14 Nov. (o.s.) 1737, Keene to Newcastle 13 Dec. 1737, B.L. Add. 32796.

40. List of British Merchant Ships Taken or Plunder'd by the Spaniards P.R.O. 94/128. Not all were either taken or plundered; see nos. 38-40.

41. H. Walpole, 'Points, to be Consider'd ...', B.L. Add. 9131, ff. 242–6. An edited version of the paper, in heavy black ink, follows this one, and may have been for the eyes of George II. On reprisals see R. Pares, *War and Trade*, pp. 46–9.

42. B.L. Add. 9131, f. 245.

43. Keene to Newcastle, 21 Apr. 1738, Newcastle to Keene, 28 Apr. (o.s.) 1738, Keene to Newcastle, 25 May 1738, B.L. Add. 32797, 32798.

44. D. McKay & H. M. Scott, *The Rise of the Great Powers 1648–1815* (1983), pp. 160–1.

45. W. Coxe, *Memoirs of the Life and Administration of Sir Robert Walpole, Earl of Orford* (3 Vols. 1798), I, p. 579. See Coxe's unprecedentedly long footnotes at this point.

46. *Gentleman's Magazine*, VIII, July 1738, p. 336 fn. (Coxe mistakenly says 1736).

47. W. T. Laprade, *Public Opinion and Politics in Eighteenth Century England* (New York 1936), pp. 394 & 396.

48. A. J. Henderson, *London and the National Government, 1721–1742* (1946), pp. 182–3, fn. 16.

49. *The Original Series ...* pp. 6–7.

50. *The Craftsman*, 11 Feb. (o.s.), 1738.

51. Newcastle to Keene, 2 Mar. (o.s.) 1738, enclosing copy letters of 22 Jan., 1 & 6 Feb., B. L. Add. 32797. Also depositions taken before Lord Mayor John Barnard, 10 Apr. (o.s.) 1738; ibid. ff. 295–6.

52. Cayley to Newcastle, 13 May 1738, P.R.O. 94/222; Keene to Newcastle, 26 May 1738, B.L. Add. 32798.

53. Keene to Newcastle, 13 Dec. 1737, B.L. Add. 32796.

54. G. J. Walker, *Spanish Politics ...*, pp. 193–206; [A. Boyer], *The Political State of Great Britain*, XLI, 1731, p. 289; Waldegrave to Newcastle, 12 Oct. 1737, Keene to Newcastle, 14 Oct. 1737, 13 Jan. 1738, B.L. Add. 32796, 32797.

55. Keene to Newcastle, 31 Mar. 1738, Newcastle to Keene, 12 April (o.s.) 1738; quotation Keene to Newcastle, 7 Apr. 1738, B.L. Add. 32797.

56. See, e.g., *Craftsman* 18, 25 Mar., 15 Apr., 3, 17 June (o.s.) 1738, 6, 13 Jan., 10, 24 Feb., 7, 21, 28 Apr., 5, 12, 19 May, 1739; Mark Akenside, *The British Philippic ...* (1739); Capt. Charles Jinkins [sic], *Spanish Insolence corrected by English Bravery; being an historical account of the many signal naval achievements obtained by the English over the Spaniards ...* (1739); the Convention debates of 1739, e.g. Chandler, *Commons Proceedings*, XI, pp. 25, 95, Timberland, *Lords Proceedings*, VI, pp. 63, 89, 95, 156.

57. *Craftsman* 3 June (o.s.) 1738. An earlier proposal was L. D., *Reasons for a War against Spain, in a Letter from a Merchant of London ... With a plan of operations* (1737, 2nd. ed. 1738). See discussion in J. Black, 'The British Navy and British Foreign Policy in the First Half of the Eighteenth Century', in J. M. Black & K. W. Schweizer (eds.), *Essays in European History in honour of Ragnhild Hatton* (Lennoxville 1985), pp. 150–1.

58. Keene to Newcastle, 11 Mar. 1737, B.L. Add. 32794.

59. Newcastle to Keene, 3 & 24 Mar. (o.s.) 1737, P.R.O. 98/129; Keene to Waldegrave, 11 Mar. 1737, B.L. Add. 32794; quotation Keene to Newcastle, 10 June 1737, B.L. Add. 32795.

60. Keene to Newcastle, 13 Dec. 1737, giving a long and valuable account of the courtiers and ministers of Spain, B.L. Add. 32796. Quotation f. 242.

61. Memorial, B.L. Add. 32796, ff. 94–109; R. Pares, *War and Trade*, pp. 43–6; R. Browning, *Newcastle*, pp. 89–91.

62. H. Walpole to Keene, 3 Sept. 1737, 31 Oct. 1737, B.L. Add. 32795, 32796; same to Newcastle, 26 Nov. 1737, P.R.O. 84/369.

63. Newcastle to Keene, 4 Nov. (o.s.), 1737, B.L. Add. 32796. For a representative treatment of the issue, see J. O. McLachlan, *Trade and Peace*, pp. 110–11.

64. Keene to H. Walpole, 4 Nov. 1737, Newcastle to Keene, 19 Jan. (o.s.) 1738, B.L. Add. 32796.

65. Stert's paper &c., 14–21 June (o.s.) 1738, B.L. Add. 32798, ff. 172–196; P.R.O. 94/131. A long account by Geraldino, from the Simancas archives, is given in McLachlan, *Trade and*

Peace, pp. 111–12. See also the very revealing comments by Geraldino on the British political context, *ibid*. p. 199, fn. 131.

66. Keene to Newcastle, 28 July 1738, 2 Aug. 1738, B.L. Add. 32798, P.R.O. 94/131.

67. Newcastle to Hardwicke, 25 Aug. (o.s.) 1738, B.L. Add. 35406.

68. Newcastle to Hardwicke, 25 Sept. (o.s.) 1738, B.L. Add. 35406; Newcastle to H. Walpole, 22 Aug. (o.s.) 1735, B.L. Add. 32788.

69. Newcastle to Geraldino, 16 Aug. (o.s.) 1738, Geraldino to Newcastle, 17 Aug. 1738, P.R.O. 94/132; Burrell to Keene, 7 Sept. 1737, B.L. Add. 327985; opinions on Asiento Company position, July (o.s.) 1734, B.L. Add. 33007, ff. 126–30. Useful discussion in J. O. McLachlan, *Trade and Peace*, pp. 114–7, E. G. Hildner, 'The Role of the South Sea Company'.

70. Keene to Newcastle, 17 June 1737, Newcastle to Keene, 23 June (o.s.) 1737, Keene to Newcastle, 13 Jan. 1739, B.L. Add. 32795, 32800. The company had paid its dues at a fraudulent rate of exchange, giving debased European coins (ten *reals* to the dollar) at the rate of only eight *reals* to the dollar, which should only have applied to the true silver dollars in which its colonial profits were made.

71. Keene to Newcastle, 15 Sept. 1738, P.R.O. 94/131. The Convention was signed on 9 Sept. 1738.

72. Minutes, 16 Oct. 1738 (o.s.), B.L. Add. 33032. Present were the Walpole brothers, Newcastle, Hardwicke, Grafton and Harrington.

73. Keene to Weltden, South Sea Company factor at Havana, 28 Feb. 1739, B.L. Add. 32800.

74. Newcastle to Keene, 5 May (o.s.) 1737, 12 Sept. (o.s.) 1737, Keene to H. Walpole, 14 Oct. 1737, B.L. Add. 32795, 32796.

75. Keene to Newcastle, 29 May 1738, 7 July 1738, B.L. Add. 32798.

76. Keene to Newcastle, 13 Jan. 1739, B.L. Add. 32800.

77. Waldegrave to Keene, 20 Dec. 1737, Newcastle to Keene, 26 Jan. (o.s.) 1739, B.L. Add. 32796, 32800.

78. Keene to Newcastle, 17 Jan. 1739, Waldegrave to Newcastle, 29 Jan. 1739, Newcastle to Waldegrave, 1 Feb. (o.s.) 1739, B.L. Add. 32800.

79. Newcastle to Keene, 8 May (o.s.) 1739, Keene to Newcastle, 9 June 1739, Waldegrave to Newcastle 18 June 1739, B.L. Add. 32800, 32801.

80. Deposition enclosed in Newcastle to Keene, 24 Mar. (o.s.) 1737, P.R.O. 98/129, General Matthew to Board of Trade, enclosed in Newcastle to Keene, 12 Sept. (o.s.) 1737, Keene to Stone (secretary to Newcastle), 15 Apr. 1738, Trevor (acting envoy in United Provinces) to Keene, 26 June 1738, B.L. Add. 32795, 32797, 32798.

9

MID-EIGHTEENTH CENTURY CONFLICT WITH PARTICULAR REFERENCE TO THE WARS OF THE POLISH AND AUSTRIAN SUCCESSIONS

Jeremy Black

'There are more tempers than that of Spain in the world, which are never to be satisfied, and the truth is the late parties at war have not got enough in more than one sense to be quiet.'
    Thomas Robinson, British envoy in Vienna, 1736
'The King of Prussia ... is determined that no German Prince shall pretend to dictate in Germany besides himself. We are unhappily got into an age of conquering monarchs disgusted with their former boundaries.'
    John Sturrock, 1743[1]

This essay will seek to examine features general to eighteenth-century international relations by considering two major wars that have received insufficient attention from British scholars and have been in general neglected in recent years. The major theme of the essay is the central importance of individual monarchs and, to a lesser extent, ministers. This is appropriate in an age when dynastic interests were a central concern of state activity and in some countries largely defined the latter. These interests were determined by the monarchs and it was generally accepted that they should do so. By placing the personal interpretation of the way in which dynastic interests should be furthered at the centre of policy, a thesis is advanced that differs from some of the more determinist conceptions implicit in social-science analyses of the causes of war.

As in most periods a rhythmic quality can be discerned in the alternate presence of war and peace in the eighteenth century. Thomas Robinson observed in November 1733, 'I am no more surprised after so many years of peace that things are revolved into their old state of war, than I should be at any man's having a good fit of sickness after a long run of health'.[2] The period from the autumn of 1733 to the summer of 1748 was one of conflict, with two major wars, the Polish Succession (1733–5) and the Austrian Succession (1740–8), involving at some stage most of the European powers. This period followed another, begun in 1721, that was generally peaceful, in which the major differences dividing the European powers were settled without serious conflict. The reasons for this difference are of considerable interest in eliciting the causes of the mid-century wars. The avoidance of war, an achievement that tends to be overlooked by historians, serves as the background to the wars which did occur.

The 1720s had not been without sustained tension involving most European states in significant military preparations. In the early 1720s conflict had appeared imminent as Austria denied Spanish dynastic pretensions in Italy and Peter the

Great kept the other Baltic powers guessing about his intentions. From 1725 to 1731 Europe was divided into two alliance systems, each of which supported its claims with extensive military preparations, though conflict was restricted to an unsuccessful Spanish siege of Gibraltar in 1727. In 1731 Britain and France nearly began hostilities, the following year a Spanish invasion of Italy was feared.[3] The failure of the powers to actually fight in this period must be attributed partly to the effects of exhaustion after the European wars of 1688–1721. Serious financial difficulties, particularly heavy indebtedness, affected a large number of states. A London newspaper claimed in 1724 that 'the carrying on of War, is in this Age grown so expensive, that the Wealth of a Country may as well be the Ballance, as the Source of its Power, since it is not a hasty Expedition, or a Field Battle, that can decide the Fate of a Government, for now the Art Military is reduced to Money; and a good Treasurer, that can find the necessary supplies, to feed, clothe, and pay an Army, regularly, has as great, and perhaps as just a share in the successful event of a War, as the most prudent and bravest General'. Viscount Perceval, an Irish peer then in Paris, doubted that France and Spain would fight in 1725, despite their differences over a serious dynastic snub — the French decision that Louis XV would marry a Polish princess rather than his betrothed Spanish princess — 'neither Kingdom being in a condition to engage though they both vapour much'. In similar vein, after a later period of costly conflict, the Bavarian envoy in London, Baron Haslang, suggested in 1768 that the ability of powers to fight, rather than the issues in dispute, was the crucial factor in causing wars. He attributed the peaceful nature of international affairs in western Europe at that juncture to the domestic consequences of the Seven Years' War and noted that there was never any shortage of pretexts if rulers wished to fight.[4]

Financial considerations were doubtless of importance both in encouraging pacific tendencies and, as in 1747 and 1762, underlining the views of ministers pressing for an end to war. However, the significance of this factor should not be pressed too hard. While it is true that states cannot fight if they lack the means to do so, it is by no means clear how rulers perceived the pressures of financial restraint and the reiterated wails of finance ministers. It could be suggested that monarchs such as Louis XV regarded the job of such ministers as one of providing funds for royal policies, rather than playing a role in their formulation. Tallard, the French envoy in London in 1701, reported that Britain was ready to fight despite being short of money and having weak credit,[5] and indeed the financial strains produced in most European states by the Nine Years' War did not prevent the War of the Spanish Succession. The serious indebtedness that followed the War of the Spanish Succession did not prevent a series of conflicts in the late 1710s, including an Austro-Turkish war and the War of the Quadruple Alliance, and did not dissuade the British from contemplating war with Russia in 1720. Financial crises seem often to have engendered not prudence, either in foreign or fiscal policy, but rashness; in the late 1710s the willingness of the Austrians to consider war in the Balkans and in Italy, of the British likewise in the Baltic and the Mediterranean, and the financial rashness that lay behind the crashes in Britain and France in 1720, the South Sea Bubble and the Mississippi Crash. It could be suggested that the latter helped to keep Europe at peace in the 1720s, but this does not appear to have been the case. The major European powers were all able to expand and put into the field or send to sea large forces during the crises of that decade. They planned for war, Britain, France and the United Provinces preparing for an invasion of the Empire and Italy in 1727 and, with the addition of Spain, 1730, Prussia an invasion of Hanover in 1729 and 1730. Financial considerations appear to have played little role in the planning. The Bavarian minister Count Preysing claimed in 1751 that it would be foolish for other states to assume that French financial exhaustion due to the War of the Austrian Succession would lead her not to defend her interests. In 1749, a year after the end of that conflict, France had threatened to intervene if there was war in eastern Europe. In 1750 Mirepoix, the French Ambassador in London, reported that Britain could not afford another war. Five years later she was to attack France. The French foreign minister at the time of the war of American Independence, Vergennes, subordinated considerations of public finance to the opportunity to attack Britain.[6] There seems to have been a substantial gap between those who assessed policy options and those who were expected to produce the means. This was in keeping with the nature of early-modern European government, ignorant of the resources at its disposal and exploitative in its policies, assuming that the necessary means would always be found.

One characteristic feature of the 1720s was the resort to international peace congresses. The Congresses of Cambrai and Soissons were linked to a significant development of the period that has been praised by historians, the system of collective security involving reciprocal guarantees. In a thoughtful and important survey Ragnhild Hatton has suggested that the period was one 'when progress was made in limiting wars and achieving a longish period of peace by conscious rational efforts ... the idea of the Society of Europe in which peace was regarded as the natural state was being transferred from the blueprints to reality on a practical level'. Hatton saw a generally rational, hopeful 'climate of opinion' that reached its apogee in congresses that served to 'deflate' problems and make them more amenable to solutions. This suggestion is of considerable importance as historians working on the nineteenth century have attributed much to the collective security and congress system of the period,[7] and because the 1720s forms an obvious contrast in this respect with the succeeding decades. Negotiations in 1731–33 were handled not through any congress, but by bilateral discussions or with the assistance of the good offices, not the mediation, of another power. This was true of the Anglo-Austrian treaty of 1731, negotiations between Austria and Sardinia and Austria and Spain, both with British participation, in 1732–3 and 1731–3 respectively, and the negotiations that sought to settle the Holstein question and led to the Treaty of Copenhagen in 1732. Though an attempt was made in the winter of 1734–5 to settle the War of Polish Succession by Anglo-Dutch good offices and though there was talk of a congress to end the war, it was instead ended by Austro-French bilateral negotiations, each power consulting neither its allies nor the neutral powers that had displayed interest. None of the contentious issues of the late 1730s, such as the contested inheritance to the Rhenish duchies of Jülich and Berg or the pretensions of various powers to the eventual Austrian inheritance, were discussed at any congress. The failure both to hold congresses and to settle disputes, such as the War of Polish Succession and the Jülich-Berg question, through the intervention of other powers represented a very different diplomatic mode to the 1720s.

Whether it also represented a different mood is unclear. It would be attractive to argue that war came in the 1730s because of the breakdown of the system of collective security and congresses or was in some ways related to it, but the evidence points in different directions. The system, if that is not too grand a term, if it ever meant much, had definitely broken down by 1725. In that year a bold approach, but conventional method, seeking the alliance of an enemy, led to an Austro-Spanish pact, the Alliance of Vienna, that destroyed the basis of the system that the effective British and French foreign ministers, Stanhope and Dubois, had sought to create in the late 1710s, namely the isolation of the power, Spain, that would not accept the views of others. Collective security sought to achieve and depended on the isolation of Spain. It was based on force, not diplomatic novelty. When Spain negotiated a viable alliance the weakness of existing Anglo-French diplomatic schemes was revealed and the two powers were forced to match Austria and Spain in the traditional race for, or rather market of, the alliance of other powers. Congresses were also perceived as unhelpful. The French first minister Cardinal Fleury suggested in 1727 that their lengthy procedures and the ease with which recalcitrant powers could prolong them made them unsuitable for dealing with European problems. This view was shared by many diplomats, such as Johann Pentenriedter, one of the Austrian Plenipotentiaries at the Congresses of Cambrai and Soissons, and was also expressed in the press, the opposition British newspaper the *Craftsman* noting in 1727, 'it is well known that Congresses are, generally speaking, no other than formal meetings of Plenipotentiary Ministers, in order to sign, in a solemn manner, what hath been privately agreed on between their respective masters; and that the great differences between princes are seldom easily and successfully concluded, when they are left to be debated in those Assemblies'.[8]

The negotiations of the 1720s, whether in the context of the congresses or not, were successful insofar as the decade saw little conflict, but they failed to produce a satisfactory solution of the problems affecting European relations. This was essentially due to the irreconcilable interests of the major powers, which the process of negotiation simply made more prominent. Spanish determination to recapture territories lost to Austria in the War of the Spanish Succession, the Emperor Charles VI's wish to ensure the indivisible inheritance of his territories by his elder daughter Maria Theresa and to obtain European guarantees for the Pragmatic Sanction, the device by which he sought to do so, and French interest in thwarting this plan were as much features of the international relations of the 1720s as of the succeeding period when they were to help to cause two wars. Bar Prussian determination to obtain a portion of the Austrian inheritance through an attack on Austria, the ambitions that led to the War of Austrian Succession in 1740 were already operative, indeed dominant, in the 1720s. Such ambitions were far from secret. In 1730 the future Augustus III of Saxony-Poland's interest in obtaining some of the Austrian dominions was referred to as a factor affecting negotiations with his father Augustus II.[9]

The Wars of the Polish and Austrian Successions were due to these irreconcilable differences but in each case conflict was postponed until the actual succession fell due. Augustus II died on 1 February 1733, Charles VI on 20 October 1740. Within seven and two months respectively war began. The decision of the powers to delay conflict until after the successions fell due partly reflected the nature of international relations in the period, and, in particular, its unpredictability and the exigencies of alliance diplomacy. No single power was strong enough to risk conflict on its own. Indeed a major reason for the avoidance of significant conflict in the 1720s was the isolation of aggressive states. Britain found the coalition she had constructed to force Russia to disgorge some of her Baltic conquests from Sweden collapse in 1720 before she could use it. Spain could not obtain support for her schemes and this played a role in forcing her to accept agreements which she disliked. In 1728 the absence of Austrian support played a role in leading her to accept the Convention of the Pardo, by which her differences with Britain and France were partially settled. The following year the failure of Austria, Saxony and Russia to support Prussia played a significant role in dissuading Frederick William I from invading Hanover. In 1730 an uncooperative French attitude prevented her allies, Britain and Spain, from attacking Austrian Italy. In order to have any prospect of success it was essential to have a strong and determined alliance, but the kaleidoscopic nature of international relations in the period was such that it was difficult to keep such an alliance in being for any length of time. Bereft of ideological bonds, most alliances were temporary expedients, reflecting personal assessments of advantage and threat by rulers confronted by a rapidly altering international system. In 1733 Austria and Russia supported the candidature of Augustus III for the Polish throne, though they had both earlier opposed it. Augustus III in turn sought his share of the Austrian inheritance in 1741. British Whig administrations supported Austrian gains in Italy in the 1700s and late 1710s, planned military action against Austrian Italy in 1727 and 1730, sent no assistance when these territories were invaded in 1733–5, but reversed their policy in the following conflict.

In 1733 and 1740–1 it was possible to create alliances strong enough for rulers to envisage successful aggressive action. Whereas in 1732 Franco–Spanish relations were such that Spain could not envisage a successful attack on Austrian Italy, the position had changed the following year. Similarly, the succession of Frederick II 'the Great' in Prussia in 1740 and his willingness to attack Austria provided France with the prospect of a powerful German ally rather than the militarily and financially weak Saxony and Bavaria whom she had negotiated with for an anti-Austrian alliance in 1732. More powerful alliances each united in a common aim made brinkmanship more dangerous. One of the more common diplomatic devices of the period was the threat of war. It was believed that an indication of ability and willingness to fight would lead to a successful resolution of differences or at least to obtaining more consideration. In 1715 the British envoy in Paris, the

Earl of Stair, suggested that a tough stance was necessary to secure satisfaction over the Dunkirk dispute with France: 'I lay it down for a principle that there is nothing makes the French think of giving us any satisfaction in this matter but the fear of a war. As long as they are persuaded that no consideration will induce our nation to come into a war, they will give us no satisfaction'.

Fifteen years later Earl Waldegrave, British envoy in Vienna, thought that the threat of force was the best way to bring Austria to terms: 'everything at present carries the face of war, but I hope that when they find that we are in earnest, and determine to stand to our point, they will consider better of it, and see that the difference is not worth contending for'. In 1742 the Spanish government urged France to move troops towards the Savoyard frontier in order to intimidate Charles Emmanuel III of Sardinia. In the Russo–Swedish crisis of 1749–50 Frederick II argued that French firmness would preserve Baltic peace, while the French foreign minister, Puysieulx, pressed him to display firmness and agree to a plan of operations with Sweden, arguing that the least sign of fear on the part of France or her allies would only lead Russia to keep its courage up and gain from a difficult position. Puysieulx also claimed that one of the surest ways for Spain to avoid war was to appear not to fear it. The effective British foreign minister, the Duke of Newcastle, argued in 1750 that France would be driven to keep the peace if Britain strengthened herself 'by measures, and alliances, pacifick, and justifiable in themselves'. In 1755 Rouillé, the French foreign minister, claimed that British aggression against France in the New World stemmed from an assurance of Spanish passivity and that Spain had to make it clear to Britain that she was ready to intervene. Active naval preparations were seen as the only way to dissuade France from aggressive action both during the Falkland Islands crisis of 1770–1 and later in the decade. The opposition London newspaper the *Monitor* suggested in 1762 that France should reduce her forces in order to ensure her willingness to keep the peace: 'they ought not to scruple to reduce their military and naval force within such limits as to give no umbrage for suspecting their intention to break the peace. War is more desirable than a peace, which by the continual alarms of hostile preparations obliges us to lie upon our arms against the surprise of an insidious friend'.[10]

Brinkmanship had its dangers, particularly when combined with the annual routine of naval exercises and military camps that led others to fear attack. Russian exercises in the Baltic, both real and rumoured, kept other Baltic powers in a state of anxiety and preparedness in the early 1720s and late 1740s. Military deployments in eastern Spain led to anxiety over a possible attack on Italy in the early 1720s, 1730, 1731 and 1732. The preparation of a large British fleet for the Mediterranean in 1731 led the French to fear an attack on Dunkirk, and French military preparations combined with rumour to produce a volatile situation with diplomats registering false reports, such as French invasions of Lorraine and Zweibrücken in 1731–2. States did not explain their troop movements generally. In 1753 the French foreign minister instructed the French envoy in The Hague that if the Dutch questioned him on the build-up of troops in French Flanders he was to reply that he had no instructions on the matter and that Louis XV was entitled to move his troops to his frontiers whenever he wanted.[11] The existence of large standing armies and of irreconcilable political differences led some commentators to feel that conflicts were likely. Perceval observed in 1724, 'If the Treaty of Cambray don't take effect I shall expect a rupture somewhere, for so many armies reinforced at so great charge will not likely be left to do nothing when the season of action comes, and subjects of discontent remain open. Princes think their money thrown away when their armies are idle'.[12] Uncertain about the actions of other powers, states had to take decisions in the knowledge that poor communications and the time necessary to prepare troops for movement would limit their ability to react promptly. The news of the death of Augustus II in Warsaw took twelve days to reach St. Petersburg. The British-inspired Austrian attempt to persuade Russia not to invade Poland in 1733 was thwarted partly by the delay attendant upon communication between Vienna, St. Petersburg and the Russian army. The difficulty of making a prompt response was exacerbated by the military problems of resting on the defensive. For logistic reasons it was often difficult to maintain large forces in border areas, and this was certainly a factor in encouraging the Swedes to advance in the opening stages of the Great Northern War in 1700. Furthermore offensive operations enabled a power to denude its garrisons in order to form an effective field army. Having put themselves in a strong position by preparing for war, it was easy for states to be tempted into benefiting from these preparations. In 1755 George II was prepared to consider war with France, the latter 'being so low, we so superior at sea, and such alacrity in the whole nation — England would never have such an opportunity'.[13]

Brinkmanship increased international tension. Tallard reported in March 1701 that the British politicians most zealous for peace nevertheless said that they could see the need for defensive preparations when all Europe was armed and they could see French troops in Antwerp and French warships ready to sail.[14] Writing of the possibility of an Austro–Turkish war, Thomas Robinson reported from Vienna in 1736, 'This Court is very apprehensive of it, but one would be almost apprehensive that the very effect of their fears of such a war might be likely to kindle one. It is from that fear that they intend to incamp this summer in Hungary'. The French envoy in The Hague suggested correctly in 1742 that the deployment of British troops in the Austrian Netherlands would bring war closer. Discussing the necessity of Austro–Russian measures to prevent a likely Franco–Prussian attack when Augustus III died, the Duke of Newcastle argued in 1753 that 'nothing would be so fatal, as . . . ill-concerted measures, which may have the appearance of provoking, without doing anything really material'. Chauvelin, one of the French representatives in London, argued in January 1793 that the enormous expenditure of the British government on military preparations proved that it desired war.[15] The pursuit of alliance partners entailed new commitments and led other powers to retaliate and compete. In March 1743 the British envoys in Vienna pressed for assurances that British troops would help Austria, the previous year Spain had urged France to send her Brest squadron into the Mediterranean, both steps that would make Anglo–French hostilities more likely.[16] The difficulty of verifying reports led to a situation of mutual suspicion. In 1743 the British Consul in Naples reported that Anglo-Neapolitan relations were in such a state with a powerful British fleet in the Mediterranean 'that a rupture may ensue from the credit of a false report'.[17] Powers could 'be deceived by the ministers of ... allies with fictitious and vain apprehensions of the warlike disposition of some princes, who did not deserve that reproach perhaps so much as those who laid it upon them'.[18] Brinkmanship could also lead powers into situations from which it was difficult to retire. A wish to influence the Polish royal election and to adopt a position that would please their Russian allies, combined with a failure to appreciate that the issue might enable France and Spain to unite and attack, led Austria to move troops into Silesia and towards the Polish frontier in 1733, whence it was difficult to move them. In 1749 the Russians found it difficult to extricate themselves with honour from a crisis provoked by their warlike moves and threats. In such a situation, fearful of the unknown consequences of backing down, it was easy to move into an unwanted war, particularly as 'some people drew a very imperceptible line between peace and war'. Puysieulx argued in April 1750 that warlike and peaceful dispositions were not contradictory. Pressing Spain to support Bourbon interests in Italy, he argued that negotiations were usually ineffective unless supported by warlike preparations: 'l'amour de la paix n'est nullement incompatible avec la résolution et les moyens de faire la guerre si elle devient indispensable. Les deux dispositions, bien loin d'être contraires, se prêtent un mutuel secours'.[19] Aggressive actions could stem partly from a defensive stance. The Russians feared in 1733 that the election of the French and former Swedish candidate for the throne of Poland, Stanislaus Leszczynski, would be followed by a French-inspired coalition of Sweden, Poland and Turkey determined to reverse Russian territorial gains from the three powers over the previous seventy years and to shut Russia off from Europe. Such a coalition would also threaten Austria. It is certain that thoughts of a Swedish reconquest of the Baltic provinces, surrendered to Peter the Great as recently as the Treaty of Nystad of 1721, were entertained in 1733 as they had been on several occasions in the late 1720s, such as on the accession of the minor Peter II in Russia in 1727.[20] It is therefore possible to view the Russian attempt to prevent the election of Stanislaus by invading Poland, and the subsequent defeat of the French force seeking to relieve Gdansk (Danzig) in 1734, as defensive moves. In a similar fashion the French seizure of the Duchy of Lorraine in 1733 and the cession of Lorraine to Stanislaus, with a reversion to the French crown, in the Third Treaty of Vienna, which ended the War of the Polish Succession, can be seen as defensive moves by the French. Francis Duke of Lorraine was already in 1733 clearly intended as the spouse of Maria Theresa, whom he was indeed to marry in 1736, and his election as King of the Romans, heir to the Emperor, was being discussed. A dynastic union of Lorraine and Austria would throw France's eastern frontier wide open and threaten Louis XIV's territorial gains. Given Austrian defeats in the period 1733–48, such a view may appear incredible, but it was not so against the background of the aggressive, expansive Austrian state of the previous fifty years. The right of self-defence in light of a presumed intended Franco–Spanish attack was made much of when Anglo–Spanish hostilities began in 1761.

Self-justification could strain credulity, as when Frederick II claimed in June 1741 that Maria Theresa had begun the War of Austrian Succession by refusing his just rights.[21] The need to establish that the other power was the aggressor in order to be entitled to support from allies played a major role in creating a situation in which nobody appeared to be responsible for wars. Oliver Goldsmith wrote in 1760, 'There is nothing more easy than to break a treaty ratified in all the usual forms, and yet neither party be the aggressor. One side for instance breaks a trifling article by mistake; the opposite party upon this makes a small but premeditated reprisal; this brings on a return of greater from the other; both sides complain of injuries and infractions; war is declared'. Bussy, the French envoy in London, reported in 1743 that the British ministry was seeking to provoke France to attack Britain in order to benefit from their defensive alliances.[22] A reading of the manifestoes of the various powers involved in the Polish and Austrian Succession Wars could induce a similar cynicism. In the case of the latter conflict this would be justified by a consideration of the ease with which powers, such as Prussia and France, disregarded their guarantees of the Pragmatic Sanction. Four months before beginning the War by invading Silesia Frederick II had reflected that 'Princes were chiefly governed by their interests ... alliances and friendship between Princes could not subsist long if the advantages were not reciprocal'.[23] The British diplomat Horatio Walpole suggested in 1735 that the French guarantee would not be 'worth a button' after Cardinal Fleury died.[24] Such a cynical interpretation would ascribe war largely to the dishonesty and ambition of those who governed states,[25] a view entirely in keeping with the historiography and political analysis of the period, which both tended to ascribe political action to the malevolent and conspiratorial actions of the few, actions that were often believed to reflect trivial personal interests.[26] In the case of the Polish and Austrian Succession Wars such an impression owes something to the conscious artifice required in order to contrive as reasonable, comprehensive and multi-faceted a dynastic claim as possible. In 1725 the Elector of Bavaria, Max Emanuel, produced a copy of the will of the Austrian ruler Ferdinand I that purported to award most of the Austrian lands to the Bavarian Wittelsbachs upon the extinction of the Habsburg male line. This was a forgery, the authentic will of 1554, which was and still is in Vienna, providing for a succession only in the event of no male or female issue.[27] The brutal contrast between such claims and earlier guarantees and between both and the actions and private expressions of government understandably induced a sense of cynicism among both contemporaries and historians. A lack of trust among the powers led to a tendency to distrust peaceful professions, and to suspect the worst. Every power was held to be secretly preparing for conflict. In 1750 Joseph Yorke was certain that the French stance in the Baltic crisis would be 'contradicting by action what she sets forth in words'. In 1791 Lord Auckland, British envoy at The Hague, was fearful of Prusso–Russian hostilities: 'I apprehend that the K. of Prussia greatly miscalculates his own force, at the same time that he prepares for war with as little principle and provocation as any professed gambler sitting down to a gaming table, and without any feeling for the miseries and murders which he is going to multiply upon the Globe'.[28]

With large permanent armed forces rulers were able to implement the aggressive schemes that they secretly planned, only restrained by prudential considerations of the need to develop as favourable an international and domestic situation as possible. There is an element of truth in such an analysis, but it is also too simple and fails to explain satisfactorily the periods of peace that the century witnessed. The manipulative interpretation of international affairs that ascribes everything to the actions of a few rulers and ministers appears increasingly incongruous as scholarly studies stress the limited royal power and governmental authority that lay behind the façade of absolutism. However, it could be suggested that foreign policy and, to a lesser extent, military affairs represent exceptions, being spheres in which royal interest was greatest, royal authority most acceptable, and, in the case of the former at least, royal control most effective. Royal authority was limited by factors inside and outside the governmental system, but in the case of foreign policy the former were absent in most European countries as diplomats neither possessed nor sought corporate independence as other officials did.

More serious limitations in the conduct of foreign policy were the problems of securing reliable information and of assessing or predicting the actions of other powers. The difficulty of ensuring that allies acted as promised was to prove a fatal problem for rulers and ministers seeking to create and manipulate an alliance system. The anti-Austrian coalition that France tried to create in 1741 from the states seeking part of the Austrian inheritance proved to be ephemeral, its successes, bar the election of Charles Albert of Bavaria as the Emperor Charles VII, transient. The British attempts to create anti-French coalitions in 1732–3 and 1743 were hamstrung by rivalries between her allies. Major powers might seek to create alliance systems, but they found it difficult to sustain them. In their eyes, and those of many historians, smaller states tended to be interested only in subsidies and trivial concerns. This was particularly marked among British commentators. In December 1740 Sturrock wrote, 'I look upon the several Princes of Germany at this juncture as so many Members of Parliament. Almost all have their private interest in view, few regard the general good of the Empire'. This analysis is less than fair to the smaller states,[29] but it stems from the undoubted problems major powers faced in constructing effective alliances. The contrast between the perception of alliances from without and the reality of tension within[30] is one that underlines the difficulty of accepting any interpretation of international relations in the eighteenth century in which events are planned, actions intended, powers manipulated. It also leads to scepticism concerning the accounts of some political scientists who appear never to have read any of the diplomatic correspondence of the period. One of the essential problems with most general treatments of early-modern European international relations is the absence of any consideration of the atmosphere in which decisions or what passed for decisions were taken. In trying to compress a vast amount of information into the compass of a book it is natural to study developments and decisions that in hindsight appeared and appear crucial. However, it is all too easy to move from that to a study in which many of the problems of the period are forgotten, and, by concentrating on a small number of developments, to make them look planned. To consider a problem and its causes is to isolate artificially a set of events, and this is particularly misleading in a period when the conduct of foreign policy in most states was not the product of discrete, developed and autonomous administrative units, but rather dependent on the unstructured and usually poorly documented world of royal intervention and court faction. In contrast diplomatic documents survive in profusion and are both accessible and well-organised. These have generally attracted most scholarly attention in the past, and studies based on them tend to support 'rational', 'purposeful' interpretations of foreign policy. Moves happen as a result of plans.[31]

It could be suggested that the bias in the available sources and the tendency to concentrate on the institutions of foreign policy and their records have led to a misplaced emphasis comparable to that caused by the isolation of certain events for study. The collapse of the Anglo–Austrian alliance in 1755-6 and the negotiation of a Franco–Austrian alliance, the so-called Diplomatic Revolution, is an important topic for study, but to approach relations between Austria and the other two powers in the years before these events simply from this perspective is misleading. In a similar fashion the Polish and Austrian Successions did not dominate the international relations of the 1720s and 1730s to the extent that certain surveys would suggest. The Polish Succession agitated diplomats well before 1733. The elective nature of the monarchy, the contentious nature of the last election and the conflicting interests of several major powers suggested that the issue might produce war. 'If King Augustus tips off, as the state of his health threatens, we shall soon have the world in an uproar on that side', observed George Tilson, a British Under Secretary in 1722. It was generally accepted that trouble would follow his death, but although this was widely reported as imminent in the 1720s, he survived until 1733.[32] Interested powers made plans, Austria, Russia and Prussia settling on a Portuguese or Polish, but not Saxon, prince for the succession in 1732,[33] but it would be mistaken to suggest that Poland dominated the thoughts of any one power. It is for example possible to make out a case for strong French interest in developing the basis for a candidature by Louis XV's father-in-law Stanislaus, but much of this can be ascribed to the activities of Stanislaus' connections and of an active French envoy, the Marquis de Monti. It did not prevent contradictory French diplomatic initiatives, such as the negotiations with Augustus II for an anti-Austrian alliance in 1732 and the interest in a Franco–Russian agreement in 1732-3. By isolating the issue of the Polish Succession it can be made to appear to dominate French eastern-European policy. A wider perspective induces caution. Poland was not the only contentious succession. In 1732 the young Frederick the Great had anticipated war over the Jülich–Berg succession, an affair which he described as having held Europe in suspense for a long time.[34]

The crucial differences between 1733, with its outbreak of a major war, and the 1720s and early 1733s, when serious differences between the major powers failed to lead to a major conflict, were the willingness of France to fight and the beginning of hostilities in eastern Europe. The latter directly reflected Russian determination to prevent any reversal of the Petrine territorial settlement. In 1719

Augustus II's minister Count Flemming had promised George I that the Poles would fight Russia if they were promised Kiev, Smolensk and a large subsidy. This projected alliance had been seen as crucial in the plans of 1719–20 for forcing Russia to return the conquered Baltic provinces to Sweden. It was Polish weakness that was central both to Peter I's conquest of these provinces and to his retention of them, just as it permitted Russia to dominate the Ukraine. Stanislaus' failure in 1733–5 was an important contributory factor to Russia's defeat of Sweden when the latter attacked her in 1741.

Russian military strength and the support of her Austrian ally ensured that the invasion of Poland in the autumn of 1733, intended as a limited operation, entailed little military risk. This was not the case for France. According to the most recent suggestion Cardinal Fleury, the French first minister, 'saw a chance to humble the Habsburgs with the minimum of risks and without France's appearing the aggressor'.[35] If it was that simple it is a little difficult to explain why France had not attacked in 1730, when Spain, Britain and the United Provinces were committed to do so also and when Austria's leading ally Russia was affected by domestic political turmoil. It is known that French foreign policy in the mid-1730s was a matter for ministerial disagreement, with, in particular, the foreign secretary Chauvelin being more in favour of action against Austria and cooperation with Spain than Fleury. The limited survival of papers for these two men has helped to obscure the debate, but it is difficult to explain why Fleury, who had supported better relations with Austria in 1727–8, and shown no enthusiasm for war with her in 1730 should have sought conflict in 1733. His relations with the principal prominent foreign proponent of war with Austria, Elisabeth Farnese, Queen of Spain, were cool. Fleury himself excused the French action on Austria in October 1733 by reference to the force of public opinion.[36] A year earlier the British envoy in Paris, Earl Waldegrave, had reported that the ministry's problems with the Parlement of Paris might lead them to war: 'I am told it was one of their projects to reconcile their domestic broils, to seek a pretence to quarrel with their neighbours, and try the event of a campaign or two, which though unsuccessful would give the ministry more quiet than the troubles they labour under at home, for it would either divert the nation from thinking of what has passed, or give the Ministers a plausible pretence to yield in several points to the Parliament, in order to join against their foreign enemies'.[37]

The idea that war or the prospect of it could be employed in order to unite a country or alter it politically was advanced on several occasions during the century. Bussy suggested in 1742 that the British government supported the move of troops to the Austrian Netherlands for parliamentary reasons.[38] However, it was rarely mentioned by diplomats commenting on the policies of states that lacked representative assemblies. On the contrary it was commonly states possessing the latter that were held to be prone to fight for domestic reasons. These states were believed generally to be unstable, and, in particular, susceptible to popular pressure.[39] The outbreak of war between Britain and Spain in 1739, the War of Jenkins' Ear, was attributed, with reason, to domestic pressures on the British government preventing the implementation of an agreement between the two powers that was otherwise satisfactory from the diplomatic point of view. Similar conclusions were reached in the case of Anglo–French relations in 1755, Secretary of State Holderness claiming 'there is but one voice in the whole nation upon this subject'.[40] The French envoy in London assumed in 1790 that public opinion would affect Pitt's policies. In 1793 the London opposition newspaper, the *Morning Chronicle*, ascribed Anglo–French hostilities to public opinion: '... we have suffered ourselves to be cajoled by a set of vehement and malignant spirits, who having rank prejudices to gratify or having tasted the fruits of former wars, pursued only the gratifications of their passions, and did not disdain the jesuitical plan of obtaining their purposes through popular delirium'.[41]

It is difficult to assess the impact on policy of public opinion, however defined, in states such as Britain, Sweden and the United Provinces where the existence of representative institutions produced a public discourse of foreign policy, and whose political structure historians have been able to probe. It is far harder to do the same for states such as France where the mode of political behaviour and the institutions of political action were different. In 1742 Sir Cyril Wych reported from Russia on domestic pressure for harsh peace terms with Sweden: 'the Russian nation will certainly insist on new and more advantagious conditions, and tho' the Czarina out of her inclination for peace and her predilection might be willing to make a peace upon the foot of the Treaty of Nystad, yet her ministry and friends cannot advise her with any security to themselves to consent to conditions which the Russian nation may think inglorious'.[42] What is unclear is how such popular views were discerned and how they affected policy. Nevertheless, it is the nature of the French political system in the 1730s that requires consideration. It is generally accepted that in 1733 and 1741 Fleury was nudged into conflict with Austria against his will, by Chauvelin and Marshal Belle-Isle respectively, but whereas there has been much work on the struggle at the French court in 1741, the same is not the case for 1733.[43] A perfectly plausible explanation for the views of aggressive ministers in 1733 can be advanced based on the favourable international situation. The British attempt to isolate France was clearly in difficulties. British attempts to settle Austro–Spanish and Austro–Sardinian disputes were clearly unsuccessful, while the Grand Alliance of the 1700s that had confronted France in the War of the Spanish Succession and been reconstituted after the Anglo–Austrian Treaty of Vienna of 1731 was in difficulties. The Dutch government was angry with Austria and Britain, while, according to Chavigny, the French envoy in London, the British ministry was on the brink of collapse over contentious domestic legislation, the Excise Crisis, and the Hanoverian monarchy was itself precarious, in danger of collapsing before national indebtedness and Jacobitism.[44] Given this situation, it was not surprising that on 20 May 1733 the French Council of State determined that war would be declared on Charles VI.

That the international situation became favourable for an attack on Charles does not mean that it 'caused' the attack. It is necessary to consider a range of factors that may have influenced opinion at the French court. Given the significance of royal and national dignity and honour in this era and of dynastic pride, considerations often advanced in the diplomatic correspondence of the period,[45] it is understandable both that Louis XV should support the royal candidature of his father-in-law and oppose the attempt to prevent it. Fleury's general opposition to war could be taken to reflect the cultural influences making for peaceful solutions to international disputes. Without suggesting that writers who criticised war, such as Archbishop Fénelon and the Abbé Saint-Pierre, were very influential, it could be argued that churchmen and lawyers did think about the legality of war and that this may have affected the mores governing military responses to diplomatic problems. Rulers were brought up to think of the justice of their actions, and this may well have influenced Louis XV and Fleury in 1733. Maria Theresa participated in the Polish partition with great reluctance. On 17 March 1733 Louis XV declared that he would not tolerate any interference with the free choice of the Polish nation. Royal honour was involved, as it had been for Philip V of Spain in 1725, when Louis XV sent back his intended bride, and, as in the latter case, the reaction was violent. The effect of this on French policy is incalculable, as is the wish to take revenge for the diplomatic isolation of France in 1731, while it is not clear what the relation between the domestic political problems of 1732 and the aggressive diplomatic strategy of the following year may have been.

The French diplomatic offensive of 1733 produced an anti-Austrian coalition. It was widely accepted that this was a crucial precondition for war. In March Frederick William I of Prussia told the French envoy in Berlin, Chetardie, that a Spanish alliance was essential.[46] And yet these diplomatic preparations did not necessitate war. That France went to war probably owed much to a conviction that she must fight for royal honour and to prevent humiliation and isolation. It could be suggested that it was this conviction that France would fight over the Polish issue that led Sardinia and, in particular, Spain to reject attempts to keep them allied to Britain and Austria. Chavigny suggested in February 1733 that the perception of French resolution was crucial in influencing the views of other powers. The Grand Vezir was not the sole European statesman who wished to know if France could be relied upon.[47] The French success in negotiating alliances played a role in encouraging other powers to support or not to oppose her. On 19 February Chetardie was instructed that Augustus II's death had occurred at a difficult time when nearly all of Europe was leagued against France.[48] By the autumn she was certain of the support of Spain and Sardinia and of the neutrality of the United Provinces and the Wittelsbachs.

If French moves can be regarded as a preparation for aggression, they were generally successful, though Sweden and Turkey refused to enter the war. If they should be viewed as an exercise in brinkmanship, they were a failure, insofar as eastern Europe was concerned, as they did not prevent Russia invading Poland and overturning Stanislaus' election in favour of Augustus III, though in western Europe they ensured Dutch neutrality. The most reasonable assessment to make of French policy is that the French were unwilling to fight without allies and, until the latter were certain, hoped that their stance would deter Austria and Russia from interfering in the Polish election under the pretext that they were protecting its liberty. Far from taking the initiative, France responded to Russian action and did not begin operations until most of the campaigning season was over. In early

September the Austrian Chancellor, Count Sinzendorf, told the Spanish envoy in Vienna that it was too late in the year for Spain to act in Italy.[49] It was only extraordinarily good weather in Italy that allowed her and her allies to conquer so much of Lombardy that winter. The diplomatic developments of 1733, like the course of the war itself, were to reveal that western European powers had only limited influence in eastern Europe. Chavigny probably got the balance in French ministerial circles right in July 1733 when he claimed that the motives for action had never been so pressing and legitimate nor the circumstances so favourable, but this did not lead to success for Stanislaus.[50] If French policy is assumed to have been concerned with the acquisition of Lorraine only, then this failure may appear inconsequential. However, aside from the fact that the French could not have predicted safely that Augustus II would predecease Charles VI in circumstances favourable for them, it is misleading to adopt a geopolitical determinism when discussing the variety of factors that affected the formulation of policy.

If a major European war on the death of Augustus II could not have been predicted safely, the same was not so true of the Austrian Succession. Plans for the partition of the Austrian lands had been drawn up and diplomats had for many years predicted conflict.[51] The German coalition that Belle-Isle was to create in 1741 had already been prefigured by France, Bavaria and Saxony in 1732.[52] The biggest bar to preparations for partition came with the end of the War of Polish Succession in 1735, for the preliminary treaty signed by France and Austria, which led to the Third Treaty of Vienna of 1738, produced an entente between the two powers centred on a French guarantee of the Pragmatic Sanction. French diplomatic support for Austria forced an unwilling Sardinia and, in particular, Spain to accept an Italian settlement less favourable than they had militarily secured. Chauvelin was dismissed in February 1737 and the most vociferous contender for a share of the Austrian inheritance, Charles Albert of Bavaria, was consigned to a diplomatic limbo, his freedom of manoeuvre destroyed by the understanding of his two powerful neighbours. Most eighteenth-century wars ended in secret unilateral negotiations. However, the terms France accepted in 1735 were completely unacceptable to her allies, and by unilaterally abandoning them she destroyed the alliance that supported her in the War of Polish Succession, not that Spain and Sardinia had failed to engage in secret diplomacy of their own. Well before the accession of Frederick II, Cardinal Polignac, the French representative in Rome, could complain that perfidy had never been so strong in the world.[53] Distrust between the powers that had plotted or acted against Austria in 1732–5 made a successful resumption of such action appear less likely. In 1738 Fleury told the Bavarian minister Count Törring that he knew as little of the views and schemes of Elisabeth Farnese as of those of the Great Mongol.[54] Törring himself was reduced to speculating about the possible effects of Fleury's apparently imminent death.[55]

Bavarian requests for French support ensured that a ready means for action against Austria was to hand. Cooperation between Bavaria and France had been a frequent feature of international relations over the previous century. Bavaria provided France with a Catholic German ally against Austria, a state able, with

French support, to resist Austrian attempts to use Imperial authority and prestige to win German support. France offered Bavaria military, diplomatic and financial support, all crucial if she were to maintain her capacity for independent action in the face of her powerful Austrian neighbour.[56] However, in the late 1730s good Franco–Austrian relations seemed to preclude the possibility of French military support for Wittelsbach claims when Charles VI died. When France guaranteed the Pragmatic Sanction she had saved the prior rights of third parties such as Bavaria, and on 16 May 1738 France secretly signed an agreement with Bavaria promising to support her just claims.[57] Nevertheless, French conduct in the negotiations over the Jülich–Berg inheritance in the late 1730s was scarcely designed to encourage Wittelsbach rulers, such as Charles Albert. The right to inherit these territories was contested by Frederick William I of Prussia and by the Elector Palatine, Karl Philipp, on behalf of his heir Karl Philipp of the Wittelsbach cadet house of Sulzbach.[58] Though she tended to support Karl Philipp, France proved willing to entertain the idea of a partition of the Duchy of Berg, a solution completely unacceptable to him, and in early 1739 the French foreign minister Amelot sought Bavarian assistance in securing this compromise. Törring was pessimistic about the possibility of French support while Fleury was in control of policy, and informed the Cardinal in May 1739 that Charles VI was too closely linked with France to be separated from her. Fleury replied that he could not be sure of future developments, but was adamant that Austro–French ties were limited to friendship. However, the late 1730s did not witness a repetition of the French diplomatic offensive against Austria of 1731–3, and it was in line with his general policy that Fleury responded to the news of Charles VI's death by assuring the Austrian envoy Prince Liechtenstein that Louis XV would observe all his engagements with Austria.[59]

It is not clear what France would have done had Prussia not attacked Austria by invading her duchy of Silesia on 16 December 1740. When the Austrian Chancellor told the British envoy in January 1741 that 'everything had been so quiet ... but for this King of Prussia', the latter retorted by arguing that France had been equally the aggressor by preventing Spain from settling her maritime disputes with Britain. Frederick II, who had become ruler of Prussia following his father's death on 31 May 1740, was surprised by French passivity.[60] Fleury was already aware that other rulers, particularly Charles Albert and Philip V of Spain, saw the death of Charles VI as an opportunity for action, but his early plans were restricted to a plan to deny the Imperial election to Francis of Lorraine, rather than to eternalise the glory of Louis XV by heeding Providence's call to re-establish a just European balance of power, as Charles Albert suggested.[61] The Prussian invasion of Silesia dramatically altered the situation by substituting action for negotiation and by forcing other European powers to define their position. It is possible to suggest that France would have gone to war with Austria anyway, but an equal case could be made out that France in 1740 was moving towards war with Britain in order to prevent the latter from conquering Spanish territories in the West Indies and, by defeating Spain, destroying any maritime balance of power. War between the two powers was widely anticipated and in

August the French sent a fleet to the West Indies to prevent British conquests. Fleury was certain that war would result,[62] and once ships had put to sea in the eighteenth century it was generally believed that hostilities might occur. The absence of the anticipated naval war between the two powers cannot be simply ascribed to the death of Charles VI. It was partly due to the unwillingness of both powers to push confrontation to the point of hostilities. The British ministry chose to regard neither the dispatch of D'Antin's fleet to the West Indies nor reported French fortification of the port of Dunkirk, in clear breach of treaty commitments, as a cause of war, although they believed it imminent and were under domestic pressure to take a strong stance.[63] The French did not attack Britain in the West Indies despite their concern over British operations there. As in the War of Polish Succession, when France had taken care not to push Britain to the point of hostilities,[64] so in 1740 an uneasy balance, short of war, was maintained.

Frederick II was unable to achieve such a balance. His invasion of Silesia was not intended as the opening move of a major European war, a step that would precipitate attempts to enforce claims on the Austrian inheritance by the other powers. Frederick hoped that Maria Theresa would respond to a successful attack by agreeing to buy him off, and in many respects his invasion can be seen as the action of an opportunist, seeking to benefit from a temporarily favourable European situation. Maria Theresa was offered, in return for Silesia, a guarantee of all the other German possessions of the Habsburgs, troops to serve in Italy or the Low Countries, support for Francis of Lorraine's imperial candidature and a cash indemnity. Subsequently Frederick proposed a partition of Silesia.[65] Frederick's opportunism can be regarded as a rash move, for though the conquest of Silesia proved relatively easy, its retention in the face of persistent Austrian hostility was to be a major burden for the Prussian state. The French envoy in Berlin felt that Frederick had attacked carelessly, without either allies or negotiations to obtain them.[66] However, the situation in 1740 appeared favourable for such an attack. From his accession Frederick's support was eagerly sought by other powers, and nothing was done to stop him when in September 1740 he attacked the Prince-Bishop of Liège in the Herstal affair, a minor dispute which demonstrated the efficacy of violence. In 1746 the Earl of Hyndford, British envoy in St. Petersburg, was to suggest that 'if the King of Prussia is always humoured, it will spoil him, and ... if he had been hindered from plundering the bishop of Liège, which was his first heroic action, he would never have taken a fancy to Silesia'.[67]

In seeking French support in June 1740 Frederick sought to use the idea that the enterprising quality of youth and their notions of heroism would make him a useful ally. His awareness of these factors does not mean that they should be discounted when considering his motivation.[68] Frederick was prepared to break agreements, but he was not unique in this and it was not necessary to ascribe his actions to an absence of religion and the company of sceptics such as Voltaire and Algarotti.[69] Combined with a duplicity characteristic of many rulers of the period, including his more religious father, was the rashness that led him to declare that he would sooner perish than desist from his undertaking, and Charles Churchill to describe him as 'acting the little Alexander'.[70] The attack on Austria was to some extent fortuitous. In the autumn of 1740 Frederick had expressed more interest in Jülich-Berg, and, just as he toyed with approaches from Britain and France, so he was clearly unsure whither to direct his aggressive interests. Had Charles VI died a year later, then it is quite possible that Frederick would have invaded Jülich-Berg already, as his father had planned to do on a number of occasions, including 1732 and 1738. The consequence might well have been a major war, but one that pitched France, as a traditional patron of the Wittelsbachs, against Protestant Prussia. That had certainly been envisaged in the late 1730s. This hypothesis is only advanced in order to suggest that the combination of Frederick's aggression, rash or prudent, and the European situation at his accession did not make a War of Austrian Succession precipitated by Prussian action inevitable. There is a markedly improvised quality about Prussian policy in the second half of 1740, necessarily so in terms of the rapidly changing European situation. The prospect of Anglo–French hostilities was of importance, as was the situation of Austria's principal ally Russia, for the Czarina Anna died three days before Charles VI, to be succeeded by her great-nephew, the two-month-old Ivan VI, and a weak and divided regency. Russian developments were arguably crucial in encouraging Frederick to invade Silesia. When the British envoy stressed Prussian vulnerability in February 1741, Frederick replied that he was certain of Russia and therefore not worried about his other frontiers.[71] In geopolitical terms the Austro–Russian alliance dramatically lessened Prussian independence. It had been the formation of that alliance in 1726 that had intimidated Frederick William I into abandoning the anti-Austrian Alliance of Hanover, and fear of Russian attack had prevented him from executing his plans during the War of Polish Succession. In the late 1730s the vitality of the alliance had been demonstrated by joint participation in a war against the Turks, a conflict in which Russia had not had its military prestige tarnished as Austria's had been. The prospect of a weakened Russia was therefore of great significance for political reasons in late 1740, but so also perhaps was the heady atmosphere of unexpected developments that produced a sense of opportunities waiting to be grasped.

Prussian aggression helped to precipitate war. Despite British pressure, the Austrians were unwilling to accept Prussian claims, arguing that the cession of Silesia would be followed by demands on the Habsburg lands from other rulers. The failure to settle Austro–Prussian differences speedily had the same effect. The Austrians failed to crush Frederick and were defeated at Mollwitz on 10 April 1741. Maria Theresa's refusal to cede Silesia led Frederick to sign the Treaty of Breslau with France on 5 June. He renounced his claim to Jülich-Berg and agreed to support the imperial candidature of Charles Albert in return for a French guarantee of Lower Silesia and French promises of military assistance for Bavaria and diplomatic pressure on Sweden to attack Russia. France and Frederick encouraged other powers to act,[72] and they did so realising the opportunities presented by what appeared to be a European system in flux. On 28 May 1741 Belle-Isle secured the signature of a treaty between Bavaria and Spain by which the latter agreed to subsidise the military activities of the former. On 19 September similar pressure ensured a defensive and offensive alliance between Saxony and Bavaria for the partition of the Habsburg lands that conferred Bohemia, Upper Austria and the Tyrol on the latter. The previous month French troops had crossed the Rhine. With some reason, Elisabeth Farnese told the French envoy in February 1742 that France alone had put the claimants to the Austrian succession in a state to act.[73]

In 1746 Henry Fielding, in his capacity as a British ministerial journalist, wrote, 'If we attentively weigh the true grounds of the present war, they must appear to be opposing the scheme of universal monarchy, framed by the House of Bourbon'.[74] Belle-Isle certainly had a plan for French domination of Europe, and in March 1743 an Austrian diplomat claimed that the Marshal was ready to put all Europe into flames to achieve his ends,[75] but his plan failed dramatically. Despite the fall of Linz and Prague on 14 September and 25 November 1741 respectively, and Charles Albert's coronation as King of Bohemia and Emperor, Belle-Isle's scheme had collapsed by mid-1742. Frederick II betrayed his allies and signed a treaty with Austria, the latter overran Bavaria, and the Russians defeated France's ally Sweden. French failure suggests that it was not possible for any one power to dominate Europe. In mid-1741 France arguably came closer to doing so than any modern European state prior to Napoleon I's France. In November 1741 Wasner, the Austrian envoy in Paris, referred to France as having taken upon herself the distribution of kingdoms and provinces. Two months earlier the Austrian minister Count Harrach claimed that Europe was in a situation of unprecedented danger. A well-developed and well-motivated alliance was able to give military teeth to diplomatic conceptions. The Habsburgs appeared prostrate, an impression reinforced by signs of support for Charles Albert in Bohemia and Austria. The traditional allies of Austria, Britain and the United Provinces, were weak and disunited domestically and unwilling to aid Austria with troops, while Austria's allies of the post-1726 period, Prussia and Russia, were respectively an enemy and affected by ministerial and dynastic instability. Russian diplomatic pressure on Frederick in early 1741 to desist from the invasion of Silesia was as unsuccessful as George II's attempt that summer to reconcile Austria and Prussia and create a powerful anti-French coalition.[76]

And yet France failed. This was due to a variety of factors including underrated Austrian resilience and Russia's refusal to enter the French system as the French envoy in St. Petersburg La Chetardie hoped. On 6 December 1741 Ivan VI was deposed and the regency of Anne of Mecklenburg swept away by a palace revolution in favour of Peter the Great's younger daughter Elizabeth. Chetardie had sought such a development, though his role was less significant than he claimed. However, French hopes that it would prove possible to direct Elizabeth's policies, in the first instance by ensuring a settlement of the war with Sweden to the satisfaction of that defeated country, proved as misplaced as French confidence in her allies. Unable to dominate Europe militarily on her own, France was forced, as was every other power considering a major conflict, to seek the assistance of others, but the very resort to war made it less easy to retain the support of allies. Powers that were willing to accept subsidies regularly in peacetime and in return promised support proved only too willing to vary their policies to meet wartime exigencies. War made the position of second-rank powers more crucial, and accordingly it led to an increase in bids for their support, a significant corrosive of alliances that tended to lack any ideological, religious, sentimental, popular or economic bonds.

The early 1740s were particularly important in this respect for they followed a period when the ability of second-rank powers to play a significant role in European affairs had been dramatically limited by the understanding between Austria and France. The relationship between the two powers in the late 1730s was an uneasy one, but it had kept Italy peaceful and prevented the Jülich-Berg dispute from leading to a European war. The alliance between Austria and Russia played a similar role in eastern Europe, particularly as Fleury did not wish to provoke Russia by pushing Swedish *révanchiste* aspirations too strongly and as the Russian victory in the War of the Polish Succession had served as a useful reminder of the inadvisability of contesting the Petrine settlement of eastern Europe. When major powers cooperated, second-rank states found their room for manoeuvre circumscribed. Good Austro–French relations were particularly important in this respect. They isolated George II in 1727–8, preventing him from resolving the apparent diplomatic impasses of the period by going to war. It is arguable that Frederick II would not have attacked Austria but for his suspicion that French promises to observe the Pragmatic Sanction would not be kept and that the Franco–Austrian understanding was about to collapse. Alliances helped to ensure that when major states fell out other powers were affected, and it was generally believed that once a war had begun, conflict would spread.[77] Frederick suggested that there would be no Baltic war in 1749 because neither France nor Britain wanted any war to break out then.[78] The 1750s brought stability to Italy with mutual guarantees of territory by the major powers. One effect of the Diplomatic Revolution was to make it impossible for Charles Emanuel III of Sardinia to play the active role in the Seven Years' War that he and the British desired. He was unable to act as the Italian counterpart of Frederick II because of agreement between France and Austria. The Austro–French alliance also limited Britain's continental options, one British Secretary of State complaining in 1757 that the two powers were 'upon the point of subverting the system of Europe, and of submitting the World to their arbitrary will and pleasure'.[79]

The apparent collapse of Austrian power in 1741 and the willingness of France to encourage other powers to claim shares in the Austrian inheritance represented a great opportunity for the second-rank states, and it was one that they seized. However, France was unable to retain the alliance of all these powers once it was clear that Austria would not collapse. The appearance of two warring blocs inspired caution and ambition in the second-rank powers. Amelot noted with reference to the Duke of Modena that minor princes were often unsure as to which way to turn.[80] Austrian military success led Charles Albert to seek a settlement with Austria, the prospect of Russian attack restrained Frederick II, while Philip V and his heir Ferdinand VI sought to negotiate a unilateral peace and Augustus III established a record of duplicity that should have gained him a reputation greater than that of Frederick. The attempt to realise the purposes of alliances through war proved to be the end of most of them.

The question of the extent to which the outbreak of the Polish and Austrian Succession wars represented the failure of diplomatic attempts to solve problems recognised as serious is an interesting one. The Duke of Newcastle, a British Secretary of State, referred in Parliament to the unsettled state of the Imperial succession as being due to 'accidents', particularly the failure to have negotiated the matter. Both of the conflicts were preceded by negotiations, but these had been essentially between powers sharing common views rather than between potential rivals. In comparison with the talks between Austria, Prussia and Russia that had produced in the Lowenwöld Convention an agreement on action for when Augustus II came to die,[81] Franco–Russian discussions over Poland were perfunctory. Charles VI proved unwilling to discuss seriously Bavarian claims on the Austrian inheritance, just as he had refused to heed seriously French opposition to the prospect of a dynastic union of Austria and Lorraine.[82] The Swedish succession produced in the 1740s lengthy discussions between the powers concerned that the heir to the childless Frederick I might, on his succession, alter the Swedish constitution. By Frederick's death in 1751 the views of the various powers were well known and this made the solution of the crisis easier. However, it is arguable that it was only Russia's failure to win the support of her allies for offensive action that prevented war.[83] St. Contest was unimpressed in 1752 by reports that plans for the Polish succession on the death of Augustus III were being discussed. He argued that they were premature as Augustus was only 56 and could live sufficiently long for any plans to be broken before his death.[84] Possibly antagonisms were too strong to make negotiating the Austrian succession a serious option. However, Britain and Austria were to be criticised for failing in 1731 to negotiate with powers that opposed the Pragmatic Sanction. In that year Thomas Pelham, the British Secretary of Embassy at Paris, argued that 'no general pacification can be made whilst France remains in the present situation with regard to the other powers, ... she is too considerable to be left alone and if left alone will always be able to embroil matters so far as to endanger the tranquillity that is now established'. The Prussian and Russian envoys in Paris pressed the point without success. Nine years later Lord Carteret was to condemn the British guarantee for having been made 'without taking the least care to adjust the differences that subsisted between the House of Austria and the other Princes of Germany'.[85] However Austria, having discovered the virtues of intransigence in 1730, when she had resisted the coalition of Britain, France, Spain and the United Provinces, was in a strong diplomatic position in early 1731, her alliance actively sought by the first three powers, and in no way obliged to yield to pressure. In a powerful and interesting recent essay Charles Ingrao has attacked Charles VI for clinging to the Pragmatic Sanction. Yet, Ingrao's preferred solution, an alliance with Bavaria and/or Saxony obtained by a marriage of Maria Theresa and possibly her sister as well with the Bavarian and/or Saxon princes, who were sons of the Josephine archduchesses, the daughters of Charles VI's elder brother the Emperor Joseph I, is fraught with complications.[86] The failure of the Congresses of the 1720s to solve, rather than merely postpone, European problems did not encourage the use of this method in the 1730s, and several rulers, most clearly Karl Philipp of the Palatinate in the Jülich-Berg question and Elisabeth Farnese over the Spanish garrisons in Tuscany and Parma, discovered that obduracy was the way to achieve their goals. The unwillingness of Charles VI to risk negotiations over an issue in which he could not be sure how far other rulers would seek to push him is understandable.

If a diplomatic solution was not seriously attempted while the powers jockeyed for position by recruiting allies, it is not surprising that war followed when the successions became vacant. A disputed succession posed a particular problem for the policies of brinkmanship followed by most powers, the attempt to obtain benefits by military preparations and the threat of force. A vacant succession lasted only for a certain period before being filled by an election and coronation. This forced interested parties, such as Russia in 1733 and Bavaria in 1741, to act speedily. It was necessary to threaten more obviously and to intervene, if intervention was judged necessary, before a certain date. The need for speed exacerbated the usual problems of brinkmanship such as rumour and the obligation to begin military preparations early were they to have any impact. In 1733 the Russians could not delay moving their troops for too long if they were to reach Warsaw by the date of the royal election. In the summer of 1741 the French had to invade the Empire, and prepare diplomatically for such an invasion, in enough time for them to contribute to the invasion of Austria that campaigning season. Once moves were made it was difficult to retract them lest that was interpreted as a sign of weakness,[87] or to control their consequences. Equally the pressure for action made it difficult to avoid moves that would serve to provoke others or vindicate claims about the malevolence of a state's intentions.[88]

An emphasis on the failings of the diplomatic system or the problems of brinkmanship in a fast-altering situation is not intended to displace the suggestion that the wars of the period cannot be simply explained with reference to 'rational factors'. It is all too easy to explain developments by suggesting the constraints of a system, to 'rationalise' and systematise both the actions of individuals and the rapidly altering flux of events, to make wars appear obvious in hindsight and predictable to contemporaries. It has been recently claimed that the Austrian ministers of the eighteenth century were dominated by geopolitical considerations even if they were unaware of them: 'the state and extent of their awareness, however, cannot confute the course of their actions, nor the compelling strategic structures that predetermined the path they chose. Rather like actors reading a new script for the first time, they simply stumbled through their lines without benefiting from the perspective that comes from familiarity with the plot'.[89] Such an interpretation permits a somewhat flexible reading of the sources, but it could equally be suggested that the historian should address himself more to the factors advanced by contemporaries: considerations of honour, glory and opportunity. In order to appreciate the decisions that were reached it is necessary to enter the mental world of the age and to consider the language that was used to discuss international relations. In 1791 during the Ochakov crisis Lord Auckland complained of 'the levity with which some people urge the war: and all because they say that the national dignity is engaged'. The *Craftsman* referred with reason in 1743 to Charles Albert's 'golden dream ... of gaining two kingdoms' and suggested that he had been intoxicated by his scheme. In 1750 the French envoy in The Hague, the Abbé de La Ville, informed the States General of the United Provinces when he sent them his letters of recall that Louis XV would not hesitate to go to war if forced by considerations of glory or in order to help his allies and maintain his engagements. 'La Gloire du Roy' could of course be regarded as a pretext, as Robinson suggested in 1755,[90] but even if that argument is to be adopted — and it is as suspect as the reductionist arguments used to explain away the significance of religion in early-modern history — it is still necessary to assess the way in which 'gloire' or 'national dignity' could serve to win support for a policy and provide the emotional impetus that might lead to war being risked. It is necessary to discard the notion that honour, glory and prestige were somehow 'irrational' pursuits and that opportunism and the absence of consistent policies were somehow less intelligent than long-term plans. Prestige and glory were the basis of the power of early-modern monarchs both domestically and in international relations. They conferred a mantle of success and magnificence that was the most effective lubricant of obedience. Most monarchs had only a limited personal interest in domestic 'reforms' or administrative change, and that which took place is often correctly linked to important ministers rather than to their monarchs. Far from being a diversion from intractable domestic problems, or a means of solving these problems, war was regarded as the natural activity, indeed 'sport', of kings. Their upbringing conditioned them to accept such a notion, and most male monarchs spent their years of peace in activities that were substitutes for war and which served to keep their minds on military matters: manoeuvres, reviews and the royal cavalry exercises for the court aristocracy known as hunts. At times of war most monarchs took seriously their role as warriors, leading their armies towards if not always into battle. Young princes, such as the grandsons of Louis XIV, were placed in the command of armies at an early age. Monarchs in the eighteenth century dressed increasingly in military uniform. The iconography of kingship, the theatre of display and ceremonial, within which monarchs lived and through which they sought to have their role perceived, stressed martial achievements. In Jacques Dumont 'le Romain's' *Allegory of the Peace of Aix-la-Chapelle* exhibited in the Paris Salon of 1761 Louis XV, portrayed as the peacegiver, is dressed in armour as Alexander the Great. On tapestries and in equestrian statues monarchs were depicted in military poses. The magnificence of ambassadorial entries was intended to reflect royal dignity and power. Past rulers who were set up as exemplary figures, such as Henry IV of France, tended to be great warriors. Military success was regarded as crucial to the reputation of contemporary monarchs.[91] This was not a misplaced feeling. It may be idle to speculate as to what the consequences for the prestige of French monarchy would have been had the Dutch crisis of 1787 been resolved in favour of her Dutch protégés by the threatened French military intervention, but it is difficult not to feel that the position of Louis XVI was weakened by the absence of any personal military glory. The theory of kingship, the ideal of monarchy placed the king at the head of his aristocracy on the battlefield, much as he led them on the hunting ground. Conscious as they were of the theory, many monarchs hearkened to the intoxicating lure of the battlefield. Although this became less attractive to the British and French monarchs of the second half of the eighteenth century, other rulers were still eager to campaign. Whether the monarchs were or not, a portion of the aristocracy could be expected to be eager for war, for a variety of reasons that included personal profit and prestige, a hope for advancement and a sense, in a society in which derogation of rank for participating in a range of economic activities epitomised aristocratic notions of behaviour, that conflict was their proper role. Following the death of Charles VI, Sir Cyril Wych, a British diplomat, noted: 'it is very well known, that the general humour and bent of the French nobility carry them all to war, whenever they can begin it with a prospect of succeeding'. A letter entitled 'Homer-War-Conquest', published in the *St. James's Chronicle* in 1792, claimed that 'the eulogy of heroes has been the constant business of historians and poets from the days of Nimrod down to the present century', and stated that Homer had 'given to military life a charm which few men can resist, a splendour which envelopes the scene of carnage in a cloud of glory, which dazzles the eyes of every beholder ... and obliterates with the same irresistible stroke the mortal duties of life and true policy of nations'.[92]

In the case of both the Polish and the Austrian Succession wars there were significant individuals and groups who wanted to fight and appear to have been relatively heedless of the consequences of a resort to war. For these people war represented not the failure of diplomacy nor a geopolitical determinism. They could read the script all too well, for war was the essence of the roles of warrior king and military nobility that they had been seeking to fulfil. It was therefore understandable that optimistic assessments of the chances of a successful war were made. Frederick II and the French aristocrats whom Belle-Isle sought to lead, Charles Emmanuel III and Elisabeth Farnese were prominent among those who were willing or eager to fight, and it was this arguably that made war likely in the 1733–48 period. It was also the case that war produced definite gains for several of the participating powers. Aside from the victories celebrated in triumphal processions and Te Deums by an age that was prepared to glory in conquest, success in war brought territorial gains that somehow appeared more real or significant than the human and financial costs of conflict. Peter the Great gained Sweden's eastern Baltic provinces, Charles Emmanuel III won much of the Milanese, Philip V avenged Austria's conquest of Spain's Italian possessions by obtaining a kingdom for Don Carlos. France won the reversion to Lorraine, Frederick II retained Silesia. None of these achievements would have been made without war, and success in obtaining benefits, even if not necessarily initial goals, presumably encouraged a resort to conflict. 'James III', the Pretender to the British throne, wrote in 1743: 'I am shocked at the thoughts of seeing iniquity triumph in the person of the King of Prussia, who I consider as the sole cause of all the confusion which has happened'.[93] It could be suggested that the relatively short War of Polish Succession (1733–5) and the significant gains it brought or brought near for several rulers, particularly Philip V who gained Naples and Sicily for Don Carlos, Louis XV who gained the reversion to Lorraine, and Charles Emmanuel III of Sardinia who was able to occupy the Milanese, encouraged a resort to war over the Austrian Succession. Several of the states which adopted an aggressive role in the Austrian Succession conflict had done well from the War of Polish Succession. Of the rulers who had remained neutral in the latter conflict, Charles Albert would certainly have acted had he felt it safe to do so. In a similar fashion it could be suggested that European peace in the period 1763–78 reflected the exhaustion produced by the Seven Years' War, its unexpected length, and the failure of the rulers who had participated to obtain their ends, win any territorial benefits or gain any glory. In contrast the power that achieved the most gains in the war, Britain, proved willing to risk further colonial struggles in the years after the Peace of Paris of 1763. The monarchs for whom the Seven Years' War had proved such a disappointment mostly lived on for some years after the conflict, Louis XV not dying until 1774 and Frederick II until 1786, while Maria Theresa sought to limit the power of her son Joseph II. In contrast Catherine II, 'the Great', who did not accede to the Russian throne until 1762, was more willing to consider war or the use of military force as an option.

The period 1730–40 saw a new generation of monarchs and ministers, many full of youthful exuberance, who had not had their enthusiasm for action or their sense of what could be achieved through war tempered by the experience of the conflicts of 1688–1721 as so many of the leading figures of the 1720s had done. Cautious Swedish ministers led by Count Horn, who had experienced the defeats of the Great Northern War, were replaced in 1738 by others keen to attack Russia, a war they got, with disastrous results, in 1741. Having seen most of his dominions occupied in the War of the Spanish Succession and then lost Sicily in the War of the Quadruple Alliance, Victor Amadeus II of Sardinia, who abdicated in 1730, had been very cautious in his last years. Unwilling to commit himself to the Hanover and Seville alliances, he denied them the invasion route into Italy that they sought. His successor Charles Emmanuel III was willing to fight and helped to bring war to northern Italy in the Polish and Austrian Succession wars. Philip V's eldest son by his second marriage (to Elisabeth Farnese), Don Carlos, who arrived in Italy in 1731 to succeed to the Duchy of Parma, was an example of a pugilistic young monarch, as of course was Frederick II. Charles Albert, born in 1697, was still a youth when war ended in the Empire in 1714. He inherited Bavaria in 1726. In contrast Bonnac, the French envoy in The Hague, reported in 1755 the Dutch hope that George II would wish to keep the peace on account of his advanced age.[94] It is important not to push the argument of youth too far. Belle-Isle was 56 in 1740, Carteret had served his diplomatic apprenticeship during the Great Northern War, Philip V had been King of Spain since 1700. Nevertheless in the case of at least Prussia and Sardinia it can be suggested that the accession of new monarchs brought major changes in the policy of their countries. In the case of Sardinia there was no alteration in geopolitical interests. The conquest of the Milanese and the gain of some of the Ligurian coastline were as much the wish of Charles Emmanuel as of his father, but the former was more willing to risk war to obtain them.

A stress on the particular views of individual monarchs rather than on a geopolitical model could be criticised as entailing a return to the traditions of eighteenth-century historiography, when great events were commonly ascribed to the often trivial interests of individuals. 'The rash measures and false steps which men are apt to be hurried into by their passions and delusive prospects of success'[95] were a frequent theme of eighteenth-century writers both political commentators and historians. They suited a moral exposition of action, the predominant one of the period. The Princess of Orange suggested in 1750 that Russian hostility towards Sweden could be 'attributed in some measure to the personal dislike Chancellor Bestuchef has to Count Tessin'. The same year Newcastle feared that the French foreign minister Puysieulx would propose 'un coup éclatant' in order to maintain his tottering position at court.[96] *The Times* claimed in 1790 that many wars had 'originated in the injustice, the animosity, or the capricious passions of individuals'.[97] Since the eighteenth century it has been usual for scholars to search for a deeper level of significance, and to adopt a timescale and set of questions that have tended to replace personal motivation by impersonal trends as a means of explanation. Historians of the nineteenth century, looking for long-term trends in the foreign policy of their countries, were inclined to adopt an approach to the subject that stressed 'rational' factors suitable for an age that saw war as a heroic struggle integral to the exemplary history of the growth of the nation states that it sought. Modern diplomatic history of the early-modern period is still greatly affected by the late nineteenth and early twentieth-century historiographical tradition, for it was then that the subject was founded, themes established and much work done. The scholars of that period tended to rely heavily on the diplomatic records, to ignore other sources and to produce work that neglected the atmosphere in which decisions were taken. It is possible that this stress on impersonal trends, though extremely valuable, has been taken too far and that it is necessary to re-examine the ideas of eighteenth-century commentators,[98] not all of whom were grub-street publicists. Diplomats and ministers seeking to explain the actions of their own and other states tended to stress personal rather than impersonal factors. It is important not to contrast the two too sharply, but there is an essential difference between geopolitical explanations that often convey a sense of inevitability and explanations, such as those in this essay, that would encourage a more diffuse and less certain approach. To stress the role of the court, of concepts of kingship and of the atmosphere in which decisions were taken is not to rely on the *deus ex machina* of the personal predilections of particular monarchs. It is rather to suggest that a subtle attempt to recreate the context in which decisions were taken cannot ignore the prevalent ideas of the period and that an examination of the views of individual rulers becomes valuable when related to this context. A study of the Polish and Austrian Succession wars would suggest that it is necessary in order to understand them to appreciate the views of individuals and groups who sought war and to realise that war was not necessarily the product of diplomatic failure but rather something that was sought because it produced what were perceived as benefits. A stress on the unpredictability of eighteenth-century international relations, and in particular problems of brinkmanship, helps to explain why rash and opportunist actions were so often necessary. Whichever approach is adopted, it is still the case that the views and actions of only a relatively small number of men are considered. 'Popular' action was not absent in the Polish and Austrian Succession wars, as the Austrians discovered to their cost when they were expelled from Genoa in 1746 by a popular uprising, but the interests or reactions of the people were rarely considered by those who took decisions. Baron Wachtendonck, the Palatine foreign minister, regretted in 1758 that the poor were obliged to suffer in the disputes of the powerful, so that the latter could obtain another inch of ground or acquire some glory. Later in the century a British tourist observed: 'Leaving Cambray at four in the morning, which was still and misty, I could not help contemplating the then silent unoccupied battlements, and solitary ramparts, so often the theatre of bloody contentions between people who could have no possible inducement to cut one another's throats, but a slavish adoption of the pride and caprice of their own tyrants'.[99]

NOTES

1. Robinson to Tilson, Under Secretary in the Northern Department, 5 May 1736, B.L. Add. 23853; Sturrock, 'Bearleader' (travelling tutor) to Lord Beauchamp, to the latter's mother, the Countess of Hertford, 25 Mar. 1743, Alnwick Castle, Northumberland papers, vol. 113, p. 218. I would like to thank the Duke of Northumberland for permission to consult these papers.

2. Robinson to Charles Delafaye, Under Secretary in the Southern Department, 18 Nov. 1733, PRO. 80/101.

3. J. Black, *British Foreign Policy in the Age of Walpole* (Edinburgh, 1985).

4. *Honest True Briton* 27 Ap. (o.s.) 1724; Perceval to his cousin Daniel Dering, 22 Sept. 1725, B.L. Add. 47031; Haslang to the Palatine minister Baron Zedtwitz, 14 June 1768, Munich, Bayerisches Haupststaatsarchiv, Bayerisches Gesandschaften, London 246; Joseph Yorke, envoy in Paris, to his father Lord Chancellor Hardwicke, 26 May 1751, Earl Harcourt, British envoy in Paris, to Charles Jenkinson, 27 Dec. 1770, B.L. Add. 35355, 32806.

5. Tallard to Louis XIV, 3, 7, 21 Mar., 2 Ap. 1701, AE. CP. Ang. 191.

6. Preysing to Haslang, [5] July 1751, Munich, London, 225; Mirepoix to Puysieulx, French foreign minister, 3 Jan. 1750, AE. CP. Ang. 428.

7. R. Hatton, *War and Peace 1680-1720* (1969), pp. 26, 22; J. Shennan, *Philippe Duke of Orléans* (1979), p. 61; R. Hatton, *George I* (1978), p. 216; F. de Callières, *The Art of Diplomacy*, edited by K. Schweizer and H. Keens-Soper (Leicester, 1983); R. Langhorne, 'The Development of International Conferences, 1648-1830', *Studies in History and Politics* 2 (1981-2); N. Rich, *Why the Crimean War?* (Hanover, New Hampshire, 1985), p. 204.

8. A. Drodtloff, Johann Christoph Pentenriedter (PhD, Vienna, 1964), pp. 227, 238; *Craftsman*, 2 Dec. (o.s.) 1727; Robert Trevor, envoy at The Hague, to Robinson, 19 Aug. 1746, B.L. Add. 23823.

9. Lord Harrington and Stephen Poyntz, British envoys in Paris, to Benjamin Keene, envoy in Spain, 1 Ap. 1730, B.L. Althorp papers, E2.

10. Stair to Secretary of State James Stanhope, 18 Ap. 1715, Edinburgh, Scottish Record Office, GD. 135/141/2; Waldegrave to Robinson, 1 Feb. 1730, Leeds, District Archives, Vyner Mss. 6018, 13463; R. Koser (ed.), *Politische Correspondenz Friedrichs des Grossen* (46 vols., Berlin, 1879-1939) 6, 496; R. N. Middleton, French Policy and Prussia after the

Peace of Aix-la-Chapelle 1747–1753 (PhD, Columbia, 1968), pp. 107–8; Bishop of Rennes, French envoy in Spain, to Amelot, French foreign minister, 14 Jan. 1742, AE. CP. Espagne 470; Amelot to Fénelon, French envoy in The Hague, 9 May 1743, AE. CP. Hollande 446; Puysieulx to Vaulgrenant, envoy in Spain, 21 Ap. 1750, AE. CP. Espagne 506; Aubeterre, French envoy in Vienna, to Rouillé, 20 Aug. 1755, AE. CP. Autriche 254; Newcastle to Hardwicke, 19 Sept. 1750, B.L. Add. 35411; Rouillé to Duras, envoy in Spain, 14 Ap. 1755, AE. CP. Espagne 517; Viscount Stormont, British envoy in Paris, to the Earl of Rochford, Secretary of State, 31 Mar., 4 Ap. 1773, 16 Feb. 1774, PRO. 78/287, 291; *Daily Gazetteer*, 11 Oct. (o.s.) 1740; *Monitor*, 27 Nov. 1762.

11. J. Black and A. Reese, 'Die Panik von 1731', in J. Kunisch (ed.) *Expansion und Gleichgewicht* (Berlin, 1986); Aubeterre to St. Contest, French foreign minister, 22 Dec. 1753, AE. CP. Autriche 252; St. Contest to Bonnac, 2 Dec. 1753, Paris, Archives Nationales (hereafter AN.) KK. 1400.

12. Perceval to Captain Worth, 24 Dec. 1724, B.L. Add. 47030; Morville, French foreign secretary, to Partyet, consular official in Spain, 5 Jan. 1726, AN. Archives de la Marine, B7, 123; J. Richard, *A Tour from London to Petersburg* (London, 1780), pp. 159–60.

13. Robinson to Newcastle, 5 Ap. 1755, B.L. Add. 32854; Le Dran memorandum, 'Sur les Causes de la rupture entre la France et la gde. Bretagne en 1755', AE., Mémoires et Documents (hereafter MD.), Ang. 41 f. 167–8.

14. Tallard to Louis XIV, 23 Mar. 1701, AE. CP. Ang. 191.

15. Robinson to Tilson, 5 May 1736, B.L. Add. 23853; Fénelon to Amelot, 23 Mar. 1742, AE. CP. Hollande 442; Newcastle to Robert Keith, envoy in Vienna, 30 Mar. 1753, PRO. 80/191; Chauvelin to Le Brun, French foreign minister, 15 Jan. 1793, AE. CP. Ang. 586.

16. Robinson and Villiers to Secretary of State Lord Carteret, 16 Mar. 1743, PRO. 80/158; Bishop of Rennes to Amelot, 5 Feb. 1742, AE. CP. Espagne 470; Robinson to Harrington, 1 Sept. 1732, PRO. 80/89; Chavanne, Sardinian envoy in The Hague, to Charles Emmanuel III, 8 Jan. 1739, Turin, Archivio di Stato, Lettere Ministri Olanda 36.

17. Allen to Newcastle, 5 Feb. 1743, PRO. 93/11.

18. French foreign minister as reported in Yorke, to Secretary of State, Duke of Bedford, 22 Mar. 1749, B.L. Add. 32816; Hautefort, French envoy in Vienna, to St. Contest, 3 May 1752, Aubeterre to St. Contest, 4 May 1754, AE. CP. Autriche 251, 253.

19. Yorke to Hardwicke, 6 May 1750, B.L. Add. 35355; Puysieulx to Vaulgrenant, 28 Ap. 1750, AE. CP. Espagne 506.

20. Robinson to Harrington, 27 July 1733, Harrington to Edward Finch, 2 Oct. (o.s.) 1733, PRO. 80/97, 95/64.

21. Earl of Hyndford, British envoy in Prussia, to Harrington, 11 June 1741, PRO. 90/52.

22. *Public Ledger*, 13 Mar. 1760; Bussy to Amelot, 22 Mar. 1743, AE. CP. Ang. 416.

23. Guy Dickens, British envoy in Berlin, to Harrington, 17 Aug. 1740, PRO. 90/48; Anon., *Sir Thomas Double at Court* (London, 1710), p. 97.

24. Walpole to Newcastle, 21 Oct. 1735, B.L. Add. 32789.

25. Waldegrave to Charles Delafaye, Under Secretary in the Southern Department, 20 Sept. 1733, Wasner, Austrian envoy in Paris, to Zohrern his London counterpart, 21 Oct. 1741, PRO. 78/204, 107/49.

26. M. D'Aube, 'Réflexions sur le Governement de France', Bibliothèque Nationale, Nouvelles Acquisitions Françaises 9513, p. 166; P. Thicknesse, *Useful Hints to those who make the Tour of France* (London, 1768), p. 155.

27. H. von Zwiedineck-Südenhorst, 'Die Anerkennung der pragmatischen Sanction Karls VI durch das deutsche Reich', *Mitteilungen des Instituts für Österreichische Geschichtsforschung* 16 (1895), pp. 276–341; W. Michael, *Das Original der Pragmatischen Sanktion Karls VI* (Berlin, 1929); C. Ingrao, 'Empress Wilhelmine Amalia and the Pragmatic Sanction', *Mitteilungen des Österreichischen Staatsarchivs*, 34 (1981), pp. 333–41; L. Hüttl, 'Die Bayerischen Erbansprüche auf Böhmen, Ungarn und Österreich in der

Frühen Neuzeit', in F. Seibt (ed.), *Die Böhmischen Länder Zwischen Ost und West: Festschrift für Karl Bosl* (Munich, 1983).

28. Yorke to Hardwicke, 25 Feb. 1750, Waldegrave to Newcastle, 19 Sept. 1732, B.L. Add. 35355, 32778; Auckland to James Bland Burges, Under Secretary at Foreign Office, 1 May 1791, Oxford, Bodleian Library, Bland Burges papers, 30. I would like to thank Richard Head for permission to quote from these papers.

29. Sturrock to Richard Aldworth Neville, 19 Dec. 1740, Chelmsford, Essex Record Office, DD By CI; Marquis de Fleury, Saxon minister, to Zamboni, Saxon agent in London, 14 Mar. 1731, Oxford, Bodleian Library, Zamboni papers III (i); Amelot to Bishop of Rennes, 16, 20 Jan., Amelot to Fénelon, 25 June, Fénelon to Amelot, 18 July 1742, AE. CP. Espagne 470, Hollande 443; Charles Albert to Baron de Wetzel, 11 May, 29 June 1742, Munich, Bayr. Ges. Dresden 821; Arthur Villettes, Resident in Turin, to Robinson, 21 Jan. 1742, B.L. Add. 23810; La Ville, French agent at The Hague, to Bussy, 12 Mar. 1743, Carteret to Robinson, 19 Aug. 1743, PRO. 107/56, 80/160; Trevor to Robinson, 26 Mar. 1746, B.L. Add. 23822; O. Feldbaek, *Denmark and the Armed Neutrality. Small Power Policy in a World War* (Copenhagen, 1980), p. 11; G. Quazza, 'I negoziati austro-anglo-sardi del 1732–33', *Bollettino Storico Bibliografico Subalpino* 46–7 (1948–9); J. Black, 'The Development of Anglo-Sardinian Relations in the First Half of the Eighteenth Century', *Studi Piemontesi* 12 (1983), p. 59.

30. Anthony Thompson, in charge of British affairs in Paris, to Newcastle, 3 Aug. 1743, Earl of Rochford, envoy in Turin, to Bedford, 14, 21 Feb., 11 Ap. 1750, PRO. 78/228, 92/58. K. W. Schweizer, Frederick the Great, William Pitt and Lord Bute: The Origin, Development and Dissolution of the Anglo-Prussian Alliance 1756–63 (PhD, Cambridge, 1975); Black, 'The Anglo-French Alliance, 1716–31: A Study in Eighteenth-Century International Relations'. *Francia* 13 (1986).

31. Black, 'Archives and the Problems of Diplomatic Research', *Journal of the Society of Archivists* 8 (1986); Black, 'British Foreign Policy in the Eighteenth Century: A Survey', *Journal of British Studies* 26 (1987).

32. Tilson to Charles Whitworth, envoy in Berlin, 27 Mar. (o.s.), 6, 13 Ap. (o.s.) 1722, B.L. Add. 37388; Duke of Liria, Spanish diplomat passing through Berlin, to Marquis de la Paz, Spanish foreign secretary, 11 Oct. 1727, Brigadier Du Bourgay, British envoy in Berlin, to Secretary of State Viscount Townshend, 20 Mar. 1728, Cyril Wych, envoy in Hamburg, to Townshend, 31 Aug., 3 Sept. 1728, PRO. 107/10, 90/23, 82/45.

33. Frederick William I of Prussia to Chambrier, his envoy in Paris, 14 Feb. 1733, AE. CP. Prusse 91; Townshend to Edward Finch, 10 Dec. (o.s.) 1728, PRO. 95/51; P. Boyé, *Un Roi de Pologne et la Couronne ducale de Lorraine* (Paris, 1898); E. v. Puttkamer, *Frankreich, Russland und der polnische Thron 1733* (Königsberg, 1937); E. Rostworowski, *O Polska Korone. Polityka Francji u Latach 1725–1733* (Cracow, 1958), French summary.

34. Monti to Villeneuve, French envoy in Constantinople, Paris, Bib. Nat., M. Fr., 7196; Frederick to Prussian minister General Grumbkow, 3 Sept. 1732, R. Koser (ed.), *Briefwechsel Friedrichs des Grossen mit Grumbkow und Maupertius (1731–59)* (Leipzig, 1898), p. 55.

35. D. Mckay and H. M. Scott, *The Rise of the Great Powers 1648–1815* (1983), p. 145.

36. Waldegrave to Newcastle, 14 Oct. 1733, B.L. Add. 32782; Choiseul-Stainville, Lorraine envoy in Paris, to Francis III of Lorraine, 15 Oct. 1733, Nancy, Archives de Meurthe-et-Moselle, 3F 87.

37. Waldegrave to Newcastle, 19 Sept., Thomas Pelham, Secretary of Embassy at Paris, to Delafaye, 19 Sept. 1732, B.L. Add. 32778.

38. Bussy to Amelot, 22 Nov. 1742, AE. CP. Ang. 416; *Bristol Gazette*, 27 June 1771; *Times*, 31 Aug. 1790.

39. Tallard to Louis XIV, 17 Mar. 1701, AE. CP. Ang. 191; Anon., 'Mémoire sur les moyens de conserver par mer la Paix ...', July 1749, AE. MD. Ang. 40 f. 165.

40. Holderness to Robert Keith, 11 Mar. 1755, B.L. Add. 9147; Bonnac, French envoy in

The Hague, to Rouillé, 14, 21 Mar. 1755, AE. CP. Hollande 488; Haslang to Count Wreden, 16 May 1755, Munich, Bayr. Ges. London 230.

41. Luzerne to Montmorin, French foreign minister, 23 July 1790, AE. CP. Angleterre 574; *Morning Chronicle*, 5 Feb. 1793.

42. Wych to Carteret, 2 Aug. 1742, PRO. 91/32.

43. Albert, Duc de Broglie, *Frederic II et Marie Thérèse* (Paris, 1883); E. Driault, 'Chauvelin, 1733–1737: Son rôle dans l'histoire de la réunion de la Lorraine à la France', *Revue d'histoire diplomatique* 7 (1893); M. Sautai, *Les Débuts de la Guerre de la Succession d'Autriche* (Paris, 1909); A. M. Wilson, *French Foreign Policy during the Administration of Cardinal Fleury* (Cambridge, Mass., 1936); R. Butler, *Choiseul I* (Oxford, 1980), 247–84.

44. Chauvelin, mémoire for royal council, 28 Ap., 1733, AE. MD. Ang. 503 f. 113; Chavigny to Chauvelin, 8 Jan., 1 July 1733, AE. CP. Ang. 379, 381; Canale, Sardinian envoy in The Hague, to Charles Emmanuel III, 4 Aug. 1733, Turin, LM. Ing. Olanda 30; J. Black, 'British Neutrality in the War of the Polish Succession', *International History Review* 8 (1986).

45. Stormont to Rochford, 31 Mar. 1773, PRO. 78/287.

46. Chetardie to Chauvelin, 31 Mar. 1733, AE. CP. Prusse 94.

47. Chavigny to Chauvelin, 16 Feb. 1733, AE. CP. Ang. 379; Villeneuve to Chauvelin, 23 Aug. 1733, Paris, Bib. Nat. M. Fr. 71793; Count Törring, Bavarian foreign minister, to Count Plettenberg. Cologne minister, 18 Mar. 1733, Münster, Staatsarchiv, Dep. Nordkirchen, N.A. 148.

48. Instructions to Chetardie, 19 Feb. 1733, AE. CP. Prusse 94.

49. Bussy, French envoy in Vienna, to Blondel, French envoy in Mainz, 12 Sept., Bussy to Chavigny, 19 Sept. 1733, Vienna, Haus-, Hof-, und Staatsarchiv, Staatskanzlei (hereafter HHStA.), Interiora, Intercepte 1.

50. Chavigny to Chauvelin, 25 July 1733, AE. CP. Ang. 381.

51. Anonymous undated partition plan possibly produced by Törring in 1733, Munich, Bayr. Ges. Wien 220; Horatio Walpole, British envoy at The Hague, to Harrington, 11 Jan. 1735, P.R.O. 84/340.

52. R. Beyrich, 'Kursachsen und die polnische Thronfolge, 1733–1736', *Leipziger historische Abhandlungen* 36 (1913); P. C. Hartmann, *Karl Albrecht-Karl VII* (Regensburg, 1985), pp. 131–3.

53. Polignac to Bussy, 23 Feb. 1732, AE. CP. Autriche, supplement 11; Robinson to Under Secretary Edward Weston, 18 July 1733, P.R.O. 80/97.

54. Törring to Charles Albert, 3 Jan. 1738, Munich, Kasten Schwarz 17190.

55. Törring to Charles Albert, 17, 23, 28 Feb. 1738, Munich, Kasten Schwarz 17190.

56. B. Auerbach, *La France et le Saint Empire Romain Germanique depuis la paix de Westphalie jusqu'à la Révolution Française* (Paris, 1912); B. Wunder, 'Die bayerische 'Diversion' Ludwigs XIV', *Zeitschrift für Bayerische Landesgeschichte* 37 (1974); F. Mathis, *Die Auswirkungen des bayerisch-französischen Einfalls von 1703 auf Bevölkerung und Wirtschaft Nordtirols* (Innsbruck, 1975); L. Hüttl, *Max Emanuel* (Munich, 1976); P. C. Hartmann, *Geld als Instrument europäischer Machtpolitik im Zeitalter des Merkantilismus* (Munich, 1978); B. Kroener, 'Von der bewaffneten Neutralität zur militarischen Kooperation, Frankreich und Bayern im europäischen Machtekonzert 1648–1745', *Wehrwissenschaftliche Rundschau* 6 (1980); Black, 'Britain and the Wittelsbachs in the Early-Eighteenth Century', *Mitteilungen des Österreichischen Staatsarchivs* 40 (1987).

57. Broglie, 'Le cardinal de Fleury et la *Pragmatique Sanction*', *Revue Historique* 20 (1882).

58. There is an interesting contemporary account of the dispute in Anon., *The History of the Succession to the Counties of Juliers and Berg* (1738).

59. Törring to Charles Albert, 9 May 1739, Munich, Kasten Schwarz, 17194; A. von Arneth, *Geschichte Maria Theresia's* (Vienna, 1863–79), I, p. 371; Sautai, *Préliminaires*, pp. 475–6; M. Doeberl, *Geschichte Bayerns* (3 vols., Munich, 1928) II, 195.

60. Robinson to Harrington, 25 Jan. 1741, P.R.O. 80/144; *Politische Correspondenz* I, 108, 119, 144.

61. Sautai, *Préliminaires*, pp. 475-6; M. Doeberl, *Geschichte Bayerns* (3 vols., Munich, 1928), II, 195.

62. P. Vaucher, *Robert Walpole et la Politique de Fleury, 1731-42* (Paris, 1924), pp. 338-41.

63. Newcastle to Harrington, 11 Sept. (o.s.) 1740, P.R.O. 43/94; Horatio Walpole memorandum, B.L. Add. 9132 f. 1; Anthony Thompson to Trevor, 10 Oct. 1740, Aylesbury, Buckinghamshire County Record Office, vol. 23; Mann, Hesse Cassel envoy at The Hague, to William VIII of Hesse-Cassel, 8 Oct. 1740, Marburg, Staatsarchiv, 4f Niederlande 657; *Politische Correspondenz* I, 51, 72.

64. Black, 'British Neutrality in the War of the Polish Succession', *International History Review 8* (1986).

65. Robinson to Harrington, 4 Jan. 1741, P.R.O. 80/144; *Politische Correspondenz* I, 179.

66. Valory to Amelot, 3 Jan. 1741, AE. CP. Prusse 115; Robinson to Harrington, 28 Jan. 1741, P.R.O. 80/144.

67. Hyndford to Secretary of State, Earl of Chesterfield, 20 Dec. 1746, *Sbornik Imperatorskago Russkago Istoricheskago Obschestva* (148 vols., St. Petersburg, 1867-1916), CIII, 154.

68. *Politische Correspondenz* I, 4.

69. Hendrik Hop, Dutch envoy in London, to his brother, 6 Jan. 1741, P.R.O. 107/49.

70. Guy Dickens, British envoy in Berlin, to Harrington, 31 Jan. 1741, P.R.O. 90/49; Charles Churchill to Neville, 11 Jan. 1741, Chelmsford, D/D By CI; Törring, Bavarian envoy in Berlin, to his father, Count Törring, 14 Feb. 1741, Munich, Bayr. Ges. Berlin 8; Sautai, *Préliminaires*, p. 187.

71. Dickens to Harrington, 4 Feb. 1741, P.R.O. 90/49.

72. Törring to father, 8, 25 Feb., 11, 25 Mar. 1741, Munich, Bayr. Ges. Berlin 8.

73. Bishop of Rennes to Amelot, 5 Feb. 1742, AE. CP. Espagne 470.

74. *True Patriot*, 6 May (o.s.) 1746.

75. Wasner to Gundel, 14 Mar. 1743, P.R.O. 107/56.

76. Wasner to Zohrern, Austrian envoy in London, 1 Nov. 1741, P.R.O. 107/50; Onslow Burrish, British agent in Antwerp, to Duke of Newcastle, 11 Sept. 1741, P.R.O. 77/87; *Politische Correspondenz* I, 374; Thomas Johnston to Sir Robert Walpole. 20 Oct. (o.s.) 1741, Cambridge University Library, Cholmondeley Houghton correspondence 3104.

77. The best work on relations between Austria and France is M. Braubach, *Versailles und Wien von Ludwig XIV bis Kaunitz. Die Vorstadien der diplomatischen Revolution im 18. Jahrhundert* (Bonn, 1952). It tends to adopt too deterministic an attitude and to suggest that the alliance was inevitable. Aubeterre to Rouillé, 9 Aug. 1755, AE. CP. Autriche 254; Holderness to Keith, 11 Mar. 1755, B.L. Add. 9147.

78. *Politische Correspondenz* VI, 338.

79. Holderness to Burrish, envoy in Munich, 26 Aug. 1757, P.R.O. 81/106.

80. Amelot to Bishop of Rennes, 6 Feb. 1742, AE. CP. Espagne 470.

81. Newcastle, 18 Nov. (o.s.) 1740, W. Cobbett, *A Parliamentary History of England* (36 vols., 1806-20), XI, p. 649; Braubach, *Prinz Eugen von Savoyen* (5 vols., Munich, 1963-5), V, pp. 235-6, 255.

82. Sautai, *Préliminaires*, pp. 72-90; Braubach, *Eugen*, V, pp. 244-5, 279, 288.

83. Newcastle to Holderness, 27 Feb. (o.s.) 1750, P.R.O. 84/454.

84. St. Contest to Hautefort, 19 Ap. 1752, AE. CP. Autriche 251.

85. Pelham to Delafaye, 17 Aug. 1731, P.R.O. 78/198; Cobbett, *Parliamentary History* XI, 641.

86. C. Ingrao, 'The Pragmatic Sanction and the Theresian Succession: A Reevaluation', *Topic* 34 (1980).

87. Amelot to Fénelon, 25 Mar. 1742, AE. CP. Hollande 442; Dickens, envoy at St.

Petersburg, to Newcastle, 19 June 1751, *Sbornik* CXXXVIII, 244; Mirepoix to Rouillé, 22 Mar. 1755, AE. CP. Ang. 438.

88. Fénelon to Amelot, 5 Ap., Amelot to Fénelon, 6 Ap. 1742, AE. CP. Hollande 442.

89. C. Ingrao, 'Habsburg Strategy and Geopolitics during the Eighteenth Century', in G. C. Rothenberg, B. K. Kiraly and P. F. Sugar (eds.), *East Central European Society and War in the Pre-Revolutionary Eighteenth Century* (Boulder, Colorado, 1982), p. 63.

90. Auckland to Burges, 19 Mar. 1791, Oxford, Bodleian, Bland Burges 30; *Craftsman* 30 July (o.s.) 1743; La Ville to States General, 15 Nov. 1750, papers of Edward Weston. I would like to thank their owner John Weston-Underwood for giving me permission to consult them; Robinson to Robert Keith, envoy in Vienna, 11 Mar. 1755, Leeds Archive Office, Vyner papers, 11835.

91. Dumont painting illustrated in P. Conisbee, *Painting in Eighteenth-Century France* (Oxford, 1981), p. 114; N. V. Riasanovsky, *The Image of Peter the Great in Russian History and Thought* (Oxford, 1985), p. 303.

92. Wych to Harrington, 2 Nov. 1740, P.R.O. 82/61; *St. James's Chronicle*, 31 May 1792.

93. James to O'Rourke, Jacobite envoy in Vienna, 7 July 1743, Vienna, HHStA., England, Varia 8.

94. For Charles Albert's policies, K. T. Heigel, *Der Österreichische Erbfolgestreit und die Kaiserwahl Karls VII* (Nördlingen, 1877); F. Wagner, *Kaiser Karl VII und die grossen Mächte 1740–1745* (Stuttgart, 1938); Hartmann, *Karl VII*; Bonnac to Rouillé, 14 Mar. 1755, AE. CP. Hollande 488.

95. *London Evening Post*, 23 Ap. 1752.

96. Holderness, envoy in The Hague, to Newcastle, 13 Mar. 1750, P.R.O. 84/454; Perron, Sardinian envoy in London, to Charles Emmanuel III, 29 Jan. 1750, AST. LM. Ing. 56.

97. *Times*, 26 May 1790; Prince M. M. Shcherbatow, *On the Corruption of Morals in Russia*, edited by A. Lentin (Cambridge, 1960), p. 61.

98. D. S. Graham, British Intervention in Defence of the American Colonies 1748–56 (PhD., London, 1969), p. 112.

99. Wachtendonck to Haslang, 21 Jan. 1758, Munich, Bayr. Ges. London 234; J. E. Smith, *A Sketch of a Tour on the Continent* (3 vols., 1793), I, 62; *Universal Spectator*, 19 Mar. (o.s.) 1743.

10

THE SEVEN YEARS' WAR: A SYSTEM PERSPECTIVE

Karl Schweizer

Historians have tended to view the Seven Years' War, perhaps the most momentous conflict of the eighteenth century, largely in terms of Anglo-French relations, as the consequence of escalating disputes between Britain and France originating in America but linked to tensions in Central Europe through strategic imperatives and the diplomatic events and complications of 1755–56. Advanced by both British[1] and Continental scholarship[2] (including the recent work of Niedhart, Kunisch and Schulin[3]), this interpretation of the war is conceptually restrictive, reflecting a tendency towards short-range unidisciplinary explanations of war causation, while ignoring the approaches of international relations and conflict research, particularly the theories of general war associated with the world system paradigms of Wallerstein, Modelski, Thompson *et al*, the great power network of J. Levy[4] and various studies examining historical patterns of warfare,[5] all of which are useful as sources of data and ideas.

It is the aim of this essay to deepen our understanding of the Seven Years' War by re-examining its origins from an international system perspective. An attempt will be made to explain the outbreak of war with reference to certain structural characteristics of the state system at that time, including power distributions, the size of the system, alliance configurations, as well as political/economic patterns and trends. It will be argued that it is not only the process of events but also the structural context within which events take place that impels powers — especially Great Powers, as the dominant actors in international politics,[6] towards open war. Seen in this light, the Seven Years' War — whatever its immediate causes — represents a deeper structural crisis within the global political system, generated by the need to readjust relations among the 'core states' in the system[7] in line with intervening changes in power distributions and in a more general sense, to resolve prewar ambiguities in the order and status hierarchy of the system itself. Thus Britain — victorious over France — emerged as a world power, with command of the sea, control over trade and hence the capacity to shape global affairs, while in Europe the war registered the superiority of Prussian absolutism over its Habsburg rival, thus consolidating Prussia's rise to major continental influence and prestige.

From its origins in the late 1400s, the European international or Great Power System had by the early eighteenth century developed into a complex of secular, sovereign states, — autonomous centers of power and decision — theoretically equal yet widely divergent in resources and strength, linked by an organized system of continuous relations: politics and economics, diplomacy and commerce, peace and war.[8] The differentially expanding power of these states, aided and accelerated by improvements in governmental, fiscal and military organization,[9] had inevitable implications both for the units within the system and for the system *per se*: as member states increased their productive potential, some portions of this growth and development were transposed to the systemic level, a process of adjustment consolidating the links between state actions and the dynamics of the system as a whole. At the same time, the international system was expanding in size and degrees of interaction. By the eighteenth century, hitherto tangentially related states and subsystems to the north and east had become more closely integrated into a competitive network of multipolarity[10] — the result of two developments: greater activity by the more recent participants — the Scandinavian states, Russia, Poland and the Ottoman Empire — and partly, the increased capabilities and enlarged spheres of activity of the western and central European states. The development of the 'western segment of the state system increasingly encompassed northern and eastern Europe as it was also enveloping or including within its scope extra-European areas. As the western portion of the system became more structured and more active, the states on its peripheries could not help but be affected'.[11] States, then, interacted more frequently, in many more contexts with appreciably greater mutual effect through relatively lesser effort, thus producing greater potential for armed conflict in the pursuit of national interests and goals. In addition, the simultaneous expansion of armed forces, combined with improvements in military technology and the greater efficiency of bureaucratic and fiscal institutions, better enabled states to mobilize their energies for war, and this in turn made warfare more likely both inside Europe and overseas.

Fundamental to this evolving pattern of international politics was the peace settlement of 1713-14 — the so-called Treaty of Utrecht which restrained France's hegemonial ambitions, strengthened the German states at the expense of imperial authority, embodied significant changes of territories and dynasties and, above all, signalled Britain's predominance in sea power and overseas trade.

While territorial expansion and conquest were the primary means to wealth and power in the agrarian-based, pre-1500 world,[12] the gradual development of a global market economy, firmly anchored in world trade, gave certain states with the necessary resources dominant roles in world trade and hence in global political affairs. Indeed, the position of a state in the world market henceforth became a principal determinant if not *the* principal determinant of its status in the international sphere. Leading powers in this new world market system of exchange according to Modelski[13] were first Portugal, followed by the Netherlands, and later Great Britain — a preponderance facilitated by a superiority in agro/industrial production, by extensive internal reforms,[14] and naval/fiscal expansion during the years of warfare against Louis XIV. 'The basic institutions of the British global system', to quote one historian, emerged in the struggle against the French; the dominant Parliament as the focus of the political system; the Navy, now Britain's largest growth industry, in firm control of the Narrow Seas, the Atlantic, and the Mediterranean (through Gibraltar); and the

Bank of England and the National Debt (1694) as instruments of economic mobilization and control.[15] Britain, newly united, had become the secure home base from which economic change was slowly shaping the forces of the Industrial Revolution that by the nineteenth century would sweep Europe and then the world. France, by contrast, declining in power though still formidable, devoted much of her national energies to the pursuit of European objectives at the relative expense of transmaritime pursuits — another factor contributing to Britain's rising imperial success.

The French wars also fostered one of the most significant developments in European politics during the eighteenth century — namely the increasing importance of colonial questions in determining the policies of the European states. 'Struggles for overseas territories, hitherto largely separate from the wars inside Europe, gradually merged into a wider network of conflicts embracing both Europe and its colonial dependencies'.[16] By the 1740s colonial wars, fought by states to strengthen their dominance over the world market economy, had become an integral part of the perennial power struggle between the European states.

For Britain after 1713, ascendancy in world trade became combined with a flexible policy of selective continental intervention designed to restrain military/dynastic ambition and maintain the European power balance established at Utrecht.[17] This meant that while territorial acquisitions on the European continent and permanent combinations were to be avoided, Britain was prepared to cooperate with like-minded states in the interest of stability and peace — the major reason for her post-Utrecht alliance with France, an alliance which would be the key stabilizing force in European politics until the 1730s.[18] Negotiated as a bilateral treaty of mutual guarantee in 1716 and broadened the following year into the Triple Alliance of Britain, the United Provinces and France, this agreement significantly aided the settlement of Austro–Spanish and later Anglo–Spanish conflicts, contributed to the resolutions of problems in the Baltic — a legacy of the Northern Wars — and promoted the conclusion of the Quadruple Alliance in 1718, thereby establishing what has been described as a 'rudimentary system of collective security for western and central Europe'.[19]

Yet Anglo–French cooperation was not to last; although France remained somewhat isolated diplomatically, and at different points in the two decades between the Peace of Utrecht and the war of the Polish Succession each of the two powers needed the other's support and had benefited from it, the interests and aims of the two states were becoming divergent. Colonial competition began to intrude more as both states recovered from the strains of war and as the relative peace within Europe enabled them to devote more attention to naval and imperial expansion. Within Europe, Britain and France still had no significant reason for conflict, though the alliance preferences of each (aside from or in addition to their mutual relationship) intruded upon *entente*, first in terms of prestige and subsequently in terms of being drawn into the disputes of other states on opposing sides.

By 1738, the success of French diplomacy in Balkan and in Imperial affairs, combined with the revival of French naval and commercial expansion, reawakened Britain's traditional suspicion of Bourbon designs. These suspicions were given added force by France's subsequent support of Spain in the latter's colonial disputes with Great Britain — support which took the form of military operations against the Dutch and Britain's ally, during the so-called Austrian Succession war that absorbed the Anglo-Spanish conflict after 1740.

The Peace of Aix-la-Chapelle which terminated this war left vital questions of relationships and territory unsettled; confirmed had been the continuous dissatisfaction of major states, the unresolved rivalry between Britain and France for pre-eminence in colonial trade, and finally the need to integrate the newly established Great Powers, Russia and especially Prussia, within the European system of states — a complex process of adjustment which would henceforth determine the pace and direction of diplomatic events.

Uneasy though the peace was, until 1754 no major conflicts developed; by degrees Europe assumed its long-accustomed shape and disposition, the immediate postwar years witnessing no sudden or dramatic rupture in the established pattern of power alignments. Prussia was still allied to France, which in turn wielded controlling influence in Turkey, Sweden and Poland — its client states in the North and East,[20] a combination opposed by Britain, the Dutch and Austria — comprising the historic 'old system', based on the Barrier Treaties of 1713 and 1715. Hovering menacingly on the periphery was the formidable state of Russia whose conflicts of interests with Prussia and France[21] correspondingly cemented its alliance with Vienna and facilitated friendly relations with Britain.[22]

But even as the dust gathered on the conference tables near the venerable spires of Aix-la-Chapelle Cathedral, Europe was, all unknowing, in a dynamic state of flux. At work beneath the uneasy facade of stability, behind the deceptive features of continuity was a subtle process of transformation in the very structure of power and interests in Europe — a process which would eventually produce a totally altered configuration of alliance groupings. Viewed in its widest context, this appears due to a long, albeit erratic, development dating back to the reign of Louis XIV,[23] reflecting the deep-seated shiftings and diplomatic convulsions which time and statesmanship had wrought. A more immediate precipitating factor — a product of the recent war itself — was the sudden rise of Brandenburg-Prussia as a first-rate military state. By seizing and successfully defending Silesia, Frederick II had consolidated his military reputation, established his state's potential for continued and accelerated growth and substantially offset the fragmentary character of Prussia's geopolitical structure.[24] Indeed it was the very magnitude of his success which signified the beginning of a new epoch — the period of dualism in German politics[25] — and more than anything determined the postwar direction or rather reorientation, of Austrian foreign policy priorities.

Intent upon reacquiring Silesia, if not re-establishing Austrian primacy within the Empire, Maria Theresa set out, after 1748, to prepare for the future conflict with Prussia by strengthening Habsburg dominions through vigorous and far-reaching schemes of internal re-organization and reforms.[26] An inevitable byproduct of this growing preoccupation with the Prussian threat was Austria's shifting focus from such traditional spheres of dynastic interest as the Netherlands and Italy, to vital areas nearer home.[27] This meant that Austria's traditional rivalry with France, dating from the time of Charles V, was beginning to lose its validity — the basic premise of Anton von Kaunitz-Rittberg,[28] director of Austrian foreign affairs after 1753 — to whom the recent war and his experiences at Aix-la-Chapelle[29] offered abundant proof that the old system of power relations was defunct, and that if Austria were ever to recover Silesia, she required a new continental ally with an effective military force — and that ally was France. The utter inadequacy of the traditional alliance with the Maritime Powers to serve Austria's new needs and objectives had become patently clear during the years 1740-1748.[30] The Dutch, weak and lethargic, were no longer reliable (without much resistance, they had relinquished numerous Barrier forts to the French),[31] while for Britain, primarily absorbed by colonial/maritime issues, Austria was simply an auxiliary in the conflict with France.[32] Unwilling to assume extensive European commitments, the British government had not only shown utter indifference to the fate of Silesia, but by threatening to withold vital support had repeatedly imposed upon Austria such policies as accorded best with *British* interests.[33] Conversely, a *rapprochement* with France, Kaunitz argued, would provide security for Habsburg possessions in Germany and in Italy as well as the Netherlands but, more important, substantially augment Austria's future military and financial strength. As a result, from about 1749 onwards, an increasingly influential element within the Austrian government (encouraged by Maria Theresa herself) advocated as eventual policy the idea of systematically detaching France from Prussia, retaining close ties of friendship with Russia, and gradually completing Frederick's diplomatic isolation[34] without meanwhile jeopardising the subsisting link with the Maritime Powers: the British and the Dutch.[35] In 1750, Kaunitz was appointed ambassador to Paris where he hoped to lay the groundwork for this programme. He established several useful and promising contacts, but on the whole his tentative proposals did not as yet impress the predominantly pro-Prussian members of Louis XV's *conseil d'état*.[36] Though having failed, temporarily, to reverse the established policy of centuries, Kaunitz by no means abandoned his views, but returned to Vienna in 1753 (to become State Chancellor) still seeing Bourbon–Habsburg co-operation as the key to Austrian revisionist schemes.[37]

Given this fundamental shift in Austria's alignment policy and long-term interests, the 'old system', consecrated by time and past success stood seriously undermined. It was to be a while, however, before this became widely recognized, and until then the 'old system' retained its established reputation, especially in Britain and Holland, as the only effective mechanism for preserving the balance of power and restricting the aggressive ambitions of France. The prime exponent of this view was Thomas Pelham-Holles, Duke of Newcastle and Secretary of State for the North from 1748. Convinced that France aimed for a resumption of war once her army and naval forces were rebuilt, Newcastle hoped to forestall French intentions through an active continental system, involving the strengthening of the Barrier fortresses in the Low Countries, the conclusion of alliances with Denmark and Spain and subsidy agreements with smaller European states.[38]

As part of the Imperial Election Scheme,[39] two such agreements were concluded — one with Bavaria in 1750 and another with Saxony a year later — though in effect neither treaty[40] could eliminate the inseparable differences between Austria and the Maritime Powers or restore to the Anglo–Austrian *entente* that spirit of cordiality and co-operation necessary for concerted action. By 1753–54, British diplomacy at Vienna — despite the special mission of Sir Charles Hanbury Williams[41] — had reached an impasse. The fundamental divergence of Anglo–Austrian views on such complex issues as the future of the Austrian Netherlands, the re-establishment of the barrier against France, and Austria's demand for a new treaty of commerce, could simply not be reconciled.[42] Since the course of the last war, as Kaunitz patiently explained to Williams, had clearly illustrated the futility of the Barrier system as a defence for the Low Countries, Austria had no intention of contributing towards the upkeep of Dutch garrisons, still less of restoring, at her own expense, those fortresses demolished by Marshal Saxe.[43] Nor in fact was she prepared any longer to tolerate restrictions imposed by the Barrier treaty upon the economic activities of her Netherlands subjects in the interests of British and Dutch merchants with their preferential tariffs.[44] Equally, if not more, divisive was Newcastle's unfortunate adoption and implementation of the ill-fated Imperial election plan, which set Germany in an uproar, further impaired Austro–British relations in the inter-war period and, in effect, confirmed Kaunitz's predilection for an agreement with France. Austria's readiness to abandon traditional hostilities against France — for over two centuries the pivot of European diplomacy — made her alliance with the Maritime Powers a liability, since at any moment Franco–British tensions might involve Austria in a war with France, the very power Austria hoped to court.[45] Obviously, Kaunitz was merely playing for time, carefully steering a middle course until his long-standing hopes for an Austro–French reconciliation could be implemented. Meanwhile, however, both Keith, the regular envoy, and Williams, by giving undue weight to any event which appeared to favour the 'old system', managed to sustain Newcastle's illusions and maintain the semblance of an alliance which in reality had already collapsed.[46] The only way of restoring to the British 'entente' the value it had lost would have been for Britain to commit herself to Austro–Russian antagonism to Prussia. This explains why Kaunitz repeatedly insisted[47] that Britain accede to the fourth secret article of the so-called 'Treaty of the Two Empresses' signed in 1746, which Newcastle, fearing hostilities with Prussia, refused to endorse.[48]

As these Austro–British deliberations extended into 1754, still without results, it soon became evident that the uneasy truce between Britain and France in North America and India was about to end. The activities of the Ohio Company and the gradual westward expansion of British colonists infuriated the French, who controlled Canada to the North and Louisiana to the South. The aggressiveness of French traders in India alarmed the British as did French fortifications of their American positions, while persistent disputes over naval prizes and titles to strategic West-Indian islands antagonized both powers. The situation everywhere was explosive.[49]

More knowledgeable about colonial affairs than is usually assumed, Newcastle was determined to defend British interests in America yet also anxious to leave scope for compromise and negotiation.[50] But under political pressure Newcastle gradually became committed to an American policy which made French counter-actions and hence steady escalation from crisis to open conflict virtually certain. Adopting the plan of operations formulated by Cumberland, the cabinet duly dispatched two regiments under Braddock with orders to attack the French (in conjunction with colonial forces) at four strategic points,[51] although formal declarations of war had not yet been issued on either side.

Apprized of these events, the French government, however reluctantly, had little choice but to send a counter-expedition, and mobilization orders were duly issued for six battalions intended to strengthen the strategic outposts along the Great Lakes. By then, however, the impromptu British offensive had already misfired. An advance into Upper New York failed to take the strategically important Crown Point on Lake Champlain, disaster struck near Pittsburgh where the French killed Braddock and two-thirds of his army, while at sea a fog-bound squadron off Newfoundland missed a French fleet conveying troops and supplies to Canada. Both countries, by sending forces to defend their colonies, were moving toward a full-scale war. Commercial and territorial competition had become armed conflict. The die was cast.[52]

More than ever, these events necessitated the consolidation of Britain's 'defensive arrangements' on the continent, partly to distract French attention from British colonial operations but also to safeguard the security of Hanover, George II's hereditary electorate — a necessary factor in Britain's strategic calculations when preparing for hostilities with France.[53] Although Englishmen often resented the union of Hanover and Britain, abandoning Hanover was strategically and politically unfeasible.[54] The Electorate's interests sometimes coincided with British interests and contributed to their furtherance while the impossibility of severing the connection insured that Hanover's interests would be considered by British administrations and, on occasion, would predominate. It also meant that Britain was obliged to make provisions for Hanover's defense and thus for continental war, by subsidies to allies, through a British expeditionary force or both.

One of the prerequisites repeatedly stressed by Kaunitz for Austria's eventual participation in the defense of the Netherlands and Hanover had been the conclusion of a subsidy agreement between Britain and Russia. As yet convinced, thanks to Keith's misleading reports, that Kaunitz could still be relied upon, Newcastle accordingly re-opened negotiations with St. Petersburg in the spring of 1755. Hanbury Williams, fresh from his latest diplomatic calamity at Warsaw, was put in charge of the mission with the coveted title of full ambassador.

Ever since the days of Peter the Great, Anglo-Russian political and particularly commercial relations had been on a generally close and friendly footing,[55] Russia depending on England for certain colonial goods while England, correspondingly, obtained from Russia the bulk of her indispensable naval stores. In addition, Russian policy ran counter to French interests in Poland, Turkey and the Baltic States which, combined with Empress Elizabeth's anti-Prussian orientation, constituted an effective barrier to Franco-Prussian military ambitions.[56] Already, in 1742, Britain had managed to secure Russian military aid against France although, in the end, the hired troops arrived too late on the scene to be of much practical use. The newly proposed subsidy agreement, in one form or another, had been the focal point of Anglo-Russian relations since the war. Closely associated with the background discussions of Britain's accession to the Treaty of Warsaw, the convention, in its initial stages, had been rejected in London partly due to the magnitude of Russia's financial demands, but even more owing to the intense parliamentary opposition to the conclusion of such treaties in time of peace.[57] Now, however, with war in the offing, the situation had changed. As before, Newcastle was not only concerned about the intentions of France, but also about Prussia, France's ally since 1741.

Whereas from about 1688 to 1714 relations between England and Prussia had been relatively friendly — though hardly close — following the accession of George I, these rapidly deteriorated. Added to policy disputes were the traditional animosities of Welf and Hohenzollern extending over generations and made particularly bitter by territorial rivalries and discordant kinship ties. Indeed, except for their brief co-operation during the Northern war, for most of the 1720s and '30s Britain and Prussia remained politically estranged.

With the accession of Frederick II in 1740, many in Britain hoped for a new era of political co-operation as well as closer social and cultural contacts between the two countries, though continuous territorial quarrels, electoral issues and personal factors thwarted all prospects of reconciliation. Intermittent attempts to improve relations persisted until 1748, when with the failure of Henry Legge's mission to Berlin[58] Britain abandoned the idea of accommodating Prussia and concentrated instead on the possibility of neutralizing Frederick's military initiative and hence danger to Hanover by means of a defensive agreement with Russia.[59] Frederick's fear of a Russian attack was well known in London,[60] and the idea of using Russia as a deterrent is a recurrent theme in Newcastle's correspondence throughout this period.[61] What first forced Newcastle's hand, prompting him to re-open (in a modified form) the Russian subsidy scheme rejected in 1749, was the urgent question of Hanover's security in 1753 — a time when Anglo–Prussian relations had virtually reached a breaking point. Rumours of Prussian mobilization were rampant,[62] and as the fear and uncertainty increased, the Hanoverian Council (under the influence of alarming news from the Prussian frontier)[63] frantically prepared and submitted a detailed defense project, calling for prompt collaboration with Austria and, above all, a subsidy arrangement with Russia.[64] The British cabinet agreed and Colonel Guy Dickens (Britain's envoy in St. Petersburg) received appropriate orders, though by August, Frederick strongly disavowed any intentions of moving against Hanover. All the same, Britain, with an eye to the future, decided to prolong the talks without specifically designating Prussia as the enemy. Subsequent disagreements both over the amount of the subsidy and over the *casus foederis* for the deployment of Russian troops outside Russia prolonged the negotiations, without result, until early 1755 when the hapless Dickens, physically and mentally exhausted, requested his recall.

Instructed to bring the subsidy treaty to a 'speedy conclusion',[65] Williams, his successor, arrived in St. Petersburg in June and promptly set about his task. Empowered to raise the amount of the subsidy, and well supplied with bribe money, he managed to complete his mission with the new Anglo–Russian agreement signed on 30 September, 1755.[66]

Though British policy was largely based on the traditional view of Russia as a mercenary power — a reservoir of troops which Britain could and should use in accordance with her interests — Russia, in responding to Newcastle's overtures, was in fact pursuing a calculated and deliberate policy of her own. Personified by Empress Elizabeth but actually formulated and controlled by her chancellor and *de facto* foreign minister, Count Alexis Bestuzhe-Riumin, this policy had far-reaching aims to which all else was to be subordinated: collaboration with Austria for the defeat and partition of Prussia, the cession of East Prussia to Russia (to be exchanged with Poland for Kurland), and finally the expulsion of French influence from Eastern Europe and that other sphere of sustained contention, Turkey. To this end, the subsidy treaty offered the perfect means and opportunity of mobilizing a sizeable force in the Baltic area, ready to attack Prussia as opportunity offered.

From the outset, the treaty had provided for action against the 'common enemy', which Russia naturally understood to be Prussia, although the negotiations had never mentioned that power by name. This unfortunate omission and the ambiguity thus created were to cause considerable trouble later when it came time to identify the target state, especially since by then Newcastle had already formulated a radically different solution to Britain's continental problem. Boscawen's attacks on French shipping had ruptured formal diplomatic relations between London and Paris in July and all-out war was now certain. Further talks with the Dutch and the Austrians throughout the spring and summer of 1755, conducted by Britain as a last-minute attempt to revive the all but broken 'old system', had been fruitless.[67] Fearful of alienating France and of lowering Austrian defenses, Kaunitz had flatly refused to despatch any reinforcements to the Low Countries, and though promising vaguely to protect Hanover, he attached such exorbitant conditions that even Newcastle became convinced of his insincerity.[68] No more satisfactory was the response of the Dutch. With their dilapidated Barrier, ill-disciplined troops, ramshackle navy and declining economy, the United Provinces were hardly prepared for an impending war. Not only was there a growing movement for all-out neutrality, but the influential pro-French Republican party, centred in Amsterdam, roundly threatened to make terms with France unless Britain took immediate and effective measures with Austria and Russia for their defence.[69] Realizing that Kaunitz's demands — apart from the expense involved — were clearly directed toward Britain's ultimate participation in Austria's revisionist plans against Prussia, the Cabinet unanimously decided on their rejection. Already, however, Newcastle's thoughts were moving in another direction. Profoundly influenced (if not disturbed) by news of Williams' mission,[70] Frederick, in June, had informally intimated an interest in discussing the current European crisis with King George (then at

Hanover),[71] while several weeks later, through an intercepted letter, it became known in London that Prussia favoured the neutralization of Germany in any future war.[72] The requested interview did not take place, though Frederick's initiative, added to Austria's undeviating recalcitrance, quickly suggested to Newcastle the possibility of utilizing the pending Anglo–Russian negotiations as a means of securing from Frederick a formal agreement for the neutralization of the continent. Since a strong continental coalition was now obviously out of the question, such an arrangement would safeguard Hanover, facilitate the abandonment of the expensive and much criticized policy of subsidizing client states and enable Britain to localize the war with France; to concentrate exclusively on the conflict overseas.[73]

As yet, the Anglo–Russian subsidy treaty had not been concluded or ratified and, judging by previous events, it could well take months, following ratification, before the cumbersome Russian military machine actually rolled into motion. Prussia, on the other hand, as the neighbour of Hanover, was at once more useful, and more dangerous, if not less expensive, than the venal Russians. So rather than prepare for a drawn-out, unpopular and costly continental war, Newcastle argued, why not simply prevent the Franco-British colonial struggle from extending to Europe by inducing Frederick to guarantee the inviolability of Hanover, while Britain, in turn, controlled the military policies of Russia?

Approved, after some reservation, by both the leading members of the cabinet and George II's Hanoverian ministers,[74] Newcastle's ideas were adopted as policy and Lord Holdernesse, then attending the King at Hanover, was consequently given leave to open negotiations with the Prussian court.[75] Frederick's reaction was initially ambivalent: although anxious to avert a general European war, he had no intention of providing unilateral guarantees for Hanover until the results of Britain's negotiations at St. Petersburg became known. Also, he was still allied to France, though admittedly a France which, throughout the summer of 1755, appeared increasingly weak and lethargic, unlikely to give him much support[76] if Prussia were attacked — a real prospect with Austria fervently scheming to recover Silesia and Russo–Prussian enmity at its height. Through his efficient espionage system, Frederick had secured a copy of the Russo–Austrian defensive treaty of 1746 and knew that certain of the secret articles were aimed expressly at him;[77] other evidence suggested a gradual Russo–Austrian link-up with Saxony, Hanover and possibly other German states — invoking visions of encirclement, Frederick's perennial fear. Given Russia's (and Austria's) chronic lack of mobilization funds, much obviously depended on outside capital — hence Frederick's intense concern with the progress of Anglo–Russian deliberations and especially the final treaty, a copy of which reached him in December 1755 along with renewed British proposals for a *rapprochement* and for the settlement of all outstanding Anglo–Prussian disputes.[78] Suddenly desperate, now that Russian mobilization was possible, Frederick promptly approved the British overtures and, in January 1756, signed the Convention of Westminster by which the contracting parties guaranteed their respective possessions and agreed to resist jointly the entry of all foreign troops into Germany including those of their present allies.[79]

Neither Britain nor Prussia, it is clear, intended to effect a change in the existing political system of Europe, regarding their convention as merely a temporary agreement, in no way incompatible with their respective alignment policies. Equally, they were fully confident of persuading their allies to accept this interpretation[80] — a miscalculation which dictated the course of the famous 'diplomatic revolution' that was to follow. First, France, indignant at what seemed Prussian duplicity and fearful of isolation, became more responsive to continuing Austrian overtures and eventually, on 12 May 1756,[81] concluded with Austria the first Treaty of Versailles. This treaty guaranteed Austria's neutrality in an Anglo–French war and the security of her territories from French attack. In addition, each power was obliged to provide 24,000 troops to the other partner if attacked. Similarly adverse was the reaction in St. Petersburg[82] where news of the Westminster Convention arrived at a critical moment — just before the ratifications of the Anglo–Russian Subsidy Treaty were to be exchanged.

The first obvious sign that British plans were afoul at the Russian court came in early 1756, when instead of receiving the expected ratification, Williams was presented with a separate declaration, one which placed a rigid interpretation on the treaty — that the Russian forces were to be used against Prussia only. Williams wisely refused to accept the document but when on 16 February, 1756 he finally received the Russian ratification, it contained a clause which, like the declaration, stated that Russia would make a diversion only against Prussia — that is to say, if Prussia attacked Great Britain or a British ally.[83] In rebuttal, Williams now pressed for a more general understanding of the treaty, arguing that it must be directed against France, not Prussia, but without success. What the British had failed to see was now obvious: the Westminster Convention had decisively altered (if not undermined) the entire basis of Anglo–Russian relations. Whereas for Britain, once Prussia came to terms, the *casus foederis* of the subsidy treaty had changed, to the Russian government (and Empress Elizabeth especially) the treaty had always been and still was primarily the instrument for an aggressive strategy against Frederick of Prussia. Thus, upon learning of Britain's reconciliation with her arch-enemy, Elizabeth inevitably concluded that the subsidy agreement, at least for Russian purposes, was no longer practical or beneficial and consequently opted for its repudiation.[84] Here she was strongly encouraged by the pro-French party, under the aegis of Vice-Chancellor Voronzov, which had emerged in 1755 and whose goal it was to overthrow Bestuzhev and the system he represented and to re-establish closer political and commercial ties with France. Through his activities, so far unofficial, Voronzov had already made some progress in this direction, but after the Westminster Convention he was able to proceed more openly, with greater advantage, and above all with the full support of the Empress. By the end of July 1756, despite the desperate efforts of Bestuzhev and Williams to salvage some part of the subsidy treaty, it became clear that Britain's political influence at St. Petersburg had collapsed while that of France (backed by Austrian influence) was in the ascendant.[85] Worse still from March onwards, the newly established 'Conference at the Imperial Court'[86] composed an extensive and systematic plan of war, calling for constant collaboration with Austria, further negotiations with France, and the formation of additional infantry and cavalry regiments as well as the full-scale mobilization of existing military units. As this Russian build-up continued into the summer of 1756, Frederick, in receipt of regular intelligence reports from Vienna, Versailles and St. Petersburg, became increasingly alarmed.[87] Mitchell, the British envoy to Berlin, did his best to soothe Frederick's growing anxiety by concealing the worst features of Williams's despatches,[88] but this worked only for a time. By the end of June, Frederick seriously suspected that Britain's influence in St. Petersburg was on the wane and that he was the imminent victim of a conspiracy being hatched by Austria, Russia and probably France. His worst apprehensions were confirmed when on 9 July Mitchell finally showed him the Russian *déclaration secrétissime* which Elizabeth had insisted he appended to the subsidy treaty prior to ratification. Frederick, the envoy reported:

> ... read it over unmoved and observed with great calmness that it made our treaty with the Russians quite useless; that as to himself he wondered why the Empress of Russia had so strong an aversion to him; that he had never done anything to deserve it and that he imputed it to the influence and arts of the court of Vienna.[89]

Not one passively to await the inevitable and failing to receive satisfactory explanations regarding Austrian military movements,[90] Frederick decided to forestall his enemies by defeating and forcing Austria to a separate peace before either France or Russia could actively intervene. Despite Britain's urgings against an immediate offensive and despite the warnings of his cabinet ministers and envoys, Frederick refused to yield and on 28 August his troops crossed the Saxon frontier. The European part of the Seven Years' War had begun.

To summarize, the Seven Years' War was the consequence of both immediate and long-term causes — immediate factors such as the ambiguities of crisis decision-making, diplomatic pressures and the destabilizing dimensions of military escalation and, in a wider context, certain processes in the global political system within which all state activity including conflict and *entente* must be viewed. Although the outbreak of war was preceded by extensive alliance and counter-alliance formations, the evidence indicates that these alignments were more a response to antecedent conditions of political instability and the anticipation of imminent conflict than determinants of war themselves. And while polarized alliance structures are often co-related with war,[91] the hostile groupings in existence by 1756 had evolved out of the rapidly shifting diplomatic patterns associated with the Diplomatic Revolution. This confirms J. Levy's observation that originally flexible alliances tend to become 'formalized and institutionalized' but only in response to already threatening war.[92] As Levy points out, '... it is not polarized or non-polarized alliances, nor the change from one to another, that lead to war. Rather, it is the underlying international and domestic conditions and events which trigger a dynamic process of escalation. This induces an anticipation of impending war by statesmen and hence their frantic search for allies, leading to rapidly shifting coalitions and ultimately to war, either directly or after the polarization of the alliance system'.[93]

It is of course possible that the *ad hoc* and secretive nature of most alliances contributes to international tensions by generating suspicion and mistrust and that the existence of alliances increases the chances of misinterpretation by decision-makers, thereby producing a high-threat environment equally conducive to war. Thus in its American setting, the Seven Years' War — certainly as regards timing — appears to have resulted from an action-reaction cycle triggered by concurrent misinterpretation on the part of Britain and France of their respective intentions. The Anglo–French response to presumed hostilities was to increase military/naval capabilities in order to deter aggression and prepare for war in case deterrence failed. These actions, evidently quite unintentionally, produced a conflict spiral which, reinforced by psychological dimensions, escalated towards open war. It was similar uncertainty regarding adversarial capabilities and intentions that prompted Frederick II's *rapprochement* with Britain while still allied to France and which, combined with belief in Prussia's offensive superiority,[94] decided his pre-emptive strike against Saxony in the summer of 1756. Both measures — the military initiative succeeding the failed diplomatic manoeuvre — brought to completion the Austro–French–Russian coalition he had hoped to disrupt and initiated the war in Europe that he had feared all along. Ultimately alliances, including the agreements operative on the eve of the Seven Years' War, are not prime determinants of great power conflicts but rather intervening variables in a dynamic pattern of conflict comprising antecedent conditions, political tensions, miscalculations and underlying systemic processes which independently contribute to war. This, in turn, suggests that the significance of specific wars lies not only in the identity and political weight of the states involved, the issues in dispute or even the flexibility and perceptual accuracy of the combatants but depends upon when these wars occur within the development of the global political system — what W. R. Thompson has called 'world system time'.[95] In this sense, the Seven Years' War, as stated earlier, must be seen as a structural crisis in the international system since it occurred in a period of transition within that system precipitated by alterations in the distribution of capabilities between the principal world powers, Britain and France. Once the global system has entered such a transition zone, 'relatively trivial incidents or seemingly minor crises may serve to tilt the structural imbalance in favour of global war'.[96]

Britain's rise to global predominance based on naval, commercial and financial superiority was resisted by France, a power economically less dynamic, resulting in a global conflict fought to resolve the issue of systemic leadership, to reorganize the framework of international economic relations and to effect a realignment of the international systems governance with the new distribution of power as registered by war. Simultaneously the growth of exchange networks and polarized alliance structures hastened the spread of conflict to Europe, the merging of continental with colonial issues and the involvement of states with widely divergent motives and aims.

NOTES

I would like to thank the Humanities Research Council of Canada and the Bishop's University Research Committee for providing generous research support and D. J. Black, Dr. John Brewer, Professor R. Hatton and Professor I. R. Christie for their advice and encouragement over a number of years. For permission to consult and cite their manuscripts, I am indebted to the following: the British Library, Public Record Office, Deutsches Zentral-archiv (Merseburg); the Duke of Devonshire and the Trustees of the Chatsworth settlement; Niedersächsisches Staatsarchiv, Hanover; Haus-, Hof-, und Staatsarchiv, Vienna and Mr. J. Weston-Underwood.

1. British literature on the Seven Years' War, though in large part now outdated, is voluminous. For listings of the most pertinent sources, see the bibliography in: R. Middleton, *The Bells of Victory: The Pitt–Newcastle ministry and the Conduct of the Seven Years' War 1757–1762* (Cambridge, 1985), pp. 238–244; K. W. Schweizer, Frederick the Great, William Pitt and Lord Bute: the origin, development and dissolution of the Anglo-Prussian Alliance 1756–1763 (Cambridge Ph.D. thesis, 1976), pp. 457–475; and *idem*, 'William Pitt, Lord Bute and the Peace Negotiations with France, May–September 1761'. *Albion*, vol. 13, nr. 3, p. 262 note 1.

2. For representative views see: A. Schaefer, *Geschichte des Siebenjährigen Krieges* (Berlin, 1874), I; W. Michael, *Englands Aufstieg Zur Weltmacht* (Berlin, 1895), V; E. Marcks, *Englands Machtpolitik* (Stuttgart, 1940), esp. pp. 131–154.

3. G. Niedhart, *Handel und Krieg in der Britischen Weltpolitik 1738–1763* (Munich, 1979); J. Kunisch, *Staatsverfassung und Mächtepolitik: Zur Genese von Staatenkonflikten im Zeitalter des Absolutismus* (Berlin, 1979); E. Schulin, *Handelstaat England* (Wiesbaden, 1969).

4. Immanuel Wallerstein, *The Modern World System*, 2 vols. (1974, 1980), *The Capitalist World Economy* (Cambridge, 1969). Theories of international conflict building upon aspects of Wallerstein's world system analysis include the 'Uneven economic growth' theory of Chase-Dunn, the power transition theory of Organski and Kugler, Doran's power cycle theory and Gilpin's theory of hegemonic war and change. See C. Chase-Dunn, 'Interstate System and Capitalist world Economy: One Logic or Two?', *International Studies Quarterly* 25 (March, 1981), pp. 19–42; A. F. K. Organski, *World Politics* (New York, 1968), ch. 14; Organski and Kugler, *The War Ledger* (Chicago, 1980); C. F. Doran, 'Power Cycle Theory and the Contemporary State System', in W. R. Thompson (ed.), *Contending Approaches to World System Analysis* (Beverly Hills, 1983), ch. 7; C. F. Doran and W. Parson, 'War and the Cycle of Relative Power', *American Political Science Review*, 74 (1980), pp. 947–65; R. Gilpin, *War and Change in World Politics* (Cambridge, 1981). An admirably concise and critical survey of this literature has been provided by J. Levy, 'Theories of General War', *World Politics*, 3 (XXXVII, 1985), pp. 344–372. For convincing criticisms that Wallerstein's interpretation of world system dynamics and global war unduly subordinates politico-military factors as a byproduct or result of the processes of capitalistic economic development see: T. Skopol, 'Wallerstein's World Capitalist System: A Theoretical and Historical Critique', *American Journal of Sociology*, 82 (1983), pp. 1075–90; G. Modelski, 'The Long Cycle of Global politics and the Nation State', *Comparative Studies in Society and History*, 20 (1978), pp. 214–235; A. R. Zolberg, 'Origins of the Modern World System: A Missing Link', *World Politics*, 33 (1981), pp. 253–81. An economy exists as Gilpin has observed, within a social and political framework that both permits and proscribes certain types of economic activities; the economy, at least in the short run, is subordinate to the larger social and political goals of the society. It does not exist in an autonomous sphere governed solely by economic laws (Gilpin, p. 133). In the modern world, the emergence of a world market economy was dependent on the pluralistic structure of the European (and, subsequently the global) political system; hence fluctuations in the character of this system (i.e. shifts in power concentrations) could cause fluctuations in important economic processes. W. R. Thompson, 'Uneven Economic

Growth, Systemic Challenges and Global Wars', *International Studies Quarterly*, 27 (1983), pp. 341–355.

5. L. Dehio, *The Precarious Balance: Four Centuries of the European Power Struggle* (New York, 1962); K. Waltz, *Man, the State and the War* (New York, 1954); R. Rosecrance, *Action and Reaction in World Politics* (Boston, 1963); G. Modelski, 'Wars and the Great Powers', *Peace Research Society Papers*, 18 (1971), pp. 45–59; Q. Wright, *A Study of War* (Chicago, 1942); F. A. Beer, *How Much War in History* (1974); L. L. Farrar (ed.), *War: A Historical, Political and Social Study* (Santa Barbara, 1978); J. S. Levy, *War in the Modern Great Power System, 1495–1975* (Lexington, 1983).

6. Interesting recent research has suggested that international war, since about 1500, has been primarily a great power activity. 'War', writes Modelski, 'can no longer be regarded as a form of activity normally distributed over the entire population of members of the international system. Rather, it is a form of behaviour peculiarly characteristic of states occupying the position of Great Powers, (and those aspiring to that rank) because it is by war that such rank is established'. G. Modelski, 'Wars and the Great Power System', in L. Farrar, *op. cit.*, p. 44. For an operational definition of Great Power status and detailed analysis of the membership of the great power system since 1495 see: J. Levy, 'World System Analysis: A Great Power Framework', in: W. L. Thompson (ed.), *Contending Approaches to World System Analysis*, pp. 183–290; and *idem*, 'Historical Trends in Great Power War, 1495–1975', *International Studies Quarterly*, 26, nr. 2 (1982), pp. 278–300. The same author has also provided the most comprehensive description available of the characteristics, patterns and trends in wars involving the major powers. See Levy, *War in the Modern Great Power System, passim.*

7. The World economy school posits two distinctive classes of 'core powers'. One group is composed of states which are mainly globally oriented or more involved in expanding and exercising political and economic influence on a global scale in contrast to their varying interests in European affairs. This group has supplied the world system's leading states, the world powers (Portugal, the Netherlands, Great Britain and the United States) during the past five centuries. The second group is composed of states that have focused much of their expansionary energies within their own immediate region (i.e. Spain, France, Sweden, Germany), usually at the expense of their ongoing but intermittent global activities.

8. On the origins and expansion of the European state system see: M. Wight, *Systems of States* (H. Bull ed.) (Leicester, 1977), pp. 113–114; G. Mattingly, *Renaissance Diplomacy* (1955), ch. 1; J. Levy, *War in the Modern Great Power System*, pp. 19–29; E. W. Nelson, 'The Origins of Modern Balance of Power Politics', *Medievalia et Humanistica*, 1 (1943), pp. 124–142.

9. S. E. Finer, 'State and Nation Building in Europe: The Role of the Military', in C. Tilly (ed.), *The Foundation of National States in Western Europe* (Princeton 1975), pp. 134–144; J. M. Bridgman, 'Gunpowder and Governmental Power: War in Early Modern Europe 1494–1825', in L. Farrar (ed.), *War, A Historical, Political and Social Study*, pp. 105–111; J. R. Western, 'War on a New Scale: Professionalism in Armies, Navies and Diplomacy', in A. Cobban (ed.), *The Eighteenth Century* (1969), pp. 203–215.

10. S. Kim, *The Quest for a Just World Order* (Boulder, 1984), pp. 28–29; M. Keens-Soper, 'The Practice of a States System', in K. W. Schweizer (ed.), *Diplomatic Thought 1648–1815 (Studies in History and Politics*, II) (1982), pp. 15–35.

11. Jane Meyer, 'The Foreign Policies of Consolidated States, Great Britain and France in the 18th Century, (Johns Hopkins, Ph.D. 1976), p. 314.

12. R. Gilpin, *War and Change in World Politics*, (Cambridge, 1981), pp. 112–132.

13. Modelski, 'The Long Cycle of Gobal Politics', pp. 217–221; cf. W. R. Thompson, *Contending Approaches*, pp. 12–13.

14. Meyer, *op. cit.*, pp. 124–132.

15. Modelski, 'The Long Cycle', p. 221; cf. R. Davis *The Rise of the British Shipping Industry* (1962), pp. 223–225; W. E. Minchinton, *The Growth of English Overseas Trade in*

the 17th and 18th Centuries (1969), pp. 99–118; G. Symcox (ed.), *War, Diplomacy and Imperialism, 1618–1763* (1973). p. 14.

16. J. B. Wolf, *Toward a European Balance of Power 1620–1715* (1970), ch. 9; E. V. Gulick, *Europe's classical balance of power* (1955), pp. 30–89.

17. J. Black, 'The Anglo–French alliance 1716–1731: A Study in Eighteenth-Century International Relations', *Francia* 13 (1986).

18. J. Black, *Natural and Necessary Enemies. Anglo–French Relations in the Eighteenth Century* (1986), ch. 1.

19. G. C. Gibbs, 'Parliament and the Treaty of Quadruple Alliance', in R. Hatton and J. Bromley (eds.), *William III and Louis XIV, Essays 1680–1720 by and for Mark A. Thomson* (Toronto, 1967), pp. 286–287.

20. L. J. Oliva, *Misalliance: A Study of French Policy in Russia during the Seven Years War* (New York, 1964), pp. 2–3.

21. See S. Horowitz, Franco–Russian Relations, 1740–1746, (Ph.D. thesis, New York, 1954), ch. 1.

22. P. Karge, *Die Russisch-Österreichische Allianz von 1746 und ihre Vorgeschichte* (Göttingen, 1887). On Anglo–Russian relations, J. Black, 'Anglo–Russian Diplomatic Relations in the Eighteenth Century', *Study Group on Eighteenth-Century Russia Newsletter* 12 (1984); J. Black, 'Anglo–Russian Relations 1714–1750: a Note on Sources', in J. Hartley (ed.), *The Study of Russian History from British Archival Sources* (1986).

23. M. Braubach, *Versailles und Wien von Ludwig XIV bis Kaunitz* (Bonn, 1952), pp. 451–456.

24. J. A. Marriot and C. Robertson, *The Evolution of Prussia: The Making of an Empire* (Oxford, 1937), ch. IV; M. Braubach, *Der Aufstieg Brandenburg Preussens 1640–1815* (Freiburg, 1933), ch. III.

25. D. B. Horn, *Frederick the Great and the Rise of Prussia* (London, 1967), p. 47.

26. For further details see F. Walter, *Die Theresianische Staats-reform von 1749* (Wien, 1958), pp. 34ff; E. C. Briocher, *Der Augstieg der Preusischen Macht von 1713 bis 1756 in seiner Auswirkung auf das Europäisch Staatensystem* (Cologne, 1955).

27. W. J. McGill, 'The Roots of Policy: Kaunitz in Italy and the Netherlands 1742–1746', *Central European History*, vol. I no. 2 (1968), pp. 136–143.

28. For a detailed analysis of Kaunitz's views on Austrian foreign policy priorities see: W. J. McGill, The Political education of Wenzel Anton von Kaunitz-Rittenberg (Harvard Ph.D., 1960). Cf. G. Küntzel, *Fürst Kaunitz-Rittberg als Staatsman* (Frankfurt, 1923).

29. W. J. McGill, 'Wenzel Anton von Kaunitz-Rittberg and the Conference of Aix-la-Chapelle 1748', *Duquesne Review*, 14 (1969), pp. 154–167.

30. 'Meynungen über das auswärtige Systema', 18 March 1749, Haus-, Hof-, und Staatsarchiv (hereafter H.H.St.A) Verträge, 102. For strains prior to 1740, J. Black, '1733 — Failure of British Diplomacy?', *Durham University Journal* 74 (1982); Black, 'The Development of Anglo–Sardinian Relations in the First Half of the Eighteenth Century', *Studi Piemontesi* 13 (1983), p. 54; Black, 'When Natural Allies Fall Out', *Mitteilungen des Österreichischen Staatsarchivs* 36 (1983); Black, 'British Neutrality in the War of the Polish Succession, 1733–1735', *International History Review*, 8 (1986).

31. For Dutch activity during the war see P. Geyl, *Willem IV en England tot 1748* (The Hague, 1925).

32. Braubach, *Versailles und Wien*, pp. 861–862.

33. D. B. Horn, *Great Britain and Europe in the Eighteenth Century* (Oxford, 1967), pp. 126–128; J. Black, 'British Foreign Policy and the War of the Austrian Succession 1740–1748', *Canadian Journal of History* (1986).

34. For the important deliberation on Austria's postwar alliance system which took place in March and April 1749 see: W. J. McGill, 'The Roots of Policy: Kaunitz in Vienna and Versailles', *Journal of Modern History*, 43 nr. 2 (1971), pp. 229ff.

35. A. Beer, Über die Österreichische Politik in den Jahren 1749–1755', *Aufzeichnungen des Grafen William Bentinck Über Maria Theresia* (Wien, 1871), pp. xii–xxxvi.

36. See the illustrative letters in H. Schlitter (ed.), *Correspondance secrète entre le Comte Kaunitz et le Baron Ignez de Koch, Sécretaire de l'Impératrice Marie-Thérèse, 1750–1752* (Paris, 1899).

37. W. J. McGill, 'Kaunitz in Vienna and Versailles', pp. 239–241.

38. For a detailed statement of Newcastle's general continental policy after 1748 see: Newcastle to Hardwicke, 25 Aug. 1749 (o.s.), B.L. Add. MSS. 35410ff. 126–137; Newcastle to Keith 22 Oct. 1753, B.L. Add. MSS. 32846,ff. 401–5.

39. For further details see: R. Browing, 'The Duke of Newcastle and the Imperial Election Plan, 1749–1754', *Journal of British Studies*, 1 (1967), pp. 28–47.

40. C. Eldon, *England's Subsidy Policy towards the Continent during the Seven Years War* (Philadelphia, 1938), pp. 2–3.

41. D. B. Horn, *Sir Charles Hanbury Williams and European Diplomacy 1747–58* (1930).

42. P. G. M. Dickson, 'English Commercial Negotiations with Austria 1737–1752', in A. Whiteman, J. S. Bromley and P. G. M. Dickson (eds.), *Essays in Eighteenth Century History Presented to Dame Lucy Sutherland* (Oxford, 1973), pp. 81–112.

43. W. Coxe, *Memoirs of the Administration of the Rt. Hon. Henry Pelham* (1829), II, pp. 469–482.

44. L. P. Gachard, *Etudes et notices historiques concernant l'historie des Pay-Bas* (Bruxelles, 1890), pp. 236–238; *idem, Historie de la Belgique* (Bruxelles, 1880), pp. 526ff.

45. D. B. Horn, 'The Duke of Newcastle and the Origins of the Diplomatic Revolution', in J. H. Elliot and H. G. Koenigsberger (eds.), *The Diversity of History: Essays in Honour of Sir H. Butterfield* (London, 1970), pp. 258–259.

46. Cf. Keith to Newcastle, 25 May, 1753 (very private) B.L. Add. MSS 32844, f. 339.

47. D. B. Horn, *Hanbury Williams*, pp. 144–145.

48. Newcastle to Keith, 29 Jan. 1754, PRO.SP. 80/193.

49. The major issues of contention are discussed in detail by L. H. Gipson, *The Great War for Empire: Zones of International Friction* (New York, 1939), vol. IV; cf. J. H. Parry, *Trade and Dominion: The European Overseas Empire in the Eighteenth Century* (1971), pp. 112–118. For French aggressive activities in the Ohio Valley see: Dinwiddie to Lords of Trade 16 June 1753, PRO.CO. 5/1327ff. 292–5; Halifax to Newcastle, 12 August 1753, B.L. Add. MSS. 32732ff. 450–1.

50. T. R. Clayton, 'The Duke of Newcastle and the Origins of the Seven Years War', *The Historical Journal*, 24 (1981).

51. S. Pargellis (ed.), *Military Affairs in North America 1748–1765: Selected Documents from the Cumberland Papers in Windsor Castle* (New York, 1936), pp. 31–35. Instructions for General E. Braddock 25 November 1754, PRO.CO. 5/6ff. 3–18.

52. For the various attempts at negotiation and the mutual retaliations which led to war, see P. L. R. Higonnet, 'The Origins of the Seven Years War', *Journal of Modern History*, 40 (1968), pp. 57–90.

53. Newcastle to Yorke 15 January 1754. B.L. Add. MSS. 32848,ff. 85–87.

54. J. Corbett, *England in the Seven Years War: A Study in Combined Strategy* (1918) vol. I, pp. 22–23, 39–40.

55. D'Arcy Collyer, 'Notes on the Diplomatic Correspondence between England and Russia in the first half of the eighteenth century', *Transactions of the Royal Historical Society*, XIV (1900), pp. 144ff; M. S. Anderson, *Britain's Discovery of Russia 1553–1815* (1958), pp. 65ff; W. Mediger, *Moscaus Weg nach Europa* (Göttingen, 1952).

56. Mediger, *ibid.*, pp. 201ff., pp. 247–249.

57. D. B. Horn, 'The Cabinet Controversy on Subsidy Treaties in time of peace, 1749–1750', *English Historical Review*, XLV (1930), pp. 463–466.

58. R. Lodge, 'The Mission of Henry Legge to Berlin', *Transactions of the Royal Historical Society* (1931), 14, pp. 1–38.

59. Newcastle to Hardwicke, 21 Sept. 1753, B.L. Add. MSS. 32734ff. 141–143.

60. 'There is no power on earth the King of Prussia respects more than Russia' (Legge to Newcastle, 17 May 1748). PRO.SP. 90/64.

61. Newcastle to Hardwicke, 6 Sept. 1751, Coxe, *Pelham Administration*, II, pp. 406–407; Newcastle to Horatio Walpole, 29 June 1754. B.L. Add. MSS. 32735,ff. 397–8.

62. Newcastle to Keith, 9 March 1753, quoted in E. Satow, *The Silesian Loan and Frederick the Great* (Oxford, 1915), pp. 276–277.

63. 'Papers relating to alleged Prussian troop movements', N[iedersächsisches] St[aats] A[rchiv] Hanover 9, Preussen 191.

64. 'Gutachten der Geheimen Räte', 23 Feb. 1753, NStA, Hanover 9, Preussen 193.

65. Hanbury-Williams' secret instructions, endorsed 11 Apr. 1755, in PRO.SP. 91/60.

66. See K. W. Schweizer, 'The Anglo–Russian Subsidy Treaty of 1755', in *Military and Naval encyclopaedia of Russia and the Soviet Union*, D Jones (ed.) (in press).

67. A. C. Carter, *The Dutch Republic in Europe in the Seven Years War* (1971), pp. 31–44.

68. Holdernesse to Newcastle, 28 May 1755, Newcastle to Holdernesse, 11, 18 July 1755, B.L. Add. MSS. 32855 f. 236, 32857 f. 1,ff. 162–164.

69. Cf. W. Bentinck to Newcastle, 22 April, Yorke to Newcastle (private), 3 June 1755, B.L. Add. MSS. 32854 f. 210, 32855ff. 312–13; Coquelle, *op. cit.*, pp. 54–60.

70. What no doubt heightened the impact were the reports arriving in Berlin of Russian military mobilization along the Prussian frontier. H. Kaplan, *Russia and the Outbreak of the Seven Years War* (Berkeley, 1968), p. 10.

71. Through a secret correspondence handled by the Duke of Brunswick, Holdernesse to Newcastle, 1 June 1755, B.L. Egerton MSS. 3428,ff. 208–209; Holdernesse to Newcastle, 7 June 1755, B.L. Add. MSS. 32855, f. 375.

72. Newcastle to Holdernesse, 11 June 1755, B.L. Add. MSS. 32857, f. 43; Holdernesse to Newcastle, 5 June 1755, B.L. Eg. MSS. 3428,ff. 208–209.

73. 'Deduction of continental measures from 1755 to April 1758', Weston MSS., Bundle I; Newcastle to Holdernesse, 11 July 1755, Newcastle to Hardwicke, 26 July 1755, B.L. Add. MSS. 32857,ff. 5, 384–385; Newcastle to Münchhausen, 25 July 1755, NStA (Hanover) Hanover 91v.

74. Newcastle to Holdernesse (entre nous), 1 Aug. 1755, Hardwicke to Newcastle, 9 Aug. 1755, B.L. Add. MSS. 32857 f. 506, 32858 f. 74; Münchhausen to Newcastle, 18 Aug. 1755, NStA. (Hanover) Hanover 91v.

75. Holdernesse to Newcastle, 14 Aug. 1755, 'Instructions for the Earl of Holdernesse', 9 August 1755, B.L. Add. MSS. 32858ff. 141, 150.

76. Frederick to Knyphausen, 9 Aug., 1 Sept. 1755, *Politische Correspondenz*, XI, pp. 241–242, 287–288; Frederick to Mitchell, 25 Aug. 1755, Deutsches Zentral-Archiv (DZA), Merseburg, Rep. 96. 32. H,ff. 243–246.

77. Frederick to Maltzahn, 1 Feb. 1753, *Pol Corr.*, IX, pp. 328–329.

78. Michell to Frederick, 28 Nov. 1755, DZA Rep. 96. 32. H.ff. 351–352; Holdernesse to Newcastle, 21 Nov. 1755, B.L. Add. MSS. 32861 f. 59.

79. For the original convention see: PRO.SP. 108/421 (Treaty Papers). It has been printed in both English and French by C. Jenkinson, *Collection of Treaties* (1785), III, pp. 54–60.

80. Newcastle to Yorke, 10 February 1756, B.L. Add. MSS. 32862 f. 430; Frederick to Knyphausen, 3, 10 Feb. 1756, *Pol. Corr.*, XII, pp. 72–73, 93–99.

81. Broglie, *L'alliance Autrichienne* (Paris, 1895), pp. 338–343, 368–374; Oliva, *op. cit.*, pp. 28–29; for the text, see A. Schaefer, *Siebenjährigen Krieg*, I, pp. 584–585.

82. Holdernesse to Williams, 26 Dec. 1755, Williams to Holdernesse, 14, 19 Feb. 1756, PRO.SP. 91/61–2.

83. Kaplan, *op. cit.*, pp. 36–56.

84. D. B. Horn, *Hanbury Williams*, pp. 267–268.

85. Oliva, *op. cit.*, pp. 14–25.

86. Kaplan, *op. cit.*, pp. 47–56. Important primary materials relating to the origin, development and function of this council may be found in: Sbornik, CXXXVI, pp. 31–33; P. J. Bartenev (ed.), *Arkhiv Kniazia Vorontsova* (Moscow, 1872), III, pp. 356–367.

87. Most of these reports or references to them are reprinted in *Pol Corr.*, XII, XIII.

They have been extensively utilized by A. Naude, 'Frederick der Grosse vor dem Ausbruch des Siebenjährigen Krieges', *Historische Zeitschrift*, 55 (1886), pp. 425–462; vol. 56, pp. 404–462.

88. Mitchell to Holdernesse, 22 June 1756, PRO.SP. 90/65.

89. Mitchell to Holdernesse, 9 July 1756, PRO.SP. 90/65.

90. Frederick to Klinggraeffen, 24, 27 July, 26 August 1756, *Pol. Corr.*, XIII, pp. 90–91, 163, 278–279.

91. J. D. Signer and M. Small, 'Alliance aggregation and the onset of war, 1815–1945', in J. D. Singer (ed.), *Quantitative International Politics* (New York, 1972).

92. J. S. Levy, 'Alliance Formation and War Behaviour: An Analysis of the Great Powers 1495–1975', *Journal of Conflict Resolution*, vol. 25, no. 4 (Dec. 1981), pp. 581–613.

93. *Ibid.*, p. 609.

94. R. A. Preston and S. F. Wise, *Men in Arms* (1979), pp. 147–151.

95. Referring to time in terms of the regular rhythms and cycles of the world systems major processes. See: W. R. Thompson, 'The world-economy, the long cycle and the question of world system time', in P. J. McGowen and C. W. Kegley, (eds.), *Foreign Policy and the Modern World-System* (1983).

96. W. R. Thompson (ed.), *Crises in the World System* (Beverly Hills, 1983), p. 100.

SELECTIVE BIBLIOGRAPHY

This brief list is intended only as an introduction to the very extensive literature available. For reasons of space English-language titles have been concentrated upon. Unless otherwise cited, place of publication is London.

The Origins of Wars

Ardrey, R., *The Territorial Imperative* (1967).
Ardrey, R., *The Hunting Hypothesis* (1977).
Aron, R., *Peace and War, A Theory of International Relations* (1966).
Bernard, L. L., *War and Its Causes* (New York, 1944).
Blainey, G., *The Causes of War* (1973).
Blanning, T. C. W., *The Origins of the French Revolutionary Wars* (1986).
Brodie, B., *War and Politics* (1974).
Brown, W., *War and the Psychological Conditions of Peace* (1942).
Bueno de Mesquita, B., 'Systemic Polarization and the Occurrence and Duration of War', *Journal of Conflict Resolution* 22 (1978).
Bueno de Mesquita, B., *The War Trap* (New Haven, 1981).
Bull, H., *The Anarchical Society* (New York, 1973).
Cantril, H. (ed.), *Tensions that Cause War* (Urbana, 1950).
Carthy, J. D. and Ebling, F. J. (eds.), *The Natural History of Aggression* (1964).
Claude, I. L., *Power and International Relations* (New York, 1962).
Clausewitz, Carl von, *On War*, eds. M. Howard and P. Paret (Princeton, 1976).
Corvisier, A., *Armies and Societies in Europe, 1494–1789* (Bloomington, Indiana, 1978).
Crook, D. P., 'Darwin on Age and Aggression', *Australian Journal of Politics and History* 29 (1983).
Dehio, L., *The Precarious Balance* (New York, 1962).
Denton, F. and Phillips, W., 'Some Patterns in the History of Violence', *Journal of Conflict Resolution* 12 (1968).
Dickinson, G. L., *Causes of International War* (New York, 1972).
Doran, C. and Parsons, W., 'War and the Cycle of Relative Power', *American Political Science Review* 74 (1980).
Durbin, E. and Bowlby J., *Personal Aggressiveness and War* (1939).
Ferrill, A., *The Origins of War. From the Stone Age to Alexander the Great* (1985).
Frank, J. D., *Sanity and Survival: Psychological Aspects of War and Peace* (1968).
Gilpin, R., *War and Change in World Politics* (Cambridge, 1981).
Goldstein, J., 'Kondratieff waves as war cycles', *International Studies Quarterly* 29 (1985).
Hinsley, F. H., *Power and the Pursuit of Peace. Theory and Practice in the History of Relations between States* (Cambridge, 1963).
Hoffman, S., *The State of War* (New York, 1968).
Howard, M., *War in European History* (Oxford, 1976).
Howard, M., *The Causes of Wars and other essays* (1983).
Howard, M., *Weapons and Peace* (1983).
Jervis, R., *Perception and Misperception in International Politics* (Princeton, 1976).

Kaplan, M. S., *System and Process in International Politics* (New York, 1957).

Kara, K., 'On the Marxist theory of war and peace', *Journal of Peace Research* 5 (1968).

Kegley, C. W. and Raymond, G. A., 'Normative Constraints on the Use of Force Short of War', *Journal of Peace Research* 23 (1986).

Kegley, C. W. and Raymond, G. A., 'Third Party Mediation and International Norms: A Test of Two Models', *Conflict Management and Peace Science* 10 (1987).

Keohane, R., 'The Theory of Hegemonic Stability and Change in International Economic Regimes', in O. R. Holsti *et al* (eds.), *Change in the International System* (Boulder, Colorado, 1980).

Keohane, R. O. and Nye, J. S., *Power and Interdependence* (New York, 1977).

Kubalkova, V. and Cruickshank, A. A., *Marxism–Leninism and the Theory of International Relations* (1980).

Levy, J. S., 'Alliance Formation and War Behaviour: An Analysis of the Great Powers, 1495–1975', *Journal of Conflict Resolution* 25 (1981).

Levy, J. S., 'The Contagion of Great Power War Behaviour', *American Journal of Political Science* 26 (1982).

Levy, J. S., 'Historical Trends in Great Power War', *International Studies Quarterly* 26 (1982).

Levy, J. S., 'World System Analysis: A Great Power Perspective', in W. R. Thompson (ed.), *World System Analysis: Competing Perspectives* (Beverly Hills, 1983).

Levy, J. S., *War in the Modern Great Power System, 1495–1975* (Lexington, Kentucky, 1983).

Levy, J. S., 'Theories of General War', *World Politics* 37 (1985).

Lorenz, K., *On Aggression* (1966).

McNeill, W. H., *The Pursuit of Power* (Chicago, 1982).

Mead, M., 'Warfare is only an invention — not a biological necessity', in L. Bramson and G. W. Goethals (eds.), *War: Studies from Psychology, Sociology, Anthropology* (New York, 1984).

Modelski, G., 'The Long Cycle of Global Politics and the Nation State', *Comparative Studies in Society and History* 20 (1978).

Montagu, A. (ed.), *Man and Aggression* (1973).

Nef, J. V., *War and Human Progress* (New York, 1950).

Otterbein, K. F., 'The anthropology of war', in J. J. Honigmann (ed.), *Handbook of Social and Cultural Anthropology* (Chicago, 1973).

Pruitt, D. G. and Snyder, R. C. (eds.), *Theory and Practice on the Causes of War* (Englewood Cliffs, New Jersey, 1969).

Sabrosky, A. (ed.), *Polarity and War* (Boulder, Colorado, 1985).

Singer, J. D., *Explaining War. Selected Papers from the Correlates of War Project* (Beverly Hills, 1979).

Taylor, A. J. P., *How Wars Begin* (1980).

Thompson, W. R., 'Uneven Economic Growth, Systemic Challenges, and Global Wars', *International Studies Quarterly* 27 (1983).

Thompson, W. R. (ed.), *Contending Approaches to World System Analysis* (Beverly Hills, 1983).

Vayrynen, R., 'Economic Cycle, Power Transitions, Political Management and Wars between Major Powers', *International Studies Quarterly* 27 (1983).

Wallerstein, I., *The Modern World System* (2 vols., New York, 1974 and 1980).

Walsh, M. N. (ed.), *War and the Human Race* (New York, 1971).

Waltz, K. N., *Theory of International Politics* (Reading, Mass., 1979).

Wright, Q., 'Design for a Research Project on International Conflicts', *Western Political Quarterly* 10 (1957).
Wright, Q., *A Study of War* (1964).
Zinnes, D. A., *Contemporary Research in International Relations* (New York, 1976).
Zolberg, A. R., 'Strategic interactions and the formation of modern states: France and England', *International Social Science Journal* 32 (1980).
Zolberg, A. R., 'Origins of the Modern World System: A Missing Link', *World Politics* 33 (1981).

International Relations 1500–1650

Adams, R. P., *The better part of valor: More, Erasmus, Colet and Vives, on humanism, war and peace 1496–1535* (Seattle, 1962).
Adams, S., 'Spain or the Netherlands? The Dilemmas of Early Stuart Foreign Policy', in H. Tomlinson (ed.), *Before the Civil War* (1983).
Allmand, C. T. (ed.), *War, literature and politics in the late middle ages* (Liverpool, 1976).
Anderson, R. C., *Naval Wars in the Baltic during the Sailing Ship Epoch 1522-1850* (1910; reprinted 1969).
Aston, T. (ed.), *Crisis in Europe, 1560–1660* (1965).
Attman, A., *The Struggle for Baltic Markets: Powers in Conflict 1558–1618* (Gothenburg, 1979).
Bayley, C. C., *War and society in Renaissance Florence* (Toronto, 1961).
Benedict P., *Rouen during the wars of religion* (Cambridge, 1980).
Bernard, G. W., *War, Taxation and Rebellion in Early Tudor England* (Brighton, 1986).
Bilmanis, A., 'The struggle for domination of the Baltic: an historical aspect of the Baltic problem', *Journal of Central European Affairs* 5 (1945).
Birely, J., *Religion and Politics in the Age of the Counter-Reformation, Emperor Ferdinand II, William Lamoraini, S. J., and the Formation of Imperial Policy* (Chapel Hill, North Carolina, 1981).
Bitton, A., *The French nobility in crisis, 1560–1640* (Stanford, California, 1969).
Bonney, R., *The King's debts: finance and politics in France 1589–1661* (Oxford, 1981).
Bowman, F. J., 'Sweden's wars 1611–1632', *Baltic and Scandinavian Countries* 4 (1938).
Brandi, K., *The Emperor Charles V* (1939).
Braudel, F., *The Mediterranean and the Mediterranean world in the age of Philip II* (2 vols., 1972–3).
Briggs, R., *Early Modern France* (Oxford, 1977).
Brightwell, P., 'The Spanish System and the Twelve Years' Truce', *English Historical Review* 89 (1974).
Brightwell, P., 'The Spanish Origins of the Thirty Years' War', *European Studies Review* 9 (1979).
Brightwell, P., 'Spain and Bohemia: The Decision to Intervene, 1619', *European Studies Review* 12 (1982).
Brightwell, P., 'Spain, Bohemia and Europe, 1619–21', *European Studies Review* 12 (1982).
Buisseret, D., *Henry IV* (1984).
Burckhardt, C. J., *Richelieu and his Age* (1970).
Carmona, M., *Marie de Medicis* (Paris, 1981).
Chevallier, P., *Louis XIII* (Paris, 1979).
Clark, G. N., *War and society in the seventeenth century* (Cambridge, 1958).

Contamine, P., *Guerre, état et société à la fin du moyen âge. Etudes sur les armées des rois de France 1337-1494* (Paris, 1972).

Corvisier, A., *Armies and societies in Europe, 1494-1789* (Bloomington, 1979).

Cruickshank, C. G., *Army Royal: Henry VIII's invasion of France 1513* (Oxford, 1969).

Davies, C. S. L., 'England and the French War, 1557-9', in J. Loach and R. Tittler (eds.), *The mid-Tudor polity c. 1540-1560* (1980).

Davies, N., *God's Playground, A History of Modern Poland* (Oxford, 1981).

Davis, J. C. (ed.), *Pursuit of Power. Venetian ambassadors' reports on Spain, Turkey and France in the age of Philip II, 1560-1600* (New York, 1970).

Davis, R., *Rise of the Atlantic economies* (1973).

Deveze, M., *L'Espagne de Phillipe IV, 1621-65* (2 vols., Paris, 1970-1).

Dickerman, E. H., 'Henri IV and the Juliers-Cleves Crisis: the Psychohistorical Aspects', *French Historical Studies* 8 (1974).

Dickmann, F., *Der Westfälische Frieden* (Münster, 1959).

Dodge, T. A., *Gustavus Adolphus. A History of the Art of War from its Revival after the Middle Ages to the end of the Spanish Succession* (Boston, 1895).

Dominguez Ortiz, A., *The Golden Age of Spain* (1971).

Duke, A. C., and Tamse, C. A., *Britain and the Netherlands*, vol. 6, *War and Society* (The Hague, 1977).

Dukes, P., *The Making of Russian Absolutism, 1613-1801* (1982).

Elliott, J. H., *The Revolt of the Catalans, A Study in the Decline of Spain, 1598-1640* (Cambridge, 1963).

Elliott, J. H., *Imperial Spain 1469-1716* (1963).

Elliott, J. H., *Europe divided 1559-1598* (1968).

Elliott, J. H., 'A question of reputation? Spanish foreign policy in the seventeenth century', *Journal of Modern History* (1983).

Elliott, J. H., *Richelieu and Olivares* (Cambridge, 1984).

Elliott, J. H., *The Count-Duke of Olivares. The Statesman in an Age of Decline* (1986).

Elton, G. R., *Reformation Europe 1517-1559* (1963).

Falls, C., *Elizabeth's Irish wars* (1970).

Fernandez Alvarez, M., *Charles V* (1975).

Fernandez Santamaria, J. A., *The state, war and peace: Spanish political thought in the Renaissance, 1516-1559* (Cambridge, 1977).

Fichtner, P. S., 'The Politics of Honor: Renaissance Chivalry and Hapsburg Dynasticism', *Bibliothèque d'Humanisme et Renaissance* 29 (1967).

Fichtner, P. S., *Ferdinand I of Austria, 1503-1564: the politics of dynasticism in the age of the Reformation* (Boulder, Colorado, 1982).

Finer, E. I., 'State and nation-building in Europe: the role of the military', in C. Tilly (ed.), *The formation of national states in Europe* (Princeton, 1975).

Fischer-Galati, S. A., *Ottoman Imperialism and German Protestantism, 1521-1555* (1959).

Geyl, P., *The Netherlands in the Seventeenth Century* (1961).

Gilbert, F., *The Pope, his banker and Venice* (Harvard, 1980).

Hale, J. R., *Renaissance war studies* (1983).

Hale, J. R. and Mallett, M. E., *The military organization of a Renaissance state: Venice c. 1400 to 1617* (Cambridge, 1984).

Hale, J. R., *War and Society in Renaissance Europe 1450-1620* (1985).

Hayden, J. M., 'Continuity in the France of Henry IV and Louis XIII. French Foreign Policy, 1598-1615', *Journal of Modern History* 45 (1973).

Holborn, H., *A History of Modern Germany: the Reformation* (1970).

Israel, J., *The Dutch Republic and the Hispanic World, 1606–61* (Oxford, 1982).

Jesperson, K. J. V., 'Social change and military revolution in early modern Europe', *Historical Journal* 26 (1983).

Jesperson, K. J. V., 'Henry VIII of England, Lübeck and the Count's War, 1533–1535', *Scandinavian Journal of History* 6 (1981).

Kamen, H., *Spain 1469–1714* (1983).

Kirchner, W., *The Rise of the Baltic Question* (Westport, Conn., 1954).

Knecht, R. J., *Francis I* (Cambridge, 1982).

Koenigsberger, H. G., *The Habsburgs and Europe 1516–1660* (Cornell, 1971).

Kouri, E. I., *England and the Attempts to Form a Protestant Alliance in the late 1560s* (Helsinki, 1981).

Livet, G., *La Guerre de Trente Ans* (Paris, 1963).

Lloyd, H. A., *The Rouen campaign, 1590–1592: politics, warfare and the early-modern state* (Oxford, 1973).

Lockyer, R., *Buckingham. The Life and Political Career of James Villiers, First Duke of Buckingham 1592–1628* (1981).

Lynch, J., *Spain under the Habsburgs, 1516–1700* (1964).

McNeill, W. H., *Europe's Steppe Frontier, 1500–1800* (Chicago, 1964).

Maland, D., *Europe at War, 1600–1650* (1980).

Mallett, M. E., *Mercenaries and their masters: warfare in Renaissance Italy* (1974).

Mallett, M. E., 'Preparations for war in Florence and Venice in the second half of the sixteenth century', in S. Bertelli *et al* (eds.), *Florence and Venice* (Florence, 1979).

Maltby, W. S., *Alba, a biography of Fernando Alvarez de Toledo, third duke of Alba, 1507–1582* (Berkeley, 1983).

Mann, G., *Wallenstein* (1976).

Mattingly, G., *Renaissance Diplomacy* (1955).

Neale, J., 'Elizabeth and the Netherlands, 1586–7', *English Historical Review* 45 (1930).

Oestreich, G., *Neostoicism and the early modern state* (Cambridge, 1982).

Oman, C., *A history of war in the sixteenth century* (1937).

Pagès, G., *The Thirty Years' War* (1970).

Parker, G., *The army of Flanders and the Spanish road 1567–1659* (Cambridge, 1972).

Parker, G., *The Dutch Revolt* (1977).

Parker, G. (ed.), *The General Crisis of the Seventeenth Century* (1978).

Parker, G., *Europe in Crisis 1598–1648* (1979).

Parker, G., *Spain and the Netherlands, 1559–1659* (1979).

Parker, G., *The Thirty Years' War* (1984).

Petersen, E. L., 'Defence, War and Finance: Christian IV and the Council of the Realm 1596–1629', *Scandinavian Journal of History* 7 (1982).

Potter, D., 'Foreign Policy in the Age of the Reformation: French involvement in the Schmalkaldic War, 1544–1547', *Historical Journal* 20 (1977).

Potter, D., 'The Treaty of Boulogne and European Diplomacy, 1549–50', *Bulletin of the Institute of Historical Research* (1982).

Rabb, T. A., *The struggle for stability in modern Europe* (New York, 1975).

Ramsay, G., 'The Foreign Policy of Elizabeth I', in C. Haigh (ed.), *The Reign of Elizabeth I* (1984).

Roberts, M., 'Gustavus Adolphus and the art of war', *Historical Studies* 1 (1948).

Roberts, M., *Gustavus Adolphus: a History of Sweden 1611–32* (1955).

Roberts, M., *The military revolution, 1560–1660* (Belfast, 1956).

Roberts, M., 'The political objectives of Gustaf Adolf in Germany 1630-2', *Transactions of the Royal Historical Society* 5th series, 7 (1957).

Roberts, M. (ed.), *Sweden's Age of Greatness, 1632–1718* (1973).

Roberts, M., *The Swedish Imperial Experience, 1560–1718* (Cambridge, 1979).

Russell, C., 'Monarchies, wars and estates in England, France and Spain c.1580–c.1640', *Legislative Studies Quarterly* (1982).

Russell, J. G., *The Field of Cloth of Gold* (1969).

Setton, K. M., *The Papacy and the Levant, 1204–1571* (Philadelphia, 1976–84).

Shaw, S., *History of the Ottoman Empire and Modern Turkey* (volume 1, Cambridge, 1976).

Silberner, E., *La guerre dans la pensée économique du XVIe au XVIIIe siècle* (Paris, 1939).

Steinberg, S. H., *The Thirty Years' War and the Conflict for European Hegemony, 1600–1660* (1967).

Stradling, R. A., 'A Spanish statesman of appeasement: Medina de las Torres and Spanish policy, 1639–1670', *Historical Journal* 19 (1976).

Stradling, R. A., 'Seventeenth-Century Spain: Decline or Survival?', *European Studies Review* 9 (1979).

Stradling, R. A., *Europe and the Decline of Spain: a Study of the Spanish System, 1580–1720* (1981).

Straub, E., *Pax et Imperium, Spaniens Kampf um seine Friedensordnung in Europa zwischen 1617 und 1635* (Paderborn, 1980).

Subtelny, O., *Domination of Eastern Europe. Native Nobilities and Foreign Absolutism 1500–1715* (Montreal, 1986).

Tapié, V. L., *La Politique de la France et le Début de la Guerre de Trente Ans* (Paris, 1934).

Tapié, V. L., *France in the Age of Louis XIII and Richelieu* (1974).

Thompson, I. A. A., *War and government in Habsburg Spain, 1560–1620* (1976).

Trevor-Roper, H. R., 'Spain and Europe, 1598–1621', in *New Cambridge Modern History* 4 (1970).

Vale, M. G. A., *War and Chivalry* (1981).

Vaughan, D., *Europe and the Turk: A Pattern of Alliances, 1350–1700* (Liverpool, 1954).

Weber, H., 'Richelieu et le Rhin', *Revue Historique* 239 (1968).

Wedgwood, C. V., *The Thirty Years' War* (1938).

Wernham, R. B., 'Queen Elizabeth and the Portugal expedition of 1589', *English Historical Review* (1951).

Wernham, R. B., 'Elizabethan war aims and strategy', in S. T. Bindoff *et al* (eds.), *Elizabethan government and society* (1961).

Wernham, R. B., *Before the Armada: the Growth of English Foreign Policy 1485–1588* (1966).

Wernham, R. B., *The making of Elizabethan foreign policy* (1980).

Wernham, R. B., *After the Armada: Elizabethan England and the Struggle for Western Europe 1588–95* (Oxford, 1984).

Wilson, C., *Queen Elizabeth I and the Revolt of the Netherlands* (1970).

Wilson, C., *The Transformation of Europe, 1558–1648* (1976).

Winter, J. H. (ed.), *War and economic development* (Cambridge, 1975).

Zeeh, E., 'The struggle for Poland's Prussian ports during the reign of Gustavus Adolphus', *Baltic and Scandinavian Countries* 4 (1938).

International Relations 1650–1792

Aalbers, J., 'Holland's financial problems (1713-33) as a consequence of the French Wars', in A. C. Duke (ed.), *Britain and the Netherlands* 6 (1978)

Anderson, M. S., *Peter the Great* (1978).

Andrews, C. M., 'Anglo–French Commercial Rivalry, 1700–1750: the Western Phase', *American Historical Review* 20 (1914–15).

Barker, T. M., *Double Eagle and Crescent: Vienna's Second Turkish Siege and its Historical Setting* (Albany, New York, 1967).

Barton, H. A., 'Russia and the problem of Sweden–Finland, 1721–1809', *East European Quarterly* 5 (1972).

Barton, H. A., 'Gustav III of Sweden and the East Baltic, 1771–1792', *Journal of Baltic Studies* 7 (1976).

Baxter, S., *William III* (1966).

Baxter, S., 'The Myth of the Grand Alliance', in P. R. Sellin and S. B. Baxter (eds.), *Anglo–Dutch Cross Currents in the Seventeenth and Eighteenth Centuries* (Los Angeles, 1976).

Baxter, S., *England's Rise to Greatness, 1660–1763* (Berkeley, 1983).

Bengtsson, F. G., *The Life of Charles XII, King of Sweden 1697–1718* (1960).

Black, J. M., '1733 — Failure of British Diplomacy?', *Durham University Journal* 74 (1982).

Black, J. M., 'George II Reconsidered', *Mitteilungen des Österreichischen Staatsarchivs* 35 (1982).

Black, J. M., 'The theory of the balance of power in the first half of the eighteenth century', *Review of International Studies* 9 (1983).

Black, J. M., 'The Development of Anglo-Sardinian Relations in the First Half of the Eighteenth Century', *Studi Piemontesi* 12 (1983).

Black, J. M., 'Sir Robert Ainslie: His Majesty's Agent-provocateur? British Foreign Policy and the International Crisis of 1787', *European History Quarterly* 14 (1984).

Black, J. M., 'Parliament and the Political and Diplomatic Crisis of 1717–18', *Parliamentary History* 3 (1984).

Black, J. M., *British Foreign Policy in the Age of Walpole* (Edinburgh, 1985).

Black, J. M. and Schweizer, K. (eds.), *Essays in European History in honour of Ragnhild Hatton* (Lennoxville, 1985).

Black, J. M., 'The Marquis of Carmarthen and Relations with France, 1784–1787', *Francia* 12 (1985).

Black, J. M., *Natural and Necessary Enemies: Anglo–French Relations in the Eighteenth Century* (1986).

Black, J. M., 'British Neutrality in the War of the Polish Succession', *International History Review* 8 (1986).

Black, J. M., 'British Foreign Policy and the War of the Austrian Succession 1740–1748', *Canadian Journal of History* (1986).

Black, J. M., 'The Anglo–French Alliance 1716–31', *Francia* 13 (1986).

Black, J. M., 'Fresh Light on the Fall of Townshend', *Historical Journal* 29 (1986).

Black, J. M., 'Russia's Rise as a European Power', *History Today* 36 (1986).

Black, J. M., 'British Foreign Policy in the Eighteenth Century: A Survey', *Journal of British Studies* 26 (1987).

Blanning, T. C. W., '"That horrid Electorate" or "Ma patrie germanique"?: George III, Hanover and the Fürstenbund of 1785', *Historical Journal* 20 (1977).

Boxer, C., 'Some second thoughts on the third Anglo–Dutch War', *Transactions of the Royal Historical Society*, 5th series, 19 (1969).

Bromley, J. S., 'The French privateering war, 1702–13', in H. E. Bell and R. C. Ollard (eds.), *Historical Essays Presented to D. Ogg* (1963).

Bromley, J. S. and Hatton, R., *William III and Louis XIV* (Liverpool, 1967).

Browning, R., 'The British orientation of Austrian foreign policy 1749-54', *Central European History* 1 (1968).

Butterfield, H., *The Reconstruction of an Historical Episode* (Glasgow, 1951).

Butterfield, H. and Wight, M. (eds.), *Diplomatic Investigations* (1966).

Carter, A. C., *The Dutch Republic in Europe in the Seven Years War* (1971).

Carter, A. C., *Neutrality or Commitment: the Evolution of Dutch Foreign Policy, 1667-1795* (1975).

Chance, J. F., *George I and the Northern War: a study of British-Hanoverian Policy with the North of Europe in the Years 1709-1721* (1909).

Chandler, D., *The Art of Warfare in the Age of Marlborough* (1976).

Clapham, J. H., *The Causes of the War of 1792* (Cambridge, 1899).

Clark, G. N., 'The character of the Nine Years War', *Cambridge Historical Journal* 11 (1954).

Clayton, T. R., 'The Duke of Newcastle, the Earl of Halifax, and the American Origins of the Seven Years' War', *Historical Journal* 24 (1981).

Cobban, A., *Ambassadors and Secret Agents: The Diplomacy of the First Earl of Malmesbury at the Hague* (1954).

Conn, S., *Gibraltar in British Diplomacy in the Eighteenth Century* (New Haven, 1942).

Corvisier, A., *Louvois* (Paris, 1981).

Cruickshanks, E., *Ideology and Conspiracy: Aspects of Jacobitism, 1689-1759* (Edinburgh, 1982).

Danielson, J. R., *Die Nordische Frage in den Jahren 1746-1751* (Helsinki, 1888).

Dippel, H., *Germany and the American Revolution 1770-1800* (Chapel Hill, 1977).

Duffy, C., *Russia's Military Way to the West* (1981).

Dull, J. R., *The French Navy and American Independence: A Study of Arms and Diplomacy 1774-1787* (Princeton, 1975).

Dull, J. R., *A Diplomatic History of the American Revolution* (New Haven. 1985).

Ehrman, J., *The British Government and Commercial Negotiations with Europe 1783-93* (Cambridge, 1962).

Ehrman, J., *The Younger Pitt: the Years of Acclaim* (1969).

Ekberg, C. J., *The Failure of Louis XIV's Dutch War* (Chapel Hill, 1979).

Eldon, C. W., *England's Subsidy Policy Towards the Continent during the Seven Years War* (Philadelphia, 1938).

Evans, H. V., 'The Nootka Sound controversy in Anglo-French diplomacy', *Journal of Modern History* 46 (1974).

Feiling, K., *British foreign policy 1660-1672* (1930).

Franken, M. A. M., 'The general tendencies and structural aspects of the foreign policy and diplomacy of the Dutch Republic in the latter half of the seventeenth century', *Acta Historiae Neerlandica* 3 (1968).

Frey, L. and M., *A Question of Empire: Leopold I and the War of the Spanish Succession, 1701-1705* (Boulder, Colorado, 1983).

Geyl, P., *The Netherlands in the Seventeenth Century, II: 1648-1715* (1964).

Geyl, P., *Orange and Stuart, 1647-72* (1969).

Gibb, H. A. R. and Bowen, H., *Islamic Society and the West* (2 vols., Oxford, 1950, 1957).

Gilbert, F., 'The "new diplomacy" of the eighteenth century', *World Politics* 4 (1951).

Graham, G. S., *Empire of the North Atlantic: the Maritime Struggle for North America* (1958).

Hall, T. E., *France and the Eighteenth-Century Corsican Question* (New York, 1971).

Harlow, V. T., *The Founding of the Second British Empire* (vol. 1, 1952).

Hatton, R. M., *Diplomatic Relations between Great Britain and the Dutch Republic 1714-1721* (1950).

Hatton, R., *Charles XII of Sweden* (1968).

Hatton, R., *War and Peace, 1680-1720* (1969).

Hatton, R. and Anderson, M. S. (eds.), *Studies in Diplomatic History* (1970).

Hatton, R. (ed.), *Louis XIV and Europe* (1976).

Hatton, R., *George I: Elector and King* (1978).

Hatton, R., *The Anglo-Hanoverian Connection, 1714-1760* (1982).

Higonnet, P., 'The origins of the Seven Years' War', *Journal of Modern History* 40 (1968).

Horn, D. R., *Sir Charles Hanbury-Williams and European Diplomacy 1747-58* (1930).

Horn, D. B., 'The Diplomatic Revolution', in J. O. Lindsay (ed.), *New Cambridge Modern History* 7 (Cambridge, 1957).

Horn, D. B., *The British Diplomatic Service, 1689-1789* (Oxford, 1964).

Horn, D. B., *Great Britain and Europe in the Eighteenth Century* (Oxford, 1967).

Hutton, R., 'The Making of the Secret Treaty of Dover, 1668-1670', *Historical Journal* 29 (1986).

Ingrao, C., *In Quest and Crisis: Emperor Joseph I and the Habsburg Monarchy* (West Lafayette, Indiana, 1979).

Jones, G. H., *Charles Middleton* (Chicago, 1967).

Kaplan, H. H., *Russia and the Outbreak of the Seven Years' War* (Berkeley, 1968).

Király, B. K. and Rothenberg, G. (eds.), *War and Society in East Central Europe* (New York, 1979).

Király, B. K., Rothenberg, G. and Sugar, P. (eds.), *East Central European Society and War in the pre-Revolutionary Eighteenth Century* (Boulder, Colorado, 1982).

Klaits, J., *Printed Propaganda under Louis XIV: Absolute Monarchy and Public Opinion* (Princeton, 1976).

Koht, H., 'Scandinavian preventive wars in the 1650s', in Sarkissian, A. O. (ed.), *Studies in Diplomatic History and Historiography in Honour of G. P. Gooch* (1961).

Kopeczi, B., *La France et la Hongrie au début du xviiie siècle* (Budapest, 1971).

Lewitter, L. R., 'Poland, the Ukraine and Russia in the seventeenth century', *Slavonic and East European Review* 27 (1948-9).

Lewitter, L. R., 'Russia, Poland and the Baltic, 1697-1721', *Historical Journal* 2 (1968).

Lodge, R., 'The treaty of Abo and the Swedish Succession', *English Historical Review* 43 (1928).

Lodge, R., *Studies in eighteenth-century diplomacy, 1740-1748* (1930).

Lojek, J., 'The international crisis of 1791', *East-Central Europe* 2 (1970).

Longworth, P., *Alexis. Tsar of all the Russias* (1984).

Lord, R. H., *The Second Partition of Poland* (Cambridge, Mass., 1915).

Lossky, A., *Louis XIV, William III and the Baltic Crisis of 1683* (Berkeley, 1953).

Lossky, A., 'France in the System of Europe in the Seventeenth Century', *Proceedings of the Annual Meeting of the Western Society for French History* 1 (1974).

McGill, W. J., 'The Roots of policy: Kaunitz in Italy and the Netherlands 1742-46', *Central European History* 1 (1968).

McGill, W. J., 'The Roots of policy: Kaunitz in Vienna and Versailles 1749-1753', *Journal of Modern History* 43 (1971).

McKay, D., *Prince Eugene of Savoy* (1977).

McKay, D. and Scott, H. M., *The Rise of the Great Powers, 1648-1815* (1983).

McLachlan, J., *Trade and Peace with Old Spain, 1667-1750* (Cambridge, 1940).

McLynn, F. J., *France and the Jacobite Rising of 1745* (Edinburgh, 1981).

Madariaga, I. de, *Russia in the Age of Catherine the Great* (1981).

Marcinowski, K., *The Crisis of the Polish–Swedish War 1655–1660* (Wilberforce, Ohio, 1951).

Middleton, R., *The Bells of Victory* (Cambridge, 1985).

Misiunas, R. J., 'The Baltic question after Nystad', *Baltic History* 1 (1974).

Murray, J. J., 'Baltic commerce and power politics in the early eighteenth century', *Huntington Library Quarterly* 6 (1943).

Murray, J. J., *George I, the Baltic and the Whig Split of 1717* (1969).

Niedhart, G., *Handel und Krieg in der britischen Weltpolitik 1738–1763* (Munich, 1979).

Oakley, S., 'Gustavus III's plans for war with Denmark in 1783–4', in Hatton, R. and Anderson, M. S. (eds.), *Studies in Diplomatic History* (1970).

O'Brien, C. B., *Muscovy and the Ukraine: From the Pereiaslavl Agreement to the Truce of Andrussovo, 1654–1667* (Berkeley, California, 1963).

O'Connor, J. T., *Negotiator out of Season: the Career of W. E. v. Furstenberg 1629–1704* (Athens, Georgia, 1978).

Oliva, L. J., *Misalliance: a Study of French Policy in Russia during the Seven Years' War* (New York, 1964).

Pares, R., 'American versus continental warfare, 1739–1763', *English Historical Review* 51 (1936).

Pares, R., *War and Trade in the West Indies 1739–1763* (Oxford, 1936).

Parry, J. H., *Trade and Dominion: the European Overseas Empires in the Eighteenth Century* (1971).

Place, R., 'The Self-Deception of the Strong: France on the Eve of the War of the League of Augsburg', *French Historical Studies* 6 (1970).

Raeff, M. (ed.), *Catherine the Great: a Profile* (1972).

Ramsey, J. F., *Anglo–French Relations 1763–70* (Berkeley, 1939).

Rashed, Z. E., *The Peace of Paris 1763* (Liverpool, 1951).

Reading, D., *The Anglo–Russian Commercial Treaty of 1734* (New Haven, 1938).

Roberts, M., 'Great Britain and the Swedish Revolution, 1772–73', *Historical Journal* 7 (1964).

Roberts, M., *Splendid Isolation 1763–1780* (Reading, 1970).

Roberts, M., *British Diplomacy and Swedish Politics, 1758–1773* (1980).

Roberts, M., *The Age of Liberty. Sweden 1719–1772* (Cambridge, 1986).

Roider, K. A., *The Reluctant Ally: Austria's Policy in the Austro–Turkish War, 1737–1739* (Baton Rouge, La., 1972).

Roider, K. A., *Austria's Eastern Question, 1700–1790* (Princeton, 1982).

Roosen, W., *The Age of Louis XIV: The Rise of Modern Diplomacy* (Cambridge, Mass., 1976).

Roosen, W., 'Seventeenth Century Diplomacy: French or European?', *Proceedings of the Western Society for French History* 3 (1976).

Roosen, W., 'Early Modern Diplomatic Ceremonial: A Systems Approach', *Journal of Modern History* 52 (1980).

Rothenberg, G., *The Military Border in Croatia, 1740–1881* (Chicago, 1966).

Rowen, H. H., *The Ambassador Prepares for War: the Dutch Embassy of Arnauld de Pomponne, 1669–1671* (The Hague, 1957).

Rowen, H. H., *John de Witt, Grand Pensionary of Holland, 1625–1672* (Princeton, 1978).

Sass, C., 'The Election Campaign in Poland in 1696–7', *Journal of Central European Affairs* 12 (1952).

Schweizer, K. and Leonard, C. S., 'Britain, Prussia, Russia and the Galitzin Letter: A Reassessment', *Historical Journal* 26 (1983).

Scott, H. M., 'Frederick II, the Ottoman Empire and the origins of the Russo–Prussian alliance of April 1764', *European Studies Review* 7 (1977).

Scott, H. M., 'British Foreign Policy in the Age of the American Revolution', *International History Review* 6 (1984).

Shennan, J. H., *Philippe Duke of Orléans, Regent of France, 1715–23* (1979).

Smit, J. W., 'The Netherlands and Europe in the seventeenth and eighteenth centuries', in J. S. Bromley and E. H. Kossmann (eds.), *Britain and the Netherlands in Europe and Asia* (1968).

Sonnino, P., 'Hugues de Lionne and the Origins of the Dutch War', *Proceedings of the Western Society for French History* 2 (1975).

Sonnino, P., 'Jean-Baptiste Colbert and the Origins of the Dutch War', *European Studies Review* 13 (1983).

Spencer, F. (ed.), *The Fourth Earl of Sandwich: Diplomatic Correspondence 1763–1765* (Manchester, 1961).

Spielman, J. P., *Leopold I* (1976).

Storck-Penning, J. G., 'The ordeal of the States — some remarks on Dutch politics during the War of the Spanish Succession', *Acta Historiae Neerlandicae* 2 (1967).

Stoye, J. W., *The Siege of Vienna* (1964).f

Stoye, J. W., *Europe Unfolding, 1648–1688* (1969).

Stuart, R. C., *War and American Thought: From the Revolution to the Monroe Doctrine* (Kent, Ohio, 1982).

Sumner, B. H., *Peter the Great and the Ottoman Empire* (1949).

Symcox, G. (ed.), *War, Diplomacy and Imperialism, 1618–1763* (New York, 1973).

Symcox, G., *The Crisis of French Naval Power, 1688–97* (The Hague, 1974).

Symcox, G., *Victor Amadeus II* (1983).

Thompson, R. H., *Lothar Franz von Schönborn and the Diplomacy of the Electorate of Mainz from the Treaty of Ryswick to the Outbreak of the War of the Spanish Succession* (The Hague, 1973).

Viner, J., 'Power versus plenty as objectives of foreign policy in the seventeenth and eighteenth centuries', *World Politics* 1 (1948).

Waddington, R., *Louis XV et le renversement des alliances* (Paris, 1896).

Westergaard, W., *The First Triple Alliance* (New Haven, 1947).

Wilson, A. M., *French Foreign Policy during the Administration of Cardinal Fleury, 1726–1743* (Cambridge, Mass., 1936).

Wilson, C., *Profit and Power* (1957).

Wolf, J. B., *Towards a European Balance of Power, 1620–1715* (Chicago, 1970).